Glorious Mud!

Fine house with relief designs on upper wall, Seiyun, Hadhramaut, Yemen (1962).

Glorious Mud!

Ancient and Contemporary Earthen Design and Construction in North Africa, Western Europe, the Near East, and Southwest Asia

Gus W. Van Beek
with Ora Van Beek

A Smithsonian Contribution to Knowledge

Published in cooperation with
ROWMAN & LITTLEFIELD PUBLISHERS, INC.

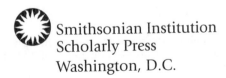

Smithsonian Institution
Scholarly Press
Washington, D.C.

Published by Smithsonian Institution Scholarly Press

P.O. Box 37012, MRC 957
Washington, D.C. 20013-7012
www.scholarlypress.si.edu

In cooperation with

ROWMAN & LITTLEFIELD PUBLISHERS, INC.

A wholly owned subsidiary of The Rowman & Littlefield Publishing Group, Inc.
4501 Forbes Boulevard, Suite 200, Lanham, Maryland 20706
www.rowmanlittlefield.com

Estover Road
Plymouth PL6 7PY
United Kingdom

Cover image: The mud-brick palace of the former Sultan in Seiyun, Hadhramaut, Yemen (1962). Photo by Gus Van Beek

Library of Congress Cataloging-in-Publication Data:

Van Beek, Gus W. (Gus Willard), 1922–
  Glorious mud! : ancient and contemporary earthen design and construction in North Africa, Western Europe, the Near East, and Southwest Asia / Gus W. Van Beek; with Ora Van Beek.
    p. cm.
  "A Smithsonian contribution to knowledge."
  Includes bibliographical references and index.
  ISBN 978-0-9788460-0-8 (hardcover : alk. paper)
1. Earth construction. 2. Earth construction—History. 3. Vernacular architecture—History. 4. Archaeology—Methodology. I. Van Beek, Ora. II. Title.

TH1421.V36 2007

693'.2—dc22   2007031118

Printed in the United States of America

⊗™ The paper used in this publication meets the minimum requirements of American National Standard for Information Sciences—Permanence of Paper for Printed Library Materials, ANSI/NISO Z39.48—1992.

Contents

Tables

Preface

This book addresses many audiences. It will inform everyone interested in architecture—professional architects and laypersons alike—especially those intrigued with the possibilities of using materials and concepts for dwellings that will conserve the environment and its resources while meeting the burgeoning demand for efficient, low-cost shelter. It will also be of value to historians and anthropologists, who attempt to understand the development of architectural and vernacular structures and their political, economic, and cultural roles in societies through time. It will speak to all who are concerned with some of the most intractable problems now challenging humanity: the population explosion throughout the world, which has resulted in a vastly increased demand for shelter everywhere, and the degradation of the earth's environments and its finite resources. Last, but by no means least, it is written for my colleagues—professional archaeologists—many of whom have little or no knowledge of mud construction.

Most archaeologists have excavated sites where stone, fired brick, or wood were the only significant building materials recovered. Often researchers experienced in digging mud structures have lacked the interest to investigate walls and other remnants with sufficient attention to detail and/or lacked knowledge of the types of construction and design that would enable them to make their reconstructions and interpretations more accurate and probable. The brilliant Egyptian architect, the late Hassan Fathy, observed that "archaeologists confined their attention to broken pots and effaced inscriptions, their austere discipline being enlivened from time to time by the discovery of a hoard of gold. But for architecture they have neither eyes nor time. They can miss architectural statements placed right under their noses" (Fathy, 1973:8). Fathy's indictment is certainly true of many archaeologists, but some of us share with him a fascination with mud construction and design. Indeed, there are a number of us who not only "see" architecture, but attempt to understand the underlying principles of design, construction, and function. As an example, I cite the late David Oates' (1967:70–96) exquisite descriptions of the construction of the engaged, mud-brick spiral columns and columns imitating palm trunks at Tell al-Rimah, Iraq, which are described in Chapter 12 of this book.

Many "mud" archaeologists, however, have not been sufficiently motivated to investigate those regions where different types of mud construction and design are still in use today. Yet the study of contemporary vernacular architecture in mud broadens our archaeological horizons with a plethora of possibilities for reconstructing mud structures. These contemporary types have significant and widespread ramifications for studies of ancient cultures, including architecture, demographics, function, and urban planning.

I should note at the outset that I am neither an architect nor an engineer, although I sometimes sense in myself a closer collegial bond to builders than to many archaeologists and anthropologists. To some it may seem audacious of me to write about mud construction without professional credentials in architecture and engineering. I have had a reasonable amount of experience in interior design and finishing crafts, but my major contribution is the unique perspective I bring to this subject as an archaeologist whose nearly 60-year professional career has been spent excavating sites in which mud was the only building material employed. This specialization was not intentional; it just happened. It may have been due either to chance or to God's will. In retrospect, I would have had it no other way!

My interest in mud construction stems from my first archaeological field work in Wadi Beihan of Western Aden Protectorate (now Yemen) in 1951. It gradually turned to wonder and excitement during the subsequent decades of research and excavations at many sites in a number of regions: the Hadhramaut valley in Yemen, Asir and Najran in Saudi Arabia, and both Jericho in the Jordan Valley and Tell Jemmeh near Gaza in the southern Levant, where I had the opportunity to study both ancient and contemporary earthen structures. I was overwhelmed by the creativity of those seventh century B.C. masons at Tell Jemmeh who erected mud-brick barrel vaults with voussoirs, or keystone-shaped bricks. These structures are the earliest known examples of voussoir mud-brick vaulting in the world. Trying to understand how the vaults were built led me to investigate types of mud-brick domes, arches, and vaults and their histories in Egypt, Mesopotamia (modern-day Iraq), and Iran.

Other discoveries at Jemmeh led to research in rammed-earth construction in Morocco. With each research effort, my wife, Ora, and I were introduced to other types of mud construction and design. To study them, we made single journeys to Yemen and Syria, as well as repeated visits to Pakistan, India, Egypt, Europe, and the American Southwest. I still marvel at the imaginative, varied, simple-to-complex designs we have seen: from the roadside wattle-and-daub tea huts in the Egyptian Delta to the six- to eight-story, mud-brick houses of the Hadhramaut; from the simple, layered walls of Baluchistan, Pakistan, to the form-built earthen walls of structures in Morocco, France, Germany, and the United States; from the host of imaginative ways of building flat or gabled roofs to the ingenious methods of vault and dome construction in the Near East as early as 3000 years B.C.

And so, to the study of mud architecture I also bring something that most contemporary architects and construction engineers either lack or regard as unnecessary for their professions—time depth. Time depth is a common trait among people who specialize in antiquity. Their familiarity with the past enables them not only to be "at home" in history, but also to view the present as a continuum from the past. In architecture, time depth means knowledge of a history of developments and adaptation of designs and construction methods to diverse environments and functional needs, all set in frameworks of varying regional traditions and individual tastes through time. In design and construction of mud structures, it is a history not only of recent centuries, but one that reaches back at least 11,000 years.

I have worked in the harsh environment of Near Eastern deserts and their fringes, as well as in the "sown" lands with their rain-fed and irrigated agriculture. I have lived for several months at a time in multistoried, mud houses on the edge of the *Rubàl-Khali*—the Empty Quarter—that great desert in the Arabian Peninsula. Those sojourns occurred during both winter, when nights were bitterly cold, and summer, when days were almost unbearably hot. The houses in which I resided were always comfortable without heaters or air conditioners. By contrast, I have also lived in newly built, thoroughly modern, concrete apartment houses and hotels in Jiddah and Riyadh, Saudi Arabia, and in Sana`a, Marib, and Aden, Yemen, where mechanical air conditioning and occasional heating were required around the clock throughout all, or nearly all, of the year to make their occupation bearable. The contrast in performance between mud and concrete is so marked that one wonders whether we are progressing or retrogressing with the vastly increased popularity of concrete in the twentieth century!

Through this intimate contact, I developed a keen interest in mud construction, marveling at the range of earthen structures from the simplest to the most complex. During excavations, I began to identify with the thought processes of the ancient builders as I unraveled their methods of construction, agonizing with them in their mistakes and delighting in their successes. Perhaps the sum of this experience, knowledge, and attitude gives me a modicum of legitimacy to deal with this fascinating yet enormous and diverse subject.

It should be obvious that I do not know all there is to know about mud construction; neither does anyone else. In this field, everyone is forever learning, and all experts I have met are eager to learn more and to share their knowledge. (Ora and I continue to learn every time we visit a country to see its earthen buildings, even when we revisit buildings previously studied.) Architects, archaeologists, ethnologists, and other specialists working in these and other countries could add examples, observations, and explanations that would greatly enrich this book.

This book, however, is not meant to be encyclopedic in content. Rather, it considers the characteristics, advantages, and disadvantages of earthen construction and describes the different ways of building with soil and mud, many of which are known to specialists but not to laypersons. It resurrects both little-known and long-forgotten building techniques that may enrich the repertoires of ideas and designs of contemporary architects and builders. Most importantly, by bringing together ancient and contemporary methods of design and construction, it illustrates the continuity and persistence of different traditions throughout that enormous segment of the world lying between the Atlantic Ocean and Southwest Asia. Note that I do not say "all countries" or even "all regions"; the regions are too vast and the countries too many for that. Were I younger, I also would have traveled to southeastern Europe, sub-Saharan Africa, Central and East Asia, Australia, and Central and South America to study the wondrous earthen structures in those regions, but there is not enough time to do everything. Thus, in the final analysis, the book is a highly personal odyssey.

I therefore invite the reader to wander with me through time and place, exploring modern and ancient earthen architecture from Morocco to India, from northern Iran to southern Yemen, and many of the countries in between. I want to introduce the wondrous things I have learned about and that enthrall me—things most tour guides never show because they themselves lack eyes to see, curiosity to investigate, and, perhaps, that sense of wonder in the sometimes simple, beautiful structures all around them.

I have accumulated a vast amount of material for this book from archaeological excavations, travels, and library research during the past five decades. In organizing it for publication, I considered two approaches. According to the current, popular approach, I could present mud architecture country by country. This would be most convenient for a reader interested in the possibilities of mud architecture and who is planning a trip to one or more of the countries covered. Such a book, however, would serve as a mud architecture tour guide and would probably resemble the genre of the "coffee table book." This type of presentation should be encyclopedic for each country, treating earthen construction and design in all provinces or states. This approach posed several problems. (1) Lacking the time and/or resources to travel systematically in each country for an extended period, Ora and I could not completely survey any country. In Pakistan, for example, research was limited to portions of Baluchistan and Punjab, as we were unable to visit the North-West Frontier, Northern Areas, or Sind. (2) The periodic breakdowns in security that many Near Eastern and Southwest Asian countries have experienced in recent decades has made field research in nearly all disciplines irregular at best and impossible at worst. (3) To have followed this approach would have made it difficult to compare construction methods.

The second arrangement—the one chosen for this book—categorizes the different components of mud architecture in the general order of construction: characteristics of design, foundations, preparing mud, types of mud wall construction, types of roofs, finishing details, and solutions to specific problems. In this approach, histories, similarities, differences, spatial relationships, and evaluations are described for each aspect of construction, providing a more understandable, holistic presentation of mud architecture through time. Unfortunately, such an approach necessitates discussing different aspects of the same buildings in several chapters. To make it easier to bring these fragments together, I have tried to cross-reference text with related illustrations when they appear in other chapters.

There are a number of first-rate books on the mud architecture of individual countries and of specific regions for readers who wish more in-depth information about those areas. I have consulted many and cited herein those most useful. I hope they will help to direct further reading.

If the information presented herein proves to be of interest, perhaps a few historical architects, construction engineers, and archaeologists will "catch fire" and decide to specialize in earthen construction, advancing systematic research in all aspects through time and broadening coverage on all continents. It is my fervent hope that others will crusade for earthen architecture to play a major role in our vastly overpopulated world where hundreds of millions of people desperately need adequate shelter. Apart from our physical selves and our garments, nothing in the world is closer to us than the houses in which we live out our days. They give us much more than mere shelter. They provide us with those basic psychological and spiritual aspects of life: stability, familiarity, security, and the joy of "nesting" in our own place!

Acknowledgments

Much information in this book could not have been included were it not for the able assistance of my wife and research partner, Ora. Whereas I primarily focused on structures, their designs, methods of construction, efficiency, and costs, Ora was chiefly interested in the people who inhabited the buildings, their lifestyles, material cultures, and symbolisms. Since joining together, we opened our eyes and minds to the strengths of each other, learning much and developing new perspectives. In particular, she taught me to put people in my ancient and contemporary buildings, and I taught her to see the sublime creativity with which those people designed and constructed their buildings.

In extremely conservative Muslim societies, wives are housed separately from the husband and male children. Social mores prohibit visiting males from meeting and speaking with wives and daughters, from entering their quarters, and even from being in the same room with them. Such mores severely restrict a male investigator's scope of research in these societies, limiting it to the culture of the male residents. The cultural domain of the females in such societies amounts to at least 50% of a household but is often significantly more when there are multiple wives with children; yet their living quarters must remain unknown to male researchers. If a balanced view of the culture is to be obtained, then the participation of a female researcher who has access to the women is absolutely essential.

Because field work in these societies was necessarily a joint effort, my research focused on the exterior features of all buildings, the overall plan of the compound, the type of construction, and the interior of the men's quarters; Ora, meanwhile, investigated the interior layout and design of the women's quarters and addressed household functions, e.g., where and how cooking, laundering, sewing, and housecleaning were conducted and by whom within the female hierarchy. Wherever we went—with rare exception—she was permitted to enter the women's quarters; there she conducted interviews and sketched the interior layout of the rooms. Without knowing a word of the language and lacking an interpreter, the warmth in her eyes and smile frequently gained Ora a welcoming reception. Wives showed her their individual quarters, introduced her to their children, gave her tours of the kitchens, proudly showed off their best dresses and jewelry, and sometimes invited her to take as many photographs as she wished. Ora provided all of the descriptions of the interiors and furnishings of the women's quarters, as well as many general observations on houses, traditions, and mores. She breathed life into our research as she has into me for so many years.

These trips were, for the most part, hard and difficult. Roads were often only tracks across broken country; many "hotels" in which we stayed will never achieve so much as a one-star rating; we went hungry when food was not available, and when it was, much of what we ate was very limited in selection and swam in grease. We were ill some of the time, and always hot and tired. Yet through it all, Ora's enthusiasm and desire to work never flagged. I cannot imagine a finer traveling companion.

I must gratefully acknowledge the Smithsonian Institution, which has provided a congenial research environment and most of the financial support for my investigations in mud architecture. In particular, I am grateful to Robert Hoffmann, former Provost and Assistant Secretary for Research, to Roberta Rubinoff, former Director of the Office of Fellowships and Grants, and to the nameless reviewers who approved our grant application, "Ancient Dwellings: Adaptations of Mud Design and Construction in the Middle East," which resulted in Scholarly Studies Grant 1233S016. This grant made possible the field research in Pakistan, India, and Yemen in 1990–1991. I also thank Francine Berkowitz, Director of International Relations and the Foreign Currency Program, for encouraging the investigations and for providing funds for earlier study trips to Pakistan and India in 1985 and 1989. Finally, I must express my gratitude to David Pawson and Ross Simons—successive Associate Directors of Science in the National Museum of Natural History—who provided travel grants for research and conferences relating to earthen architecture from the Research Opportunity Fund.

I am especially indebted to the Smithsonian's National Museum of Natural History, where I serve as a staff archaeologist and Curator of Old World Archaeology in the Department of Anthropology. I have enjoyed shared interests, camaraderie, and support of both colleagues and administrators for 47 years. I am deeply grateful to Dennis Stanford, Chairman of the Department of Anthropology during the writing of this book, who relieved me of many duties so that I might devote more time to this task, and who never ceased to encourage me to press on. I must single out for special recognition and thanks, William (Bill) Melson, Department of Mineral Sciences, who serves as Staff Geologist of the Tell Jemmeh excavations and with whom I have collaborated for four decades in earth and artifact studies. Apart from being a distinguished scientist in petrology, he has always been one of my most intellectually stimulating colleagues. Many times during discussions of material analyses, I have experienced one of those wonderful, euphoric moments during the give-and-take of conversation when new compelling insights emerge. To me, this is the intellectual process at its best. Through Bill Melson, I was introduced to Leon Richter, Geologist and Earthquake Specialist, Nuclear Waste Technical Review Board, and through him to I. M. Idriss, University of California at Davis, an engineer specializing in construction to withstand seismic activity, both of whom kindly read and made valuable suggestions on my paper "Ancient Methods for Minimizing Earthquake Damage at Tell Jemmeh," which served as the basis of much of the discussion of this subject in Chapter 14. The conclusions, however, are my own.

I am grateful to friends in New Mexico, USA, where I learned about classic American adobe. With more than characteristic southwestern warmth, they shared their knowledge and experience, their brickyards where they made adobe bricks, the buildings they had designed and built, the problems involved in preserving ruins built of adobe, and overriding all, their contagious enthusiasm for earthen buildings. What excellent teachers and friends they are: Thomas Caperton, former Director of New Mexico Monuments, now retired; the late Paul Graham "Buzz" McHenry, Jr., the "Dean of Adobe"; Nathan Kaplan, Albuquerque architect; Robert Nestor, Santa Fe architect; Richard Levine, owner of New Mexico Earth, a major adobe brickyard in Alameda, New Mexico; Stan Huston, whose Huston Construction Company builds magnificent rammed-earth homes; Kathie and Jeff Jasper, who worked with Huston in building their rammed-earth home near Edgewood, New Mexico; and Joanne and Cameron Hoover, who shared their lovely adobe home and their adobe experiences with us!

I also thank two persons who have supplied information about rammed-earth buildings in the Greater Metropolitan Washington region, USA. Clare Cavicchi, Historic Preservation Planner of the Maryland National Capital Park and Planning Commission, provided informative documents on "Oakmont," the rammed-earth house in Cabin John, Maryland. Gardiner Hallock, Manager of Restoration at Historic Mount Vernon, informed me of the rammed-earth structures built at Mount Vernon and elsewhere in Virginia in the early nineteenth century, kindly supplied copies of relevant correspondence of François Cointeraux, Bushrod Washington, and Thomas Jefferson and various articles, and scanned a photograph of Bushrod Washington's greenhouse. Both greatly enriched my knowledge of the distribution and history of rammed earth in my own region.

I must acknowledge a host of people abroad who made the field research profitable and pleasant. Field investigations in countries with different cultures and languages succeed in proportion to the interest and quality of assistance provided by local people. During field work, Ora and I could not possibly have asked for more than that which we received from those who helped us. Indeed, their planning and concern for our research, willingness to travel with us, and service as interpreters enabled us to accomplish more than we had dared to hope.

In Pakistan, Mohammed Mohsin Qazi, a geologist by training and then the Assistant General Manager of the magnificent Serena Hotel in Quetta, Baluchistan, arranged our itinerary and used his vacation time to travel with Ora and me on most of our trips. As a member of a distinguished Pathan family and an extraordinarily beloved person in his own right, he opened doors that would otherwise have remained closed to us, shared his intimate knowledge of the region, peoples, and cultures with us, and interpreted the Pashto language for us. He, his lovely wife, Shawar, and their children frequently shared their home and food with us. During a weeklong, citywide curfew in Quetta in 1991 when guests were confined to the hotel, they managed to transport us every day from the hotel to their home and back again safely through all the checkpoints.

In India, Pradeep Mehendiratta, Director of the American Institute of Indian Studies (AIIS—the largest U.S. cultural institution overseas), obtained the necessary permission from the Government of India and the state governments for my research. He organized our journeys with the assistance of AIIS regional directors and state officials according to his vast knowledge of India and my research needs. In times of fatigue, Pradeep Mehendiratta and his family nurtured and strengthened Ora and me, sharing the warmth of their home with us. At different times, M.A. Dhaky, Director for Research, and Research Scholar Krishna Deva of the AIIS Center in Varanasi, Papu Rao, AIIS Regional Director in Madras, and M.K. Raval, then Director of Archaeology, Gujarat State in Ahmedabad, traveled with us, translated for us, and taught us about the customs, art, and architecture of their respective regions of India. It was a genuine treat to travel with these learned, congenial companions.

In Yemen, the late Mohammed Bafaqih, Director General of the Organization of Antiquities and Libraries, whom I had met 30 years earlier in the Hadhramaut valley when he visited the Smithsonian's expedition camp, greatly facilitated my research by arranging an extended trip through the interior of Yemen. I also acknowledge my archaeological colleagues in Yemen who helped in many ways: Jean François Breton, then Director of the French Archaeological Mission in Sana`a, shared his long experience in excavating in Yemen, took Ora and me on an afternoon field trip, and accepted us into his family; Jurgen Schmidt and his staff at the German Archaeological Institute, including especially Burkhard Vogt, then excavating at ancient Marib, assisted me in investigating the ruins of the contemporary mud buildings on the piggy-back tell at Marib; David Warburton, then Director of the American Institute for Yemen Studies, Sana`a, shared the facilities of this increasingly important center for American research and personally introduced us to Sana`a. I also acknowledge the architects and engineers for the United Nations Educational, Scientific, and Cultural Organization (UNESCO) who kindly answered my questions regarding construction and shared with me many results of their research, especially M. Blane, whose drawings showing the damage to Beit Jarhum in Shibam were the basis for the simplified and normalized drawings of the building's exterior and interior.

In France, Hubert Guillaud, Secretary General of CRATerre (Center for Research and Application of Earthen Buildings) in Grenoble, introduced us to the Center and its splendid training program and experimental work in earthen construction techniques. He marked our maps locating the finest examples of *pisé de terre* (rammed earth) and provided us with copies of relevant descriptive sheets of rammed-earth structures made in the detailed survey of these structures in France. We spent a delightful afternoon discussing rammed-earth architecture and its origin and development with Hugo Houben, Director General of CRATerre in Villefontaine. Locally in Dolomieu, Guy Gardien and Michele Maillot taught us about construction practices and the history of *pisé de terre* buildings there and gave excellent directions on the country roads to the rammed-earth church in Charancieu.

In Germany, Georg Jochen Güntzel invited me to lecture on my research in earthen architecture at the Lippe School of Architecture and Design in Detmold. As the ranking specialist in rammed earth in Germany, he directed Ora and me to as many of the finest examples of these structures as we were able to visit. He and his wife, Hanne, introduced us to Renaissance (half-timber) houses in Detmold, in neighboring towns, and in Detmold's remarkable Open-air Museum of Historic Renaissance Buildings, most dating from the sixteenth to the nineteenth centuries. They also hosted us in their home with kindness and warmth. In Weilburg, Heike Kurzius-Schick and her late husband, Eduard Kurzius, spent the better part of two days taking us to see all of the rammed-earth houses in town. She also arranged for us to visit Traude Gudrun, who owns and lives in a six-story rammed-earth apartment house—the tallest such building in Europe—and who gave us a tour of the house from basement to attic and showed us through her own lovely apartment. In Auerbach–Benshein, historian Claudia Gröschel and architect Peter Hartnagel discussed the beautiful Fürstenlager—a former prince's summer residence—which they were restoring. How can we repay so many wonderful people for such kindnesses, except perhaps with deepest thanks and an unending bond of friendship? So Ora and I hope it will always be.

The production of a book of this scope inevitably rests on the talents and dedication of many persons. Foremost, I thank my editor, Meredith Ray McQuoid, for her tireless attention to detail and for understanding my heart and spirit while substantially paring down my prose. I also thank our dear friend Robin Turner for assisting my wife Ora in reviewing and making valuable suggestions toward the final text.

I am much indebted to those who have given of themselves and their time to assist in illustrating this book with photographs and line drawings, and I express my gratitude here. Virtually all of the photographs and floor plans in the book are mine, and usually the year that a photograph was taken by me is included in its figure caption (e.g., years were not documented for most of the Tell Jemmeh photos). Some photographs of layered mud and rammed earth from South America and the Jordan Valley were given to me by colleagues Betty Meggers, South American archaeologist, and Ram Gofna, Israeli archaeologist. Sources of photographs taken by others are nearly always acknowledged in their figure captions. Many photographs are in my personal collection, and in some cases the names of photographers have been lost to memory. Of the photos taken by me, many are important because they are now archival; e.g., the structures photographed either no longer exist or have significantly deteriorated from their conditions of 40–50 years ago. This is especially true of many of the Hadhramaut buildings, which deteriorated badly from lack of maintenance during the period of Communist rule, 1969–1989.

For processing and printing the photographs, the following organizations and individuals are primarily responsible. The successive chiefs of Photographic and Printing Services of the Smithsonian Institution's National Museum of Natural History (NMNH)—Jack Scott, Victor Krantz, and Carl Hansen—and their staffs, including the late Henry Solomon, processed my black-and-white films and made fine prints for the book, sometimes from negatives of marginal quality. On a few occasions, I sought the assistance of Lorie Aceto, formerly Deputy Director of Photographic and Printing Services in the Smithsonian, and Mary E. McCaffrey, of Photographic Production Control, to print negatives that otherwise did not respond to my efforts. Carl Hansen, Don Hurlbert, John Steiner, Daniel Portnoy, and Jim Deloreto taught me the art of scanning color slides and producing black-and-white prints with a Nikon scanner, Adobe PhotoShop software, and an Epson Stylus Pro printer. They also answered more questions and solved more problems than should ever be asked of anyone. Chip Clark of NMNH Imaging created high-resolution digital versions of well over a hundred slides for this book and also for archival purposes.

The Scientific Illustrators of NMNH's Department of Anthropology assisted greatly: the late George Robert Lewis prepared several line drawings; Marcia Bakry digitized and improved many layout sketches and recreated all the maps from my initial sketch versions. Other drawings were made by Tell Jemmeh architects David Sheehan and Brian Lolar, who are the finest archaeological architects I have known, and I am especially proud of their work. I have also modified the working drawings of Beit Jarhum in Shibam, Hadramaut, Yemen, prepared by M. Blane for UNESCO, copies of which were given to me by UNESCO in Seiyun (also in the Hadramaut), to suggest the principal features of the building before deterioration; I was aided in this effort by Ralph Chapman, former Head of the Morphometrics Laboratory for NMNH's Department of Palaeontology. I also acknowledge the drawings of the Tell al-Rimah Temple (Iraq) features by the late David Oates, the most knowledgeable archaeologist/architect specializing in ancient Mesopotamian mud design and construction. All are credited in the text or figure captions. I am responsible for the floor plans of buildings sketched in the field, brick bonding sketches, and all other uncredited drawings. For those interested in how such things are done, I used a Summagraphics Professional Digitizer, DesignCAD 2-D software program, and laser printer.

Margaret Dittemore, head of NMNH's John Wesley Powell Library of Anthropology, spent hours researching bibliographic data for my reference sources and finding answers to many other queries that arose during editing. My esteemed colleague in the Department of Anthropology, Betty Meggers, greatly assisted with final review and preparation of the manuscript text for the staff of Smithsonian Institution Scholarly Press.

Finally, I thank all whose interest in learning more about the diverse aspects of mud architecture results in their desire to read this book. I hope it will be as enjoyable to read as it was to write.

Gus W. Van Beek

Introduction

Mother Earth! From earliest times, soil has been an intimate part of human life. It is tilled for food. It is cultivated for expansive lawns and gardens of brilliant colors. It is the source of exotic gems for adornment and minerals for advanced technology. It has provided us with vessels of exquisite beauty, such as the Greek black- and red-figure pottery of the sixth to the fourth centuries B.C., as well as plain, undistinguished cooking pots. It has given us "gods" or idols, statues of heroes and figurines endowed with magic, and at the same time toys for children's entertainment. It has been regarded since antiquity as beneficial to the health and beauty of the human body in the forms of baths, packs, and poultices. Although we are not always aware of it, the earth is with us every minute of our lives.

Most of us remember how delightful it was to play with mud when we were children. We mixed soil and water, shaped gooey mud pies and mud balls, made dolls and animals, and even occasionally permitted our creations to dry. Perhaps it is the great appeal mud has for children that inspired an English ballad composed by Michael Flander and Donald Swann in 1952. The song is sung by a male hippopotamus to a female hippopotamus, with the following chorus:

> Mud! Mud! Glorious mud!
> Nothing quite like it for cooling the blood!
> So follow me, follow,
> Down to the hollow,
> And there let us wallow in glorious mud![1]

Adults sing and enjoy this ballad, not only because it is clever and fun, but perhaps also because it reaches deep into distant childhood memories of our playing in mud.

To most adults, however, mud is a messy, unpleasant substance that only means trouble. Who really enjoys walking through mud? When driving the car on a muddy road, is there anyone who does not dread the helplessness of skidding out of control? Or who has not borne the frustration of a car stuck in mud, with wheels spinning futilely, burrowing themselves deeper and deeper in the mire?

These unpleasant experiences shape adult attitudes about mud and are reflected as derogatory and negative expressions in our everyday speech:

a stick-in-the-mud	an old fogy, a bore
as ugly as a mud fence	something or someone entirely lacking in attractiveness or beauty
(so-and-so's) name is mud	someone unworthy of consideration, or who is doomed
to muddy the water	to confuse, to complicate
as clear as mud	something totally obscure
mud-slinging	making malicious remarks or disgraceful imputations
"Here's mud in your eye!"	a drinking toast, possibly made in the anticipation of becoming slightly inebriated, less clear, and carefree[2]

For travelers in Africa and Asia, these commonly shared attitudes are reinforced by the unsightly mud hovels that define the poverty areas in urban centers and that degrade the countryside near airports in many countries. At best, people view mud construction as "primitive" or as temporary shelter for the poorest of the poor, relevant only for frontier regions in bygone days. This view—now held throughout the world—has led those people who have climbed a rung or two on the ladder of prosperity to replace their traditional mud homes with far more expensive "modern" houses of concrete or fired brick.

Today the construction of mud buildings is all but inconceivable in nearly all cities of Europe, the Americas, Africa, and Asia, where the urge to be "modern" (i.e., of the late twentieth and early twenty-first centuries) is overwhelming. Being stylish and having status in the community is worth the added costs and reduced comfort of living in so-called modern houses.

In reality, mud construction can be strikingly beautiful and elegant, and it has provided humankind with the most inexpensive and efficient shelter the world has ever known. This explains its long history and continuing use in many parts of the world. Even so, most people are unaware of the magnificent mud buildings in southern Arabia and of the houses designed and constructed by the late Hassan Fathy in Egypt and elsewhere in the Near East from 1937 until his death in 1989.[3] Few people know of the exquisite adobe homes, designed and constructed by world-class architects, that continue the tradition of mud construction in the southwestern USA. These feature-laden houses rank in quality and costs with those of the wealthiest suburbs and country estates around major North American cities.

Because of its many positive attributes, mud as a building material needs to be reexamined and, perhaps, rehabilitated. This and succeeding chapters discuss historical developments in mud construction, the properties of mud as a building material, construction methods, and means of preserving mud structures.

TERMINOLOGY

In dealing with mud construction, I use simple terminology insofar as possible. There are several basic terms that occur frequently, some of which I narrowly define to be more precise; these follow below. Less frequently used terms are defined in the chapters where they occur. Measurements of bricks described herein are given in the order of length × width × height and are in metric units.

Wattle-and-daub: Spaced vertical poles or narrow boards interwoven horizontally with twigs, saplings, or reeds to form a rigid, basket-like framework into which mud is pressed. Mud is applied to both sides of the framework to make a solid wall, normally about 10–20 cm thick. In the southwestern USA, this type of construction is known as "jacal."

Layered mud: Walls built of uncompressed slabs of mud piled on top of one another to form a layer of about one-fourth to one-sixth the intended height of the wall. After two or three days, when a layer is dry, another layer is laid on top, and the process continues until the wall reaches full height. In Iraq, which comprises most of ancient Mesopotamia, archaeologists have commonly mistranslated the Arabic word *tauf* as "rammed earth" or "*terre pisé.*" *Tauf,* however, is more correctly rendered as "layered mud," because the mud is neither deliberately compressed nor contained in forms. In Iran it is called *chineh.* In the southwestern USA it is known as "puddled mud" or "coursed adobe," as it was used by native peoples there and in northern Mexico before Europeans came to North America. "Cob" is similar to layered mud in mixture and layering but is beaten with narrow boards or other tools; it has a long history in England, northern Europe, and Australia.

Rammed earth: Soil that has been as fully compacted as possible by tamping or pounding, either inside sturdy wood or metal forms to build walls, or in constructing broad platforms or sloping revetments without the use of forms. Forms prevent the soil from collapsing along the edges of walls when tamped and maintain a uniform wall thickness during the ramming of the soil. The French term *pisé de terre* (also *terre pisé,* or simply *pisé*) is frequently used in Near Eastern archaeological literature. It is derived from *terre* (earth) and *pisé,* from the Latin verb *pisare* (to beat or pound), referring to the same basic method of construction known in English as rammed earth.

Mud brick: As used herein, embraces all modular building units, irrespective of size, shape, and method of molding (i.e., hand- or form-molded). This includes mud balls.

Mud ball: Construction using rounded balls of mud. The physical distinctions between these and other hand-molded bricks of the Neolithic period are slight, because mud balls are the basic shape from which most handmade bricks are formed. The shaping process is much the same as that used in preparing most hand-made bread: it begins as a ball of dough, which is manipulated into any of a variety of shapes.

Adobe: Commonly used in the New World for mud-brick construction. It is a Spanish word borrowed from Arabic, *aṭ-ṭob,* which literally means "the mud" and is used throughout most of the Arab world for "mud brick." (For "coursed adobe," however, see entry for layered mud.) The Arabic "*ṭ*" has an emphatic sound that, when spoken rapidly, approaches a "d" sound, so that it came to be rendered "adobe" in Spanish. The Spanish borrowed the word from the Moors, a North African people from Mauritania, who conquered Spain in the eighth century A.D. It may be argued that we should adopt the word "adobe" for mud construction worldwide, following Hispanic and southwestern U.S. usage, because the word "adobe" possesses a mystique and elegance altogether lacking in the English word "mud." If replacing "mud" with "adobe" makes this fantastic building material more acceptable to the public, we should adopt it immediately.

In many instances I take issue with archaeologists' usage of certain terms of earthen architecture because they have not dealt critically with the terminology, often resulting in misinformation and lack of useful detail. Owing to the dearth of information in their publications, one cannot discover the types of materials used and the specific construction methods employed, as in the following examples. (1) The common use of the term *terre pisé*, or rammed earth, among some archaeologists where there is no evidence of forms and true compacting or ramming of the soil in buildings. (2) The use of sand as a leveling layer beneath walls of mud brick or baked brick and stone floors; there are very few references in the literature describing the composition of wall courses and floor bases. Yet today, sand is one of the most common materials used for leveling. Is it possible that in the Near East, where sand has always been abundant, ancient builders did not use this technique? (3) Most archaeological reports describe a wall finish as "plaster"; one can look in vain for a defining adjective in the text. If there are photographs of plaster, one can sometimes distinguish the difference between an unpainted mud plaster and a white plaster, but the latter is indistinguishable in its composition and may be lime plaster, gypsum plaster, or simply whitewash.

In a professional life devoted to archaeological research in many facets of culture, I have never been more frustrated than during the study of mud construction because of the lack of details in literary sources. I have systematically worked through many primary sources, chiefly archaeological excavation reports, and also such secondary sources as scholarly papers and semipopular accounts of excavations, learning much less about mud architecture than if the subject were sculpture or common pottery. Features are not described; detailed photographs are meager and are seldom more than suggestive because accompanying text explanations are lacking. Indexes—if they exist at all—are hopelessly inadequate. Archaeologists have largely ignored research on earthen construction and have been remiss by failing to describe and to publish fully the details on such sites. With few exceptions, research has been neglected on materials used in mud construction, on building methods, and in seeking parallels for construction and design features.

It may come as a surprise to colleagues that mud design and construction address many of the same areas of knowledge as pottery but add some new questions. Our understanding of mud architecture will continue to be limited until archaeologists and archaeological architects devote more curiosity and imagination to this subject in the field and laboratory. Materials should be identified with certainty, the size of layers and the weight and size (length, width, height) of bricks accurately calculated, and construction described in step-by-step detail. Care must be taken to observe and record in words, drawings, and photographs all aspects of design and construction, and archaeologists must associate structures within their study sites with those at other sites.

GEOGRAPHICAL REGIONS DEFINED

The world has changed much since I first began my archaeological career and research in earthen architecture. Political strife has altered boundaries in the Levant and Middle East and continues to do so. Over the years I collaborated with colleagues of many varied nationalities. Without fail these collaborations resulted in greater understanding on both personal and scientific levels, and I was always delighted to meet and learn from fellow enthusiasts of historical or contemporary earthen architecture. I have endeavored to maintain a neutral scientific focus in discussions of our research in regions in which memories are long and boundaries remain in dispute. It has long been the custom in reporting archaeological research to use the term "Near East" instead of "Middle East," and I continue that practice despite the now ubiquitous usage of the latter in current political debate and news headlines. Whereas the countries of North Africa, Europe, and the New World should be obvious, two important regions of focus are defined as follows:

Near East: Turkey, Syria, Lebanon, Israel, Jordan, Iraq, and all countries of the Arabian Peninsula.
Southwest Asia: India, Pakistan, Afghanistan, and Iran.

Because these regions are little known to most "Westerners" and because most local place names do not appear on maps in atlases, we have included several regional maps in Appendix A that show locations of villages and sites we investigated.

THE BEGINNINGS OF MUD CONSTRUCTION

Throughout humanity's tenancy of the planet earth, nature in its diverse environments has provided shelter for us from locally available materials: trees in the forest, bundles of grasses and straw in the grasslands, reeds in the marshes, stones from fields and stream beds, caves in hills and mountain ranges, and soil almost everywhere. As people became increasingly knowledgeable about their environment and developed greater mastery of earth's resources through accident, imagination, and experiment, they created an array of useful structures from these and other new materials. Consider, for example, the sophistication of design and the empirical knowledge of locally available materials in the present-day reed buildings, with their soaring vaulted roofs, constructed by the Marsh Arabs on the man-made islands of reeds at the confluence of the Tigris and the Euphrates rivers in southern Iraq (see Figure 11.4). Or examine the engineering skill of the Pre-Pottery Neolithic A builders of the circular tower at Jericho (Figure I.1) in the southern Levant's Jordan Valley (the area now known variously as the West Bank territory or Palestine). Built entirely of rubble (field stone, not shaped or dressed by a mason), with a mud plaster finish, it still stands about 9 m high and has an interior stairway of 22 steps. It is the earliest-known substantial stone structure in the world, having been built about 11,000 years ago.

Among these materials was mud, a combination of thoroughly mixed soil and water, baked by the sun. Scholars cannot pinpoint the time when mud was first used for construction, but it surely occurred in the dim recesses of prehistory. How did it happen? Someone may have gotten the idea of mixing soil and water and putting it in the sun to dry from observing how mud dried and cracked in river beds and ponds after water had disappeared. Perhaps our early ancestors heaped

Figure I.1   Circular rubble tower of Pre-Pottery Neolithic A, circa late ninth to early eighth millennia B.C., at Jericho in the Jordan Valley of the southern Levant (1984).

mud to make wind breaks before their caves, or daubed and chinked their dwellings of twigs, reeds, grass, or stone with mud to prevent the cold winds of winter from blowing through, thus beginning what would become wattle-and-daub construction. Or perhaps some of those ancestors examined the highly complex mud dwellings of such insects as wasps and termites, which suggested the possibility of using mud for their own houses. Other scenarios are, of course, possible, but none can be verified because, due to weathering and erosion, no remains of these earliest structures have been found.

By about 10,000 years ago, builders had improved mud mixtures by adding temper, such as straw, grasses, sand, tree bark, tree leaves, or dung, to the soil. At some point, they learned to place the mixture in the sun and bake it. Thus they developed a new material in which different substances—soil, tempering material, and water—were combined, shaped, and then baked by the sun's heat.

Mud can be classified by the kinds of soil used, such as clayey soils, sandy soils, and humus. Each kind varies in suitability for construction purposes, a subject that is discussed in Chapter 5. Mud may also be classified by methods of shaping: non-modular forming or modular forming. To the former belong wattle-and-daub, layered mud, and rammed earth, in which mud and soil are laid in more-or-less formless masses. Some kinds of non-modular construction, such as wattle-and-daub and layered mud, appear to be the earliest and most commonly used, probably because they are the easiest and quickest to build. In modular forming, mud is shaped into individual modules or units, mud balls or mud bricks, of approximately the same size. This category can be further divided by the method of production: hand-molded or form-molded. The historical trend of these types of molded units is similar throughout most of the world. It began with hand-molded mud balls and moved to plano-convex bricks and to rectangular thumb-impressed bricks in the earliest time periods. About 5000 years ago, form-molded bricks appeared in square and rectangular shapes and in a considerable variety of sizes. Many form-molded bricks were also made for highly specialized, custom installations, such as voussoirs (keystone-shaped bricks) for arches and vaults and other odd-shaped bricks for spiral columns.

DEVELOPMENTS IN THE NEAR EAST AND MEDITERRANEAN REGION

I consider Jericho (Tell es-Sultan) in the Jordan Valley (see Appendix A, Map 1) to be the type site for mud construction from the Mesolithic (tenth millennium B.C.) to the beginning of the third millennium B.C., because it has preserved the most complete sequence of settlements with mud buildings. The following examples of mud construction in Jericho and contemporaneous developments in other regions of the Mediterranean basin and the Near East summarize the major developments in mud architecture from the Mesolithic to the present.

Mesolithic (Natufian) Period

At Tell es-Sultan in Jericho, the first evidence of human occupation is from the Mesolithic, known in the Levant as the Natufian (late tenth millennium B.C.; carbon dated 9140 B.C. ± 90 years). A structure built on a platform consisted of posts and mud, indicating wattle-and-daub construction (Kenyon, 1981:272–274). To provide a perspective chronology, this development at Jericho may have occurred only 2000 years or so after people migrated from northern Asia to the New World, marking the beginning of human occupation of the Americas, although some scholars would place their entry somewhat earlier.

Epipaleolithic Period

This period (early ninth millennium B.C.) was transitional between the Natufian and the Pre-Pottery Neolithic cultures. It featured small, hut-like structures with walls made by piling up mud balls, probably built by nomadic or seminomadic groups (Kenyon, 1981:18, 225, 675–676). So far as we know, these are the first modular mud bricks made by humankind. Mud balls appear throughout human history in diverse times and places and are still in use today. In one area of Tell es-Sultan, a series of post holes associated with sandy floors probably indicates the ongoing use of wattle-and-daub construction (Kenyon, 1981:274).

Neolithic Period

Pre-Pottery Neolithic A (late ninth to early eighth millennia B.C.)

This marked the first clearly defined town at Jericho. Characteristic structures were one-room circular houses on stone foundations, generally recessed a little below ground level with steps leading down from the outside to the mud floors inside, and probably covered with domed or conical roofs. All were built of plano-convex bricks shaped flat on the bottom and convex or arching on top, and commonly measuring about 25 × 12.5 × 9 cm (Kenyon, 1981:152, 230, 269, 275–276, pl. 152a). Near Eastern archaeologists sometimes refer to units of this particular shape as "hog-back brick" (see Figure 5.18). This type of brick undoubtedly began as a mud ball, which was elongated and molded to the hog-back form. There is also evidence of wattle-and-daub construction continuing in occasional use during this period (Kenyon, 1981:51). The great stone tower at Jericho, described above, was built in the second phase of Pre-Pottery Neolithic A and continued to exist into the sixth millennium B.C.

Pre-Pottery Neolithic B (eighth to sixth millennia B.C.)

In Jericho, houses with interior courtyards surrounded by rectangular rooms were introduced. Handmade rectangular brick appeared for the first time with thumb-impressions arranged in a row of chevrons—not really a "herringbone" design as described in most publications—to increase the surface area of the brick and to improve the keying[4] of the mud mortar between the courses (see Figure 5.19). These bricks are generally about 42 × 12 × 8 cm. Mud floors and interior walls were finished with burnished mud or lime plaster. It was during this period at Jericho that human skulls were removed from the dead, covered with plaster, and had cowrie shells inserted in the mud-filled eye sockets, so that the skull more closely resembled the head of a living person. Sometimes these skulls (without other bones) were set upright beneath the room floor in a corner, turned as if to look diagonally across the room. Thin statues of marl in human form (another hallmark of the period) also appeared at this time.

Settlements found at such sites as Aşikli Hüyük and Haçılar in Turkey dating from the same period also feature rectangular buildings constructed with hand-shaped, rectangular, straw-tempered mud brick measuring to 72 × 28 × 8 cm (Todd, 1966:139; Mellaart, 1970a:3–7). The walls and floors were plastered with mud or lime, and many featured painted designs. At Çatal Hüyük, however, heavy, dressed wooden beams were used in building houses and shrines (Mellaart, 1967:63–64), and these may be the earliest known use of substantial post-and-beam framework. The "curtain" walls covering the framework were constructed of rectangular mud bricks, commonly 32 × 16 × 8 cm (Mellaart, 1967:55–56). Wooden framing was employed more frequently in buildings of the late seventh millennium B.C., but it was gradually replaced by all mud-brick construction in later periods at the site. Bricks were made in wooden molds, apparently the first known use of standardized modules in the Near East. Especially notable were the features of the shrines, which included not only wall paintings but also plaster reliefs, rows of cattle horns set in mud benches, and statues (Mellaart, 1967:65, 78).

Hand-formed mud bricks were also used in Iran at such sites as Ganj Dareh and Ali Kosh. At the former, in levels D, C, and B, rectilinear buildings were constructed with plano-convex brick and with layered mud (locally called *chineh*) (Smith, 1972:165–168). In all building phases at Ali Kosh, handmade rectangular mud bricks were used, curiously without properly bonded courses, but structures were finished with mud plaster in the middle and later phases (Hole et al., 1969:34–47). Meanwhile, rectangular buildings of layered mud predominated in Mesopotamia, as for example at umm-Dabaghiyah and at Tell Maghzaliyah (Kirkbride, 1972:6; Yoffee and Clark, 1993:7–9, 12).

Pottery Neolithic A and B (sixth and fifth millennia B.C.)

The Pottery Neolithic A period at Jericho marks the introduction of pottery making and a change in the types of dwellings built, which were little more than subsurface pits with layered-mud walls. These changes represent a clear break with the traditions of preceding material cultures at the site (Kenyon, 1981:138).

After a gap of perhaps two or three centuries, a different culture ushered in Pottery Neolithic B, which was characterized by new pottery styles and by a revival of rectilinear buildings in architecture. Kenyon (1981:96, pl. 95a,b) reported that dwellings were constructed of plano-convex, bun-shaped bricks measuring 40 × 45 × 12 cm, mud balls 16 × 16 cm round, and other hand-shaped variants, such as elongated ovals measuring 18 × 9 × 8 cm. Layered-mud construction was occasionally used at Jericho throughout Pottery Neolithic B.

In Turkey, the last phase at Haçılar (ca. 5600–5400 B.C.) also featured large rectangular houses built on stone foundations, some with walls about 1 m thick. Mud bricks were square, measuring 50 × 50 × 10 cm, or oblong and slightly plano-convex, 46 × 26 × 10 cm. Screen or privacy walls about 1.5 m high partitioned space within the houses and were built of wattle-and-daub instead of mud brick (Mellaart, 1970a:11–14; 1970b: figs. 12a, 19a,b). During the same period in Iran, at Tepe Sabz, walls of rectilinear buildings were made of hand-formed, white bricks measuring from 20 cm to 35 cm square × 10 cm high, with occasional rectangular bricks 50 × 20 × 10 cm, and were constructed on pebble or cobblestone foundations. White layered-mud walls were sometimes also used during these phases (Hole et al., 1969:57–60).

Mud brick is known to have been used in Mesopotamia at Choga Mami and Tell es-Sawaam about 5000 B.C. (J. Oates, 1969:116; Lloyd, 1984:71–72). Earlier examples of brick eventually may be found in Iraq, because it is unlikely that mud brick—the more convenient module—would have been unknown there when it had already been in use for several millennia in neighboring Turkey and Iran. The tradition of constructing rectangular buildings of layered mud continued through the Hassuna Period at many Mesopotamian sites such as Hassuna,[5] Matarrah,[6] Yarim Tepe, and Kültepe (Lloyd and Safar, 1945:272–276; Braidwood, 1952:6; Merpert and Munchaev, 1973:93–114; Bader, 1993:11). During the subsequent Halafian Period, however, circular domed houses of layered mud were the predominant architectural form (Lloyd, 1984:74).

In Iran, layered mud—not *pisé*—also appeared as a building material during the fifth millennium B.C. at Sialk (Ghirshman, 1954:32), and its use continued through the fourth and third millennia B.C. at Tepe Hissar (Schmidt, 1937:106, 157). It is not known if layered-mud construction persisted through succeeding millennia in Mesopotamia. In the Levant and Egypt, layered mud rarely, if ever, was used after the Neolithic period, having been replaced by mud brick in all applications.

Chalcolithic Period and Bronze Age

Hand-formed mud brick continued to prevail in the Levant through most of the Chalcolithic Period (fourth millennium B.C.), probably until about 3100 B.C., when the first mold-made brick became dominant in Egypt and Palestine at the beginning of the Early Bronze Age (ca. 3200 B.C.). Throughout the third millennium B.C., the fortification walls of Jericho were constructed and reconstructed of mold-made rectangular brick measuring about 35 × 25 × 5 cm. In Mesopotamia, occasional form-molded mud brick appeared as early as 5000 B.C., but it did not come into general use until the fourth millennium B.C. Curiously, in the Early Dynastic period (ca. 2650–2350 B.C.), a revival in the use of handmade plano-convex brick occurred in the unique Oval Temple at Khafaje, near Baghdad (Lloyd, 1984:95–96). Why builders would sacrifice the convenience and efficiency of form-molded brick is difficult to understand. One possible explanation is that there may have been cultic traditions or ritual requirements, which were evoked in the construction of this peculiar temple. The development of brick types at Jericho is paralleled by similar developments at Sialk III in Iran (Ghirshman, 1954:35).

In the fifth and fourth millennia B.C., rectilinear structures again prevailed in Mesopotamian construction, although sporadic examples of circular buildings appeared, the most notable of which is the "Round House" of level XI at Tepe Gawra. This structure is very large, with a diameter of slightly more than 18 m, walls 1 m thick, and enclosing 17 rooms (Lloyd, 1984:75–76).

By ca. 3100 B.C., arches and vaults were already being built in Egypt. In a First Dynasty artisan's tomb at Helwan (Emery, 1961, fig. 90), two entirely different methods of mud-brick vault construction—radial- and pitched-brick vaulting—were fully developed. One must presuppose a period of some years during which these methods were devised and perfected, perhaps as much as a century. The most creative period of vaulting design in the history of architecture occurred in Egypt during the Pyramid Age (ca. 2600–2500 B.C.), when many styles were used successfully, including (surprisingly) interlocking vault bricks (Fisher, 1924:114–120, figs. 107, 108). Egyptian builders also constructed tomb structures with walls that were decorated with intricate recessed panels stepped in three or four levels of recessing in section after section (see Figure 9.11). During the late third millennium B.C. and throughout the second millennium B.C., masons in Mesopotamia erected vaults and domes of mud brick. They also elaborately decorated temples with mud-brick engaged columns, shaping the bricks in complex, ingenious patterns to form spiraled columns and to imitate palm trunks (Oates, 1967; see Figure 12.30).

Throughout the Levant during the Middle Bronze II period (eighteenth to sixteenth centuries B.C.), the most common fortification system featured a revetment built of rammed earth, sometimes faced with stone or lime plaster, and surmounted by a vertical wall of mud or stone (see Figure 8.1). Form-built rammed earth was certainly known in China in the mid-second millennium B.C. and probably in the western Mediterranean region during the Roman Republic.

Later Developments

In the seventh century B.C. at Tell Jemmeh near Gaza, the earliest known vaults of keystone-shaped bricks, or voussoirs, were built with variable arcs or curves over rooms of different widths (see Figure 11.44; Van Beek, 1987:102–103). These heavy vaults were used to support the upper floor of a building. Rectangular mud-brick vaulted corridors with cleverly designed, small, vaulted internal air ducts connected to wind towers appeared in San Simeon, the Christian monastery at Aswan, Egypt, in the seventh century A.D. (see Figure 11.15; Appendix A, Map 2). Domes and vaults are discussed in detail in Chapter 11.

Fired brick arrived late in the Greek and Roman world. It became widely employed in Europe only about two millennia ago, although examples sporadically appeared 5000–4000 years ago in Mesopotamia in ziggurats, streets, courtyards, and floors of rooms exposed to water, such as bathrooms. In towns and cities of the Indus Valley civilization, such as Harappa[7] and Mohenjo-Daro, Pakistan, dating in the second half of the third millennium B.C., enormous fired-brick buildings predominated, which, surprisingly, were erected on large, solid platforms of mud brick, demonstrating the strength and carrying capacity of mud brick. The earliest known Greek building in which fired brick was used, for columns, is a Hellenistic palace at Nippur in southern Mesopotamia of the early third century B.C. (Robertson, 1969:235). At Pompeii in Italy, a basilica was built near the end of the second century B.C. with fired-brick columns, covered with stucco (Robertson, 1969:268–269). The construction of walls using fired-brick facings began about the time of Augustus in the late first century B.C. and subsequently became quite popular during the Empire (Robertson, 1969).

Early in the Christian Era (third to fourth centuries A.D.), multistoried houses were already being constructed at Shabwa in the western Hadhramaut valley of Yemen (see Appendix A, Map 3); these are the precursors of the magnificent six- to eight-storied mud brick houses of Shibam in the central Hadhramaut today. Although most of these "tall houses" date from the nineteenth and twentieth centuries, a number of them were built during the sixteenth and eighteenth centuries and many are still in use today (Figure I.2).

Layered mud either survived through time in some regions of the Near East or was rediscovered during recent centuries, because it seems to have staged a striking resurgence during the last 1000 years or so. Fine town walls, houses, and other structures were built of layered mud during recent centuries in many parts of Saudi Arabia and Yemen (see Figure 7.18). In the Asir region of Saudi Arabia, mud layers with a convex or rounded profile on the outer surface give walls the appearance of long pillows or bolsters piled on top of one another (see Figure 7.11). Farther south, in northern Yemen, sometimes mud layers are sharply profiled on the outer

Figure I.2 The tall houses of Shibam in the Hadhramaut valley, Yemen (1962), most of which are still occupied today.

Figure I.3   Layered mud that resembles overlapping wood siding, Marib, Yemen (1991).

surface, sloping down and outward in cross-section and resembling wood siding (Figure I.3). These layer designs retard erosion and add charm to structures as the ever-changing play of light and shadow continually alters the appearance of the walls. Occasionally the profiled outer surface serves as a key to hold smoothly finished mud plaster. Layered mud is also extensively used today in eastern Iran, Afghanistan, Pakistan, and neighboring regions to the north for constructing walls of all kinds of buildings.

From at least the twelfth century A.D. onward, form-built rammed earth—or *terre pisé*—has been widely employed for all types of structures in Morocco: houses, shops, palaces, stables, and fortifications. Especially noteworthy are the enormous city walls of Rabat and Tiznit (Figure I.4; see Appendix A, Map 4) and of other cities, as well as the huge royal stables at Meknes. It has continued in use in many parts of the world to the present, including Europe, North and South America, and Australia.

In our time, mud-brick construction in the Near East is epitomized by the beautiful and imaginative buildings designed by the late Hassan Fathy (Figure I.5). His structures include buildings of virtually all functional types found in Near Eastern towns today: houses, shops and shopping arcades, theaters, schools, and mosques. This variety of mud structures has occurred elsewhere before, but no one else has provided such a carefully planned, unified response to the demands of twentieth-century activities, and few have achieved the wondrous designs, inner harmony, and simple beauty of Fathy's creations. Mud has thus provided shelter for humankind for at least 11,000 years.

MUD CONSTRUCTION IN THE NEW WORLD

The earliest migration of peoples to the Americas from Asia occurred at least 15,000 years ago. The types of shelter they used are unknown, but they probably sought protection from the elements in caves or built shelters of skins, grass, wood, stone,

Figure I.4   Form-built, rammed-earth city wall, Tiznit, Morocco (1982).

Figure I.5   Hassan Fathy (right) and Ora Van Beek seated in front of a *mashrabiyeh* screen on the roof of his apartment in Cairo, Egypt (1977).

and mud as they did in later times. Curiously, in North America during the past 2000 years, patterns of development in mud architecture were surprisingly similar to much of what occurred in the ancient Near East. In pre-contact times, before the coming of the Spanish about the middle of the sixteenth century, Native American groups in what would become the American southwest and Mexico had already used a number of methods of building pueblos—mud balls, layered mud (i.e., puddled mud or adobe), and hand-formed mud bricks—as in the following examples. At the Coronado State Monument at Bernalillo, New Mexico, the walls of a room were interpreted to have been built with mud balls by the Tewa Indians ca. A.D. 1325 by Thomas J. Caperton, former Director of the New Mexico State Monuments (personal communication, 26 August 1994; see also Santillanes, 1994).[8] In the multistoried structure known as Casas Grandes, Chihuahua, Mexico, dated ca. A.D. 900, the walls were constructed of layered mud (McHenry, 1984, fig. 2.57). Hand-formed bricks were used during the Pueblo III period (ca. A.D. 1050–1300) in a few walls in the Speaker Chief's house in Cliff Palace at Mesa Verde, Colorado, and form-molded bricks were extensively used in many of the adobe walls in the large pueblo known as Fourmile Ruin in eastern Arizona, dating to A.D. 1250–1450 (Johnson, 1992).

How can the use of similar types of mud construction in the Old World and in the New World be explained? Mud balls and layered mud were among the earliest methods of construction in the ancient Near East, and their use has continued into the present in the Near East, Central and Southwest Asia, and possibly elsewhere in northern and northeast Asia, indicating an ongoing technology through time. Is it possible that the migrating peoples brought these techniques from their original Asiatic homeland to the New World? This question cannot be answered until we have sufficient evidence for the use of these methods of mud construction during the intervening millennia between their departure from Asia and the first millennium A.D. Although diffusion of these methods from Asia remains a possibility, it cannot as yet be regarded as more than a very remote one.

On the other hand, it is possible that these methods independently emerged in Asia and in the New World, as a result of experimentation in each region. The plasticity of mud permits it to be shaped by hand in an array of diverse forms. The simplest, most basic shape is the mud ball; when lifting mud with both hands, the hands naturally form it into the round shape of a ball. In due course, it seems that the more curious and creative householders experimented in pressing mud balls into different shapes, or in heaping up layers of mud to build houses more easily, speedily, or efficiently, according to the prevailing ideas at the time. I incline to the latter interpretation although keeping in mind that evidence might appear that supports the former.

MUD ARCHITECTURE FOR TODAY AND THE FUTURE

Many of the design and specialized construction techniques mentioned in this introduction and brief history are being employed anew in our time, and still others await discovery, which I am hopeful this book will stimulate. Creative young architects and builders are producing mud buildings that are sources of aesthetic delight. Others are working with urban planners and anthropologists in programs focused on teaching people of overpopulated and impoverished lands to build inexpensive, efficient, and attractive mud houses for themselves. The explanation for this phenomenon lies in the properties of soil and the nature of earthen construction, which are discussed in Chapter 1.

NOTES

Gus W. Van Beek, Department of Anthropology, National Museum of Natural History, Smithsonian Institution, Washington, D.C. 20560-0112, USA. Ora Van Beek, Silver Spring, Maryland 20902, USA.

Reviewers: Amihai Mazar, Institute of Archaeology, Hebrew University of Jerusalem, Jerusalem, Israel 91905. William G. Melson, Department of Mineral Sciences, National Museum of Natural History, Smithsonian Institution, Washington, D.C. 20560-0112, USA. Lawrence E. Stager, Department of Near Eastern Languages and Civilizations, Harvard University, Cambridge, Massachusetts 02138, USA.

1. I am indebted to two Smithsonian colleagues, the late Vincent MacDonnell, who learned of my interest in mud and taped a copy of this ballad for me, and Michael Robinson, who provided details about its composition.

2. This interpretation of the phrase is suggested by Boswell's (1931:598) use of the word "muddy" in *The Life of Samuel Johnson*. According to Boswell, Johnson says of his clergyman friend, Mr. Charles Congreve: "Not that he gets drunk, for he is a very pious man, but he is always muddy."

3. Hassan Fathy (1900–1989) was born in Egypt to a prominent and wealthy family, yet he anguished over the plight of the poor. His dream was to create communities of well-designed mud buildings for the lower and middle classes, the beauty and comfort of which would ennoble the human spirit. He persuaded the government to build a new community across the Nile from Luxor; as designer and builder, he created a unique and magnificent village there. He also transformed depressed communities of squalid mud huts into attractive mud brick villages whose buildings had singular beauty and utility with their rounded corners and soaring domes and vaults; he proudly said of his town planning and buildings, they had "a surprise every way a person turns!" (H. Fathy, personal communication, 1977). When the wealthy saw his buildings, many engaged him to build summer homes for them. He also built a mosque complex at Abiquiu, New Mexico, USA.

4. "Keying" here refers to the adherence of the mortar to the brick surface. A key for plaster (mentioned later in the book) refers to irregularities in a wall's surface (planned or not) that help plaster adhere to it.

5. Lloyd and Safar (1945:272–276) described layered mud at Hassuna as "adobe," which prevailed from level Ib through level X and was thereafter replaced by "rectangular sun-dried brick." It may be that at least some of the "adobe" walls may have been built with mud balls; see his description on p. 273. In his revised book *The Archaeology of Mesopotamia*, Lloyd (1984:70) described the construction as *pisé*, by which I understand "layered mud."

6. Braidwood (1952:6) translated *tauf* as "packed mud."

7. One story ranks among the worst examples of human destruction and looting of an ancient site. During the nineteenth century, the British engineers who were building a railroad in Punjab robbed fired brick from buildings of ancient Harappa to provide ballast for several miles of roadbed. The site was reduced to a series of hillock-like mounds separated by deep meandering valleys. The engineers destroyed forever any archaeological hopes of a full stratigraphic record of the development of the site; of producing a comprehensive, integrated plan of the city and its many building phases; and of understanding the organization of this major urban center.

8. Subsequent findings indicated that Caperton's interpretation of mud-ball construction with soft-ball sized units at this site was inconsistent with the historic walls at the site; the current interpretation is that the "balls" of mud were actually akin to basketball-sized masses roughly formed into bread-loaf shapes, which resulted in coursed-adobe construction (Richard Reycraft, Chief of Preservation, New Mexico State Monuments, personal communication, 7 February 2007).

Part I

OVERVIEW OF MUD CONSTRUCTION

Chapter 1

Advantages of Mud Construction

Earthen buildings have provided a number of important advantages to people in every nation throughout history, and still do so today.

LOW COST

Mud structures are cheaper to build than any other form of shelter except reed or grass buildings, sod houses, or caves excavated in the earth. The raw materials required for earthen construction are readily available in most countries at little or no expense: soil, water, straw or sand, and sunshine. No energy intensive activities, such as kiln firing of brick, manufacturing cement, harvesting forests, and milling timber—all of which consume vast quantities of energy produced by burning wood, coal, oil, or gas—are required. Wright (1978:22) has noted that making a concrete block of the same volume as a mud brick requires 300 times more commercially produced energy!

Of natural building materials, mud offers the widest range of building costs, ranging from very modest to quite expensive. In the southwestern USA, both poor and wealthy people live in adobe houses, while much of the middle class tends to live in "faux adobe"—conventional American frame houses covered on the outside with cement stucco and painted to resemble adobe houses. Yet there are also many middle-class families, of varying income levels, who live in true adobe houses of varying sizes and appointments. In many localities, there is a price range in adobe for every budget.

At the high end of the cost scale are luxury homes in the American southwest, for example in the greater Albuquerque–Santa Fe (New Mexico) region, costing US\$500,000– \$2,000,000 (~\$200.00/ft^2 or ~\$2152.00/m^2). Designed and built by brilliant, creative architects who take advantage of the plasticity of mud in imaginative ways, many of these houses are intimate, harmonious masterpieces, subtly exposing delightful surprises at every turn. In the Old World, the tall houses in the Hadhramaut of Yemen are probably the most costly because of their multiple stories

Figure 1.1   A very low cost, one-room "beehive" domed house, Fah, Syria (1994).

and design features, yet they are considerably less expensive than the fine American adobe houses.

At the low end of the price scale, for example, is a small, one-room, mud-brick house—known as a "beehive" house—in Fah, a village northeast of Aleppo in northern Syria (Figure 1.1). This traditional type of house once predominated in a north–south band approximately 80 km wide that extended from about 100 km south of Aleppo northward into eastern Turkey. Each house (or room) is square, about 25 m², with walls commonly about 5 m long and 60 cm thick, and roofed with a corbelled, slightly conical, mud-brick dome. In 1994 prices, this one-room house cost 2000 Syrian pounds ($47.62) to build, which amounted to about $1.90/m² (~$0.18/ft²).

Figure 1.2 Foundation of house under construction, for which cost estimates were obtained from the masons, Hauta, Hadhramaut, Yemen (1991).

In the same compound is a newly built concrete house that is twice the size (50 m²) of the one-room beehive house. This house, which is shaped like a rectangular box and roofed with a concrete slab, cost 12,500 Syrian pounds ($297.62) to build, i.e., 250 Syrian pounds/m², which converts to about $5.95/m² (or ~$0.55/ft²). Thus, for the same amount of space, one pays more than three times as much for a concrete house as for the mud-brick beehive house. Although labor costs and the cost of living in Syrian villages are extraordinarily low by standards of western industrialized nations, building a one-room beehive house of mud brick in the USA—with much higher labor costs, including a concrete slab, American-made wooden doors and window frames, and utility services—would probably cost about $5000–$6000.

An example of a higher priced mud dwelling is a large, four-story house in Hauta, a rapidly growing settlement east of Shibam in the Hadhramaut of southern Yemen. The house was under construction and the ashlar[1] foundation was almost finished in November 1991 (Figure 1.2). The foundation measured 14.25 m × 14.25 m, an area of 203.06 m². When completed, the house was to have four stories, for a total area of about 812.25 m². During a break in their work, the masons told us about the costs (in riyals) of materials and labor for this large house. Without segregating all costs between specific materials and labor, they recited figures shown in Table 1.1. The local exchange rate at the time was $1.00 = 26 riyals (which was the market rate,

Table 1.1 Materials and labor costs of a large, well-appointed house in the Hadhramaut, Yemen, in 1991.

Building elements	Riyals	U.S. dollars (in 1991)
Specific items		
100 Stone blocks (foundation)	1,100.00	42.31
100 Mud bricks	400.00	15.38
Wooden doors and windows	3,000.00	76.92
Overall costs		
Building construction	533,000.00	20,500.00
Ramad (lime plaster)	355,333.00	13,667.00
Total of overall costs	888,333.00	34,167.00

not the official government rate). This yielded a total cost then of $34,167 ÷ 812.25 m² = $42.06/m² (or $3.91/ft²).

Covering a building with lime plaster—the finest surface finish for earthen buildings—is quite expensive, amounting to as much as two-thirds of the construction costs of a house. To save money, many Hadhramis cover only about 35% of the building—including the roof, parapet, and the lowest 1 meter of the outer surface of the walls from the ground upward, as well as the floors and stairways inside the structure—with lime plaster, and the remainder is covered with mud plaster (see Frontispiece). The cost of lime plaster for this house is now reduced:

$$355,333 \text{ riyals} \times 35\% = 124,367 \text{ riyals} = \$4783$$

The total cost then drops to

$$533,000 \text{ riyals} + 124,367 \text{ riyals for lime plaster}$$
$$= 657,367 \text{ riyals, or}$$
$$= \$20,500 + \$4783 \text{ for lime plaster} = \$25,283.$$

Thus, the cost per square meter with only 35% covering of lime plaster is

$$\$25,283 \div 812.25 \text{ m}^2 = \$31.13/\text{m}^2 \text{ (or } \$2.89/\text{ft}^2).$$

The differences in the cost per square meter between the Syrian and Hadhramaut examples primarily reflect both the complexity of the building and the prevailing labor costs in each region. Throughout most of Africa and Asia, however, labor costs tend to more closely resemble those of the north Syrian villages than those of the Hadhramaut. Even the higher costs of labor in the Hadhramaut are still very much lower than those of the USA and other developed countries, where virtually all construction is done by expensive hired labor. For example, building costs in an Israeli kibbutz (for concrete block or precast concrete slab buildings) are calculated to be about $700/m² (~$65/ft²; Hayim Porat, member of Kibbutz Re'im, pers. comm., 1978).

In the USA, building a house of mud is a perfect "do-it-yourself" project if one has an abundance of enthusiasm, unlimited perseverance, the ability to follow instructions, and the necessary rental equipment. Those who "do-it-themselves" in building with mud will find labor costs primarily confined to crafts requiring registered tradesmen, such as electrical wiring and plumbing. In any case, the total costs will be considerably cheaper. Lydia and David Miller, of Rammed Earth Institute International, observed, "For the 'do-it-yourselfer' rammed earth is probably simpler and requires much less cash outlay for materials than orthodox construction of frame, brick or tile." (Miller and Miller, 1982:39.)

The importance of such a low-cost building material should transcend nearly all other considerations among the so-called Third World nations, which are economically depressed in varying degrees. Most of them are "have-not countries," because they lack the necessary raw materials—such as iron, wood, cement, and oil—to meet their modern construction, transportation, and industrial needs. They must import these items, thus spending their precious hard currencies. Among these countries, inexpensive mud housing can alleviate some of their critical economic problems by greatly reducing the need to import building materials. Such a course frees their reserves of precious hard currencies to meet other societal needs, such as education, health services, and development of the economic infrastructure.

Besides people of the Third World, those in developed countries can also benefit from mud construction. Consider the astonishing rise in housing costs in the USA since the early 1970s. It is now extraordinarily difficult for an increasing number of young and middle-aged people to purchase a home in urban areas, where modest homes cost $230,000–$400,000 (or even more in many areas), because high demand has inflated land values and led to soaring construction costs, even when mortgage loan rates are relatively low. In urban areas, most condominium apartments are priced beyond the financial resources of many families when selling price, mortgage loan rates, and condominium operating fees are combined. Rising housing costs and taxes coupled with much more slowly rising personal incomes puts home ownership beyond the reach of more and more families in one of the richest nations of the world. The 1990 U.S. census disclosed that among families not presently owning a home, 11% of American renters—only one family in nine—had any prospects of ever owning a home. So much for the "American Dream." In varying degrees, a housing crisis prevails not only in the USA, but in many other countries of the industrialized world as well. At the same time, for the large outlay of funds required, one frequently gets substandard materials and shoddy workmanship. A cheap shot? Not really. Visit a few houses under construction, and carefully examine the materials and craftsmanship of a typical $300,000–$500,000 house in any metropolitan area—including the greater Washington, D.C. region—and critically evaluate their "quality."

Mud construction requires an investment of physical or mechanical energy, i.e., labor by the human body or by machines. If a family decides to build their mud house all or in part by themselves, they will make for themselves a comfortable, durable home while saving considerable money. Indeed, a mud-brick house can be constructed by one person who is willing to follow instructions carefully and to work physically hard during spare time for several months. McHenry (1980:119) noted that a three-room house of 600 ft^2 (55.8 m^2) with a 10 in (25 cm) wall thickness, requires 3000 mud bricks, each measuring $14 \times 10 \times 4$ in ($35 \times 25 \times 10$ cm) and weighing about 35 lbs (~16 kg). With good weather, materials and equipment at hand, and working only with shovels, wheelbarrows, and wooden molds—no sophisticated mechanical equipment or fossil energy—two people could make 500 such bricks a day; thus, making 3000 bricks represents six days' work. To lay 3000 bricks requires another eight days of the two workers, for a total of 14 days! Varying either the number of workers or the size of the house provides other interesting results. If workers make only 200 bricks a day, 3000 bricks will require 15 days. One person could build all walls of a 600 ft^2 (55.8 m^2), three-room house in about four weeks, or six workers could erect the walls of an 1800 ft^2 (163.50 m^2) house in 13 days. A house built on stone or concrete foundations with walls 24 in (60 cm) thick and laid in English bond (see Figure 9.5) would require about 4000 bricks. If an eight-course mud-brick foundation is used, about 5500 bricks would be needed. One person building a house with stone or concrete foundations would need at least 44 working days, or two people at least 22 working days. For a house with mud-brick foundations, one person would probably require at least 60 days, or two persons at least 30 days.

Soil quarried on one's own property is free, and water and straw or sand are read-ily available at little cost even in urban areas. If one wished to speed the digging of foundation trenches and the quarrying of soil, one could hire an operator with a backhoe, which requires a cash outlay. If this work is done in the old tradition with the help of friends and neighbors, some funds would undoubtedly be expended for food and drinks for the workers.

Although exterior and interior walls alone do not a house make, they represent one of the major components and costs in construction. Mud walls should be finished with plaster of mud, lime, or cement (stucco), the cost of which ranges from nothing for mud walls, to considerable for stucco; plasters are discussed in Chapter 12.

Roofs and floors are less expensive than walls. Of the many possible types of roofs, at least two are made of mud. (1) The traditional flat roof is carried by heavy wooden beams (known as "vigas" in the southwestern USA) or, occasionally, by a primary steel I-beam, which supports wooden cross beams—increasingly com-mon in Punjab, Pakistan (see Chapter 10). (2) Vaulted and domed roofs require only careful workmanship and mud brick; domes and two types of vaulting can be erected without any type of scaffolding or interior support. These are a challenge to do-it-yourselfers but are well worth the effort because of their beauty, efficiency, and modest costs (see Chapter 11).

Beautiful, serviceable floors can also be made of mud by several methods. Still needed are doors, windows, trim, cabinets, and utilities services, which represent a minor portion of the total cost of a house built in most countries of southwestern and southern Asia, but which are a considerably greater portion of total costs in the USA and Europe. These details and building techniques are discussed in Chapter 13.

Building with a maximum amount of mud construction considerably reduces the cost of houses and other structures. Urban renewal programs using mud architecture can help solve the serious housing problems of much of the world. Perhaps the most imaginative example of public housing is "Domaine de la Terre," a community in l'Isle d'Abeau, Villefontaine, about 30 km southwest of Lyons, France. The com-munity consists of 65 homes arranged in 12 sections or units consisting of 5–10 ad-joining houses, which are attractively sited on planned, meandering streets. About 300 people live in these houses. The project was conceived by a group of young ar-chitects who received their training at the School of Architecture of the University of Grenoble, some of whom later founded the Center for Research and Application of Earthen Buildings (CRATerre). Ten teams of architects each created differing designs, resulting in aesthetically varied modern dwellings built using either of the three major types of mud wall construction: (1) rammed earth; (2) compressed, stabilized earthen blocks (mud brick); or (3) an earth–straw mixture laid in layers (layered mud). The total cost of the project was estimated by the Association pour la pro-motion de l'Institut international de la construction in terre dans la Ville Nouvelle d'Isle d'Abeau (1987:1–8) to be 25,000,000 francs (~$4,625,347 at 1997 exchange rate), or 3100 francs/m² = $574/m² ($53.30/ft²). Since the community's founding in 1985, a strong unity and community spirit developed among the residents, and was manifested in community government and the production of community festi-vals attended by many visitors. The Domaine de la Terre project demonstrated that mud construction can provide millions the opportunity to live in good, affordable houses of comfort and beauty.

COMFORTABLE INTERIOR TEMPERATURE

Soil has proven to be the most suitable building material in harsh, arid environments (as well as in environments with seasonally changing climates) because of its thermal retention properties. This comes as no surprise to those who dig in their gardens on hot summer days and are revived by the coolness of the soil in their hands; similarly, we marvel at the relative warmth of the soil when certain chores require digging below the frost line during the freezing days of winter. In deserts where the midday heat can kill human beings who lack protection, many animals seek holes and burrows underground, which enable them to survive both summer heat and winter freezes in comfort. When surface soils reach a temperature of 150°F (65.6°C), the earth a mere 18 in (45 cm) below the surface is a comfortable 60°F (15.6°C). Surely early humans—in company with many subterranean friends—discovered these characteristics of the soil early during their tenure of our planet and sought comfort for themselves in holes in the earth, whether in caves or in roofed pits.

Technically, thermal retention is not the same as "insulation." Insulation refers to nonconducting materials. In modern houses, a wide variety of substances, such as fiberglass, mineral wool, polystyrene, urethane boards, and perlite, use nonconducting air spaces to inhibit the passage of heat and cold. Actually, soil ranks among the poorest conductors of heat. Fathy (1973:45–46) listed the comparative thermal conductivity of several common building materials. These figures express the number of calories of heat (cal) that each material transmits per minute for each square centimeter of wall thickness; the lower the number, the less heat that is conducted by the material, and the greater the comfort inside.

Mud brick (with 20% fine sand) = 0.22 cal/min/cm^2
Mud brick (with 80% coarse sand) = 0.32 cal/min/cm^2
Baked brick = 0.48 cal/min/cm^2
Hollow concrete block = 0.80 cal/min/cm^2

Another measurement determines rate of heat transfer between the inside and outside of walls (Table 1.2). This shows that the thermal conductivity of rammed earth is about one-third that (or less) of other construction materials according to Lee (1937:31).

Lee's data were based upon idealized wall thicknesses for the material used (and probably for the common building practices at the time). Almost no one builds

Table 1.2 Differences in thermal conductivity among rammed-earth and various types of thick conventional walls.

Wall type, with typical width and components	Thermal Conductivity (Btu/h/ft^2)[a]
Rammed-earth wall, 27 in thick	0.10
Fired-brick wall, 12 in thick, with plaster on wood lathe	0.24
Limestone or sandstone, 12 in thick, with plaster on wood lathe	0.33
Frame wall, 12 in thick, with wood sheeting, studs, wood lathe, and plaster	0.35

[a] Btu (British thermal unit) = quantity of heat required to raise temperature of 1 lb of water by 1°F at a specified temperature (as 39°F).

with 12 in (~30.5 cm) thickness of fired brick now. In moderate and upscale town-houses being built near our home in Maryland, USA, walls consist of one brick veneer against a thin insulating blanket, plus 3 × 2 in (~7.5 × 5 cm) wooden framing, plus ¾ in (~ 2 cm) drywall, for a total thickness of about 6–6½ in (~15.2–16.5 cm). Nonetheless, despite the extra thickness of the rammed-earth wall in the comparison, it is not the thickness of the wall that matters but the material and its preparation. Temperature extremes (both hot and cold) race through hard crystalline materials such as glass, fired brick, concrete, and concrete block—which absorb and release heat quickly—but make their way very slowly through soil, no matter whether it is soft or hard, loose or compact. Thus earthen houses absorb and release heat very slowly, the insulating properties of mud leveling the heat gain and loss. Houses built with the "sharper" materials in the comparison table tend to follow the temperatures surrounding the walls with much lower insulating ability.

Mud actually absorbs, retains, and dissipates heat slowly. But heat retention, like insulation, spells comfort for people. Figure 1.3 illustrates the results of experiments conducted by an Iranian research center investigating the performance of housing materials in an arid environment during the 1970s. It shows the temperatures inside two buildings identical in size and shape, erected side-by-side, one of which was constructed of prefabricated concrete and the other of sun-dried mud brick. Note that the exterior temperature changed by about 22°C (39°F) during a 24 h period, peaking at 35.4°C (95.7°F) at about 3 PM. The temperature inside the concrete building climbed from a low of 18.6°C (65.5°F) to a high of 39.9°C (103.8°F) at

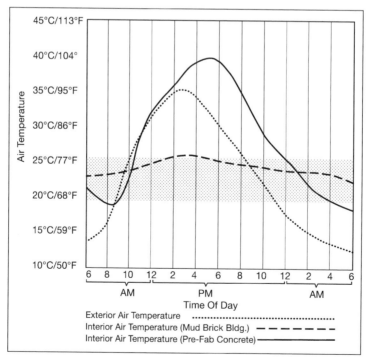

Figure 1.3 Comparison of exterior and interior temperatures (°C) for two houses—one of concrete and one of mud brick—in Iran during a 24 h period.

about 5:45 PM, 2½ h after the maximum exterior temperature was reached. Inside the mud building, however, the temperature fluctuated only 3.2°C (5.9°F), from a low of 22.5°C (72.4°F) to a maximum of 25.7°C (78.3°F), peaking at the same time as the maximum exterior temperature. In other words, the highest temperature inside the mud-brick building was an astonishing 14.2°C (25.5°F) cooler than the highest temperature inside the concrete building! The temperature zone of maximum comfort for people (stippled area in Figure 1.3) falls between about 19.7°C and 25.8°C (67.5°F and 78.4°F).

Slightly different structures were used in a thermal comfort study in Egypt in 1964 (Fathy, 1986:40–41, figs. 5–8). Among the test buildings were (1) a mud-brick building with walls 50 cm thick, roofed with a mud-brick vault and dome, and (2) a concrete building with prefabricated concrete panels 10 cm thick for both walls and roof. On a March day, the outside air temperature ranged from 12°C (53.6°F) at 6 AM to 28°C (82.4°F) at 2 PM and returned to 12°C (53.6°F) at 2 AM. The temperature inside the mud-brick building varied from 21°C to 23°C (69.8–73.4°F), with a range of only 2°C (3.6°F) during the 24 h period! This very small range is due to the heat retention characteristics of earth, the thickness of the mud walls, and the characteristics of vaulted and domed mud roofs. The temperature in the prefabricated concrete building reached 36°C (97°F); that was 13°C (23°F) higher than in the mud-brick building and 9°C (16°F) higher than the maximum temperature outside.

Not surprisingly, similar results were obtained in a New World research project by Fitch and Branch (1960:139). They measured the interior temperature of an adobe house in the southwestern USA on a summer day. While the outside temperature ranged from a low at 2 AM of 64.9°F (18.3°C) to a high at 2 PM of 105°F (40.6°C), the interior temperature of the adobe house ranged from a low at 2 AM of 74.8°F (23.8°C) to a high at 2 PM of 80°F (26.7°C). Whereas the outside temperature varied by 40.1°F (22.3°C) throughout a 24 h period, the temperature inside the adobe house varied only 5.2°F (2.9°C), a range nearly identical to that in the Iranian experiment illustrated in Figure 1.3.

We can vouch for these results. We visited a beehive-domed house in Fah, Syria, mentioned above (Figure 1.1), at about 10:30 one morning in April, when winter rains and gusty, cold winds alternate with sunny days. That day one of us (GVB) was wearing a wool sweater over a corduroy shirt and carrying a flannel-lined nylon jacket. Three houses were in the compound—the corbelled, domed beehive mud house, a flat-roofed mud house, and a new, concrete house with a concrete-slab roof. We examined and measured the beehive house in detail and then quickly visited the flat-roofed house, both of which were very comfortable whether standing up or sitting on the floor. After we finished with the mud houses, the owner proudly invited us to see his new concrete house. Inside, the damp cold was startling and immediately led to putting on and zipping up the flannel-lined jacket; even then, the chill penetrated our clothing. In all three buildings, the windows were closed; only the door to each house was open during our inspection. As we left the concrete building and removed our jackets, we asked the owner if his concrete house was hot inside during the summer. "Very hot," he replied, "We all sleep outside on the roof!" The only benefit the owner derived from his concrete house was a show of affluence in being able to afford such a costly home. What he sacrificed was year-round comfort for himself and his family.

Mud construction provides stable interior temperatures in regions of extreme heat and cold without air conditioning or large heating systems. A mud house with walls 2 ft (0.6 m) thick, a well-insulated roof, and minimum-heat-gain doors and windows would have an indoor temperature range varying no more than about 6°–8°F (3.3°–4.4°C) year-round in most of the USA without central heating and air conditioning! The Millers, who lived in a rammed-earth house in Greeley, Colorado, never required air conditioning during summer and reported that their heating bills are about one-half to one-third those of a house of the same size built of conventional materials (Miller and Miller, 1982:42).

Reducing dependence on major cooling and heating equipment effects great savings on utilities, irrespective of the type of fuel used. These savings are considerable in the USA where every conceivable utility cost and tax is passed on to the consumer. The savings are less, of course, for all who live in countries where utility costs are kept artificially low by government subsidies; nonetheless, any reduction in energy use enables those governments to use the saved energy funds for other national purposes. Apart from this sometimes enormous financial benefit, the homeowners would also enjoy years of much greater comfort in the interior climate of their mud home—a climate unequaled in houses built of any other known construction material.

BEAUTY AND FLEXIBILITY

Buildings that are beautiful and aesthetically pleasing gladden the human spirit. This fact has been lost in most urban buildings constructed after 1950, and we see them everywhere. In the USA, one city is much like the next, with rectangular, box-like structures with rows of monotonous windows or colored-glass panels extending from the street to the roof resembling a tawdry trinket. These buildings tend to be functional warehouses for cubicles, computers, and their unfortunate inhabitants. The trouble is that we cannot get rid of them. If a composer writes a symphony that is not well received, the symphony is retired from the repertory. If an artist paints a canvass that does not appeal to museums, gallery owners, and the public, it is returned to the studio where it is either destroyed, filed away in a closet, painted over, or displayed on the wall if it still pleases the artist. It is different with buildings because they are so expensive. Once built, they cannot be retired no matter how ugly they are, and they remain eyesores degrading the community for decades. For this reason, it is desirable that architects and construction engineers design harmonious structures that awaken us to their beauty and visual surprises, so that our spirits will be uplifted daily.

Mud construction can produce strikingly beautiful and functionally efficient structures. For most people, their experience with mud buildings has been limited to the poverty areas around nearly every city in Asia, Africa, and parts of the Americas. Built of mud, scraps of wood, cardboard, sacking, sheet metal, glass, or any of a number of other components scrounged by the occupants, these ugly shelters give the impression that all mud construction is dirty and primitive. Most people doubt that such a common, unsophisticated substance could produce anything of beauty.

In the Asir region of Saudi Arabia and the Hadhramaut valley of Yemen are magnificent and charming mud houses of traditional designs, built by nameless ma-

Figure 1.4 Tall house finished with attractive decorative devices including finials, dentils, quoin corners, pilasters, and lattice fencing. Seiyun, Hadhramaut, Yemen (1962).

sons, who often added new imaginative features (Figure 1.4). In Egypt, several Near Eastern nations, and New Mexico, USA, Hassan Fathy employed mud brick to build country houses, shops, schools, and mosques (see Figure 2.10)—even complete towns in some cases—with voluptuous domes, lofty vaults, and soaring arches that excite our eyes and raise our spirits. Also in New Mexico, Paul Graham McHenry, Nat Kaplan, Stan Huston, and Bob Nestor— among others—design luxurious, warm homes that enfold and comfort us with their soft lines, textures, and the subtle play of light and shadow.

Earthen structures are often more architecturally attractive, colorful, and majestic than buildings of wood, fired brick, or stone. Indeed, if one aspect of beauty consists in the harmony between structure and landscape, buildings of earth can equal or surpass those of fired brick or stone in blending and nestling into their surroundings. They often appear to have grown from the earth and to have been there forever (Figure 1.5).

Figure 1.5 Mud-brick town nestled at the base of a cliff in the Hadhramaut valley, Yemen (1991).

The secret of the beauty of mud construction is its plasticity, texture, and mass. For example, sharply angled corners that prevail in wooden, stone, and fired brick construction often give way in mud structures to smooth, rounded corners of walls both inside and out, and rounded exterior and interior door and window openings in walls. One must see their merging gradations of light and shadow, and feel the rounded areas to appreciate the softness of walls. In addition to their gracefulness, rounded corners are more functional than sharp corners, which may be accidentally chipped and broken by people, equipment, and vehicles striking them. We were visiting Hassan Fathy in 1977 at his roof apartment in an historic Ottoman apartment building in Cairo when a group of students of architecture and urban planning from Stuttgart, Germany, arrived unannounced to pay homage to our host. Hassan immediately began an impromptu lecture: "When you design, throw away your T-squares! There are no straight lines in nature; everything is curving! We have no straight lines in our bodies; when we hug a loved one, our arms form circles, not rectangles." He was, of course, correct in emphasizing the preeminence of the curve in nature; we are accustomed to it and comfortable with it. Is it any wonder that our eyes are delighted by the curving elements in mud architecture?

The plasticity of mud also makes possible many decorative devices that not only relieve the austerity of buildings but also add interest and surprise (Figure 1.6). These devices include such features as (1) the paneling of walls in single or multiple stages (see Figure 9.14); (2) columns with fluting that resemble ancient Greek styles (Figure 1.7), or with designs that imitate natural forms such as palm trees and spirals (see Figure 12.30); and (3) relief decorations, on both outer and inner wall surfaces and on ceilings, that commonly feature geometric or floral forms in low relief (Figure 1.8; see also Frontispiece). An attractive design employed in the former Sultan's Palace in Seiyun, Hadhramaut, Yemen, are the thin ridges forming a delicately pointed arch above each window (Figure 1.9). Sometimes panels and designs in low relief are painted a different color (pale pink for example) from the rest of the wall or from the background, which provides striking beauty (Figure 1.10).

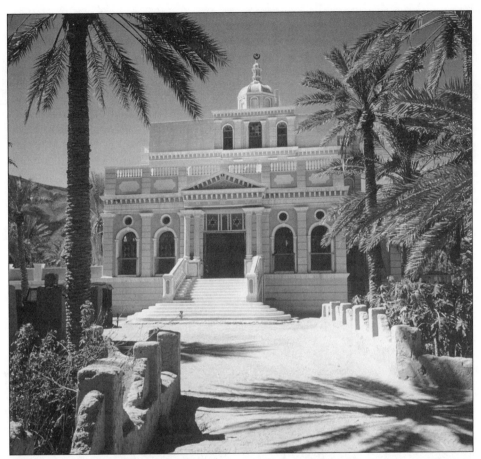

Figure 1.6 The abandoned al-Kaf house (which later became a hotel) in Terim, Hadhramaut, Yemen (1961).

The mass of a mud building, which almost always is hidden by plaster and sometimes by paint, nevertheless displays a uniformity of material and color. From the outside of a building, in the recessing of windows and doors, one can see a suggestion of wall mass that inspires confidence and assures safety. When one enters a house and sees the actual thickness of the wall when passing through the door, or when sitting in a window seat that is entirely within the wall, one immediately senses security and peace that comes from being out of harm's reach.

Mud is remarkably flexible in its adaptability to the demands of different kinds of structures. Most types of buildings with specialized functions can be constructed of mud brick: market stalls, small manufacturing plants, fortifications, temples, mosques, monasteries, churches, schools, hospitals, theaters, ice houses, service stations, hotels, chateaus and manor houses, farm houses, barns, and stables; exceptions include structures such as bridges, large manufacturing plants, and probably buildings exceeding 10 stories in height, although we have no firm data on height possibilities. Yet the ubiquitous high-rise buildings that frame the skylines of virtually all American, European, and Asian cities have their counterparts in the tall, mud-brick houses of

Figure 1.7   Column and ceiling decoration in the al-Kaf house in Terim, Hadhramaut, Yemen (1961).

the Hadhramaut valley in southern Yemen. From the beginning of the Christian era, tall houses built to several stories were similar in basic construction to our high-rise structures in employing basic post-and-beam and curtain wall construction.

Moreover, fired-brick construction and its decorative elements can be duplicated in mud brick: brick-for-brick, bond-for-bond, molding-for-molding, and some building techniques can be rendered better and faster in mud construction. For example, classical architecture sometimes features marble buildings with cornices decorated with cyma moldings—horizontally concave moldings curving down and outward, then reversing the curve to become convex (somewhat in an S-shape)—and with one or more fascia moldings (flat horizontal bands) below. This can be produced in mud brick, and is commonly covered with lime plaster. An excellent example is the front property wall of the former Sultan's Palace in Seiyun, Hadhramaut (Figure 1.11). Note how harmoniously it joins similarly decorated capitals of the engaged piers below. Another attractive decorative design is open lattice work on top of privacy walls and porches. In the Hadhramaut valley, the diagonally set,

Figure 1.8 Recessed niche with mud relief decoration in layered-mud wall, Punjab, Pakistan (1989).

Figure 1.9 Detail of pointed-arch reliefs trimming windows and open lattice work at top of the walls of the former Sultan's Palace in Seiyun, Hadhramaut, Yemen (1962).

Figure 1.10   Country house with pinkish plaster on wall panels, Hadhramaut, Yemen (1962).

Figure 1.11   Cyma recta molding with fascia moldings below; broken corner of cornice discloses sun-dried mud brick inside. Property wall of the former Sultan's Palace, Seiyun, Hadhramaut (1991).

crisscrossing bricks are very thin (see Figures 1.9, 3.58). In the abandoned refugee town north of Jericho in the Jordan Valley, bricks of normal thickness were used to create a somewhat similar zigzag design topping a wall (Figure 1.12). To increase privacy, the openings between the bricks are sometimes filled with mud to make a solid yet decorative wall (Figure 1.13).

Figure 1.12 Open zigzag design on porch wall in the abandoned (in 1967) refugee town north of Jericho, Jordan Valley, southern Levant (1978).

Figure 1.13 Closed zigzag design on porch wall in refugee town north of Jericho, Jordan Valley (1978).

Figure 1.14   Property wall of layered mud, south of Lahore in Punjab, Pakistan (1989).

Nearly any free-form structure that can be constructed with poured concrete can also be built of rammed earth. Compare any poured-concrete arch (see Figure 8.23 for example) with the rammed-earth arches of the royal stables at Meknes in Morocco from the late seventeenth to eighteenth centuries (see Figure 8.36). A serpentine wall, like those of ancient Egypt (Clarke and Engelbach, 1930:213, fig. 259), can be built around a single lot or around a city block. Massive city walls can be erected. Round, fortress-like towers can be added to the corners of a house. There are few inherent limitations in mud construction—most apparent limitations derive from lack of imagination.

STRENGTH AND DURABILITY

Appearances can be deceiving. Sun-dried mud walls may not appear to be as strong and lasting as stone, fired-brick, or concrete walls; however, mud walls are extraordinarily strong and durable, and rammed-earth structures are the strongest of all.

During our travels in Punjab, Pakistan, with Waseem Ahmad (Senior Chemist of the National Museum in Lahore, Pakistan), we examined several layered-mud walls defining property boundaries (Figure 1.14) and also the walls of village houses.

Figure 1.15   Outer face of fired-brick wall showing insufficient cement mortar, Punjab, Pakistan (1989).

Ahmad informed us that the high fortification walls around prisons in Pakistan are constructed of layered mud because they are harder to breach and more secure than fired-brick, concrete block, or stone walls and that it is virtually impossible to dig through a thick mud wall without mechanical tools, because of the wall's hardness.

By contrast, fired-brick and stone walls in Pakistan and India are much easier to break through. Masonry blocks are typically laid without using a full bed of mortar on the bedding and between rising joints. A continuous bead of mortar is laid only on the front edge of the bedding and rising joints (on the outside face of a wall), which are visible to all (Figure 1.15). On the more infrequently seen inner face of the wall, instead of a continuous bead of mortar, only small piers of mortar are placed at the corners and in one or two places between the corners. With only a screwdriver, bottle opener, or metal rod, one can pry or break out the small concrete piers of mortar, wiggle the brick with fingers, and pull it out of the wall. When several bricks have been removed in this manner, a prison inmate can easily crawl through the hole to escape.

How strong are earthen walls? A bullet can penetrate only 4–5 cm. The Millers tell of a parked, unattended pickup truck that rolled down a slight grade, leveling a small tree and eventually hitting the front wall of a rammed-earth house (Miller and Miller, 1982:41). The stucco on the exterior surface of the wall was scratched, but no

Figure 1.16   Vaulted storage buildings (left) and stone mortuary temple (right) at the Ramesseum, from thirteenth century B.C., Luxor, Egypt (1977).

damage occurred to any of the art objects on wall-mounted shelving directly inside the point of impact. The front end of the pickup truck, however, was damaged.

Barring major earthquakes, if mud plaster on earthen walls is kept in good repair, earthen buildings have extraordinarily long lives. In archaeological time, they far exceed wooden structures in longevity and equal or surpass that of fired brick. At Luxor, Egypt, for example, major sections of the pitched-mud-brick, vaulted storage buildings of the Ramesseum surround the mortuary temple of Ramses II on three sides. These structures were constructed in the thirteenth century B.C., making them more than 3300 years old (Figure 1.16). In Shibam, Hadhramaut, Yemen, the six-story, mud-brick house known as Beit Jarhum is between 400 and 500 years old (see Figures 3.55, 3.56), whereas the former Sultan's Palace in Seiyun, Hadhramaut, is more than 100 years old (see Figure 3.60). At Rabat, Morocco, the old city wall of rammed earth dates from the seventeenth century (see Figures 8.24, 8.25). These examples, all fully exposed to the weather, have survived because they were well constructed, well maintained, and/or massive.

The strength and survival of mud and earthen buildings stem from the great compression of the soil, which increases in hardness as it dries, so that it resembles stone. Indeed, earthen walls are sometimes said to be built with "handmade stone." I discovered this characteristic of mud walls early in my archaeological career. Working with a handpick consisting of an adze-like blade and a small mason's trowel, I had attempted to define the individual mud bricks and smoothing walls that had been exposed to air for 24 hours or more, only to discover that the bricks were as hard as stone!

The density of the soil also makes the walls soundproof, a highly desirable feature missing in most recently built apartments, condominiums, and hotels in the USA. Mud walls are also fireproof; only the wooden, plastic, and fabric furnishings are destroyed by fire, leaving the earthen walls intact. At worst, they may be partially baked—"at worst" because baking reduces the insulating quality of earthen walls. Fire-proofing, however, should make the homeowner eligible for considerably lower fire insurance rates. Additionally, mud walls discourage habitation by insects and rodents if basic rules of cleanliness are maintained.

What more could one ask? A fine, do-it-yourself medium that is cheap and yields unsurpassed comfort. A plastic substance that is ideal for creative design and construction. A versatile construction material that is suitable for building structures of diverse function and design, and which are pleasing to the eye. A material that is fireproof, soundproof, strong, and enduring. It sounds perfect, does it not? Well, almost. There are a few problems; however, imaginative solutions for these problems have been developed by masons throughout history, which we explain in subsequent chapters.

NOTE

1. Ashlar masonry is composed of "dressed" (hewn or squared) stone blocks.

Chapter 2

Factors in Building Design

Building designs derive from a combination of several factors: (1) local environment, (2) cultural mores, (3) regional building traditions, (4) function, and (5) human creativity, which vary in importance through time and depend upon the political, economic, and cultural situation. The first three factors are general in nature and apply to all structures in the same environment, in the same culture, and in closely related cultures. When one factor changes, it is likely that building designs will also change in response to the demands of the factor at that moment in time. The fourth factor, function, is specific, and it may be of greater importance in structural design, sometimes overriding in part the design influence of the general factors. Modifying and often altering the effects of these four factors is the fifth, human creativity. Creativity is a universal human trait appearing in all areas of human thought and activity. It emerges unexpectedly in certain individuals, sometimes with little or no apparent development, and we conclude it is probably of genetic origin, aided by training, education, the mores and values of the society, and chance. The works of creative individuals often exert enormous influence, even revolutionizing major aspects of culture, including architecture. Perhaps we should add a sixth factor—human preference, which primarily impinges upon the fifth factor, creativity. No matter how imaginative, suitable, and attractive a building design may be, it must find acceptance by the people if it is to become a lasting part of the building tradition. Even if a design never achieves this distinction, individual aspects of it may be incorporated in the tradition.

Each of these factors is complex enough to merit its own book-length treatment, which is not possible here. Instead we provide a few examples of each to illustrate their interaction and importance in designing structures.

ENVIRONMENTAL CONSIDERATIONS

Many facets of the environment influence building design and the placement of structures:

Figure 2.1   Barren mountains and flat land with layered-mud compound and houses in northern Baluchistan, Pakistan (1990).

Figure 2.2   Deteriorating layered-mud property wall bordering flat, agricultural land in the region between Lahore and Harappa in Punjab, Pakistan (1989).

- Climate, including the mean seasonal and daily temperatures, humidity, frequency and distribution of rainfall, and site elevation.
- Geology, including amount and characteristics of rock and soil types.
- Vegetation cover in kind and extent.
- Topography of the proposed building site.
- Location and orientation of the proposed structure on the site.
- Physical history of the specific area, including occurrences of tornadoes, hurricanes, floods, and seismic events.

The environment determines in varying degrees what materials will be used in construction. Throughout history, if an area has an abundance of trees yielding timber suitable for building, wooden houses predominate. In hill country and areas with readily available stone that can be quarried, stone buildings prevail. In plains and marshy areas where there are no forests, groves, or sources of stone, then mud, sod, reed, or grass structures will predominate. In antiquity, materials used in

building were generally limited to those available near the building site. Human in-
genuity and a growing technological base enabled creative individuals to overcome
environmental limitations by developing special processes for modifying raw materials. These technological processes today provide us with fired brick, cement and
concrete, metals, glass, and plastics for construction. Global distribution systems
now make possible the transport of building materials to people everywhere who
can afford the costs. In this manner, we transcend the historically limited supplies
provided by the regional environment.

The effects of contrasting environments on mud house design can be seen in two
regions of Pakistan (see Appendix A, Map 5) where mud buildings prevail in all
but the major cities: the Baluchistan plateau (Figure 2.1) in the west-central region,
which adjoins Afghanistan on the west, and the river valleys and plains of Punjab
(Figure 2.2) in the east-central region, bordering western India.

The Baluchistan plateau is an arid tableland with an elevation of 1600 m above
sea level at Quetta, the provincial capital, with high mountain ranges in the far
north and east. (All climate data for Quetta were obtained from Canty & Associates'
Weatherbase, 2004b.) Average annual precipitation for the province is sparse, about
230–240 mm, although it is somewhat higher in the mountain regions, where some
of the winter moisture falls as snow. Monthly average precipitation in Quetta ranges
25–51 mm for December through April and 0–13 mm for May through November.
Unlike other regions of Pakistan, Baluchistan does not have a fertile monsoon
season. The average number of days with rain is just 20.3 annually: the months of
December through May average 1–4 rainy days per month; June through November
average 0.2–0.9 rainy days per month. Temperatures in the Quetta area during July
range from an average high of 34°C (94°F) to an average low of 18°C (65°F), and
January temperatures range from an average high of 10°C (50°F) to an average low
of -2°C (28°F). Trees and lush fruit orchards flourish on some mountains and in in-
termontane valleys. Yet most of Baluchistan is like the plains and hill slopes around
Quetta, where vegetation is mostly scrub growth, wild grasses, and weeds, and these
areas are usually brown by May.

In Punjab near the Ravi River, the elevation is 215 m above sea level at Lahore,
the provincial capital—considerably lower than elevations in Baluchistan. (All
climate data for Lahore were obtained from Canty & Associates' Weatherbase,
2004a.) Average annual rainfall in this agricultural zone bordering the river is
518 mm. July and August are monsoon season, averaging 155 mm and 135 mm
of monthly precipitation, respectively; monthly average precipitation for the
rest of the year ranges 3–64 mm, with October through December being driest.
In dry years, Punjab's minimum rainfall is sufficient to yield a crop of wheat,
whereas Baluchistan's minimum produces only dust. Punjab is warm, with a
yearly average high of 28°C (84°F) in Lahore. Summer temperatures range from
an average low of 28°C (84°F) to an average high of 38°C (102°F) with dry
winds; the highest temperature on record is 48°C (120°F) in June. Winters are
mild, with temperatures ranging 8°C–18°C (48–65°F). Irrigation agriculture is
intensively practiced on the alluvium of the valleys and plains of Punjab. Salt
is leached continuously, leaving a white efflorescence on the ground surface, as
well as on fired-brick and mud structures. (Salt also characterizes the soils of
Baluchistan, but to a lesser degree.)

Table 2.1   Structural and design modifications reflecting climatic differences in two regions of Pakistan. (Layered-mud walls are of the same thickness in both regions for structural and insulating purposes.)

Design feature	Baluchistan	Punjab
Roof type	Mostly flat; few shed and gabled in high country	Nearly all flat
Roof material	Mud flat roofs; tin and aluminum shed and gabled	Mud flat roofs; rarely metal
Roof features	Flat roofs inside parapet, often with drip molding Shed and gabled roofs overhang walls 30–50 cm	Flat roofs inside parapet, often with drip molding
Roof stairs	Narrow (5–10 cm) board with cut steps, to shovel snow from roof	Exterior mud stairway or wood ladder
Curbing at wall base	Primarily of mud; sometimes massive, serves as benches	Of mud or fired brick; fewer and smaller
Cooking area	Outdoors in summer, sometimes roofed; indoors in winter	Entirely outdoors, open air

These differences in climate between Baluchistan and Punjab have resulted in differences in the features and design of layered-mud structures typical of each region (Table 2.1).

By comparison, the Hadhramaut in Yemen (see Appendix A, Map 3), with an elevation of about 915 m above sea level, is slightly hotter in summer and has colder nights in winter than Punjab. Rainfall is minuscule. Roof stairs are permanent and are located inside the building to give access to the flat roof, a major activity area year-round. The cooking area is primarily indoors, although some families cook on the roof during summer. Walls are much thicker in the Hadhramaut owing to the multistoried design of houses, but the walls become thinner as they ascend to higher stories. Except for domes in cemeteries, all roofs are flat in the Hadhramaut (Figure 2.3).

EFFECTS OF CULTURAL MORES

Traditional values also influence house design and construction. Baluchistan is tribal in traditions and culture, not only in the countryside and small villages, but in major urban centers, such as Quetta. The major tribal groups are Baluchis, who occupy the center and south of the province, and Pathans, who live in the north and west, but these locations are not exclusive to either tribe. Today, Islam increasingly shapes the society and social mores with very conservative—fundamentalist—ideology, customs, and practices. Yet many professionals and intellectuals are liberal in their interpretation of faith and practice in daily life. Consider a few examples of accepted cultural mores that particularly affect building design.

From the points of view of philosophy, community traditions, and attitudes, families and homes may either turn outward to the neighborhood or turn inward on themselves for privacy. People of the Western world generally tend to lead open lives; those who can afford the extra land surround their houses with open space, sharing with their community a view of their property, the comings and goings of

Figure 2.3 The Hadhramaut valley at Seiyun, about 305 m below the flat, rock-covered plateau. The dark vegetation consists of date palms. Not visible are the vegetable garden plots near the base of the cliffs. The Sultan's Palace is left center; the *suq* (market) is the open area with small shops to the right. All buildings are of mud brick and have flat roofs (1962).

family and visitors, and the outdoor activities of the family. Most houses in the USA turn outward, commonly without privacy walls; indeed the building codes of most American cities make it unlawful to build a fence more than 6 ft high. Civic pride and the residents' willingness to accept responsibility for the community almost always accompany the "open" type of residential area. The appearance of the neighborhood is taken seriously by these communities; the residents—except perhaps those of economically depressed areas of inner cities—expect all houses to be well maintained, lawns to be well groomed, and both vacant lots and streets to be clean and free of rubbish. Citizens also expect the local government to maintain public property and streets and to provide convenient waste disposal services.

Western attitudes contrast markedly with the "privacy" concept of Mediterranean and Near Eastern societies. The prevailing style of family living in these societies is closed, walled-in, and private; the garden, lawn, house, and family activities are closed to the community and the world. A house may be built along the perimeter of the entire property, surrounding a central courtyard as in ancient Rome, or it may have an enclosed courtyard at one end. Alternatively, residences of wealthy families may be surrounded with lawns and gardens, as in the West, but the entire property would be enclosed by a privacy wall 2.75 m tall or higher (Figure 2.4), often topped with broken glass, spikes, or barbed wire to ensure privacy and to deter intrusion.

Despite the emphasis on privacy, householders generally keep their courtyards and other property inside the high wall immaculate. Without giving notice, we visited courtyards and houses in Pakistan, Yemen, and Syria where the earthen floor had been freshly sprinkled with water to harden the surface and to allay dust, or where a

Figure 2.4   Layered-mud property wall. The chimneys show the location of the building inside the wall. Pishin, Baluchistan, Pakistan (1990).

concrete floor had been recently washed. We observed grounds that commonly were without so much as a fragment of plastic or twig littering the area—so clean that one could eat off the floor. We were invited into houses where all household utensils such as churns, pots, and pans were clean and neatly arranged (see Figure 3.3) and where bedding was neatly folded and stacked on chests against the wall (see Figure 3.50).

In stark contrast to the immaculate condition of properties inside the privacy walls in most Muslim communities throughout Southwest Asia and the Near East, the appearance of the neighborhood and immediate area outside the enclosure walls is of little or no interest to the inhabitants. Vacant lots between estates are repositories for garbage and rubbish, such as weeds, discarded automobile tires, broken concrete blocks, plastic bottles, tin cans, and plastic bags (Figure 2.5). Streets are unpaved and often potholed and rutted, resembling lanes in a shantytown of poverty-stricken people rather than attractive streets bordered by houses of the well-to-do. There is no civic responsibility for the appearance of the neighborhood's public areas. Both the desire for privacy and the lack of civic pride contribute to the type of house designs that people living in these cultures choose.

Many societies of the world are organized around the extended family, where married sons, their wives, and children live with the sons' parents in a large house, or in smaller, individual family houses nearby or surrounding the parents' home in a large family compound. Traditionally, children revere their parents and care for them when they are unable to take care of themselves. All wage earners in the extended family commonly pool their earnings in a family treasury controlled by the patriarch. In general, the extended family requires either a large house with many rooms, a small apartment house, or a cluster of smaller, expandable structures within a family compound. The tall-house compounds, each belonging to one family, in Seiyun, Hadhramaut, Yemen, are an example of the latter. Occasionally the tall houses are joined to one another at the third or fourth level by an enclosed bridge spanning the street to permit easy communication between houses with privacy (Figure 2.6).

By contrast, throughout most of Europe and North America, the nuclear family as the basic unit in society has weakened and often is fragmented. For various reasons, families have become so mobile that they no longer support a family group housing

Figure 2.5 A former palace compound with rubbish and blocks outside the property wall in Nuqub, Beihan, Yemen (1991).

Figure 2.6 Mud-brick-walled bridges connecting houses of extended families at the fourth-floor level, Seiyun, Hadhramaut, Yemen (1991).

cluster; children leave home to attend school, go to distant places for jobs, or become psychologically isolated from parents, thus creating independent family segments away from the core family. This results in diminution of loyalty, interdependence, and unity in the core family. In these societies, individual houses or apartments shelter each independent segment of a family, often in a location distant from other related family segments. The size, income, and needs of each family segment largely determine the size of the house, the number of rooms, and space functions. Although this is true to some extent in most societies, the emphasis in the West is on independence, often resulting in isolation from the nuclear family.

In Muslim countries, polygamy continues as a traditional family institution, although the number of wives is limited to a maximum of four at one time. Yet in some Muslim countries monogamy is a long established tradition, and even within the polygamous societies there are many monogamous marriages, especially among the more educated citizens.

There is also a tradition of female modesty, which is becoming increasingly prevalent with the spread of Islamic fundamentalism. The modesty codes apply to females beginning with the onset of puberty and include a number of aspects. One is Purdah—the wearing of plain, drab clothing from the top of the head to the feet, including a veil, so that the woman's physical appearance cannot entice men.

Another tradition is gender separation. In many Muslim societies, women often live either in separate quarters in the home or in a separate house where men are not permitted to enter. In some countries, women can be in the same room with men if they remain behind a barrier, such as a *mashrabiya*—a decorative, lattice-work screen—where they can see and hear without being seen. In the privacy of their quarters, many women dress as they please, and younger women might choose to wear blouses and jeans. In some countries, women do not go shopping; in others, they may go with their husband or in the company of other women, especially female members of their extended family. Secular and liberal Muslim governments, however, do not enforce modesty codes, and a few actually forbid them in their cities, where most women dress like European and American women.

The traditions of polygamy and modesty have a major effect on house design and construction. Special plans have developed through time to accommodate this lifestyle. In rural and urban Baluchistan, men commonly have two or three wives. Wives, older daughters, and young children are housed separately from the men, either in a series of rooms in the house or in their own women's building. The husband and other males in the family live segregated in their own series of rooms or in a men's building. In the Pathan tribal areas of Baluchistan that we visited, those who could afford to build two houses had separate buildings for male and female family members, with duplicated facilities such as sitting rooms and sleeping quarters in each building (see Figures 3.13–3.15). In the traditional large, fortress-type houses of the Pathans, women had separate rooms under the same roof. When men and women have separate buildings, a room is kept in the women's house for the husband's nocturnal visit to one of his wives.

Foreign women are occasionally invited to visit the wives and children, although they or their husband may refuse such a request; male guests are never accorded this privilege. Among the Pathans, the female member of our team (OVB) was generally invited to visit the women, to meet each wife and her children, to be shown their rooms, handiwork, and cooking areas; clothing, jewelry, and cosmetics were often discussed. In their quarters, women did not cover their faces. Some even permitted OVB to photograph them and their children. By contrast, the Baluchis in the village of Pandran, south of Kalat, denied permission to visit the women's quarters, even though the request was made on OVB's behalf by the sheikh's personal representative who accompanied us in Baluchi tribal area.

Although some Baluchis had compounds with separate buildings for husbands and wives, those that we visited all had separate rooms within the same building, duplicating functional areas (see Figure 3.7). Yet we visited a Pathan complex at Khanai where the mother of the male householder was installed in a third separate building (see Figure 3.11). Whether in separate buildings or in gender-specific rooms within the same building, the number of buildings or rooms required to house a family is more than doubled because each of the wives has a separate room (shared with her children, if any). Having twice as many buildings and facilities requires both larger plots of land and more funds for building and maintenance.

In Punjab, on the other hand, monogamous marriages are common. Although still segregated, women lead more open lives with less rigid adherence to purdah and with freedom to work in the presence of men, to move around the village, and to shop in the market. In a monogamous marriage, a husband shares the same room and a double bed with his wife, and their children occupy a separate room. Most village houses in Punjab, therefore, consisted of only two bedrooms (and sometimes a third room for storage), with all food preparation done out in the courtyard (see Figures 3.1, 3.2, 3.4).

Throughout Pakistan, and indeed everywhere in the Muslim world in both rural and urban areas, one can see property boundary walls enclosing barren plots of land. The primary function of the boundary walls is to establish property ownership when land is acquired, and these walls are usually erected before dwellings or business structures are built. A property wall surrounding a home and courtyard

Figure 2.7   Layered-mud property wall of an estate in Punjab, Pakistan (1989).

also serves to assure privacy for the family so that no one can see the females of the household. Walls may be a mile or more in total length when they enclose large estates or country properties. Such walls are commonly 2–4 m high (Figure 2.7).

INFLUENCE OF TRADITION

Building traditions exist for hundreds and even thousands of years. Consider classical Greek architecture with its formalized building designs and decorative orders. The formative period can be traced to the Late Helladic period, ca. 1600–1100 B.C., with some elements going back to the third millennium B.C. or earlier. By the seventh to early sixth centuries B.C., Doric and Ionic orders were already established, with each order undergoing minor developments to reach its definitive style in the fifth and fourth centuries B.C., respectively. The first Corinthian capitals appeared during the last decades of the fifth century B.C. These orders in turn produced many variations through the Hellenistic and Roman periods, and later found a welcome home throughout Europe. Eventually they came to North America, where they have experienced cycles of being in or out of architectural favor.

There are many examples of the persistence of building traditions. A little-known example is the shape of mud bricks in different regions. By 3000 B.C., the use of rectangular brick was firmly established in Egypt, and this preference has continued throughout history to the present. About the same time, square brick became the norm in ancient Mesopotamia (modern Iraq) and neighboring regions, Iran on the east, and Syria on the west. The square shape has prevailed in this region from antiquity to the present. This, of course, does not mean that the Egyptians never used square brick, or that the Mesopotamians (Sumerians, Assyrians, Babylonians, and their neighbors) never employed rectangular brick; both Egyptians and Mesopotamians used the opposite forms for terminating brick courses, for bonding, and other special situations. What is important to note is the strength and endurance of different building traditions, despite the many close contacts between these regions through which numerous cultural features were shared or borrowed.

The same phenomenon occurs in house designs in many other places. The most common and enduring plan in the Mediterranean basin and the Near East is the courtyard house. The basic plan consists of an interior courtyard surrounded by rooms on two, three, or four sides. The courtyard house apparently first appeared in Pre-Pottery Neolithic B in the Near East about 8000–10,000 years ago. It has continued through the ages since—in the Near East, Egypt, Greece, and Italy—and still prevails, although many one- or two-story houses with surrounding yards have appeared in the last century.

From about 2000 years ago to the present in Arabia, there has been a tradition of multistoried houses. These include the remaining tall, mud-brick and fired-brick houses of Sana`a, Yemen; the layered-mud houses of four- and five-stories at Marib, Yemen; and the ubiquitous three- and four-story houses in the Hadhramaut, Yemen, and in the Asir region, Saudi Arabia. The tall house culminates in the seven- and eight-story, 100- to 500-year-old "skyscrapers" of Shibam in the Hadhramaut. Are these remnants of earlier traditions or do they represent a design created to suit lifestyles of recent centuries?

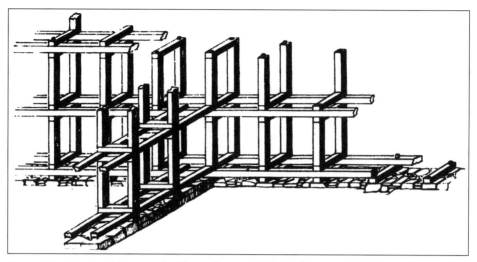

Figure 2.8 Structural framework of heavy beams of `*ilb* (jujube) wood from building K at Mash-gha, Wadi Idim, Hadhramaut, Yemen, dating from the second to fourth centuries A.D. (Adapted from Seigne, 1980: pl. 8. For the variety of techniques of joining beams in the Palace at Shabwa, see Seigne, 1992:134–143, fig. 12b.)

In cities today, tall buildings reflect economic necessity, due to the high cost of land, and the desire to concentrate many activities in the central city. One builds upward when it is not feasible to build outward.

Most ancient peoples sought to live on tells, whose natural height provided greater safety from attackers' weapons, from invasion and occupation, and from animal predators that might harm children and livestock. Because the flat surface of a tell was limited in area, it was more preferable to live in tall houses jammed close together than it was to have a house in the surrounding fields below, where protection from enemies was lacking. In antiquity, dwelling on tells reflected a primary concern for security. Yet the height of the tell also made tall houses several degrees cooler; they received more breeze, and in the shade cast by neighboring houses they received less heat from the sun (see Figure 7.1).

Archaeologists and architects have wondered when the tall-house design appeared and where it originated. There is considerable evidence of two-story buildings in the Old World, but archaeologists and archaeological architects have been reluctant to suggest taller structures. Yet in mud architecture there is ample reason to reconstruct multistoried buildings based on the ratio of wall thickness to height by using actual ratios found in existing tall houses in the Hadhramaut. The most notable features of the contemporary Hadhramaut tall buildings relevant for archaeological reconstructions are:

1) a choice of foundation types (either perimeter or hole types), reaching depths from about 1.6 m for perimeter foundations, to 2.0–3.5 m in hole excavations for basements,

2) the surprising thinness of tall mud brick walls (ca. 86 cm at the base), and tall form-built rammed earth walls (75 cm) at the base, and

3) the systematic thinning of the walls from the lowest floor to the highest floor, e.g., in the mud brick house from 86 cm to 23 cm, and in the rammed earth house from 75 cm to 40 cm, by means of using different sizes of mud bricks, and reducing the interior width of the rammed earth forms as the walls ascend.

These data free us to reconstruct structures of various heights.

Excavations during the 1970s and 1980s by the French Archaeological Mission in Yemen, under the direction of Jean-François Breton, at Shabwa, capital of the ancient kingdom of Hadhramaut, and at Mashgha in Wadi Idim about 225 km east of Shabwa, yielded surprising discoveries. By no later than the second century A.D., and possibly earlier, tall houses were already being constructed at Shabwa (Seigne, 1992:111–164) and Mashgha (Breton et al., 1980:22–32). These buildings were post-and-beam structures with curtain walls of brick, and they reached at least four stories in height (Figure 2.8). This means that nearly 2000 years ago the Hadhramis were already living in tall houses, and this design apparently became a regional tradition that has continued to the present. These tall houses anticipated the basic design of twentieth century skyscrapers. The major differences in twentieth century construction are the substitutions of (a) structural steel or concrete beams for the massive beams of wood and (b) various other materials—glass, metal, or veneers—for the brick curtain walls.

The tradition of roofing structures with mud-brick vaulting reaches back into the fourth millennium B.C., when an example with two different types of vaulting—radial and pitched-brick—appeared fully developed in a First Dynasty tomb at Helwan, Egypt. By the middle of the third millennium B.C. in the Pyramid Age, Egyptians were experimenting with many styles of barrel vault construction methods and design techniques; simultaneously, radial and pitched-brick vaults were being erected by the Sumerians in Mesopotamia. By the eighteenth century B.C., mud-brick radial vaulting appeared among the Canaanites in Israel. A third type of vault construction—rib or strut vaulting—was invented in Iran, probably early in the first millennium B.C. In the seventh century B.C., the first known example of mud voussoirs—keystone-shaped bricks—in pitched-brick vaulting appeared at Tell Jemmeh, Israel. The technique of substituting fired brick for mud brick in pitched-brick vault construction appeared not long before the beginning of the Christian era in the Fayum oasis of Egypt and again in the ninth century A.D. Buddhist monastery southeast of Patna in Nalanda, Bihar State, India (see Appendix A, Map 6). Magnificent examples of pitched-mud-brick vaulting appeared in the sixth century A.D. Monastery of San Simeon on the west bank of the Nile River at Aswan, Egypt, which continued in use until the thirteenth century (see Chapter 11).

Interestingly enough, the two earliest methods of mud-brick vault construction have been continuously employed in buildings south of Aswan from antiquity to the present, but few archaeologists knew of them. These methods were brought to the attention of contemporary archaeologists and architects by Hassan Fathy (1973:6–12), who employed the techniques in constructing numerous handsome houses, shopping arcades, schools, and mosques in northern Egypt, throughout the Near East, and at Abiquiu, New Mexico, USA. These examples illustrate the strength of the tradition of mud-brick vaulting as a means of roofing buildings when timber and iron for beams are wanting.

From these examples, we see the force of inherited tradition that unites ancient and contemporary builders. Although earlier building techniques are occasionally rediscovered and applied by architects of today, many techniques now used are new, independent inventions; yet they reflect thought processes and problem solving exercises likely also experienced by builders in antiquity.

FUNCTION

All buildings are constructed to perform one or more functions. Some structures are designed as all-purpose buildings. A typical example of a multifunctional structure is the large meeting hall, which is designed to accommodate a range of activities, such as dances, indoor sports, exhibitions, trade shows, and all types of meetings—political, academic, educational, and religious. Such a hall consists mainly of open space, with a minimum of interior piers or columns to support the roof and without permanent accoutrements or furniture, for maximum adaptability.

Most buildings, however, are erected to meet fewer specific needs and functions. Market or bazaar structures throughout North Africa and the Near East are very much the same, generally consisting of a long building of moderate depth divided into small stalls by party walls (Figure 2.9). Sometimes the stalls are entirely open on the front, at other times a door and a glass window pane constrict the size of the entrance. The shop front will always be fitted with a pivoting, folding, or retractable door for security when closed. Individual shops are generally owned by a family and operated as a family business; sometimes a wealthy family will own several shops scattered throughout the market.

A mosque (Figure 2.10), church (see Figure 11.14), or synagogue may have specific requirements in orientation, in equipment for prayer (either kneeling space or seats; open seating or restricted seating by gender), preworship washing, baptistries,

Figure 2.9 Barrel-vaulted mud-brick shops designed and newly built by Hassan Fathy at New Gourna, Luxor, Egypt (1977), awaiting finishing touches and vendors.

altars, arks, structures for preaching, choir lofts or stalls, musical instrumentation, and symbolic structures such as minarets and steeples.

A building designed as a cinema or movie house in Egypt may be somewhat similar to one in India and one in the USA, although the environment and cultural mores of each country are almost totally different. A cinema anywhere has a specific function, requiring a building designed with a stage or screen area, a large area for audience seating, and an administrative section at the front where tickets, and sometimes refreshments, are sold.

Other buildings with specific functions include hospitals, and specialized industrial structures such as factories, service stations, etc. Houses also have a clear, easy-to-understand function as the shelter or "nest" of the family. Yet, like bird nests, houses can be built in a seemingly infinite number of designs to meet all demands of the culture and family.

HUMAN CREATIVITY

Human creativity plays a major role in building design and construction techniques. Most new ideas are the product of an individual. However, in an age of increasingly complex technologies, one person's idea is often developed by a team or group because of the interrelationships with other fields that demand specialized knowledge. Yet it is usually an individual who formulates the initial concept and receives credit for the discovery or invention, as we know from Nobel Prizes and other awards and honors of today.

In ancient architecture, we know of some individual builders by name, whom history has credited with significant achievements. In Egypt, Imhotep built the first pyramid—the Step-Pyramid of Djoser, the first king of the Third Dynasty (ca. twenty-sixth century B.C.)—at Saqqara. He took the *mastaba*, a traditional tomb type that was shaped like a mud bench, transferred the medium from mud brick

Figure 2.10   Mosque at Abiquiu, New Mexico, USA, built by Hassan Fathy (1989).

to small stone blocks, and piled a series of *mastabas* on top to form a six-stage pyramidal structure. Two thousand years later, he was regarded by the Egyptians as a god who also performed miracles of magic and medicine. Another brilliant architect in ancient Egypt was Senmut, who constructed near Luxor one of the most beautiful structures surviving from antiquity, the mortuary temple of Queen Hatshepsut of the fifteenth century B.C. Among the Greeks, in the fifth century B.C., Ictinus designed the Parthenon at Athens with his assistant, Callicrates, who later designed the Temple of Athena Nike on the Acropolis; and Mnesicles designed the Propylaea and Erechtheum of the Acropolis. During the following century, Pythius and Satyrus were the architects of the Mausoleum at Halicarnassus in Turkey, which consisted of a pyramid built on top of a Greek temple and was regarded as one of the seven wonders of the ancient world. The chief monument of Byzantine architecture is the Haghia Sophia in Istanbul, constructed by Anthemius of Tralles and Isidorus of Miletus and inaugurated in A.D. 537. In the sixteenth century A.D., during the Ottoman renaissance, Mi'mar Koca Sinan designed more than 200 domed buildings from Budapest to the Arabian Peninsula, with the vast majority in Turkey.

Although we know the names of other creative builders of earlier times, most remain nameless. So far as I know, not a single ancient mud architect's name has come down to us. Yet it is to the imagination, trial-and-error testing, and persistent tinkering of those ancient innovators that we are indebted for so many basic inventions in mud construction: the development of the form for making identical mud bricks; the diverse ways of building with mud; the methods of constructing corbelled domes and the various types of vaults and arches; the techniques of erecting multistoried buildings; the almost infinite varieties of relief and carved decorative designs, as well as various types of mud and lime plasters and finishes.

Creative individuals are still with us today, developing new techniques for mud construction and adapting the latest products of diverse technologies to enhance the comfort, opulence, and longevity of mud buildings. It seems to me that most of these achievements are coming from imaginative adobe architects, engineers, and architects in the southwestern USA, where interest is keen and where a supportive and often affluent clientele demands houses with style, quality, and conveniences equal to or better than the finest homes of wood, fired brick, or stone.

Vitruvius Pollio, the great Roman architect who served Augustus Caesar in the late decades of the first century B.C., wrote ca. 27 B.C. the most important architectural treatise surviving from antiquity, *De Architectura* (*On Architecture*), which served as the "bible of architecture" until Byzantine times. In it he described the qualities by which all buildings are judged, and this applies to mud architecture also:

> Therefore the test of all building is held to be threefold: fine workmanship, magnificence, architectural composition. When a building has a magnificent appearance, the expenditure of those who control it, is praised. When the craftsmanship is good, the supervision of the works is approved. But when it has a graceful effect due to the symmetry of its proportions, the site is the glory of the architect. His work is duly accomplished when he submits to receive advice from his workmen and from laymen. For all men, and not only architects, can approve what is good. (Vitruvius Pollio, 1934 [translation]: vol. 2, bk. 6, chap. 8, ¶ 9–10.)

With all of the sometimes conflicting factors shaping the designs of buildings, it is understandable why such a multiplicity of styles exists throughout the world. Near Eastern building designs provide examples that clearly reflect these factors.

Chapter 3

A Sampling of Near Eastern and Southwest Asian Building Designs

In our field research in Pakistan, India, Syria, and Yemen, we described a number of buildings—chiefly houses—with sketch plans and photographs to illustrate the variety of designs. These houses can now be better understood in the context of the environmental, cultural, architectural, and functional characteristics of each region.

PAKISTAN

In Pakistan, consider the contrasts among a Punjab house plan (Figure 3.1; Appendix A, Map 5), two Baluchi house plans from Pandran (see Figures 3.7, 3.10), and Pathan house plans at Khanai and Qila Skarnah, Baluchistan (see Figures 3.11, 3.14).

In Punjab, monogamous families in the villages typically lived in compounds in which a property wall enclosed a rectangular courtyard, with a "broad" house built into the rear courtyard wall on the narrow side, opposite a single gate giving access to the courtyard. These broad courtyard houses of layered mud usually consisted of two or three rooms arranged side-by-side (Figure 3.2): (1) an adult bedroom for husband and wife, with a mud chest or closet in one corner; (2) an adjacent connecting bedroom for the children, furnished according to the number of children with single or bunk beds lining the walls (Figure 3.3), and (3) sometimes a third room to serve as a storeroom or stable. Courtyard walls were typically about 2.0–2.5 m high, which corresponded to the height of a normal room. The supporting roof beams of the house were laid onto the courtyard wall and the house's front wall, thereby saving the effort and expense of building a separate rear wall for the house.

In the courtyard houses we visited, all rooms were entered from the courtyard and none had windows (Figure 3.2). The cooking area was outside, occupying one side of the courtyard (Figure 3.4). Near the gateway at the opposite end of the courtyard, often was a one-room storage structure. Opposite the cooking area were the well, walled bathing and bathroom areas, pigeon house, chicken coop (Figure 3.5), and an open area near the gate for cows and other animals. Some courtyard houses had a circular granary in this area also (see Figure 13.34). All structures were built of

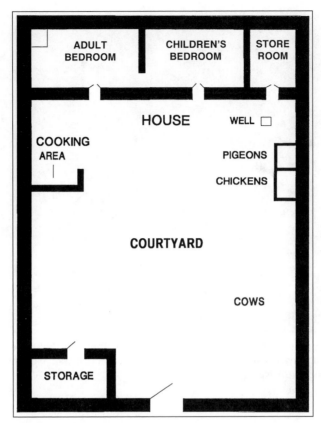

Figure 3.1   Floor plan of typical courtyard house in Punjab, Pakistan (1989).

Figure 3.2   Courtyard house, Punjab, Pakistan (1989). Door on left opens to the adult bedroom, and one on right opens to the children's room. Wall on extreme left marks the end of the house and defines the family courtyard.

Figure 3.3   Children's bedroom in courtyard house, Punjab, Pakistan (1989). The family's fine vessels, utensils, and souvenirs are neatly displayed on shelves on rear wall. Note two painted bands of floral design below shelves.

Figure 3.4   Courtyard cooking area, Punjab, Pakistan (1989). Note delicate curved design in mud extension over fireplace, which shields fire from wind. Courtyard wall has a storage box (with slatted door) and arched storage niches.

Figure 3.5   Pigeon house on left and chicken coop on right in courtyard, Punjab, Pakistan (1989). Upper surface of the latter is decorated with row of scallops, above, and stylized tongue pattern, below, in mud plaster.

Figure 3.6   Relief decoration of stylized leaves in mud on courtyard wall, Punjab, Pakistan (1989).

layered mud and many had naturalistic or geometric relief designs carved on house walls and other structures in the courtyard (Figure 3.6). The small, broad houses like this in Punjab typically occupied less land and were less expensive to build than the separate family units built by Baluchis and Pathans in Baluchistan.[1]

Layered-mud houses at Pandran, in the higher, mountainous areas of Baluchistan, reflected arrangements for polygamous families. A house we termed "Pandran 1"

(Figure 3.7) was a two-story structure with a large gate opening into a barnyard with a roofed stable and storage area. A right-angled mud stairway led to a second floor, where the stable roof served as the floor of the upper story (Figure 3.8). Arranged in an L-shaped plan were a broad, open-air terrace and the family quarters—the men's rooms on the long side of the "L" and the women's rooms on the short side—followed by a common kitchen (Figure 3.9), which stood alone because the family had a male cook. The men's rooms were distinguished from the women's rooms by a mud arch in relief above each doorway, projecting out about 5 cm from the wall surface (see Figure 13.17). The men's reception room was at the end, adjoining a roof terrace, and it was there that we were received by an assembly of 10 men. Unfortunately, OVB was not permitted to visit the wives or see their quarters in this house.

"Pandran 2" (Figure 3.10) was a more modest, one-story compound. The gateway gave access to a barnyard where the livestock were kept, and from there, a second gate on the left led to the inner courtyard and the house. The inner courtyard, paved with concrete, featured an open-air cooking area and a washing basin. Although neither the husband nor the sons were present at the time of our visit, OVB was welcomed into the women's rooms.

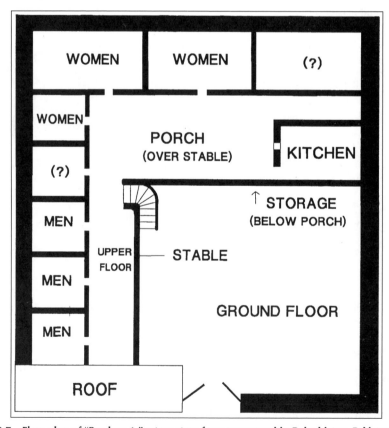

Figure 3.7 Floor plan of "Pandran 1," a two-story farm compound in Baluchistan, Pakistan (1990).

Figure 3.8   Stable (left), stairway to second-floor living quarters (center), and storage bays (right), Pandran 1, Baluchistan, Pakistan (1990). Note small windows high on the walls of the upper floor for privacy.

Figure 3.9   Kitchen on upper floor, Pandran 1, Baluchistan, Pakistan (1990).

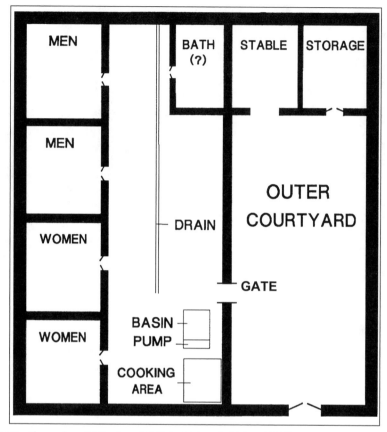

Figure 3.10   Floor plan of "Pandran 2," Baluchistan, Pakistan (1990).

In the Pathan-dominated areas we visited, the layered-mud compound most comparable to the Baluchi compounds at Pandran was one at Khanai (Figure 3.11). We were attracted to this compound while passing by because we saw two men constructing a new privacy wall. The purpose of the new wall, we learned, was to make room for enlarging one side of the women's house and the courtyard. Both men—the owner of the house and his brother—were amateurs: they were slower than professional masons and less rigorous in using good construction techniques. For example, the wall was being built on sloping terrain without a foundation, and the builders made no attempt to keep the mud layers level (Figure 3.12). Inside the compound was a front courtyard with a well. On one side of the courtyard was the men's house with three rooms. Oriented at a right angle on the adjacent side of the courtyard was the women's house with bedrooms and a workroom containing a cupboard and sewing machine. Outside, an extension of the rear wall of the women's rooms provided a windbreak for a cooking area with a tandoor (oven). Behind the women's rooms was a rear courtyard and a one-room house, oriented with the men's rooms, where their elderly mother resided.

At Qila Skarnah was a two-house, layered-mud complex owned by a man of considerable wealth.[2] The men's house (Figures 3.13, 3.14), the smaller of the two,

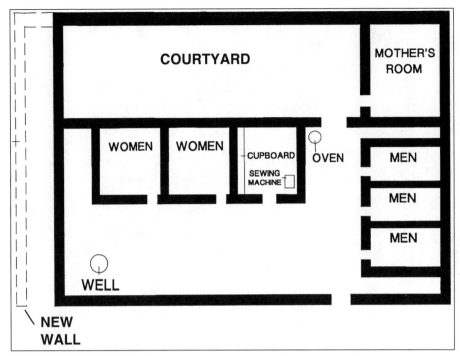

Figure 3.11   Floor plan of Pathan compound at Khanai, Baluchistan, Pakistan (1990).

Figure 3.12   Building a new privacy wall of layered mud on sloping ground, Khanai, Baluchistan, Pakistan (1990). Note sloping layers and lack of foundation trench.

Figure 3.13   Men's house in compound at Qila Skarnah, Baluchistan, Pakistan (1990). Layered mud wall is behind house.

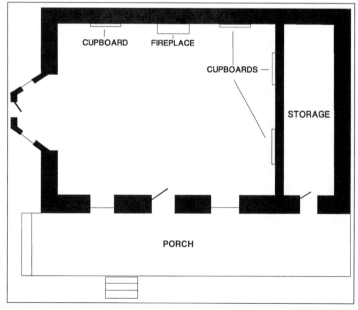

Figure 3.14   Floor plan of men's house in Qila Skarnah, Baluchistan, Pakistan (1990).

had a full porch in the front from which two doors opened into separate rooms. The larger was the living room (and sleeping area at night) and the smaller one a storeroom. A three-sided, apsidal alcove on one end of the living room served as a side entrance to the house through a narrow door; inside, the spacious opening in the living room wall was crowned with a broad, pointed arch. Crown moldings shaped from mud added elegance to the junction of the walls and beamed ceiling. The room was heated by a fireplace that was built into the wall and decorated in an English country style. Niches in the walls housed built-in wooden cupboards, providing convenient display or storage functions without occupying floor space. This was one of the relatively few surviving buildings in Baluchistan with a gabled roof.

The women's house was larger than the men's because it needed to accommodate more persons. Upon being invited to visit the women, OVB was warmly received by the first (or senior) wife, who provided introductions to the second wife and to their children, as well as to the husband's unmarried sister. From a central doorway, a long hallway at a right angle gave access to a row of four rooms. Each of the three women occupied a room that was large enough for herself and any children. At one end of the row was the husband's room, an attractively decorated room with one of his prized shotguns hanging on the wall (he was renowned as a hunter); here he would spend the night with the wife of his choice. Behind this house in the courtyard was the cooking area with a series of rectangular ovens (see Figure 13.33); a long mud wall shielded the area from strong winds, and rows of spaced holes in its lower section functioned to regulate the draft as well as to admit some light (Figure 3.15).

Near the men's house was a guest house in ruins. It originally contained at least three rooms and probably functioned during British colonial times as quarters for traveling British government officials and distinguished visitors (this region was part of India before Pakistan's independence). Each room among its remains had a fireplace decorated with parallel mud ridges, not unlike designs in plaster or wood on eighteenth- and nineteenth-century fireplaces in England and North America

Figure 3.15 Women's house, from rear courtyard, in compound at Qila Skarnah, Baluchistan, Pakistan (1990). Low rows of holes in wall (right) regulate draft and admit light in cooking area on the other side; trench (center foreground) provides drainage from main house.

(see Figure 13.30), and crown moldings of carved mud, on one of which traces of blue paint could still be seen.

At Hanna, near Quetta, we visited a small, two-story, men's guesthouse of layered mud beside the main road (Figure 3.16). The house was finished on three sides with mud plaster painted white. The rear wall was left without plaster and showed the mud layers loaded with small stones (see Figure 5.5). Outside, an enormous mulberry tree shaded an area enclosed by a layered-mud wall on two sides, with a built-in mud bench on the inner face of each wall (Figure 3.17). It must have been a delightful place to while away a summer afternoon. Fronting on the road at ground level, the house had a small storage room with its own entrance (Figure 3.18). Behind this was another small room with a mud bench on the rear wall and a broad opening to the shaded yard in the side wall. This area may have served as an alternate meeting and conversation place during times of inclement weather. A ladder here gave access through a trap door in the ceiling to the upper room, perhaps as an emergency escape route, because normally one would have climbed to the second floor (or exited from it) by an external flight of stairs leading from the front of the house up to the roofed, open porch directly above the ground-floor storage room. From the porch, one entered the only habitable room in the house. It had a window in each of the four walls and was sparsely furnished with a single bed and a table. According to the owner, this was where he entertained male visitors, played cards with friends, or spent the night when he so desired. Following a path up the slope, he took us to the family complex, which included a second house for him and beyond that a separate building for his wives; we split up in an attempt to investigate both. The man's second house was a one-room dwelling with printed

Figure 3.16 Two-story men's guesthouse at Hanna, Baluchistan, Pakistan (1990). The owner is coming down the path to meet us from the women's house behind this one.

Figure 3.17 **Pleasant outdoor sitting area under mulberry tree at men's guest house, Hanna, Baluchistan, Pakistan (1990).**

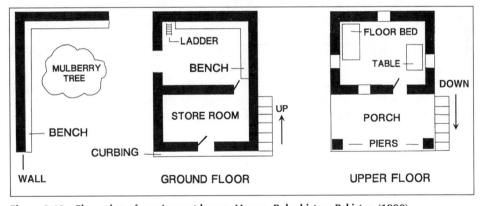

Figure 3.18 **Floor plan of men's guest house, Hanna, Baluchistan, Pakistan (1990).**

fabric covering the ceiling and interior walls decorated with a continuous row of travel and nature pictures taken from calendars; GVB remained in the man's house while OVB visited the wives, who were cooking outside, though OVB was not invited to visit their quarters.

Narrow houses consisting of one room each are seen occasionally in Pakistan. In the Hanna Valley northeast of the Cantonment section of Quetta was a group of about 20–25 mud-ball houses built by Afghan refugees of the Mulaher tribe (see Figure 5.14). The house plans were simple (Figure 3.19), typically consisting of a

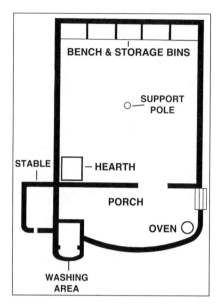

Figure 3.19   Floor plan of Afghan refugee's mud-ball house in Cantonment section of Quetta, Baluchistan, Pakistan (1991).

rectangular room about 4–5 m long × 3 m wide. One entered through a single door-way right of center in the front wall from a mud-walled porch with a side entrance. This arrangement prevented anyone from looking into the house. In one house we visited, the "door" was a piece of canvas that was attached to the roof and draped downward to cover the entrance; when necessary for the door to remain open, the canvas was gathered and stashed onto the roof over the doorway (see Figure 13.15). The room was sheltered by a gabled, thatched roof carried by a ridge pole that ex-tended from the front wall to the rear wall and that was supported by a single verti-cal pole in the center of the room. An old canvas tent covered the thatched roof to provide extra protection. Inside, a single kerosene lamp hung from the ridge pole. Although there were no windows in the room, four holes—each about 10 cm in diameter—pierced each of the side walls at different heights above the floor to pro-vide both ventilation and opportunities to see outside. Against the rear wall of the room was a long, bench-like storage structure of mud about 60 cm high divided into three compartments, two that were empty and a third that was filled with canned goods. On top of this bench-like structure was neatly folded bedding piled about 75 cm high. A shelf mounted on the side wall held piles of clothing. To the left of the doorway in the corner of the room, a hearth was sunk in the floor for warmth and indoor cooking during inclement weather (see Figure 13.26).

The raised, open porch measured about 2 m long × 3 m wide, corresponding with the width of the house. Unlike the house, the porch wall was built primarily of mud balls with some rectangular mud bricks, all roughly coursed. Its front wall was about 1.5 m high and featured an apsidal projection in the right front corner. The apsidal wall was finished at the top by a series of crenels and was roofed with tree limbs, bamboo, and a capping layer of mud. This small chamber served as the washing area for dishes, laundry, and the inhabitants. It contained a low platform on which stood three goatskin water bags and a pot with a lid. The apsidal wall had three rounded holes about 10 cm in diameter that served as windows. Adjoining the apsidal alcove was an addition that served as a stable for the family's livestock: sheep, goats, and chickens. It was roofed with bamboo and had three ventilating holes in its long wall (see Figure 5.14). The porch contained a cooking area opposite the entrance to the main room and a bread oven (consisting of a large globular pot) buried in the ground immediately left of the entrance from outside. Although our visit was spontaneous, the house was spotlessly clean and tidy.

Two fortress structures of layered mud, one about 100 years old in Qila Skarnah (Figure 3.20) and a new one in Bostan, illustrate the force of building traditions. Fortress houses and compounds are rectangular in plan, usually two or three stories high, and feature a round tower at each corner with a number of narrow gun ports near the top to defend the house. The Qila Skarnah house was about 30.5 m long and about 5.3 m high. About a meter below the parapets were two rows of gun ports to increase target coverage. The upper row consisted of horizontal holes to cover more distant targets; the lower row featured narrow vertical slits with sloping bottoms to protect the base of the house walls. Entrance to the house was gained through a large doorway in the center of the front wall. The doorway was framed by mud pilasters reaching to within 61 cm of the top of the wall. The inner side of each pilaster curved to form an arch above the doorway and continued upward to frame a rectangular panel at the top. This decorative entrance was protected from water by a short roof projecting from the wall over the doorway.

The newly built fortress house in Bostan, about 20 km northwest of Quetta, was designed so that the parapet at the top of each corner tower sloped downward, overhanging the wall, to serve as a drip molding to carry rain away from the tower walls (Figure 3.21). The rifle ports on the towers and long walls were not real in this structure but were instead stylized decorations. They consisted of configurations of four or five narrow, vertical niches placed midway in the height of the tower and walls, but nowhere did they pierce the walls.

Other authentic fortress houses (like that in Qila Skarnah) exist in Najran, Saudi Arabia, where they are also built of layered mud (Figure 3.22). The largest and most beautiful example is the former Sultan's Palace, in Seiyun, Hadhramaut, Yemen (see Figure 3.60). This style of building was quite common in the Near East and

Figure 3.20   Fortress house with gun ports in corner towers, Qila Skarnah, Baluchistan (1990).

Figure 3.21   New fortress-style house with decorative, nonfunctional towers and gun ports, imitating the design of earlier fortress houses, Bostan, Baluchistan (1990).

Figure 3.22   Layered-mud fortress compound, Najran, Saudi Arabia (1968).

Southwest Asia before World War II, when it functioned as a fortress during episodes of tribal warfare. Fortress houses originally were designed to defend against guerilla hit-and-run attacks that frequently occurred in tribal societies as recently as only a few decades ago throughout southern Arabia. The form is rarely seen in new construction because peace and greater security have eliminated its need, although it has historical interest and considerable beauty. The recent house built in Bostan reflects nostalgia for this design.

During our first visit to Quetta in 1989, Mohammed Mohsin Qazi—our research guide, translator, and friend—took us north to the town of Pishin to see the residence built by his great-grandfather, who died in 1918. At the time of our visit, it was the home of Jennifer Qazi, second wife of Mohsin's grandfather. The house had been the principal residence on a very large estate that comprised 121 hectares of rich farm land, and which included a beautiful small mosque in Moghul style for the family's use, many shops, ice houses, and side buildings containing 128 rooms, the remains of which (we were told) could still be seen. To give an idea of its magnitude early in the twentieth century, Mohsin's great-grandfather is said to have fed some 5000 local people daily![3]

The original residence was a charming Victorian cottage (Figure 3.23) built of fired brick laid in very hard mud and lime mortar. Renovation of the parlor in 1991 disclosed some of the details of the original building: a blocked-up fireplace, the fired-brick voussoirs of the arched windows, and several slender wall niches (which at some time in the past had been plastered over) between the arched windows.

One of the most exciting sections of the house was the closed-off upper floor. This floor, constructed between 1900 and 1910, was a major addition that extended from the ground behind the original cottage upward and over it. The roof of the original cottage was entirely removed. The new, second story was built of sun-dried mud brick with mud floors, which may have been finished with lime plaster, although we saw no traces of lime plaster. The addition originally consisted of a five-room apartment for Mohsin's great-grandfather, two enormous reception rooms, a solarium, a covered porch on at least two sides with a veranda, and a canopied outside staircase (Figure 3.24).

The great earthquake that totally destroyed half of Quetta in 1935, killing about 25,000 people, also damaged the upper story of this house in Pishin, about 57 km away. The canopied stairway, solarium, and veranda collapsed on the west side of the house, as well as the bathroom of the apartment on the east end. The two reception rooms and three rooms of the apartment survived with their roofs intact; this amounted to about 75% of the original addition. Yet because of vertical cracks in the walls at the outside corners of the south reception room, the upper story was locked and abandoned, never to be used again. During the passage of 56 years between the earthquake and our third visit (in 1991), no maintenance was undertaken either inside or outside. The exterior mud plaster remained in good condition except for a few minor eroded areas, none larger than about 400 cm². The original paints, though faded, survived on the walls and niches of the reception rooms, as well as on the exterior wall protected by the porch, and allowed us to imagine the original beauty and elegance of this addition.

During our visits to the house in 1989 and 1990, Jennifer Qazi expressed concern that the upper story might someday collapse and destroy her house. When this topic arose during our 1991 visit, we eagerly offered to check the stability and condition of the upper story, and Jennifer accepted. Entrance was gained by means of a ladder on the back of the house through an enlarged opening that had once been a window in the south reception room.

Three arched doorways joined the two reception rooms (Figure 3.25), and two arched doorways gave access to the screened north porch (Figure 3.26). The corrugated tin roof was gabled at right angles to the long dimension of the addition and was carried by heavy, gnarled and rough-hewn wooden beams. The ceiling was formed of milled boards laid side-by-side and varnished (see Figure 10.10). There were large arched niches with shelves for books or other small objects, and small

Figure 3.23   Qazi house in Pishin, near Quetta, Baluchistan, Pakistan (1990).

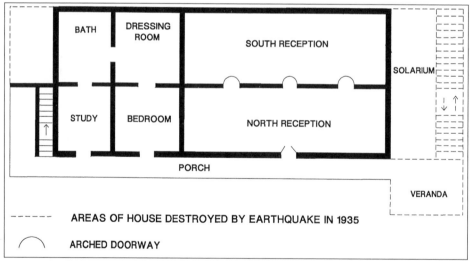

Figure 3.24   Floor plan of mud-brick second story of the Qazi house, Pishin, Baluchistan, Pakistan (1991).

apsidal niches rimmed with pointed arches in the end walls of the reception rooms. The original mud floor had become powder-dry, and when the enlarged window through which we entered was open, the wind raised a veritable dust storm in the rooms. According to Mohsin, the floors were originally covered with red oriental carpets, the walls brightened by red velvet hangings, and the ceilings clad with mirrors to greatly increase the brightness of the rooms. The wall coverings were later replaced with paint—rose color, with a yellow band extending upward from the

Figure 3.25   Reception rooms connected by arched doorways on second story of the Qazi house in Pishin, Baluchistan, Pakistan (1991). Note soil floor.

Figure 3.26   Ora Van Beek on original screened porch with painted walls, outside reception rooms on second story of the Qazi house in Pishin, Baluchistan, Pakistan (1991).

floor to about 61 cm—and a wooden ceiling replaced the mirrors. The walls of the screened porch still preserve the original blue paint and yellow trim.

This second-floor addition of mud brick may be the only surviving mud-brick structure in the Quetta region; all other mud buildings appeared to be built of layered mud. The only way to ascertain the type of construction in older buildings is to search for structures whose plaster is damaged, revealing the wall underneath, and this requires either long residence in the country or a great deal of luck during short-term visits.

Apart from domestic structures, we investigated several specialized buildings: (1) the new customs post of the Baluchistan government at Beleli, north of Quetta (see Figure 3.27), the construction of which we studied in 1989; (2) a new strip shopping center with three shops at Kuchlagh, also north of Quetta (see Figure 3.29); and (3) mosques, including roadside prayer areas such as one at Mastung, south of Quetta (see Figure 3.35).

When we examined the layered-mud customs post at Beleli a second time in 1991, 16 months after it was finished, its employees were busily collecting duty from the truck traffic on the road between Kandahar, Afghanistan, and Quetta, Pakistan (Figure 3.27). This visit provided a fine opportunity to see how the building was faring, what if any modifications had been made during use, and whether any damage had resulted from neglect and/or weather. The room on the left served as the business office, and the room on the right was used as a staff room for food preparation, rest, and sleep (Figure 3.28). A fired-brick outhouse (toilet building) was situated a short distance from the building, where the mud-plaster pit was located during construction. A large mobile water tank was parked near the eastern end of the porch.

The brick floor that was laid during construction in 1989 had since been covered with concrete. In the right rear corners of both rooms, curbed washing areas had been constructed, each with a drain pipe piercing the rear mud wall. Wastewater was unwisely permitted to collect in two pools outside on the ground close to the

Figure 3.27 Customs post from southeast corner, 16 months after completion, in Beleli, near Quetta, Baluchistan, Pakistan (1991). Low curb "wall" in foreground defines an outdoor prayer area; outhouse is on left.

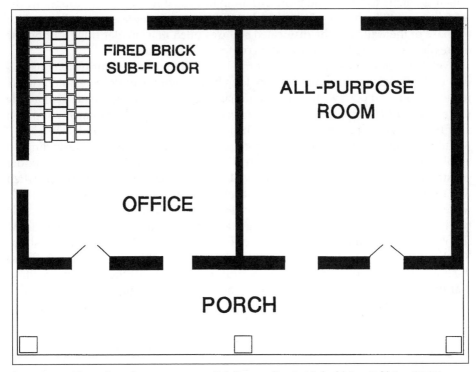

Figure 3.28 Floor plan of customs post at Beleli, near Quetta, Baluchistan, Pakistan (1990).

building walls—unwise because, with time, the water eventually seeps downward, softening and weakening the foundation. The mud mortar used to seal wooden window frames was loose and falling out in many places, permitting daylight to be seen between the wall ends and the frame. At least three of the glass panes were missing, and the resulting openings had been covered by paper or plastic.

At 2286 m in elevation, this region is very cold during the winter months, often with periods of heavy snow or rain. The winter of 1990–1991 was quite severe in northern and central Baluchistan, yet the mud roof appeared to be performing nicely (see Figures 10.4–10.6). A hole had been cut through the ceiling and roof of the office to accommodate a rectangular-shaped tin can whose ends had been removed (see Figure 3.27) to serve as the chimney of a free-standing stove in the middle of the room. Near the top of the wall, a mud patch filled the hole where the electric line had originally entered. The new line entered the front of the house from across the highway—a high bamboo pole on the far side of the road and another attached to the edge of the porch roof lifted the electric cable sufficiently high to clear trucks and buses passing beneath.

All corners of the office, except the one adjacent to the doorway, had rat or mouse holes immediately above the floor, which had been dug through the walls. Groundwater run-off had eroded the mud plaster at the base of the west wall. Unfortunately the building site was not raised above the surrounding terrain; run-off water tended to flow toward the building rather than away from it, thus adding further stress (albeit gradual) to the foundation. An animal, probably a dog, left gouges in the west wall made by its toenails when digging a concave depression in the earth at the base of the wall, and the dislocated soil was piled in a circular ridge around the depression as a wind-break for winter comfort and protection.

Overall, the building was suffering from a lack of maintenance. During its construction we had asked the head mason how long he thought the building would last. He replied, "About 60 years with good maintenance. If the government had spent a little more, it would last at least 100 years!" Given the building's deteriorated condition after two years, the mason's estimate of its longevity is probably too high.

The fledgling market at Kuchlagh stood about 20 m off the road, providing an ample parking lot, much like a small, strip shopping mall in the USA. It was under construction when we first stopped by in 1990 and was in partial operation when we last visited it. The structure—built entirely of layered mud—consisted of a large, walled compound with a single entrance (Figure 3.29). The enclosed area had only two large stacks of mud bricks, suggesting that it would be a lumberyard or a building supply business requiring considerable open storage space. Three one-room shops had been built side-by-side in the front right corner of the compound, parallel to the highway. The front wall of the shops continued the line of the enclosure wall, so that the shops were all inside the compound. A porch shading the shops extended beyond the line of the enclosure wall (Figure 3.30). The roof of the porch was supported at the front by seven well-spaced, fired-brick piers. Wooden beams carried the roof from the piers to the wall; some were crooked and curved and others were, at best, almost straight. One of the more crooked beams had broken and shifted posi-

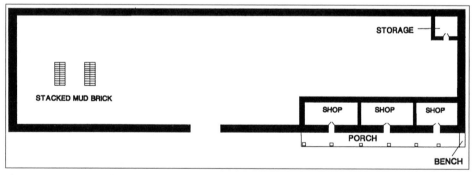

Figure 3.29   Layout of layered-mud roadside market in Kuchlagh, Baluchistan, Pakistan (1990).

Figure 3.30   The partially built layered-mud market at Kuchlagh, Baluchistan, Pakistan, with planned shops shaded by porch roof (1990).

tion, causing the mud roof to sag badly (Figure 3.31). An attractive mud bench closed the far right end of the porch and provided a shady place for three or four persons to sit. Each shop had a single door. Mounted in the front wall to the right of each door was a glass window providing natural light inside and giving the proprietors a good view of the outside; there were no other windows in the shops. A locked storage building stood in the rear corner inside the compound.

Village mosques in Baluchistan are small, rectangular buildings, with the *qibla*—the device indicating the direction of Mecca in Saudi Arabia—rendered as a small apsidal structure roofed with a half dome. Small windows often were placed just below the flat roof to provide interior light and ventilation with privacy. Other typical features were two elaborate corner towers extending upward and resembling finials; their placement and general design derive from Moghul minarets—towers from which the call to prayer is sung. Mosques in these villages typically were enclosed by boundary walls whose tops were decorated with large, globular mud balls about 30 cm in diameter, occasionally arranged in pyramidal form, spaced about 60–100 cm apart around the entire wall (Figure 3.32). In some mosques, such as one at Raisani, the decorative mud balls on the boundary walls were molded into deep scallops and other shapes (Figure 3.33). The use of mud balls apparently was confined to religious buildings in Baluchistan, but we were unable to discover its symbolism. Mud plaster on mosques was often painted white.

In addition to the traditional, enclosed mosques, open-air mosques or prayer enclosures are found along the highways, providing places where devout travelers can stop for their daily prayers (Figures 3.34, 3.35; see also Figure 3.27). Built of layered-

Figure 3.31   Failed roofing beam in porch of market at Kuchlagh, Baluchistan, Pakistan (1990).

Figure 3.32   Village mosque without windows, between Mastung and Kalat in Baluchistan, Pakistan (1990).

Figure 3.33   Mosque on estate at village of Raisani in Dhardhar, Baluchistan, Pakistan (1990). Note scalloping at top of boundary walls.

mud walls commonly about 1 m high, those we encountered were often decorated on top with mud balls, like the enclosure walls of village mosques, and enclosed a rectangular area. The *qibla* was a small, rounded or rectangular section projecting outward from the walled area on the side facing Mecca, and the single entrance was in the opposite wall. If attendance warrants and funds are available, these prayer enclosures are often replaced by traditional, roofed mosques.

INDIA

Our major research in India was centered in Gujarat State (see Appendix A, Map 6), which is representative of a larger region comprising much of Sind in Pakistan and

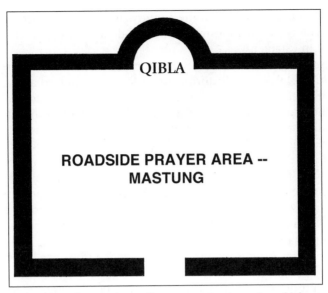

QIBLA

**ROADSIDE PRAYER AREA --
MASTUNG**

Figure 3.34 Ground plan of open-air Muslim prayer structure along highway near Mastung, Baluchistan, Pakistan (1990).

Figure 3.35 Open-air prayer structure with a mud ball decoration on each corner, both sides of entrance, and in center of curved wall of the *qibla*, near Mastung, Baluchistan, Pakistan (1990).

the southern part of Rajasthan in India. Gujarat is characterized by flat topography, and its environment is identical to that of Sind, featuring very hot summers, warm winters, and rains of the southwest monsoon. The two areas share many similarities in material culture and a common history going back to at least the third millennium B.C. Religious differences, however, are great: Sind is Islamic, and Gujarat and Rajasthan are primarily Hindu and Jain, but they also host a large Muslim population. These religious systems create political differences that frequently lead to strife. Marriage customs also differ; virtually all Indians are monogamous, sharing many similarities with monogamous Muslim families but fewer with those Muslims who practice polygamy.

In Gujarat, around Bhuj, and in the countryside south of Madras, chiefly in the area of Pondicherry, we investigated wattle-and-daub houses, which are dealt with in more detail in Chapter 6.

Some house designs in the villages and rural areas of Gujarat were very similar to those in Punjab, Pakistan, featuring an enclosed compound and a broad house plan of two or three side-by-side rooms whose rear wall is the back wall of the compound. Modhera, about 100 km northwest of Ahmedabad, is the site of a revered sun temple of the twelfth century A.D. that receives tens of thousands of local visitors and tourists annually. The small village near the temple was typical of many communities in the region. One typical house consisted of three rooms arranged side-by-side, two of which provided living space for family members (Figure 3.36) with the third used for storage. The owner and his wife lived in one room, and their son and his family lived in another. Both of the inhabited rooms contained the same basic household equipment: a hearth, three or four mud chests or closets, two or three mud granaries, and a row of storage jars (Figure 3.37). The middle room, serving both families, housed a large churn suspended from a ceiling beam, a grinding stone, and storage jars and cabinets. Operating the churn required two persons rotating it with ropes (see Figures 12.11, 12.12). A porch extended across the front of the house for shade; here the adult women were busily cleaning rice, while the daughters were polishing brass vessels in preparation for the annual *Diwali* festival.[4] In the courtyard in front of the house was a stable and open area for the animals. A single broad gate, wide enough to admit a cart, gave entrance to the compound.

In contrast to the broad houses similar to those in Punjab, we also saw narrow dwellings just one room wide. The most attractive narrow house that we visited was in the center of Charada, a village near Surendranagar, about 95 km southwest of Ahmedabad. This house was small, measuring about 7.3 m long (front to back) by about 5.5 m wide (Figure 3.38). Its outer walls tapered upward from a thickness

Figure 3.36 Three-room house in Modhera, Gujarat State, India (1991). Doorways for two rooms are just visible behind family, under the covered porch.

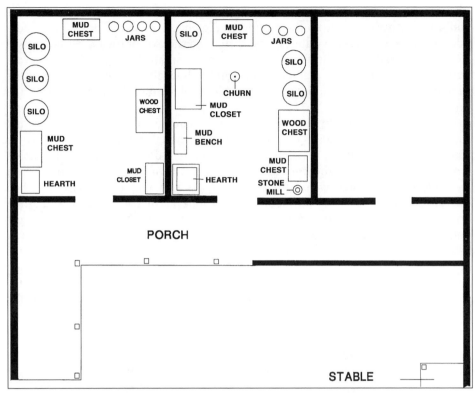

Figure 3.37   Floor plan of three-room house in Modhera, Gujarat, India (1991).

Figure 3.38   Narrow house in Charada, Gujarat, India (1991).

of 30 cm at the base to 20 cm at the top. It stood on a mud platform with three built-in steps ascending from the ground to the entrance. A gabled roof featured a ridge beam set on the side walls at a right angle to the axis of the house, and it was covered with red, half-cylindrical, ceramic tiles of small diameter. The front wall featured two mud bins or planters built against the wall, one on each side of the wide doorway; each was adorned with an identical symbol painted in red on the front surface (Figures 3.38, 3.39).

The house—occupied by a single individual—contained two rooms measuring about 2.5 m deep and almost 5 m wide that were separated by a mud party wall with a narrow doorway. A column in the front room supported the ridge beam of the gabled roof. On the right side of the front room was a portable hearth, and a drum hung on the wall; on the left side against the party wall was a charpoy (a typical Indian bed consisting of a frame strung with tapes or light ropes). The back room served as the kitchen and storage area; it had two shelves extending most of the length of the rear wall to display plates and vessels. A wooden frame that projected from the left wall held neatly folded bedding, and in the left rear corner stood a cylindrical mud granary. Along the rear and right walls, a low, raised platform (about 30 cm high) extended into the room about 50 cm. Upon these were stacked pots, boxes, and wooden staffs. A massive mud stand with two heavy piers and a heavy wooden top stood on the platform and was attached to the wall on the right; this held pots for water.

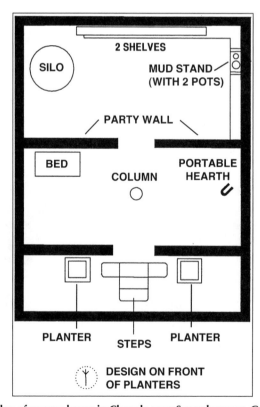

Figure 3.39   Floor plan of narrow house in Charada near Surendranagar, Gujarat, India (1991).

In Jangi, a village near Bhachau, about 86 km east of Bhuj in Gujarat, we visited a potter's house that was built in the narrow style, similar to that of the Charada house. It measured about 4.6 m wide by 6.1 m deep, with walls 33 cm thick. Like the Charada house, the gabled roof sloped to the front back rather than to the long sides (Figure 3.40). From front to back, the space was divided into three areas of about equal depth (Figure 3.41): (1) The front segment consisted mostly of an open porch, occupying about two-thirds of this area; the left third was allocated to the kitchen, whose front wall extended about 61 cm beyond the edge of the porch. (2) The middle room featured a bench for water vessels in the left rear corner and a wooden cupboard with two doors on the back wall. (3) The rear room contained a large wooden chest centered on the back wall. From the porch, a doorway about 1.3 m wide and about 1.6 m high with double wooden doors opened into the middle room. A long vertical niche framed each side of the doorway. A window, 30 × 30 cm between the niche to the right of the doorway and the end of the wall (on right when facing the house from the front) provided light and visibility to the front room. Another window of the same size was centered in the front wall of the kitchen near the cooking area. There were no windows in the long side walls.

The characteristics of Gujarati houses can be summarized as follows. Mud-brick and wattle-and-daub construction predominate, yet fired brick is rapidly becoming the most popular building material. Broad houses, composed of side-by-side rooms, are more common than narrow houses, with rooms from front to back. Roofs are commonly gabled and covered with red ceramic tile. Indoor cooking is common as is the use of mud-built furnishings, such as granaries, chests, and closets. Hand-applied mud plaster with a repeated swirl motif on the ground immediately before the house, continuing on the porch floor or the mud walls is a frequent decorative device.

SYRIA AND JORDAN VALLEY

The northern and eastern regions of Syria feature flat, treeless plains stretching from the western, mountainous zone to the Euphrates River, one of the most important

Figure 3.40　Potter's house in Jangi, near Bhachau, Gujarat, India (1991).

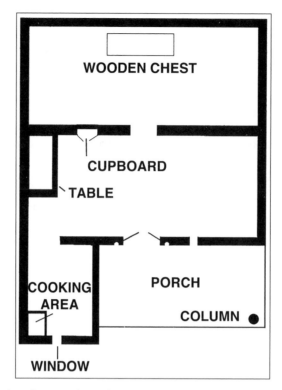

Figure 3.41   Floor plan of potter's house in Jangi, Gujarat, India (1991).

rivers in the ancient Near East (See Appendix A, Map 7). Cold in the winter and scorching hot in the summer, most of these plains are agriculturally marginal without irrigation systems. Because of the wide range in temperature, mud construction provides the most delightful interior climate. In many regions, building stone is not available, and the absence of easily accessible timber inevitably led to use of the corbelled mud dome for roofing. When the mud domed roof first came into use in Syria is still not known.

Contemporary mores in Syria differ considerably from those of other Muslim countries due to government policy. Monogamy is the prevailing family style. Purdah—the veiling of women—is not practiced in Syria, although it is tolerated for visiting conservative and fundamentalist Muslim women. Syrian women rarely wear the traditional long, colorful dresses except in villages; elsewhere they dress in western-style clothing. Tolerance of Christian minorities prevails and is picturesquely represented by the display of Easter symbols—bunnies, baby chicks, and eggs—in hotel lobbies and of Christmas symbols—plastic Santa Claus figures and Christmas trees—in restaurants and hotels. We have not seen these symbols in public places in any other Muslim country of the Near East or Southwest Asia.

Square, domed (or "beehive") mud-brick houses traditionally dominated villages in the Aleppo region of northern Syria. The largest town of beehive houses was Taftanaz, where some 4000 domed houses sheltered a population of 16,000 people as recently as the 1950s (Copeland, 1955). In 1994, we visited several beehive villages within about 75 km of Aleppo—namely Fah (Figure 3.42), Diyarah, Vivin, Slamin, Suron, and Susiyan. Such houses in this region were rapidly disappearing as people became more affluent and chose to build concrete houses. Few if any new ones were being built, and many of the older ones served as stables or general-purpose storerooms. When people no longer occupied the houses, care and maintenance rapidly declined, erosion began, and gradual disintegration followed.

A beehive house consisted of one room roofed with a corbelled dome that resembled an old-fashioned beehive (see Figure 1.1). When a family's space needs increased—e.g., a son married and brought home his bride or a growing family required a larger kitchen—a room was added on one side that connected with the first room through a large, arched doorway. This arched doorway was generally planned and built into the house wall during its original construction. In case a third room might eventually be needed, the second room also featured a preplanned arched doorway in the same location as that in the original house. Each arched doorway was blocked with mud brick and plaster until such time as a new adjoining room was required. Each domed room that was added to the original house in this manner created an ever longer row house. Most dwellings consisted of one to three rooms (Figure 3.43), but we saw as many as seven joined rooms (Figure 3.44) in the village of Susiyan.

In Fah, one of the typical beehive houses we studied had a room measuring about 4.4 m square (Figure 3.45). The outer walls ranged 65–75 cm thick to carry the weight of the dome, yielding an interior space approximately 3.75 m square. The dome began about 2.5 m above the floor, its base resting on the side walls and squinches—the curving, fan-shaped mud-brick supports in each corner (see Chapter 11 for details). This added 3 m or so to the height of the house. A single doorway with a wooden door gave access to the house in the right corner of the front wall as one faced it from outside, a location common in other beehive houses of the area.

In most houses like this one, the walls of the lower, square portion sometimes had one window, generally in the front wall if it was in a row but occasionally in the outside end wall. Usually the inner walls featured several niches, some of which were arched with a span of one meter or more. Some niches were large enough to contain a built-in wooden cabinet, as in the Yehya Billal family's beautiful home (in Susiyan) where three large niches were so used (Figure 3.46). Small holes, 15–20 cm in diameter, extended through the walls not far above the floor to provide ventilation and to enable a seated person to look outside. These holes could be

Figure 3.42   The village of Fah near Aleppo, Syria (1994).

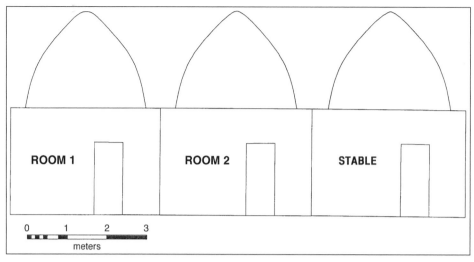

Figure 3.43 Three-room, domed house in Slamin, Syria (1994).

Figure 3.44 Seven-domed house in Susiyan, Syria (1994). The small bathroom in front of the third and fourth domed rooms (from left) is drained by the meandering channel in the courtyard (center foreground). Sixth and seventh domed roofs are in state of disrepair.

closed by sealing them with mud or by stuffing them with plastic or cloth to reduce drafts in cold weather. When closed off on the outside, they could serve as niches to hold small items. When a family had a refrigerator, it was kept in the main room unless the kitchen was located in another room or a separate building.

A large, mud-brick building with five or six domes of the Syrian type (Figure 3.47) was located in Wadi Farah, west of Jiftlik in the West Bank territory of the Jordan Valley (see Appendix A, Map 1; Ram Gofna, Israeli archaeologist, Tel Aviv University, pers. comm., 1999). We did not visit this building but learned of it from Dr. Gofna, who had studied it. He shared some of his findings with us, and the photograph he provided revealed other interesting things. The domes varied in size, with larger ones over the large rooms and smaller ones over corridors or other small spaces. When the large room projecting out from the front left side was constructed, an arched doorway was built into its south wall. A careful look at this wall (in Figure 3.47) reveals the mud-brick arch blocked with mud bricks and sealed with lime

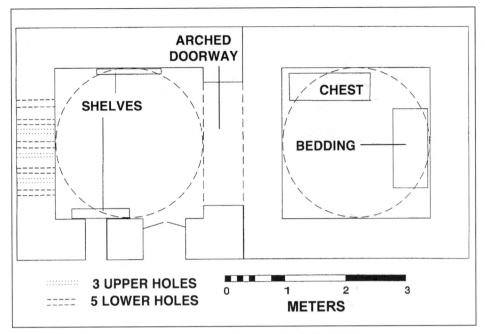

ARCHED DOORWAY

SHELVES

CHEST

BEDDING

⋯⋯⋯ **3 UPPER HOLES**
‒ ‒ ‒ ‒ **5 LOWER HOLES**

0   1   2   3

METERS

Figure 3.45   Floor plan of two-room, domed house in Fah, Syria (1994).

plaster. Apparently the owners planned to attach another room on this side at a future date, creating a longer L-shaped plan; at such time, the blocked doorway would be opened to connect the rooms. The entire building was probably covered with lime plaster at one time, as evidenced by numerous remnants on the facade and west side; the lime plaster on the domes appeared to be intact.

In Beir al-Helu, a village just south of Tell Brak in northeastern Syria, a house with a low, rounded-hip roof attracted our attention (Figure 3.48). This "pillow" type of roof was fairly common in the region. The house was rectangular in plan, with its long dimension divided into three parallel rooms. A porch area on the front reduced the depth of the middle room and gave access to each side room. Room 1, on the left when viewed from the front, was the salon, an all-purpose room (Figure 3.49). It had three windows, one in the front wall, a second in the side wall toward the rear wall, and one in the rear wall, each covered with shear white curtains and a white valance with red edging. The lower walls were painted with a green band about 60 cm high. The band rose in each corner to form a triangle whose apex extended upward to the ceiling as a narrow corner band about 5 cm wide. This corner design was probably derived from the "horns-of-the-altar" motif (see Figure 7.16) of the ancient Near East. (The decorative motif of a painted "horn" in each corner of a room may have signified it as a haven for those who entered; see further discussion and examples of this in Chapter 7, "Architectural Features and Variations" section.) The floor was covered wall-to-wall with oriental rugs; back cushions or bolsters lined the walls, and small individual cushions were scattered on the rug. A cradle swinging from a stationary frame held a sleeping infant and was entirely covered with cloth netting to protect against insects. Room 2, the middle room opening onto the

Figure 3.46 Interior of second domed room viewed through arched doorway originally built in the wall of the first room of the Yehya Billal family home, Susiyan, Syria (1994). A cabinet occupies the large niche in the right wall. The floor is covered with a striped bedouin rug with a woven carpet on top. Pillows for leaning against the wall serve as the sofa in floor cultures.

Figure 3.47 Multiple-domed house in Wadi Farah, west of Jiftlik in West Bank of Jordan Valley (1968). Front facade (in full sun) faces south. Note faint outline of brick-filled archway in front extension of house. (Photo courtesy of R. Gofna; used with permission.)

Figure 3.48 Three-room house with rounded "pillow" roof in Beir al-Helu, south of Tell Brak, Syria (1994).

porch, was the bedroom where the family slept on thin mattresses or pallets on the floor. A high stack of bedding, tidy and attractively disposed, occupied most of the length of the party wall between rooms 2 and 3. Room 3 to the right of the porch was primarily a storeroom for bedding, which was neatly folded and piled in stacks against the right and rear walls (Figure 3.50). The party wall was painted in the same green color as in room 1 but featured rosettes and stars, and there were three calendar-type pictures hanging on the wall, covering some of the painted designs.

The most striking feature of the house was the rounded roof design resembling a stretched low dome or pillow. On top of the primary beams were tin sheets, followed by smaller poles laid at right angles on top, and a layer of reeds placed at right angles on the poles. On the reeds, thick straw was heaped high over the mid-section of the house, gradually tapering in thickness to a sharply defined overhang at the roof's edges. Upon this pile, a 10 cm layer of mud was laid, its weight compressing the straw, and gradually extended to the overhang. The finished roof

Figure 3.49   Salon with cushions against walls for sitting, two or three layers of carpeting, and a covered cradle, Beir al-Helu, Syria (1994).

was very smooth, and the slope on all sides drained water quickly; the overhanging roof directed run-off water well away from the outer surface of the walls. Projecting mud-covered wooden beams above the windows served as drip moldings to protect the window sills from erosion. Mud benches were built against the entire length of the front wall, not only to provide a comfortable place to sit in the late afternoon and early evening, but also to protect the base of the walls from erosion by groundwater run-off.

YEMEN

In contrast to the similarities in house designs in eastern Pakistan and western India, the house plans of Yemen are entirely different from those of India, Pakistan, and Syria. Most houses in Yemen are built vertically rather than horizontally. Traditional mud houses in Baluchistan, India, and Syria seldom if ever have more than two stories, and the overwhelming majority are one story. In Yemen, most houses are single-family homes ranging from one to four stories in height, but in some areas—such as in the Hadhramaut valley—they reach as high as eight stories.

Why build a tall house? In the western world we build vertically because of the lack of available land and its resulting high costs within urban centers. In Yemen, however, the availability and price of land is not such an important consideration. For example, in the Hadhramaut, communities hug the wadi cliffs and stand on the scree slopes while country estates occupy relatively little space in the date palm orchards. We believe the most obvious advantages of tall houses were the ease of

Figure 3.50   Storage room with neatly stored bedding, Beir al-Helu, Syria (1994).

mounting a defense against attacks, the impenetrability of mud walls by bullets, and the likelihood of catching stronger and more frequent breezes, especially in the afternoons.

In our five-week trip across Yemen in 1991, we first visited the modern town of Marib, east of Sana'a, near the edge of the great sand desert Ramlat al Sabatein (an arm of the Rub' al-Khali; see Appendix A, Map 3). Nearby, the ruins of Marib Town occupied the top of a piggy-back tell situated on one end of ancient Marib, the largest pre-Islamic tell in the southern Arabian Peninsula (Van Beek, 1974). This enormous site was once the capital city of Saba' or Sheba, where the famous biblical Queen of Sheba[5] lived and ruled. The piggy-back town was abandoned after heavy destruction caused by repeated bombings during Yemen's civil war of the 1960s and by two earthquakes in 1982 (see Figure 7.1). Its ruinous state offered a fantastic opportunity to examine in detail the construction of buildings in the area (see Chapters 4, 7). Near the tell, we visited a house being built of layered mud by a young man for his family next to the home of his parents (Figure 3.51). It was square in plan, each side measuring 9.25 m in length, and was to consist of at least two stories. The first floor was roughed in, and construction of the second floor had just begun, as evidenced by the openings in the upper walls defining window locations. The ceiling was constructed of nicely squared wooden beams with plywood sheeting above. The first-floor entrance led through a short corridor into a larger hall, which gave access to all rooms on this floor (Figure 3.52). There were two rooms across the front, two across the back, and a middle room along the right side; directly opposite on the left side were a small storeroom and a stairwell with a square pier in the center, which formed the inner support for the stairs and landings leading to the upper floor.

Figure 3.51 Two-story layered-mud house during construction, Marib, Yemen (1991). Front entrance is on right side; small square windows on near side light the stairway inside.

After Marib, we proceeded to the Hadhramaut valley of Yemen, the most distinctive valley system in southern Arabia because of its physical characteristics and its social and economic traditions. Before Communists seized power in 1969, the valley was agriculturally self-sufficient. Its imaginative flash flood irrigation systems were designed to distribute run-off water quickly to prepared field plots, and its well irrigation systems reached abundant water only 9–12 m below the surface. It had also enjoyed prosperity resulting from a 500-year-old tradition of male migration to lands around the Indian Ocean, where many made their fortunes as traders and distributors. Money was sent back home to families in the Hadhramaut and later was also brought back for retirement. This enabled the men to build tall houses for their families, in keeping with the tradition of multistory houses going back to at least the second century A.D. These tall houses are unique in their style and among the most beautiful and famous examples of mud architecture in the world.

During the autumn and winter of 1961–1962, one of us (GVB) organized and directed a research team in a five-month walking archaeological survey of the Hadhramaut. The magnificent architecture that the team saw almost daily in this great valley system inspired GVB to plan a return trip at some time in the future to study the tall houses. The opportunity was finally realized during our trip across Yemen in 1991.

The first city in the Hadhramaut that we studied was Shibam, a walled, mud-brick city of tall houses reaching as high as eight stories, with most ranging between five and seven stories (Figure 3.53). In the suburbs outside the walls, houses were usually three or four stories high. Indeed, when viewed from some distance from the city, the tall houses separated by narrow streets reminded us of the view of lower Manhattan's skyscrapers when approached by ferry; the difference was primarily one of scale (see Figure I.2).

Towns and villages in this region are usually built at the base of the scree of the cliff face to avoid destruction by unusually high flash floods. Shibam is located in the wadi itself, near the southern cliff. The town now stands about five meters higher

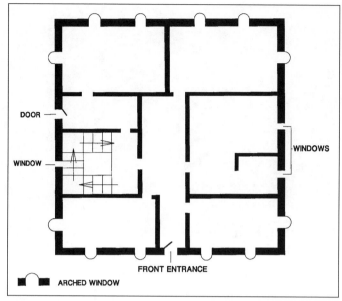

Figure 3.52   **First-floor plan of two-story house in Marib, Yemen (1991).**

than the wadi floor, perhaps on the accumulated debris of earlier structures or possibly on a hidden rock outlier extending from the southern cliff. After two flash floods destroyed Shibam at the ends of the thirteenth and sixteenth centuries A.D., dams were built upstream (to the west) to divert flood waters away from the city.

In 1991 there were about 500 houses in the walled city, most of which dated to the nineteenth and early twentieth centuries, although several were from the eighteenth century and at least one house, Beit Jarhum, was built in the sixteenth century. These buildings were not apartment houses, as one might think, but single-family homes. (Until about 1969 they belonged to the wealthy and were costly and well appointed.) The closely sited houses were generally arranged in blocks along streets aligned east–west and north–south. Many of these "streets" were so narrow they could not accommodate a Jeep or loaded camel, and a few allowed passage of nothing wider than a motor scooter (Figure 3.54).

Shibam had a mud-brick city wall about 3 m high. Although it no longer had any defensive value, during times of tribal warfare in previous centuries and in the early decades of the twentieth century it provided a measure of security from enemies. By the 1950s, however, its primary benefit was to keep children and animals within the city and to limit access by potential intruders. Outside the city wall on the south side, a row of buildings fronted on an asphalt road, neither of which existed in 1962. A single gate near the southeast corner provided entry into the city, and most vehicles parked in the open area just inside the gate. Two markets and seven mosques served the commercial and religious needs of the population. To the east of the city gate were the palaces of former Sultans, which had become housing for government and UNESCO offices.

Water for domestic needs in Shibam historically was obtained from a well about 90 m across the wadi opposite the city gate. It was carried back to town by the

Figure 3.53 City of Shibam in the Hadhramaut valley, Yemen, with the tallest mud houses in the world (1961).

womenfolk in vessels on their heads or transported by asses in goatskin water bags. Between 1970 and 1990, piped water was installed in the houses. Although this provided a welcome convenience for residents, it created serious problems for many of the tall houses because the installation of water pipes was not accompanied by a sewerage system to carry off wastewater. Moreover, the tendency to use considerably more water when it is conveniently delivered by pipes than when it is transported from a well in bags, jerry cans, jars, or tins is only human nature.

During the archaeological survey of 1961–1962, water for the research team's tent camp was transported from a well in two goatskin bags on the back of an ass, making two or three round trips every other day. Average water usage was seven gallons per person per day, which sufficed for drinking, cooking, bathing, and washing the dishes and laundry. Water usage typically increases at least eight to ten times that amount when piped water is available in semi-rural areas, and even more in Near Eastern cities.

Once piped water was installed in Shibam, the amount of wastewater produced by the town's residents vastly increased. Lacking sewer lines, people relied on the traditional disposal method; wastewater was poured through one or more holes in the wall where it entered a meter-long pipe or trough that dumped it into the middle of the earthen street. Little runoff occurred because the city was built on relatively level ground; thus the standing water was left to soak into the narrow earthen streets, where it eventually reached the mud-brick foundations of a number of houses. There it softened the mud brick, causing some sections of the houses—especially the corner areas—to settle, which led to the cracking of walls. Without shoring, these buildings would eventually collapse. To remedy that, many tall houses in Shibam had sloping mud-brick buttresses built with recessed heavy wooden beams that reached to the second floor, where they supported heavy wooden lintels in windows (see details in Chapter 14).

Less serious but aesthetically unpleasing, water pipes were mounted on the outer surfaces of walls to the height of the fifth or sixth floor. Like similar pipe installations

Figure 3.54 A narrow "street" in Shibam, Yemen (1991).

in older buildings seen in Europe, they created ugly, dark vertical lines that detracted from the harmony of the buildings. In this regard they were almost as offensive as rooftop TV antennas, which have marred the beauty of the skyline of Jerusalem and other beautiful, historic cities.

The United Nations Educational, Scientific, and Cultural Organization has organized an international campaign to preserve Shibam as a conserved, living city, somewhat like Colonial Williamsburg in Virginia, USA, but on a less grand scale. In 1991, UNESCO staff members were analyzing problems and seeking solutions relating to the stabilization, conservation, and restoration of the tall houses, the traditional market, and other structures in the town. They were negotiating the purchase of one of the tall houses, Beit Jarhum, to be the first restoration project. To that end, they were thoroughly examining the structure of the house, and had prepared "as is," or existing, floor plans and elevations. Abdul Rahman al-Haddad, Director of the Organization for Historic Monuments and Sites of the Government of Yemen, presented GVB with a set of the plans and elevations of Beit Jarhum, as well as a copy of Ronald Lewcock's book *Wādī Ḥaḍramawt and the Walled City of Shibām* (Lewcock, 1986).

Situated in the southwest quarter of the city, Beit Jarhum is six stories tall and typical of mud-brick houses in Shibam (Figure 3.55). It is believed to be the oldest house in the town, having been built in the sixteenth century. The main entrance to the house was recessed in its north wall (see Figure 13.18). Inside, the stairwell occupied the northwest corner (Figure 3.56). It featured a solid rectangular pier around which the stairway wound upward with three flights of steps between each floor; above the fourth floor, straight flights of steps led to the fifth and sixth floors. The first and second floors of the house served as stables and storerooms, and an outside entrance in the east wall provided an additional access to these floors. Because there were no courtyards in the compact town, livestock were kept on the first and second floors. (The occasional sight of a goat looking out a second floor window was an amusing surprise to us!) Both floors also provided storage space.

The basic floor plans of the structure were dictated by the major load-bearing walls. The third and fourth floors shared a similar plan with minor modifications; both floors had two large, all-purpose rooms serving as reception rooms (*majlis*), salons, or sleeping areas. The third floor was the men's floor where male visitors were entertained and business was conducted. The fourth, fifth, and sixth floors belonged to the family.

The third floor reception room or *majlis* was typical (Figure 3.57); it measured 6.5 × 3.5 m with two floor-level windows in the north wall and three in the east wall. These windows were at floor level because, in floor cultures (unlike the "chair culture" of the West), everyone sits on mats and pads on the floor and leans on bolsters or cushions against the walls; windows at this level allow inhabitants to look outside while seated. Elaborately carved wooden shutters covered the windows. Above these, just below the ceiling, were four small rectangular windows (two each in the north and east walls) to admit more light into the room. These smaller windows were fixed and never shuttered; some of them retained the traditional thin slabs of alabaster instead of glass. Two wooden cupboards were recessed in niches in the south wall, and a smaller recessed niche containing a small wooden cupboard was centered in the west wall. Above and to either side of the latter were empty, arched recessed niches. The ceiling was supported by two beams—a central beam 4.25 m long that extended from the north wall to a cross beam. The intersection was carried by a plain wooden column and capital, and the central beam was carried by an identical column midway along its length.

In the southwest corner of the fourth floor were the kitchen, a bathroom, and two storerooms. The kitchen, the only one in the house, measured 4.3 × 4.2 m. Beyond the kitchen was the *hammam*, or bathroom, with a Turkish-style toilet. This

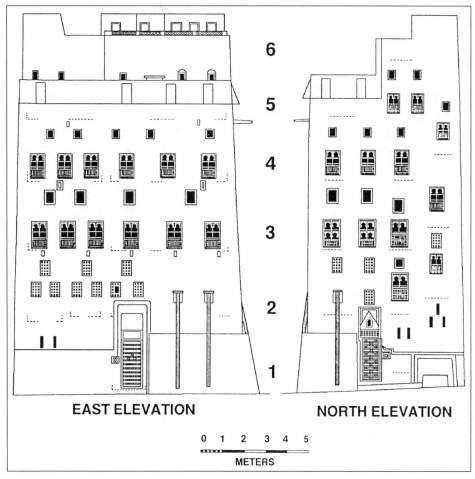

EAST ELEVATION   **NORTH ELEVATION**

0 1 2 3 4 5

METERS

Figure 3.55   Exterior view of Beit Jarhum in Shibam, Yemen (based on working drawing by M. Blane for UNESCO, 1990).

consisted of a shallow basin recessed in the floor, equipped with two pedestals to stand on when squatting and a waste hole behind. Similar toilets were located on the third and fifth floors.

The fifth floor *majlis* was moved westward and stood in part over the winding stairwell of the lower floors. The open space thus created on the east side and northeast corner of the fifth-floor plan became an open, L-shaped terrace or porch. The sixth floor was actually the roof, which provided additional open space, a terrace, and three small rooms, all for family activities. Both open terraces had walls about 1.5 m high for safety and privacy.

Terrace floors and walls of the fifth and sixth stories were fully covered with lime plaster. A lime-plastered drain channel in the floor about 10 cm wide carried rain and wastewater runoff through a vertical slit in the terrace wall to an outside drain spout (these were typically either metal or wooden). The coping of the terrace walls consisted of open work fashioned with small mud bricks set in an X pattern and

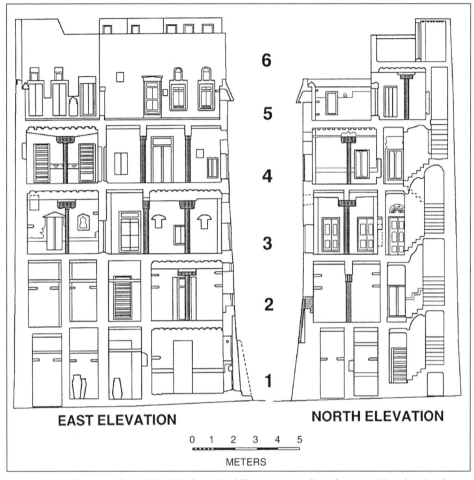

EAST ELEVATION   **NORTH ELEVATION**

0 1 2 3 4 5
METERS

Figure 3.56   Cross-sections of Beit Jarhum in Shibam, Yemen (based on working drawing by M. Blane for UNESCO, 1990).

capped with a single course of brick. The wall was reinforced at intervals with piers, each of which featured a box-like niche near its top (for holding objects in use when the inhabitants were occupying the terrace, such as oil lamps, bottles, etc.) and was finished with a conical top (Figure 3.58). In each of two corners of the terrace where it overlooked the lane below, three short tree limbs about 4–5 cm in diameter had been set diagonally across the corner into the adjoining walls to provide steps up to the top of the wall. These were used by workmen to climb over the wall onto their moveable platforms for repairing or replastering the outer surface of the walls. (Many of the newer houses did not have rooftop rooms but instead featured a small, covered shelter only over the stairway, which was easily recognizable by its characteristic sloping roof that ended abruptly at a narrow doorway.)

The position of the toilets shifted from against the west wall on the fifth floor to a distance of one meter from the wall on the third floor, with the one on the fourth floor located in between. All three toilets emptied into a narrow, vertical shaft built

Figure 3.57 Third-floor *majlis* (salon) of Beit Jarhum in Shibam, Yemen (1991). Straight ahead is north wall, with intricately carved window shutters; small upper window on left retains an alabaster pane, the traditional window material used in the Hadhramaut region. In west wall (on left) are open doors of small wooden cabinet in recessed niche.

Figure 3.58   Coping of roof terrace wall with niche in pier of Beit Jarhum in Shibam, Yemen (1991).

into the outer wall of the west side. In some houses this disposal shaft—variously referred to as a "waste chute" or "long drop"—was partially enclosed in the wall with rectangular, window-like openings, but in Beit Jarhum it was left open (Figure 3.59). At the base of the shaft, waste from the toilets fell onto a flat platform about

Figure 3.59   Open toilet disposal shaft in Beit Jarhum in Shibam, Yemen (1991).

waist high, upon which ash or lime was sprinkled daily. Periodically the waste was scavenged to fertilize the field crops in the wadi.

As in Beit Jarhum, wastewater from the kitchens and run-off water from the roofs of most houses were channeled through lime-plastered holes in the exterior walls

Figure 3.60 The mud-brick palace of the former Sultan in Seiyun, Hadhramaut, Yemen (1962). The palace is more than 100 years old.

and pitched away from them by metal or wooden spouts 75–100 cm long (see Figure 10.8). It was intended for the water to hit the ground approximately in the middle of the street, where a narrow, shallow drainage channel ran.

Another highlight of our research in the Hadhramaut was the former Sultan's Palace in Seiyun, which had become the archaeological and ethnological museum for the region (Figure 3.60). Built more than 100 years ago, this fortress house is a square, six-story building featuring circular towers at the corners, each of which was roofed with a small dome topped with a finial.

Directly below each row of the palace's floor-level windows, the wall was offset inward about 5 cm to reduce wall thickness and weight as it extended upward. The small ceiling windows and the large rectangular windows occupied these offset sections of wall. On each of the three upper floors, there were 11 rectangular windows in the facade plus three in each circular corner tower. A pointed arch in low relief above each rectangular window was painted light to medium blue. The front enclosure wall of the palace featured square or round, engaged piers with four-stage capitals. The terrace walls on the upper floors were finished in a style similar to that used in Shibam's Beit Jarhum, featuring mud bricks arranged in an X pattern below the coping.

We have described traditional house designs ranging from modest, one- or two-room village houses of peasants to elaborate, many-roomed houses of the wealthy from a selection of Near Eastern and Southwest Asian countries. The varied designs address specific needs as defined by a locality's physical environment, culture, tradition, and function, yet they are no more than a tiny sample of the seemingly infinite range of possible house plans. As for house designs typically found in the

Western world, in addition to traditional southwestern pueblo, mission, and territorial styles, we strongly believe that nearly any popular single, semidetached, or townhouse design can be rendered in mud, whether traditional, ranch-style, split-level, colonial, or modern. Earthen construction may not be suitable for buildings of more than 10 floors, although this remains to be demonstrated. But it can be used successfully for all townhouses, relatively small four- to six-floor apartment buildings, neighborhood cinemas, and small to medium-sized shopping centers with their variety of specialized shops that dot nearly every community.

NOTES

1. The Pathans (also known as Pashtuns) and Baluchis are two of the different ethnic tribes that constitute the citizenry of Pakistan. Both groups are predominantly Sunni Muslims. Pathans are the second largest ethnic group in Pakistan and are the majority in northern Baluchistan. Originally an Eastern Iranian people, they speak the Pashto language and live in a contiguous geographic area across Pakistan and Afghanistan. Also originally from Iran, Baluchis are the majority in southern and eastern Baluchistan. They tend to be independent and nomadic throughout a region across southern Pakistan and Iran. They adhere to clan structure and speak several languages, chiefly Balochi and Brahui.

2. This gentleman derived his large income from fruit orchards and was renowned as a great hunter, an important honor in Baluchistan reflecting the man's status.

3. Hyberbole? Not really. Whereas feeding 5000 was one thing, housing them would have been another. The workers would today be considered day laborers, but they brought along their wives and children. These families typically had their own dwellings offsite, but they were fed by the estate owner a modest daily meal of one or two dishes.

4. The *Diwali* festival, or "festival of lights," marks the coming of winter and the sowing of seeds.

5. The Queen of Sheba was known for her remarkable visit to the court of King Solomon, as described in the Bible (I Kings 10:1–13; II Chronicles 9:1–12).

Part II

PREPARING TO BUILD

Chapter 4

Layout and Foundation

While the design and specifications of a structure are being planned, the building code (if one exists) of the local government should be consulted.[1] Near Eastern governments generally do not have building codes as stringent as those imposed by European and North American jurisdictions. In the southwestern USA, where adobe is a traditional building material, codes reflect a high level of knowledge and understanding of adobe construction. The New Mexico [USA] Earthen Building Materials Code (New Mexico Commission of Public Records, 2003)—which now encompasses the former New Mexico Code for Unfired Clay Masonry, meaning "adobe"—has been a model often used by other jurisdictions. This section of the New Mexico Administrative Code (14.7.4 NMAC, 2003) is overly conservative in some aspects, but it remains a dependable guide for builders where local governments lack specific codes governing mud structures. From prospective builder to archaeologist, anyone seriously interested in mud construction should read *Adobe and Rammed Earth Buildings: Design and Construction* (McHenry, 1984) and *Adobe: Build It Yourself* (McHenry, 1985). Chapter 15 of the former deals with New Mexico's building codes for earth construction and includes extraordinarily sensible suggestions by McHenry—based on his knowledge of mud construction worldwide—for a model code, which should be universally adopted. Anyone exploring the possibility of constructing an earthen residence should inquire about their local building code requirements; in the absence of a section specifically covering adobe or unfired clay masonry, they should request that the New Mexico code be considered.

In the USA, pursuing the option of mud construction outside of the southwestern region requires educating citizens, trade unions, and financial institutions, as well as local, state, and federal governments. Increasing concerns about the environment and natural resources among our citizens, a growing outcry against flimsy, shoddy construction with traditional wood and masonry, and the ever increasing costs of conventional housing must open our minds and our cultural and economic institutions' policies to accept new concepts. All governments should encourage earthen construction because it contributes to a cleaner and healthier world environment, it is more comfortable to live in and cheaper to build, and it can be completely recycled. A growing number of books deal with mud construction and offer guidelines for "do-it-yourselfers," architects, builders, urban planners, and local and national governments. Those that are especially interesting and useful are cited in each chapter.

BUILDING ORIENTATION AND SITE PREPARATION

Once land is acquired and the building site is selected, the orientation of the structure must be decided upon. Orientation plays a significant role in determining interior comfort and energy conservation. Variables such as solar radiation, heat retention characteristics of construction materials, and the location and size of door and window openings affect the interior temperature of buildings. Ideally, a building should be oriented to expose roof and walls to maximum heat gain in winter and minimum heat gain during summer. The general rule-of-thumb for most regions in the northern hemisphere is to place the major openings facing south-southeast, which provides more direct solar energy for faster heating during winter mornings, and to situate fewer and smaller openings facing north-northwest, which reduces heat gain during hot summer afternoons. If the landscape features tall trees to the west of a building, solar radiation on the walls and roof will be further reduced during the summer and the structure will also be somewhat shielded from the chill northwestern winds in winter.

Optimum placement and orientation of a structure will also vary with size, characteristics, and position of the building site as well as with the topography and climate of the area, and often compromises must be made. The size and shape of the lot, nature of the terrain and soil, presence of rock outcrops or trees, pattern of prevailing winds, development plans of the urban or suburban neighborhood (which often accommodate only minimal change), and other considerations may not permit reorienting a house at will. At the planning stage, consultations involving the architect, the builder, an environmental specialist, and the homeowner are strongly recommended to decide upon the most advantageous compromises to bring maximum comfort and costs savings for the dwelling's future occupants.

After orientation is decided upon but before construction begins, the land must be prepared by grading if necessary. The ground should slope slightly away from the entire house site to prevent ponding of water that may spill from the roof and drain spouts and to keep groundwater run-off from approaching the base of the mud walls. Additionally, high areas may be cut down and low areas filled. Soil removed from a high area can be transported to level a low place so that no soil ever goes to waste. All filled areas must be tamped and filled several times to make certain that the surface is firm to minimize settling. Similarly, all soft spots—such as the surface of previously filled pits—must be checked, filled, and tamped one or more times until solid. Proper grading, together with devices discussed in Chapter 14, will assure a dry, long-lasting, and structurally sound building.

TO BUILD WITH OR WITHOUT A FOUNDATION

Mud walls, like any other types, can be built directly on the ground without foundations, and a majority of world housing constructed by both amateurs and professionals has been erected in this manner throughout human history. Generally, the ground is leveled, and the mud walls are laid directly on it. Although easier and quicker to erect than buildings with foundations, structures without foundations are more vulnerable to differential settling, erosion from run-off water covering the lowest course or two of the wall, upward absorption of ground moisture by capillary action, movement during freeze-and-thaw cycles, and earthquakes. These conditions, singly or in combination, guarantee a relatively short life for any structure built without a foundation. Walls weaken at the base and, if not repaired, will crack, then gradually lean outward, and eventually fall. (See Chapter 14 for detailed descriptions of problems derived from the lack of a foundation.)

Nevertheless, walls are often built conforming to the natural lay of the land without alteration. For example, amateur masons building layered-mud structures—especially property walls—often forget or ignore the principle of horizontal structuring and instead lay mud courses of the same thickness parallel to the sloping surface (see Figure 3.12). Such sloping walls crack more frequently while drying and are always more unstable. Despite these obvious disadvantages, such walls dot the countryside in Baluchistan and Punjab, Pakistan, and in southern Arabia because they are constructed more quickly and save time and money (Figure 4.1).

Almost any layered-mud property, boundary, courtyard, or privacy wall not built on a foundation and in need of repair can usually be rebuilt or repaired as cheaply and easily as it was erected. Walls that support structures, however, especially mud-brick walls, are more complex, expensive, and time-consuming to repair; and rammed-earth walls are practically impossible to repair. Therefore, all buildings that are expected to be long-lasting and structurally sound should have proper foundations.

Figure 4.1 A layered-mud property wall built on the ground surface without a foundation, in Dudhian, near Harappa, Punjab, Pakistan (1989).

EXCAVATION TYPES

From antiquity to the present, there have been two major types of subsurface excavations for foundations: (1) narrow trenches to accommodate the foundation of a building's walls and (2) a large excavated hole to accommodate the base of an entire building.

Trench Foundations

Narrow foundation trenches are laid out and dug along the projected perimeter of the building and within the perimeter for all other major load-bearing walls. The rest of the building, including floors, lies either on the natural surface, on compacted fill brought in to level the ground, or on any of several types of bases for floors. After the foundation is built up to ground level or slightly above it, the spaces between the foundation material and the sides of the trench are backfilled with soil, which is tamped down as it is put into the trench. Walls built on trench foundations resist possible settling and buckling (which are possible with heavy earthen walls) because the backfilled foundation trench provides lateral support. Most foundations for small structures such as houses are of this type.

Before excavation begins, stakes are driven into the ground at the outside and inside corners of each wall to define the line of the foundation. A string is then tied to one stake, drawn tightly, and tied to the other stakes defining the outside perimeter; this is repeated with stakes on the inside perimeter.

How wide and deep should the trench be? Consideration must be given to (a) the ratio of wall height to wall thickness and (b) the weight of the wall on the foundation. McHenry (1984:138) created a table showing the weight of adobe walls in pounds per linear foot for various ratios of wall height and thickness. The minimum foundation width required by the New Mexico code is the sum of the thickness of the outside house wall plus an additional 2 in (5 cm) on each side. Thus, a wall 12 in (30 cm) thick plus the extra widths totaling 4 in (10 cm) requires a minimum foundation width of 16 in (40 cm); a wall 24 in (60 cm) thick plus an extra width of 4 in (10 cm) requires a minimum foundation width of 28 in (70 cm). Additional trench space along the sides of the foundation wall is needed for foundations that are deep (below the frost line), for placing forms if the foundation is to be built of rammed earth or concrete, or for working space for the masons if mud brick, fired brick, stone, or concrete blocks are to be used. For an adequate foundation, its depth (and thus the trench) must be at least 8 in (20 cm) in areas without winter freezing; elsewhere it must be as deep as the frost line. In most regions of the USA, the frost line is 30–36 in (77–92 cm) below the surface. Interestingly, some of the ancient foundation trenches at Tell Jemmeh, which is in a zone without sustained freezing, are wider and deeper than those required by the New Mexico code by an additional 8–12 in (20–30 cm).

Foundation trenches can be excavated by one or several persons with picks and shovels, but they can be dug much faster and more efficiently by a backhoe. Hiring one with an operator is more costly, but if time is important or manpower is scarce, the backhoe is worth every dollar it costs. Until mechanized excavation machinery was developed in the twentieth century, foundation trenches had to be dug manually, and thus they were wider to enable a laborer to work efficiently. Whether dug manually or by machine, the trench must be straight enough to accommodate a straight foundation and should be somewhat wider than the planned width of the foundation. Foundations today tend to be centered in the trench, leaving about the same amount of space between planned wall surfaces and trench sides. In antiquity, however, the wall was often built close to either the outer or inner side of the trench, leaving the greater space along one of the faces of the foundation for the mason's work. The floor of the trench should be firm and level, so that the foundation will be uniformly strong and stable. All soil removed in digging the trench should be kept near the trench for backfilling and compacting after the foundation wall reaches ground level.

In erecting building walls, all mud layers and courses of mud brick should be horizontal, irrespective of the slope of the ground. On sloping ground, therefore, builders should excavate a trench with a horizontal bottom. They should dig the foundation trench in the higher ground to the depth below the lowest point on the surface of the lower ground (which should be below the frost or freeze line), so that adequate foundations can be constructed in the trench with horizontal mud layers or mud-brick courses. If this is not feasible, on sloping ground the trench can be dug with a series of steps whose bottoms are all below the freezing line; the wall can then be built on these steps in horizontal courses or layers.

Hole Foundations

Some ancient mud-brick buildings were built in large, excavated holes so that their lower level was below ground. Three structures at Tell Jemmeh were built in excavated holes more than 1.5 m deep: a rectangular, mud-brick-vaulted building of the early seventh century B.C. and two circular, mud-brick granaries of the late fourth to third centuries B.C. We excavated the larger circular granary (Figure 4.2) and the vaulted building (Figure 4.3) completely but only partially excavated the second granary.

This type of foundation is familiar to many of us today because it is the form employed for houses and office buildings with basements and for underground parking lots. The most obvious difference from the ancient system is the use of deep pilings for additional support in contemporary large buildings.

With this type of construction, the base of the walls and lowest floor rest on the leveled earth or on piers at the bottom of the hole. Occasionally, the orientation of the sides of the foundation hole does not closely correspond to the major axes of the projected building, thus when finished the building would appear to be turned slightly inside the hole. When this occurs, one corner of the structure may stand against one side of the foundation hole, with little or no backfill required at that point, and an adjacent corner of the building may be as much as 50–100 cm away from the side of the hole, requiring considerable backfilling and compacting.

In the three Tell Jemmeh buildings, the excavation of the foundation hole was neither precisely measured nor neatly done, so the width of the backfilled areas around the structure walls varied considerably. In the seventh-century vaulted building, for example, the backfilled space ranged in width from 5 to 44 cm. Why the building was turned slightly during construction is unclear. The planned orientation may have been altered very slightly during or after excavation of the foundation hole, or a careless mistake may

Figure 4.2   Overall view of large mud-brick granary, Tell Jemmeh, Israel, third century B.C. The ground surface is at the level of the interior ledge on the right side of the circular wall.

Figure 4.3   Overall view of Rooms A, B, C (top), and part of E of the pitched-brick vaulted building built by the Assyrians during the reign of Esarhaddon, Tell Jemmeh, seventh century B.C. Room E is beneath the broken vault in the foreground.

have been made in digging, or an impediment may have been discovered when the foundation courses were laid, such as a soft area below the wall (Figure 4.4).

The larger of the two circular granaries was built in a foundation hole shaped in cross-section like a pail—i.e., the hole was smaller in diameter at its base and splayed outward 25° as it rose to meet the ground surface (Figure 4.5). This was clearly a custom excavation designed to fit the planned construction of the wall, which was a single brick wide in the lower courses but increased to one and one-half bricks wide in the middle courses and to two bricks wide at ground level. Soil was backfilled and tamped each time one or two courses of bricks were laid to support the walls as they gradually increased in height, width, and weight. As with contemporary construction, the builders had to start in the bottom of the hole and raise both the outside walls and the load-bearing inside walls simultaneously.

ARCHAEOLOGICAL EVIDENCE OF FOUNDATIONS

From reading the published reports on archaeological excavation of Near Eastern sites in which mud was a major construction material, one would think that nearly all mud walls were built on the ground surface, because subsurface foundations

Figure 4.4   Backfilled foundation trench (under 50 cm arrow) of the Assyrian vaulted building at Tell Jemmeh. The top of the light-colored soil, into which the trench was cut, marks the ground surface at the time the structure was built.

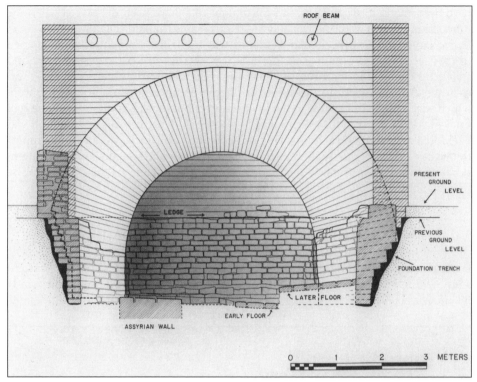

Figure 4.5   Pail-shaped foundation hole (circular foundation trench, in side view, shown in black) in a reconstructed cross-section drawing of the granary at Tell Jemmeh, third century B.C.

are rarely mentioned or illustrated. Actually the opposite is true; many mud walls had foundations laid in prepared foundation trenches. Unfortunately, excavators seldom documented them, probably because they did not look for a foundation or they excavated in a manner that destroyed the evidence. Foundation trenches are often elusive even to those who diligently seek them, and we have all missed them.

Some foundation trenches at Tell Jemmeh were very narrow and difficult to recognize. One was missed in a square where GVB was supervising the excavation in 1970, our first year at the site. This was the first wall discovered after excavations began and, because the soil and the characteristics of mud brick in the site were as yet unfamiliar, it was difficult to identify the edges of individual bricks in the bonded courses (about which more will be said later). This wall, of the early fourth century B.C., was built in a narrow trench so that one face of the wall stood flush against one side of the trench, with a space of no more than 1.5–3 cm between the other wall face and the other side of the trench. Four years later, while excavating farther along where the wall passed through a balk (in this case, an unexcavated mass of intact debris), supervisor Diane Fenicle discovered the foundation trench, which added greatly to our understanding of the stratigraphy. Later when reviewing color slides made during initial excavation, the thin backfill of the foundation trench was more easily recognizable. Figure 4.6 is a better illustration that features another wall with a narrow, ragged, foundation trench.

Figure 4.6 Narrow foundation trench, which was not immediately recognized, Tell Jemmeh, fifth century B.C.

The search for and recognition of foundation trenches (a) enable the assignment of structures to their correct building phases and (b) prevent the misdating of excavated buildings. If mistakes are made in assigning a building to the correct phase, errors will be introduced in the plan showing all buildings in a given settlement. Such errors are significant. They impair cultural reconstruction and interpretation of successive settlements and their associated ceramics, architecture, paleography, and chronology; as a result, incorrect interpretations can subsequently become fixed in the literature. Detection of substantial foundation trenches, however, also informs a researcher about the level of skill and craftsmanship of ancient builders.

MATERIALS USED FOR FOUNDATIONS

> Foundations … are to be dug down to the solid and in the solid, as may seem proportionate to the amplitude of the work, of a breadth greater than that of the walls which shall be above the ground; and these foundations are to be filled with as solid structure as possible.
>
> (Vitruvius Pollio, 1931 [translation]: vol. 1, bk. 1, chap. 5, ¶ 1.)

Foundations for earthen buildings may be constructed of several different materials: (1) mud—in the form of layers, rammed earth, or bricks; (2) stone—either ashlar masonry, rubble, or gravel; (3) poured concrete, concrete blocks, or fired brick; and (4) reused materials of earlier, ruined buildings.

Mud

A foundation of untreated, sun-dried mud is not permitted by the New Mexico building code because of concern that ground moisture will eventually soften it and lead to structural failure. Irrespective of modern concerns, both ancient and contemporary builders in the Near East and Southwest Asia frequently constructed fine, long-lasting structures with mud foundations. The most astonishing examples are the mud-brick foundations of five- to eight-story houses in Shibam, Hadhramaut, Yemen (see Figure 3.53), many of which are more than 200 years old. The masons who built them understood that mud walls, as well as those built of other materials, require adequate foundations to avoid uneven settling, cracking, and erosion. Even in the Near East where the alternating expansion and contraction of soil during the freeze–thaw cycle is minimal or does not occur at all, better buildings were constructed with substantial foundations. Surprisingly in many of those structures, the walls were part of the foundations; i.e., they were built in the foundation trenches and continued to the level of the second floor, maintaining the same type of bonding and dimensions from bottom to top.

Typical examples at Tell Jemmeh were two contemporary walls of the tenth century B.C. built in trenches 45 cm and 50 cm deep, respectively. A layer of clean, yellow sand was spread over the bottom of each trench before the foundation walls were begun, and when the wall height reached just above ground level, the trenches were backfilled with clean sand instead of soil. Both walls were in excellent condition when we exposed them (see Figure 14.27). There was no evidence of softening or erosion of the large bricks of walls 29 and 35, which measured $59 \times 35 \times 10$ cm and $56 \times 35/37 \times 11$ cm, respectively. Indeed, these bricks were among the most perfect we uncovered at Tell Jemmeh. When the sand was removed from the trench, we could see the scars left by the laborer's hoe-like tool, and could determine that he had dug the trench moving from west to east, about 3000 years ago! The function of sand-filled foundation trenches is discussed in Chapter 14.

In Shibam, Hadhramaut, Yemen, the six-story house known as Beit Jarhum rests on a composite foundation consisting of several different materials (Lewcock, 1986:96). The foundation trench for a house such as this would have been dug to a depth of 1.2–1.6 m (or until a hard layer of soil was reached) and would have been 1.3–1.75 cm wide. By rule-of-thumb, foundation trenches for these buildings are usually made 1½ times the width of the foundation walls at their base. Incidentally, the thickness of the house walls of Beit Jarhum at ground level measured only 0.86 m! That a solid mud-brick foundation wall less than one meter thick could carry six stories of heavy mud-brick walls, furnishings, and inhabitants is quite remarkable.

The bottom of the trench was filled with a layer of manure about 3 cm thick. Covering the manure was a layer of rock salt about 8 cm thick, which absorbs moisture from the soil and eventually becomes rock hard. Logs of `ilb wood (also known as the jujube tree *Zizyphus spina-christi* L.) about 10–20 cm in diameter were laid lengthwise side-by-side, then small stones were inserted to fill the interstices and level this wooden platform. `Ilb, a tree native to southern Arabia, is a near-perfect wood due to its considerable hardness and its resistance to termites, other insects, and rot. A final layer consisting of a mixture of lime, wood ash, and water covered the wooden platform. These materials are said to make an extraordinarily strong and hard base for house foundations. The masonry foundation began on this platform, about 0.84–1.15 m below the surface.

If the foundation is of mud brick, it continues above ground level, imperceptibly becoming the outer mud wall of the house. Although some who can afford the greater expense prefer stone to mud foundations, many houses are erected on complex mud foundations, such as Beit Jarhum, which has survived for at least 450 years. Straw is not used for constructing foundations because it is very expensive in the Hadhramaut; at the time of our visit, UNESCO was already experimenting with various locally available tempering materials, such as sand, in place of straw.

Boundary and privacy walls of layered mud are commonly built with mud foundations. In Quetta, Pakistan, we had an opportunity to study in detail the construction of a mud wall surrounding a residential lot on two sides (the other two sidewalls were fired brick). Two professional mud masons from Uzbekistan were hired by the owner to build the walls, which were to be 2.8 m high and 45 cm thick. The foundation trenches were to be 62 cm wide and 30 cm deep.

The masons laid out two parallel strings just above the ground surface with stakes 62 cm apart to mark the edges of the foundation trench (Figure 4.7). The chief mason, sighting down from above the line, carefully sprinkled a line of wood ash with his thumb and first finger directly below the string (Figure 4.8). He repeated this operation under the second string and then removed the stakes and strings. Both masons dug the foundation trench as defined by the ash lines, keeping the walls of the trench vertical (Figure 4.9). They left a considerable amount of loose soil in the bottom of the trench and poured water into it with a garden hose. By the next morning, the water had softened all lumps as well as the bottom of the trench so the masons could dig an additional 15–20 cm, thoroughly mixing the soil. From time to time they tramped the mud in the entire trench barefooted. By alternately adding and compacting more soil, the masons gradually filled the trench with mud to ground level. (This was the only compacting of mud that was done in constructing the layered-mud wall.) When the trench was filled, they quickly leveled the top of the wet mud and then left the foundation to dry. The drying period was expected to last three or four days before wall construction began, although this length of time is variable depending on the season of the year.

Ashlar, Rubble, and Stolen Materials

Stone foundations of both ashlar and rubble were common in antiquity and remain so today, especially in hilly and rocky areas where stone is readily available. Ashlar—dressed blocks of stone—was used less because of the greater cost and time consumed by quarrying, transporting, and dressing the blocks, even though it provides greater strength and durability. The blocks are either laid on the surface or built up in trenches, generally extending above the surface to protect the base of the mud walls from both ambient ground dampness and runoff water, which otherwise would soften and undercut the walls. If the foundation is of rubble, it continues upward to 0.5–1 m above ground level, where the mud wall of the house begins.

The top of a stone rubble foundation must be leveled if the mason is to lay truly horizontal mud layers or courses of mud brick over it. This is accomplished either by leveling the stones themselves or by applying a mud or lime mortar layer of varying

Figure 4.7   Fixing the string line for one side of the layered-mud foundation wall, Quetta, Baluchistan, Pakistan (1990). Note chunks of previous layered-mud wall, which will be dissolved and reused in the new wall.

Figure 4.8 Sprinkling wood ash in the foundation trench directly below the string to mark the line of the foundation, preparatory to removing the string, at the Qazi house in Pishin, near Quetta, Pakistan (1990).

thickness to compensate for small irregularities. Ashlar foundations are generally dry laid, i.e., without mud mortar, thus allowing the mass and dressing of the blocks themselves to provide the stability.

Sometimes ashlar blocks are removed from walls and foundations of abandoned buildings that were still standing or are robbed from buried structures in ancient sites (Figure 4.10). In archaeological sites with ashlar construction, many and sometimes all the blocks have been stolen, including those from the foundations, leaving only empty or nearly empty trenches, which are referred to in archaeological circles as "robber trenches." Archaeological architects often have only these empty trenches to reconstruct the plans of buildings. This has been the fate of many noble Greek and Roman structures as well as accessible buildings elsewhere with quality masonry.

Marble and limestone blocks robbed from ancient structures were reused to build houses (Figure 4.11) and shops, or they were burned in lime furnaces to make plaster for house walls and paved floors. Practical common folk seldom cared about nearby ancient monuments except when they served as "quarries" for already-dressed stone blocks.[2]

The robbing of fired brick, particularly to acquire antique bricks from old houses, occurs when a property owner or a scavenger decides to reuse or sell them, or when derelict structures lack community protection. Reusing fired bricks requires considerable work in cleaning the brick, especially in chiseling off the old mortar. Rubble walls are easier to disassemble when built with mud mortar but require considerable care to pull down when they were laid dry without mortar. Solid, dense mud

Figure 4.9 Smoothing the base of the foundation trench, at the Qazi house in Pishin, near Quetta, Pakistan (1990).

Figure 4.10 Ashlar corner of an offset in an ancient fortification wall, Marib Town, Marib, Yemen (1991). The blocks of the upper courses and adjacent sections of the wall have been stolen.

Figure 4.11 Reused ashlar in an abandoned house in Marib Town (1991). Note pre-Islamic architectural designs incorporated upside down in the wall: on the right, a frieze of stylized ibex facing forward; on the left fragments of two dentil-like panels, the larger of which was probably cut from column capitals.

bricks can be removed from walls if they are not of enormous size, the mortar is not too hard, and the mortar joints are relatively wide. In 1977, we witnessed Hassan Fathy's boys' school at New Gourna, near Luxor, Egypt, being disassembled and the mud bricks being carted away to be reused elsewhere. On the other hand, when specimen mud bricks of different sizes and time periods at Tell Jemmeh were promised for the Israel Antiquities Authority and the Smithsonian Institution, their removal proved extraordinarily difficult and time-consuming. Many of these bricks were very large, individually ranging 25–71 kg in weight, and the mortar joints were so thin that a brick on either side of the target brick had to be destroyed to gain sufficient working space to undercut the target brick. Thus, an easier way to reuse mud is to pull down the wall, soak the chunks in water overnight, and make layers or mold new bricks the next day or so.

Ashlar foundations were occasionally used for important mud brick buildings, as, for example, in ancient Greece (Robertson, 1969:4). In recent centuries these foundations have become increasingly popular in northern Yemen for walls constructed of either layered mud or mud brick. We visited a new layered-mud house under construction near the abandoned piggy-back tell at Marib (see Figure 3.51). This house stood on a foundation about one meter high consisting of three courses of ashlar. Nearby, Marib Town occupied the top of the piggy-back tell situated on one end of the largest pre-Islamic tell in the southern Arabian Peninsula. Many buildings in the ruined and abandoned town also stood on foundations built of pre-Islamic stones robbed from the ancient site. The foundations and walls were built of limestone blocks that frequently bore ancient south Arabian tooling marks, architectural motifs, and Old South Arabian inscriptions. These ashlar foundations were commonly about 1–2 m high, but in many instances they continued upward as stone walls extending as high as the third story (Figure 4.12). Layered-mud or mud-brick walls were then built on these stone walls for the uppermost two or three floors, sometimes extending to the parapet.

We also saw several new mud houses under construction not far to the east of Shibam in a settlement known as Hauta. There we witnessed a group of masons finishing a stone foundation (see Figure 1.2) built of small, slightly irregular ashlar. Laid in concrete mortar, it reached slightly more than one meter above ground level in four completed courses and was about 60 cm thick.

Rubble foundations are generally laid with mud or lime mortar. The latter enhances their stability and longevity. On the other hand, terrace walls of rubble are commonly laid dry so that drainage from the buttressed earth can pass through the interstices; this prevents the build-up of water pressure behind the wall, which otherwise would destroy it.

Few if any houses were built entirely of rubble, however, because tall rubble walls lack strength and are notoriously unstable in strong winds and earthquakes. Therefore, most remains of rubble walls that are less than one meter or so high almost certainly served either as foundations or the lower areas of walls that carried mud superstructures in the ancient Near East. Superstructures of most buildings founded on rubble were built of mud brick, layered mud, or rammed earth; in due course, virtually all were destroyed by neglect, abandonment, warfare, or erosion, leaving only the stubs of walls. When these are excavated, archaeologists generally find only the foundations and little or nothing of the superstructure. Reconstructions of the appearance of these buildings when they were inhabited are chiefly based on (1) what can be learned from careful and detailed observation of the excavated ruins, (2) better preserved structures in other sites in the

Figure 4.12 **Pre-Islamic ashlar blocks reused in house walls, capped with mud-brick walls, Marib Town, Yemen (1991).**

Figure 4.13   Newly built layered-mud house with rubble terrace walls and rubble foundations of the courtyard wall, Baluchistan, Pakistan (1990). Note overhanging reed bundles that protect wall tops and divert rainwater from base of walls.

region of about the same date, and (3) analogies with functionally similar current buildings.

Rubble foundations are still favored in most regions of the world where layered-mud buildings are constructed. In Baluchistan, where winters are marked by rain and snow, small rounded stones are carefully fitted and laid dry (Figure 4.13). The foundation walls may continue to 50 cm or more above the ground.

In Iran, laborers dig the foundation trench to a depth of about 46 cm, and to a width slightly greater than the projected thickness of the wall. The removed soil is mixed with burnt lime and water, and a layer about 15 cm thick is poured into the bottom of the trench. Rough stones about 15–20 cm in diameter are thrown into this soil–lime mixture and another layer is poured over the stones; this process is repeated until the trench is full. After setting for three to four weeks the foundation is as hard as rock, and construction of the superstructure walls can begin (Wulff, 1966:108). (This is similar to the Roman method for constructing a concrete foundation, to be discussed in the next section).

Buildings of form-built rammed earth in Morocco occasionally stand on rubble foundations. Between Agadir and Goulimine (also spelled Goulimime or Guelmim), we saw a rammed-earth wall of a shopping center under construction and still lacking mud plaster; the wall stood on a well-designed rubble foundation that reached about 15–20 cm above ground level.

Packed rock and gravel foundations are becoming more common in the southwestern USA because they are (a) less expensive to construct and (b) permit the ready percolation of water if the soil beneath the foundation trench is able to absorb it (Figure 4.14). If the subsoil does not readily drain, the bottom of the trench is graded (or a narrow graded channel is dug in the bottom) to conduct water to a dry well or drainage area some meters away from the foundation. Alternatively, the foundation trench is filled with a mixture known as the "base course" in highway construction, which consists of two parts sand to three parts gravel and is compacted in the trench (McHenry, 1984:138–140). McHenry successfully used this type of gravel foundation in several houses he built in Corrales and Albuquerque, New Mexico.

Figure 4.14 Loose rock foundation for a rammed-earth wall at Jasper House, Edgewood, New Mexico, USA (1995).

Poured Concrete

Poured concrete was first used by builders in Rome late in the second century
B.C. for the platforms on which the temples of Concord and Castor were erected
(Robertson, 1969:234). Subsequently, this revolutionary material seems to have
been used primarily for constructing foundations, walls, arches, vaults, and domes
in the Roman world. Using pozzolana cement—a mixture of volcanic earth from
Pozzuoli (near the areas of Rome and Naples), lime, and sand—the Romans
developed a true concrete that was hard and waterproof. An aggregate of broken
fragments of stone or bricks and pozzolana cement (Singer, 1979:407, 410, fig.
378D) was commonly used in structures including the walls, vaults, and domes
of such famous buildings as the Pantheon. Foundations were made by pouring
this concrete into wooden forms, much as is done now. Today, concrete ranks as
one of the most widely used foundation materials in the world. Gravel and sand
are added to the present-day mixture, and steel reinforcing rods are set in place to
strengthen the mass.

For adobe, the New Mexico building code requires "a continuous concrete footing at least eight inches thick and not less than two inches wider on each side than
the projected walls. All foundation walls which support adobe units shall extend
to an elevation not less than six inches above the finish grade, which are known as
"stems." Foundation walls shall be at least as thick as the exterior wall" (McHenry,
1984:209). McHenry illustrates three types of concrete foundation systems: (1) a
conventional spread footing; (2) a combined, monolithic footing and slab; and (3)
a pyramidal foundation, strengthened with reinforcing rods and mesh (McHenry,
1984:139, fig. 9.2a,c,e).

Reused Walls

In the Near East, and until relatively modern times in the Western world, surviving
sections of walls from ruined or partially destroyed mud-brick and stone buildings
were frequently integrated into new construction. With careful examination and
probing of the remains, a mason would determine whether the surviving walls
were sound, and if so, which sections and courses could be reused. It is advantageous to build on earlier walls because they have settled and are stable. If the
orientation of the walls of the proposed building entirely or partially corresponds
with the sound, earlier walls of the ruin, the builder could use the latter either as
a foundation or as an integral part of the superstructure of the new building. If
stretches of some courses were in good condition when others were not, a mason
would remove the bad courses down to the uppermost good course to provide a
solid base. Sometimes an additional course or two would be removed to accommodate the coursing of the new mud bricks, especially if they were of a different
thickness. It seems that ancient masons deliberately sought good walls of earlier
periods to build on, sometimes even changing the orientation of their proposed
building to make use of them. At Tell Jemmeh, for example, the town fortifications
of the seventh century B.C. were constructed directly above the earlier walls of the
eighth century B.C., set off from the line of the latter by 11 cm in the area where
they were exposed.

Figure 4.15 A sound section of a light-colored, eleventh century B.C. Philistine wall served as the partial foundation for a tenth century B.C. wall of darker brick that had been built over it (above the row of three white tags), Tell Jemmeh, Israel.

Erected above the largely destroyed twelfth century B.C. Philistine pottery kiln at Tell Jemmeh was the north wall of an eleventh century B.C. mud-brick building. In turn, it also became a ruin, but this structure was found to be sound in some stretches by a tenth century B.C. builder, who decided to use part of the old wall as a base for a 1.8 m stretch of new wall (Figure 4.15). The builder apparently removed bricks from some courses; those courses may have been damaged or it may have been necessary to adjust spacing to suit the thickness of the new, thinner bricks. When the tenth century B.C. wall was excavated, we discovered that it had been built over the stub of the eleventh century B.C. wall, which it both incorporated and used as a foundation.

NOTES

1. Although builders typically are familiar with local building codes, the client should also be familiar with what is required so as to make certain that code requirements are followed. For a "do-it-yourselfer," knowing, understanding, and adhering to code is absolutely essential.

2. This is what happened to the Parthenon, whose marble blocks were being burned by local citizens to make lime plaster for their houses and walks. This tragedy in part motivated the UK's Lord Elgin to save as many marble sculptures as possible by purchasing them with his own funds. We owe our opportunity to admire these reliefs—now on display in the British Museum—to his taste and farsightedness. Without his caring, most of these sculptures would have been destroyed.

Chapter 5

Soils and Mud

Through more than 10,000 years, builders have acquired a great deal of empirical knowledge about soil, the basic material in all earthen architecture, which has been passed down through generations of masons to the present. This knowledge includes how soil is selected, quarried, and prepared for use in construction. The quality of mud construction largely depends upon the type of soil used, the type and proportion of temper used to reduce plasticity, the duration of the sun-baking process, and the quality of craftsmanship in all stages.

TYPES OF SOIL

Although soil types vary by locality and region, most soils can be used to build earthen structures, including Nile River black silt and sandy, clayey, gravelly, and loessial soils (Rosen, 1986).

Excellent soil for construction is often found in river beds and along their banks. These soils consist predominately of silt, with lesser amounts of sand, and clay. Heavy clay is less desirable because it shrinks while drying. Hassan Fathy (1973:198) noted that bricks made of pure clay and molded while very wet showed severe cracking soon after molding and shrank about 37% during drying. Clayey soils also are known to shrink and crack in layered-mud and rammed-earth construction.

It is unfortunate that many European archaeologists have continued to use the term "clay" instead of "soil" when describing earthen construction. This is misleading and incorrect because clay is only one component of soil, and in a relatively pure state it is unsatisfactory for construction. A simple, inexpensive, on-site test kit can determine the approximate proportions of clay, silt, and sand in any soil. There are also a number of simple hand tests—requiring nothing more than a soil sample, a glass jar, and water—that can reveal the excesses and deficiencies of a particular soil and its suitability for construction (McHenry, 1984:48–49).

Loess is a fine-grained, loamy soil that is transported by winds and often deposited hundreds or thousands of miles from its place of origin. It is the predominant soil in the Tell Jemmeh region, apparently having come from North Africa and the Sinai. Jemmeh loess has been reworked from the Quaternary to the present (Melson and Van Beek, 1992). Loess makes excellent mud bricks that are dense and strong and that have clean, sharp corners and edges. It can be molded in a wide range of shapes and sizes; indeed, some of the largest mud bricks used in the ancient Near East were made of loess soil at Tell Jemmeh.

The Roman architect Vitruvius recommended that "bricks are to be made of white clayey earth or of red earth, or even of rough gravel. For these kinds, because of their smoothness, are durable. They are not heavy in working, and are easily built up together" (Vitruvius Pollio, 1931 [translation]: vol. 1, bk. 2, chap. 3, ¶ 1). He also noted (1931: vol. 1, bk. 2, chap. 3, ¶ 4) that certain soils behave like pumice and are useful for making fine bricks:

> Now in Further Spain there is a town Maxilua, and also Callet, in Asia there is Pitane, where bricks, when they have been made and dried, swim in water if they are thrown in. Now it seems that they are able to swim because the soil from which they are drawn is like pumice. Thus, since it is light, when made solid by the air it does not admit nor drink up moisture into itself. Therefore since these bricks are of a light and open property, and do not allow the humid potency to penetrate into the body, of whatever weight the body shall be, it is compelled by Nature to be upheld by water like pumice-stone. So indeed they have great advantages because they are not heavy in buildings, and when they are being made, they are not dissolved by storms.

The deep brown, organic soil of grasslands in the midwestern USA and in the Ukraine is not good for making mud brick because it lacks clay and is loose and crumbly. However, it has proven useful for creating shelter when blocks of sod—soil with grass—have been cut and piled to make earth lodges and sod houses. We recall GVB's mother's account of living in a sod house during one winter at the beginning of the twentieth century in Saskatchewan, Canada, where GVB's grandfather had decided to homestead. She remembered the sod house as cozy and warm during the frigid, harsh, Canadian winter. In New Mexico, cut blocks of sod, called *"terrónes,"* measuring about 36 × 18 × 18 cm, are still used in building today.

For rammed earth construction, the recommended soil composition is 70% graded sand and 30% clay (Miller and Miller, 1982:40). Soil with this ratio is uncommon in nature, so quantities of sand, fine aggregates, or clay may have to be brought to the building site and mixed with the local soil to achieve these approximate proportions. Fortunately, rammed earth as well as layered mud construction is surprisingly tolerant of variations in soil composition.

QUARRYING SOIL

An enormous amount of soil is required to build town fortifications and building walls. Soil for mud construction is usually obtained by quarrying as near the building site as is practicable, because transporting it is time-consuming and costly. Nonetheless, soil has also been quarried in wadis and fields outside the area of habitation (and sometimes from beneath the site) for the buildings in a settlement. Bricks, walls, and structures made of soil from such locations are almost always "clean," i.e., they do not contain artifacts. At Tell Jemmeh, an entire vaulted building from the seventh century B.C. was built of "clean brick," proving that the bricks were made of soil quarried off the tell; they even may have been molded off-site. If mud bricks are manufactured off the site, their fragility adds to problems of transport, whether by hod carriers or pack animals. Quarry pits, therefore, have been (and still are) dug wherever there is suitable soil, and they occur in all shapes and sizes. Slopes are sometimes sliced and pulled down, or caves are dug in embankments to provide soil.

In contemporary villages and towns in the Near East where mud construction prevails—and where civic pride in public areas is not a primary concern—enormous quarry pits are frequently excavated in vacant lots, front yards, backyards, and even in the streets. We observed an astonishing quarry pit in one of the villages in the Hadhramaut during our archaeological survey in 1962. The pit, which was more than 2 m in diameter and of equal depth, had been dug near the edge of the narrow dirt road through the village to provide soil for a new mud-brick house.

In Near Eastern sites or "tells," whose considerable depths consist of the remains of many superimposed occupations, soil for rammed earth was commonly taken from irregular areas on the top of the natural butte when the site was first occupied or, later, from debris left by previous settlements. Alternatively, a portion of the required soil was sometimes obtained by cutting into the slope to create a horizontal or slightly inward-sloping shelf to serve as a base for the revetment or wall. Soil was also probably obtained from a moat-like ditch dug at the base of a site. Such actions, which are still common today, inevitably destroy the sequence of cultural deposits. Few activities depress and frustrate archaeologists more, because what has been destroyed can never be recovered.

In these ancient tells, soil was also frequently quarried from pits dug in vacant lots, courtyards, lanes, and from ruined buildings near the new construction site (Figure 5.1). Sometimes only the largest artifacts—those that would protrude from a brick—were removed from the soil, leaving all kinds of smaller objects to be incorporated in the brick mixture—sherds, bones, glass, metal fragments, etc.—which may belong to different historical periods because the quarry pit is often dug so deep that it cuts into and through the debris of successive earlier ruins. The artifacts incorporated in bricks may be of significance in themselves or in illustrating the movement of objects in a site after their initial deposition. In excavating structures built with dirty bricks, archaeologists must break up and sift all bricks removed so that artifacts can be recovered.

At Tell Jemmeh, dirty bricks from the collapsed superstructure of a large circular storage building or granary of the late fourth to third centuries B.C. contained sherds from the preceding 900 years of occupation. Among them were two sherds from a juglet made of fine ware sometime between 650 and 550 B.C. that had been imported from the Greek Islands in the Aegean Sea. Three years after this discovery, a vaulted building dating from 675 B.C. was excavated about 20 meters southwest of the granary. There we discovered a pit (Figure 5.2) that had cut through the north wall of Room F and the vault, and also into the debris left inside the room after the building had been abandoned and covered with yet more debris. When we excavated inside that room, we found three sherds that joined the two recovered from the granary built 300 years later! The juglet, which belonged to the period of the vaulted building, enabled us to reconstruct what happened. The granary builders likely dug a number of

Figure 5.1   Excavating an old quarry pit at Tell Jemmeh, Israel.

pits near the construction area to obtain soil for brick making, including the one that cut deeply into Room F of the vaulted building. At least two of the East Greek juglet sherds were in the soil carried off to make granary bricks, but three others remained in the room fill. For archaeologists, this is an especially interesting example of the horizontal and vertical movement of objects within a site (Figure 5.3).

Rammed earth also was made with artifact-laden soil taken from earlier habitation areas without being cleaned. Vast numbers of fragments of pottery, glass, bone, metal, etc., can be found in the old, rammed-earth city walls of Rabat, Morocco, proving that dirty "occupation debris" had been quarried from nearby trash dumps for the construction of the massive wall (see Figures 8.24, 8.25). By contrast, the revetment at Tell Jemmeh was built of clean, artifact-free sandy silt from the wadi floor or river bed and transported to the site, probably from a maximum distance of 400 meters (i.e., within a radius of a quarter of a mile).

For optimum durability in all types of earthen construction today—wattle-and-daub, layered mud, rammed earth, and mud brick—the soil should be screened to remove fragments of limbs, plant roots, bones, artifacts, and garbage. Small stones should also be removed for mud-brick mixes, although they can be tolerated in layered-mud and rammed-earth mixes. The screen's mesh should be at least 1 cm but never larger than 2 cm, tightly stretched and nailed or stapled to a wood frame (made from boards 5 × 10 cm or greater), and reinforced at the corners with wooden blocks or steel corner braces. The framed screen can be leaned against practically any open structure or mounted on supporting posts driven into the ground (Figure 5.4). Soil is then tossed against the screen a shovel-full at a time so that the finer material collects behind the screen, ready for mixing. Nevertheless, sometimes houses

Figure 5.2   Soil quarry pit cutting through the north wall and into room F of the Assyrian vaulted building of seventh century B.C., Tell Jemmeh, Israel.

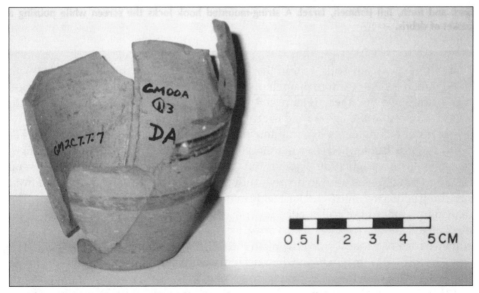

Figure 5.3   East Greek juglet sherds (square 2C) from mud bricks of the granary, late fourth to third centuries B.C. The 2C sherds join sherds (square 00A) from the pit in Figure 6.2 in room F (seventh century B.C.), their original provenience, at Tell Jemmeh, Israel.

Figure 5.4   Soil-sifting screen mounted on two pipes, permitting the operator to shake the screen back and forth, Tell Jemmeh, Israel. A string-mounted hook locks the screen while pouring a basket of debris.

are built of very stony soils. Soil in the Hanna Valley in Baluchistan is loaded with stones ranging 2.5–4.0 cm in diameter. The unplastered rear wall of the layered-mud men's house we saw there (Figure 5.5) revealed that the layers were loaded with stones. As a result, the layers were irregular in shape and size.

When soil requirements of a building project are too large to be met locally, additional soil may be quarried elsewhere and transported to the site. At an Afghan refugee settlement with a population of about 100,000 near Muslimbagh, Baluchistan, several thousand mud houses were so densely built that they presented an almost solid front stretching perhaps a mile (~1.6 km) wide in the embayment of a mountain range. The tremendous amount of soil needed for constructing this settlement was quarried on the flat land about a mile (~1.6 km) away. Extensive quarrying along both sides of the entrance road had transformed the plain into eroding badlands.

If a builder uses imagination when deciding where to quarry soil, the site can be improved by (1) leveling, i.e., cutting down high places and filling low places, and/ or (2) by digging a basement or cellar, a series of dry wells to improve drainage, or even a swimming pool. Such site improvements provide quantities of surplus soil for mud construction—sometimes enough to build the entire house.

Figure 5.5 Unplastered rear wall of a men's guest house at Hanna, near Quetta, Baluchistan, Pakistan (1990). Soil in this region is laden with small stones, which were not screened out before the mud was mixed and formed into layers.

TEMPERING MATERIALS

Tempering materials are commonly added to the mixture of soil and water in clay-rich soil to reduce plasticity. It makes the mixture less sticky and more workable, and it aids in holding the worked mass together and in reducing crack formation while the forms are drying. Chaff, or chopped straw, is universally preferred as temper in the Near East, yet in some places—such as southern Egypt—it is scarce and therefore quite expensive. In such places, masons use sand (the preferred temper in the USA), chopped grasses or weeds, certain kinds of tree bark, finely ground potsherds, or soapstone, to name a few alternatives. In building the village of New Gourna in Egypt, Hassan Fathy used both sand and straw, employing a ratio of 1 m³ soil from the valley floor plus 1/3 m³ sand plus 45 lb (20.4 kg) straw; this mixture produced 660 bricks from molds that measured 24 × 12 × 8 cm (Fathy, 1973:198). Manure is occasionally added to the mix because it is said to produce a very strong brick (Clarke and Engelbach, 1930:208), but in most Near Eastern countries, manure is of more value for other applications, such as an additive to the final coat of mud plaster, fuel for bread ovens, or fertilizer for fields and gardens.

The best way to determine if the ratios between soil and tempering agents are suitable is to try different mixtures of ingredients and make test bricks. McHenry (1984:57) describes a simple hand test that can be performed during mud mixing. Load a mason's trowel with the mix and tilt it to an angle of about 45°. If all of the mix slides off readily, it is acceptable; if most slides off, but some sticks to the trowel, there is too much clay in the mix, so more temper should be added.

Not all mud construction requires tempering agents. Layered-mud walls are often built with a mixture of only soil and water, especially in areas of heavy, gravelly soil. In the Asir region of Saudi Arabia and in northern Yemen, the base coat of mud plaster includes a considerable amount of straw, but the final coat omits straw for a smooth finish (see Figure 12.8). Similarly, rammed-earth construction does not require temper in the core structure, although it may be used in the plaster.

In the southwestern USA, a 3%–5% (by weight) asphalt emulsion or portland cement is sometimes added to the mud mixture, primarily to protect mud brick from damage by heavy rain while drying. Such brick is referred to as "semi-stabilized brick." A waterproof mud brick, produced if the amount of asphalt emulsion or cement is increased to 6%–12%, is known as "stabilized brick" or "treated brick" (Smith and Austin, 1989:15). Stabilized brick is grayish in color because of the cement and is much less attractive than regular, untreated mud brick. McHenry (1984:75) observed that stabilizing agents are not only expensive, but when added to the brick mixture, they may inhibit the bonding of the brick into a solid mass; they also make it impossible to recycle mud brick for eventual use in future construction.

Soils for rammed-earth construction are essentially the same as those used for making mud brick, i.e., most soils will do. Patty (1942) noted that at least 80% of the soil types on farms throughout the USA are satisfactory for making rammed-earth walls, and that only one-third require the addition of sand. The acceptable range of clay content for rammed earth is wider than that for mud brick, ideally 15%–18%, although higher clay content is said to increase durability and to provide a greater degree of waterproofing (McHenry, 1984:98). The remaining material may be sand or other aggregate and silt. Others recommend a mixture of 70% sand and 30% clay, and additional sand can be mixed in to bring the composition to this ratio (Miller and Miller, 1982:40). The soil should be screened to remove foreign matter such as plant roots and decaying materials. Once clean, it can be piled to await construction.

Rammed-earth builders in the southwestern USA often use stabilized soil for strength and better resistance to erosion. The preferred additive is 5% cement. One such builder adds 10% cement to the soil used for the first 10–16 in (25.5–40.5 cm) of wall immediately above the concrete slab to protect the wall from dampness (Smith and Austin, 1989:47).

Because clays and cement do not mix well together, soil with minimum clay content is best if stabilized soil is to be used. The cement must be thoroughly mixed with dry soil, either by hand with a hoe, by a front-end loader pushing the soil back and forth on a clean flat surface, by a concrete mixer, or by a pug mill—a chamber featuring a spiral shaft resembling an Archimedes screw. After this dry combination is thoroughly mixed, a little water (about 5%–10% by volume—approximately the same amount of moisture that is found naturally in a pile of soil) is added, and the ingredients are thoroughly mixed again.

Soil that has been piled for some time may be used without adding water if no cement or asphalt is to be added. But if the soil's wetness approaches that used in layered construction (very wet, just to the point where the water does not appear or run off), it will stick to the tamping tool and squirt when beaten, making compacting difficult or impossible. McHenry (1984:99) described an easy test for moisture content:

First (the soil) should appear damp, but not wet. A handful of the soil may be squeezed into a firm ball readily by hand. In this test, a soil with too high a moisture content will feel sticky and will not form a firm solid ball when squeezed. On the other hand, if too little moisture is present, the soil will not compact and hang together at all. The successful compacted soil ball will be firm and solid, but neither hard nor sticky. The hand compacted ball may be dropped onto a firm surface from a distance of approximately 3 ft (1 m). If the soil ball shatters the moisture content is adequate. If it does not, too much moisture is present.

TOOLS AND EQUIPMENT

The basic tools are the same as those used for laying fired brick and concrete blocks. A do-it-yourselfer planning to build a house or any other structure of mud should always purchase first-rate tools, such as those used by tradesmen, because they are better made, well balanced, longer-lasting, and thus cheaper in the long run. Recommended tools and their function are listed:

Tool	Function
Stakes and string	To layout the lines of building foundations accurately, and to keep layers and courses straight and level.
Plum bob and spirit level	To keep construction vertically plumb and horizontally level.
Square	To keep walls and openings with 90° angles.
Chalk line	To identify lines for construction activities.
Carpenter's rule and/or measuring tape	To measure accurately.
Wooden lathes and rigid pieces of wood	To make various measuring devices whose length is exactly the planned width of a wall (e.g., 2.5×5.1 cm or 1×2 in), allowing efficient verification of wall width and uniformity.
Heavy duty hoe with square blade, and spare handles	To dig foundation trenches, to mix soil or mud mortar, to grade the landscape, etc.
Trowel	To spread mortar and plaster, and to clean spills and run-downs of mortar on the wall (the best tool for smoothing horizontal and vertical earth surfaces).
Sledge hammer	To drive stakes, etc.
Claw hammer	For framing and to drive nails in forms, trim, etc.

Brick chisel, wood chisels, machete, and small axe	To cut and trim bricks, prepare wood joints, and cut various items.
Buckets, baskets, or wheelbarrow	To mix and to carry soil, mud mortar, mud bricks, and everything else needed at the building site.
Lumber, for rammed earth	To make forms.
Sheets of plywood, if steel forms with wooden panels are used	To serve as inserts in forms.

Many of the tools in this list do double duty, and because improvisation is a rule among builders, not all of these items are absolutely necessary in non-mechanized mud construction.

Mechanized mud construction is virtually unknown in the Near East and Southwest Asia, but it prevails in the USA, Europe, and Australia. Power tools and machines considerably reduce the amount of manual labor required, which is a major cost in industrialized nations. They also make construction much faster and more efficient, especially in moving and mixing materials. In the USA, where rental of major mechanical equipment is common, the following items should be considered: (1) a backhoe for excavating the foundation trench; (2) a cement mixer for mixing concrete for the foundation and slab (although one should certainly consider purchasing ready-mixed concrete to be delivered to the site) and for mixing soil, temper, and water for mud bricks and mud plaster; (3) a front-end loader (such as a "Bobcat") to transport the mud mix to the brick molds and to carry bricks, flooring, and roofing materials as well as other heavy items to the building site—it can also be used in rammed-earth construction, to mix soil, to carry it, and to dump it in the forms; (4) a compressed-air-driven tamper for rammed earth.

MIXING MUD

For most types of construction, the mixing—or mud—pit should be adjacent to the building site (the exception is when making mud bricks). If space allows, the pit should be parallel to the intended wall, separated from the foundation trench by a space or path just wide enough to leave a dry and easy work area for the masons. Mixing mud adjacent to a well, water pipe, or garden hose can also be a distinct advantage because it minimizes the laborious task of transporting water, which for mud construction should not be saline.

Layered mud requires very little water because the mixture must be very stiff and thick. An efficient mixing pit for layered mud is about 2 m wide by almost the length of the wall (see Figure 5.11). To be ready to lay, the mix must be stiff enough for the shovel to cut a slab of mud that will hold together as it is lifted and passed to the hands of the mason. In Pakistan, a long-handled shovel with a scooped or rounded blade is used to cut slabs of mud and to pass them to the mason.

For mud brick, the mixing pit should be adjacent to a large, flat, barren, and traffic-free area where the molded bricks can be laid out to bake in the sun. The pit size usually ranges from approximately 2 m in diameter (or square) to about 2 m wide by 3–5 m long. Water is added to the soil only until the mixture is sufficiently stiff to be poured into forms and leveled (Figure 5.6). Workers mix the mud to a depth of about 30 cm, alternately turning it over with a shovel and treading it with their bare feet until it has a fine consistency (Figure 5.7). Depending on the custom of the locality, mixing is sometimes done in a wheelbarrow with a shovel or hoe or in a concrete mixer.

A major commercial brickyard in New Mexico, Richard Levine's New Mexico Earth, mixes mud in a motor-driven machine with a hopper for soil, and a pug mill to mix the ingredients and to move the mixture to a discharge outlet, where it falls into a large, shallow mud pit. A front-end loader then scoops up the mud, transports it, and pours it into wooden forms (McHenry, 1984:27–28).

If a layered-mud wall begins to disintegrate or is about to be replaced, the masons knock it down carefully so that it falls adjacent to the new building site. We witnessed the demolition of two property walls around the Mohsin Qazi home in Pishin, near Quetta. The masons took advantage of vertical cracks in the old wall by enlarging them until the sections leaned slightly. After undercutting the base of the wall, they repeatedly pushed on one section in unison until it began to rock slightly. As the rocking movement increased, they pushed harder until the section fell (Figure 5.8), breaking into large and small chunks. Sections that could not be conveniently toppled were broken with a shovel (Figure 5.9). The masons built a dike from the largest chunks of the fallen mud structure to define the perimeter of the mixing pit. After moving the remaining pieces into the diked area, they smashed all the large

Figure 5.6 A suitable mud mixture for making mud brick, mixed in a concrete mixer and transported by wheelbarrow at an adobe workshop, Coronado State Monument, Bernalillo, New Mexico, USA (1995).

Figure 5.7 Masons treading mud in mixing pit at the Qazi house in Pishin, near Quetta, Baluchistan, Pakistan (1990).

Figure 5.8 Felling an old layered-mud wall by pushing down a section, Qazi house, near Quetta, Pakistan (1990).

Figure 5.9 **Using a shovel to destroy the wall chunk by chunk, Qazi house, near Quetta, Pakistan (1990).**

chunks inside the pit (Figure 5.10) and then filled the pit with water, leaving it to stand overnight (Figure 5.11). By the next morning, the chunks had dissolved and the mud was ready for mixing. Thus, mud from the demolished structure provided the building material for a new one.

Soil can be quickly and easily recycled, and it costs nothing! By contrast, the destruction of a building in the industrialized world requires a wrecking or dynamite crew to level the structure, bulldozers to scoop up the debris and to load it on trucks, which haul it to a landfill where much of it will probably remain for hundreds and thousands of years without returning to nature. Apart from degrading the environment and consuming vast quantities of energy, the process of destroying and disposing of a conventional twentieth century building costs a great deal of money.

Some earthen construction does not involve mixing soil with water. Soil used in rammed-earth construction in Morocco is laid pile-dry, utilizing only the natural dampness within the soil pile. In the southwestern USA, a small amount (5%–10%, by volume) of water is added to the soil only if dry cement is included in the mix.

MAKING MUD BRICK

Mud brick is shaped either by hand-molding or form-molding. The former process produces an irregular module, painstakingly shaped one brick at a time; the latter yields modules of identical shape and size by pouring and screeding mud into single or multiple molds or forms. Both types of mud brick occur in a variety of shapes and sizes.

Figure 5.10 Chunks of destroyed layered-mud wall occupying the area of the long mixing pit for the new wall, Qazi house, near Quetta, Pakistan (1990).

Figure 5.11 Mason adding water to the mixing pit for a layered-mud wall, Qazi house, near Quetta, Pakistan (1990).

Hand Molding

Hand-molded brick first appeared in the Near East about 10,000 years ago and continued into the fourth millennium B.C., when it was gradually replaced by form-made brick. Hand-molded bricks range in shape from spherical mud balls to more elongated modules. Although mud balls have been largely ignored by archaeologists and architects, they have played, and continue to play, a larger role in construction than many have imagined.

Mud Balls

The use of mud balls in construction was documented (and seen for the first time by GVB) during the 1961–1962 archaeological survey in the Hadhramaut, Yemen. There, the survey team saw a number of badly eroded structures resembling long walls (Figure 5.12). These structures were commonly triangular in section, preserved to a height of one meter or so, and they formed rectangular enclosures on the valley floor. What was their function? They were too long to be house walls and too short and lacking in mass to be defense walls. Although they might have served as courtyard enclosures, only once were remains of domestic buildings found nearby. In cross-section, these structures appeared to have been built of coursed, small, hand-molded mud balls, starting with a ridge and then covered with several sloping layers of more mud balls on each side. They seemed to resemble those of the Epipaleolithic, the transitional period between the Mesolithic (Natufian) and Pre-Pottery Neolithic A at Jericho, ca. 10,000 B.C.

Questions about the function and date of these structures went unanswered for weeks after their discovery. One day when working in Wadi Bin Ali, a southern tributary of the Hadhramaut, GVB happened on a scene that solved the mystery.

Figure 5.12 Long since worn-away, ridges built of mud balls previously delineated irrigated field plots in the Hadhramaut, Yemen (1962).

Two men were cleaning an irrigation canal consisting of a trench about 3 m deep in the wadi floor. Removal of silt that precipitates in the canal from flash flood runoff is necessary to maintain a gradient for the efficient flow of water. One man worked in the bottom of the canal while the other stood on the surface near its edge. The man inside the canal scooped up a double handful of mud, pressed it into a roughly shaped ball, and tossed it to his companion on the surface above. Obviously they found it easier and more efficient to dispose of excess mud by tossing it to ground level than by loading it into containers and hauling it to the surface with ropes. Upon catching the mud ball, the laborer placed it in an ever lengthening and rising ridge. These ridges, triangular in section, formed boundary walls around individual field plots serviced by a canal, preventing the allocated irrigation water from flowing out of the plot (Figure 5.13). These new mud balls bore a distinct resemblance to those previously seen in ancient ridges and to the mud balls frequently used in the prehistoric Near East.

During our research in Pakistan in 1991, in the Cantonment area of Quetta, we discovered a community of about 25 narrow, rectangular one-room dwellings built in recent months by Afghan refugees (see Chapter 3). All were constructed of mud balls about 10–13 cm in diameter, which were laid in courses with a considerable amount of mud mortar and covered with mud plaster (Figure 5.14; see also Figure 5.16).

Other examples illustrate wide geographic usage. In Niamtougou, Togo, West Africa, traditional round houses have been constructed from softball-sized mud balls that were flattened, molded, and smoothed to form a layer of the wall. Successive layers were added and welded together until the desired height was reached (Morris, 1973). Mud balls have also been used in Iran, according to Hans Wulff (1966:108–109, fig. 161). Although he mistakenly described the process as *terre pisé*, the cross-section of the wall clearly shows mud balls laid without the benefit of forms. In the 1990s it was believed that walls of mud balls had been constructed in the fourteenth century A.D. by Tewa Indians of the southwestern

Figure 5.13   Mud-ball walls enclosing garden plots to permit timed allocation of irrigation water to each plot, Wadi Bin Ali, Hadhramaut, Yemen (1962).

Figure 5.14 Afghan refugee's house built of mud balls and awaiting mud plaster, Cantonment area near Quetta, Pakistan (1991).

USA at Kuaua, a site now protected on the grounds of the Coronado State Monument near Bernalillo, New Mexico. Under the leadership of the Coronado Monument staff in 1994, volunteers built capping walls of mud balls over the original walls to preserve them from erosion and to enable visitors to see replicas of early mud-ball walls (Santillanes, 1994). At this site, we made mud balls and began constructing the walls of a small room while participating in an adobe workshop (Figures 5.15, 5.16).[1]

Also as part of the adobe workshop, we joined an effort at Tecolote, a village south of Las Vegas, New Mexico, where the community was repairing and restoring its adobe church that had been built in 1844. During the intervening 150 years, some additions and many repairs had been made. On the front wall, where the white plaster had been stripped off, we could see two areas where mud balls had been applied to the adobe brick to level the surface, filling areas that were not plumb (Figure 5.17).

Why mud balls? They are the most natural form of mud modules. Putting both hands in a mixing pit and lifting as much mud as two hands can hold, one naturally compresses and shapes the mass, which roughly assumes a spherical shape because a ball is the easiest shape for human hands to form. Mud balls intended for construction typically range about 10–20 cm in diameter. They can be individually carried to the building site, or, as happened in Yemen's Hadhramaut and at Coronado National Monument demonstrations in New Mexico, they can be tossed to a designated "builder," who places them on the wall. While mud balls are still wet, they are placed on well-dampened ground along the line of the wall, thus eliminating the time-consuming drying phase, which requires 2–3 weeks for mud brick. They may be left round or can be pressed or compacted into place by hand (see Figure 5.15). When pressed with the hands, each ball changes its shape to conform to the space left by adjoining balls.

Figure 5.15 Walls being constructed of mud balls at an adobe workshop demonstration, Coronado National Monument, Bernalillo, New Mexico, USA (1995). The man on right is forming a mud ball; the man on left is ready to catch a thrown mud ball; the woman is flattening mud balls and shaping their sides.

Figure 5.16 One-room, demonstration mud-ball house (adjacent to wall in Figure 5.15) awaiting mud-plaster coating. Coronado National Monument, Bernalillo, New Mexico (1995).

Mud balls should never be laid in a row across the wall's width, because the lines thus formed will be areas of weakness that may eventually become cracks. All mud balls should be laid in a random pattern and compressed so that no straight lines

Figure 5.17 Flattened mud balls filling shallow depressions in a wall to level the surface before plastering, Virgin Dolores Church, Tecolote, New Mexico, USA (1995).

are created. When a course of mud balls is complete, a little water is sprinkled on it, a layer of mud mortar about 2 cm thick is spread over the balls, and a second course is immediately pressed in place. Because the mortar tends to dry quickly, both it and each succeeding course should be laid in increments of about 1 m. No more than two or three courses should be laid in a day, to allow the wall to dry before the next few courses are added a day or so later. Each day when the wall has begun to dry, its outer and inner faces should be trimmed of excess mud with the hands, a trowel, or a shovel so that the wall is straight and the faces are clean. A mud ball wall should also be covered with plaster to protect it from weathering.

Other Hand-Shaped Forms

Other hand-molded, plano-convex types of mud brick are simply mud balls that have been rolled, elongated, or flattened in the same way a baker shapes a ball of bread dough by hand to desired forms. Many of these shape variations are discussed in the Introduction, such as hog-back (Figure 5.18), chevron thumb-impressed (Figure 5.19), and bun-shaped forms. The houses in Djenné, Mali, were traditionally built of cylinder-shaped mud modules about the size of a soft drink can (Maas, 1990:20–22). Hand-molding is a slow process, because each brick is individually formed to the desired shape and size. Uniformity in hand-molded bricks is at best approximate. Nevertheless, it is remarkable that some of the first shaping techniques have persisted to the present.

Figure 5.18   Handmade "hog-back" brick of the Pre-Pottery Neolithic A period (late ninth to early eighth millennia B.C.), Jericho, southern Levant's Jordan Valley. (Courtesy Basil E. Saffer, Brick Museum, General Shale Products, Johnson City, Tennessee, USA.)

Figure 5.19   Handmade, thumb-impressed, rectangular brick of the Pre-Pottery Neolithic B period (early eighth to sixth millennia B.C.), Jericho, southern Levant's Jordan Valley. (Courtesy Basil E. Saffer, Brick Museum, General Shale Products, Johnson City, Tennessee, USA.)

Brick Molds and Molding

The preferred seasons for making bricks in Europe in ancient times were described by Vitruvius (1931 [translation]: vol. 1, bk. 2, chap. 3, ¶ 2):

> Now bricks are to be made either in the spring or autumn, that they may dry at one and the same time. For those which are prepared at the summer solstice become faulty for

this reason: when the sun is keen and overbakes the top skin, it makes it seem dry, while the interior of the brick is not dried.

We learned in Dolomieu, France, that local builders traditionally prepare the soil for *terre pisé* construction in the spring and autumn, which also roughly corresponds to the major building seasons for mud construction in the ancient Near East, which occurred after planting and again after harvest.

The use of wooden molds for brick-making replaced hand-molding in the Near East by about 3100 B.C. and has prevailed to the present. Bricks molded in ready-made forms offer important advantages. They are uniform in size and shape, which results in stronger, more attractive, and more stable walls. Although they take longer to make, the result is a larger, denser, and standardized module for easier construction. Furthermore, forms are generally made of wood in a variety of sizes and shapes; most are square or rectangular, but occasionally they are made in unusual configurations to accommodate special applications.

A wooden mold commonly consists of four boards—for example, 5 × 10 cm or 5 × 15 cm boards—one for each side of a frame and without bottom or top. Thinner boards—e.g., 2.5 cm thick—are commonly used in the Near East, but these neither keep their sharp edges nor last as long as heavier stock. Single-brick molds predominate, and although multiple-brick molds occasionally appear, the latter are in much greater use in the southwestern USA (Figure 5.20). Molds last longer if they are strengthened and made more rigid. This can be achieved via assembly with dovetail joints or other devices, such as one or more corner straps securely screwed on each outside corner of the mold. Handles make the molds easier to remove and carry, and these simply may be extensions of the side boards that are reduced in size to fit the hand more comfortably (Figure 5.21), or they may be created by fitting the extensions with a dowel-shaped crosspiece on each end, especially for multiple-brick molds (see Figure 5.22). The inner surfaces of the mold should be smooth to ease removal of the newly molded brick. A wooden mold should also be soaked with water on its inner surfaces so that minimal water is drawn from the brick by the wood. Metal-lined wooden molds or rigid iron molds release the brick with less damage to corners and have a longer useful life than wooden molds.

Lacking bottom boards, frame-like molds are usually placed on the ground and filled with mud that is sufficiently stiff to maintain its shape with minimal settling. Special attention is given to packing the corners to make well-formed bricks. After the mold is filled, the mud is leveled; a smooth, straight-edged piece of wood or metal that is wider than the mold is carefully pulled across the top to remove excess mud and to make a flat smooth surface. The filled molds are left in place until the bricks show signs of shrinking or separating from the mold.

If the mud mixture is very wet when poured, it will require longer to dry (from a few hours to overnight) before the mold can be safely removed. This slows the brick-making process unless additional molds are available; however, a more liquid mix produces brick with greater density. If the mud mixture is stiff (less liquid), more time will need to be spent in mixing it thoroughly, but the mold is often ready to remove after an hour or so.

One-brick, two-brick, and four-brick molds are generally used for do-it-yourself brick-making, because one person can easily fill and remove forms of this size

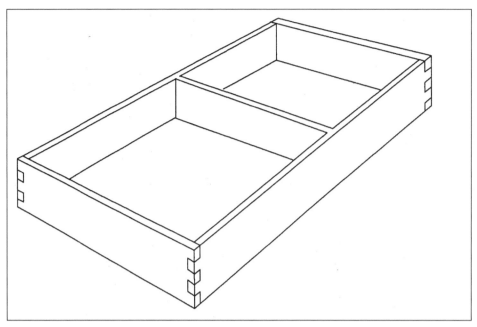

Figure 5.20   A two-square-brick mold.

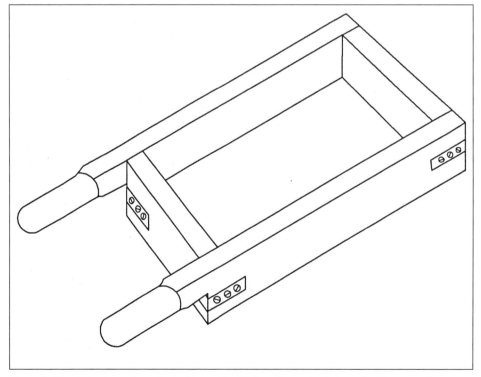

Figure 5.21   A single, rectangular-brick mold with handles and reinforced with corner braces.

Figure 5.22 A series of gang or "ladder" molds each making eight bricks, New Mexico Earth Company, Alameda, New Mexico, USA (1994).

without help. Commercial mud-brick brickyards use a ladder-like form that makes 8 or 10 bricks at a time; 100 8-brick forms laid side-by-side produce 800 bricks in a series of mixture pourings in one production event (Figure 5.22). Two persons can efficiently remove an 8-brick ladder form, one lifting each end. It is then necessary to carefully trim any excess mud from the brick and to wash off any residue remaining in the mold.

How many bricks can be molded in a day? The rate of production is governed by a number of factors: proximity of mixing materials; number of persons involved in brick-making, and their strength, stamina, and efficiency; size and weight of bricks being made; size of layout space for drying, etc. It is widely accepted in the Near East among traditional mud masons that a brickmaker can produce about 100–150 bricks per day, either working alone or as one person's share in a team effort.

In antiquity, quotas seem to have been set by the royal superintendents of brickmaking. When the Israelites were residing in the Delta of Egypt and building mudbrick warehouses for the government in the thirteenth century B.C., Moses began agitating for permission to let them leave Egypt. Ramses II—the Pharaoh—responded by commanding "the taskmasters of the people and their foremen, 'You shall no longer give the people straw to make bricks, as heretofore; let them go and gather straw for themselves. But the number of bricks which they made heretofore you shall lay upon them, and you shall by no means lessen it.'" (Exodus 5:6–8, Revised Standard Version).

Laying mud brick was also subject to quotas in antiquity. Max Mallowan (1966: vol. 1, p. 82), who excavated Nimrud (ancient Calah, in Mesopotamia), noted:

> Those who have practical experience of building in the Near East will know that one man can comfortably lay 100 bricks in one day; this is what we reckoned when we built one of our expedition houses in Syria. And it is remarkable that a Babylonian letter of the 7th century B.C. reveals that this was the accepted rate of bricklaying in Assyrian

times, for the letter complains that a rate in excess of that is too much. 'We are doing the work on the weir (a wall or dam to raise water to the fields), the work here is difficult. The daily quota of bricks is severe upon us. One man per day and one hundred and ten bricks!' It follows on this basis that 100 men can lay a million bricks in 100 days.

To avoid slowing construction due to shortages, it is necessary to make at least the same quantity of bricks as are used in a day. The production rate of 100 bricks per day is, of course, not immutable. Smaller bricks can be made and laid in greater numbers, while larger bricks can be produced and laid in smaller numbers. It is easier and faster to make a standard Egyptian brick, which measures $23 \times 11 \times 8$ cm and weighs about 4.1 kg, than to make a typical New Mexico adobe brick, which measures $14 \times 10 \times 4$ in ($35.5 \times 25.5 \times 10$ cm) and weighs about 40 lb (~18.6 kg). In a Philistine working day of the eleventh century B.C., it is very unlikely that the best brick maker—working alone in mixing, molding, and trimming—could have made more than 50 of the bricks at Tell Jemmeh, each measuring $56 \times 36 \times 13$ cm and weighs about 52.7 kg!

As in all construction with concrete or cinder block, fired brick, or lumber, loss of some materials occurs due to breakage or other mistakes, and this also applies to mud brick, which is more fragile than most other materials. It may crack if stacked improperly; it may break if dropped or when being trimmed; it will soften or dissolve completely if accidentally soaked with water. A group of young people in California built a round adobe house enclosing about 900 ft² (83.64 m²). They molded 2000 bricks by using 25 tons of soil for brick and mud mortar, laid 1200 in actual construction, and lost approximately 300 due to cracking (Kahn, 1973:67), thus 1500 bricks were required to complete the project. A loss rate of 20% seems reasonable, and should be factored in when calculating the number of bricks needed for a specific job. Fortunately, broken mud bricks can be collected and thrown back into the mud pit, where they dissolve and provide more new mud for reuse; the only real loss is the inconvenience and time required to produce the new mud bricks.

Pressed-Earth Blocks

Another mud module used in building is the pressed-earth block. One type is made by a small, hand-operated press known as a Cinva-Ram,[2] which has been used to produce blocks for buildings in the southwestern USA, South America, Africa, and elsewhere, often by the U.S. Peace Corps. The Cinva-Ram is portable, weighs about 64 kg, and produces one brick at a time. Other types of pressed blocks are made in gasoline- or diesel-powered hydraulic presses in the USA. These are large units generally towed behind trucks; they produce 2–14 blocks per minute of standard sized New Mexico adobe but can be modified to make other sizes. Soil is placed directly in the pressing chamber of the Cinva-Ram or in a hopper, which feeds it into the pressing chamber on the larger machines. Under great pressure the soil is compressed into a dense block and then discharged. Some blocks require no curing or sun-baking and are available for immediate use; others are baked for up to 10 days in the sun. Apart from being mass produced, they have a high compressive strength (from 500 to 1600 psi) and resist fracture. In most parts of the world, such machines are counter-productive because of an abundance of cheap manpower to make bricks. In the USA, however, labor is expensive, so mechanical presses offer a viable alternative for manufacturing building modules.

DRYING BRICKS

The ground surface of the drying area should be level, smooth, and clean—i.e., it should be free of small stone, gravel, and trash so that the underside of the brick will be evenly supported and smooth. If the ground is uneven, mud may flow out from under the form onto the ground, resulting in a brick of uneven thickness. The drying area should be protected from normal pedestrian and animal traffic and activities, so that the bricks will not be trampled on and damaged or destroyed while drying. In nearly every ancient mud-brick site excavated by archaeologists, and in every present-day brickyard in the Near East, a few mud bricks will bear the footprints of small animals—such as dogs and cats—that crossed the drying brick and immortalized themselves (Figure 5.23).

Most bricks bake in the sun, but if the sun is quite hot and there is considerable wind, the bricks may dry too quickly, causing them to crack (as Vitruvius noted above). In such a climate, it is preferable to dry them in the shade for a few days. Drying bricks are quite vulnerable to rain and to freezing temperatures. If rain threatens, they should be covered with plastic sheeting until the rain ceases. Care must also be taken to divert run-off water from flowing along the bottoms of the bricks. As noted in the "Tempering Materials" section, stabilizers such as asphalt emulsion or portland cement are sometimes added to the mud mixture to enhance weather resistance or to make the bricks waterproof.

Molded mud bricks should be arranged efficiently for drying. In one typical layout pattern, two rows of bricks are set close together, leaving an aisle on each side of the double row, and this is repeated across the width of the drying area.

After the molds are removed, the bricks should be cleaned of any lumps on the surfaces. These can be caused, for example, by the splashing of mud when adjacent molds were filled. This is back-breaking work because each brick must be cleaned by hand while the worker is in a stooped position. Optimally, each brick is turned over every three or four days to expose another side to the sun so that drying will proceed equally (Figure 5.24). Yet such turning and trimming are not always done. In the Hadhramaut, relatively thin bricks are sometimes left without trimming.

Drying normally requires three to five weeks, depending on the thickness of the brick and the weather. The most astonishing drying times for mud brick are those cited in ancient Italy and Tunisia by Vitruvius (1931 [translation]: vol. 1, bk. 2, chap. 3, ¶ 2), who suggested that bricks "will be more fit for use if they are made two years before. For they cannot dry throughout before…. [T]he citizens of Utica [the Canaanite, or Phoenician-Punic, city in Tunisia] use no bricks for building walls, unless the magistrate has approved them as being dry and made five years before." This surely ranks among the most amazing examples of overkill!

Nonetheless, the brick must be thoroughly dry before it can be used in construction. Because a vast quantity must be available when construction begins, the brick-making process continues for weeks, and the drying area correspondingly

Figure 5.23 Fragment of mud brick with footprint of dog, Tell Jemmeh, Israel.

grows. Such areas may be quite large, sometimes more than 1000 m², and resembling a gigantic checkerboard (Figure 5.25).

Dried mud bricks should occasionally be tested as a means of quality control, especially if their soils were taken from different places, if errors might have occurred in the proportions used in the mixtures, or if any unusual change in weather occurred during the drying period. McHenry (1984:80–81, figs. 4.16, 4.17) describes a simple field test that anyone can do to determine whether the bricks' performance will be satisfactory:

> **Damp Test:** If a brick is dampened slightly, and a finger rubbed over the damp spot, the resistance of the brick to moisture can be somewhat determined. The degree of softening of the surface will be inversely proportional to the clay content.
> **Knife Penetration Test:** The point of a common pocketknife with a small blade (⅜ in. by 2 in.) may be pressed into the side of the brick. If the brick is dry and well made the knife will not penetrate more than ⅛ in. If the brick is not dry, even though apparently dry on the surface, the knife will penetrate deeply.

Figure 5.24 Mud bricks turned to stand on edge for thorough drying, Hauta, Hadhramaut, Yemen (1991).

Figure 5.25 Mud-brick drying field, Hadhramaut, Yemen (1962). Note the minimal trimming and cleaning of bricks.

Drop Test: A dry brick may be dropped, on its corner, onto firm ground from a height of approximately 3 ft. The shock of striking the corner will set up stresses in the brick and indicate in-plane weaknesses or will shatter from dampness. This will approximate the modulus of rupture test, at least for toughness. In the case of a good brick, little if any damage occurs, other than a slight chipping of the corner. If the brick is not totally dry, or has weak structural planes from a lack of mixing homogeneity, it will shatter or break along planes of weakness.

Figure 5.26 Blocks of stacked mud bricks, Hadhramaut. Little breakage can be seen even with these relatively thin bricks.

STACKING BRICKS

When dry, bricks can be used immediately, but they are generally stacked until enough are accumulated to build all or a significant part of the structure. Stacking also frees space in the molding–drying area. Mud bricks are easily broken and must be handled carefully. Unless they are well formed, relatively smooth, and stacked on a level surface, any unevenness will cause fracturing as additional bricks are stacked on top.

In the Near East mud bricks are generally stacked on edge leaning against a wall, occasionally in a "block" of three to six layers or, in some areas, in a conical pile. In the Hadhramaut, the block pile is used almost universally, with the bricks stacked obliquely on edge, a horizontal stack serving as a "bookend" on each end, and a course of horizontal bricks capping the block (Figure 5.26). By stacking in this manner, most of the weight of successive bricks rests on the narrow edges, with a minimum of weight and stress falling on the large surfaces.

Stacking in a conical pile is accomplished by standing three to five bricks on edge in a triangle, square, or circle leaning against one another. Other bricks encircle the standing group and lean against them. As circles are added, other bricks are placed on top of those below, edge to edge, forming an upper tier. Stacking often continues until the conical pile is more than two meters in diameter and nearly two meters high. In the area of Sheikh Othman, a town near Aden, Yemen, the flat coastal plain is dotted with such piles (Figure 5.27). Both types of stacks permit the wind to pass between the individual bricks, continuing the curing process.

We have rarely seen mud bricks in the Near East stacked horizontally—i.e., flat with their large surfaces together—as fired bricks are usually stacked in American lumber yards, but two such stacks come to mind. One was in the Delta of Egypt and the other was in a compound at Kuchlagh, Baluchistan, Pakistan. In both instances,

Figure 5.27   Conical stacks of mud bricks, Sheikh Othman, near Aden, Yemen (1962).

the bricks were relatively small and lightweight, approximating common American bricks in size and shape.

ARCHAEOLOGICAL CHARACTERISTICS

It may be difficult for people who have not worked with mud brick to understand how hard and dense it is when dry. When mud brick is first uncovered in an archaeological excavation, it has the hardness and consistency of a block of cheddar cheese, because it has absorbed dampness from the surrounding soil when buried. At this stage, a mud brick can be damaged easily or even destroyed by scraping it with a trowel or by striking it with a small handpick. At one time or another, most professional archaeologists (including GVB) have inadvertently cut into or even through a wall without recognizing damp mud brick. After bricks have been exposed for 24 hours, they can be gently scraped with a trowel and brushed lightly with a slightly stiff brush to reveal the individual bricks and all mortar joints. This is the time when most bricks should be prepared for both photography and drawing.[3] Otherwise, they continue to harden until, after a week or so, they are so hard that the sharpened flat blade of a handpick can hardly "shave" the surface or a trowel scrape it with any efficacy. Indeed, one type of brick at Tell Jemmeh (referred to as chocolate brick because of its dark brown color) contains more clay than in common mud brick and is a mass of quick-drying lumps. This brick must be cleaned or "dressed" immediately after exposure to the air; otherwise, after 24 hours of drying, the lumps cannot be dressed with either a trowel or sharpened pick. Any attempt to do so dislodges lumps, leaving large pits in the brick even with the most gentle hand work.

At Tell Jemmeh, a large pit was discovered that had cut through a wall on one side, exposing an area of about 4 m². At the time, little thought was given to dressing the exposed bricks, because they were turned about 35° on their sides and simply appeared to have fallen. During the next field season a year later, GVB began to suspect that this undressed mass of brick might shed light on what appeared to be a mud-brick vault in the adjacent square. The task of dressing the wall with a handpick and trowel was assigned to Van Tries Button, a member of the work crew. The brick had become so hard that Van worked three days on its surface until, regrettably, his hands were a mass of blisters. By then, it had become apparent that the bricks had not fallen but were solidly mortared in place. Cleaning the sides of this pit thus provided valuable insights into construction methods of the original mud-brick vaulting, erected in the seventh century B.C. Unfortunately, by not dressing the bricks in the pit immediately upon their exposure, the task became excruciatingly laborious.

NOTES

1. Scientific theories and interpretations often need to be adjusted as new evidence is brought to light. Subsequent investigations at Kuaua revealed that the dried demonstration mud-ball walls did not closely match actual historic walls at the site because the softball-sized mud balls used for the demonstrations were too small. The current interpretation is that large, bread-loaf or basketball-sized handfuls of plastic mud were used to create the coursed-adobe walls for structures at this site (Richard Reycraft, Chief of Preservation, New Mexico State Monuments, personal communication, 7 February 2007). Although the demonstration walls constructed at the Coronado State Monument were found to be inconsistent with the original ancient construction, the process of building them was not without merit. It introduced workshop participants to this method of construction used elsewhere in the world and effectively showed them, hands-on, how it was actually accomplished.

2. Developed by the Inter-American Housing and Planning Center, Bogotá, Colombia.

3. A good archaeological architect will not draw a brick until all four corners—or if a corner is missing, the sharply defined broken edges—can be seen clearly.

Part III

METHODS OF EARTHEN WALL CONSTRUCTION

Chapter 6

Wattle-and-Daub

OVERVIEW OF WALL CONSTRUCTION METHODS

Four major types of earthen wall construction prevail in the vernacular architecture of Southwest Asia, the Near East, North Africa, and Europe:

Wattle-and-daub: Quick and easy to build, this type of construction involves pressing or squeezing small amounts of mud into a woven framework of reeds, wooden boards, or limbs and sticks; it can be built by one or two people; its useful life is relatively short compared to other methods, although when employed in half-timber construction it has a much longer life; it does not produce as comfortable an interior temperature as that provided by more substantial methods of mud construction.

Layered mud: In the simplest method of building substantial walls, slabs of mud are aligned to form layer upon layer until the desired height is achieved; it requires from one to three workers, but less expertise is needed than for either the rammed-earth or mud-brick methods; it provides less interior comfort than rammed earth or mud brick and is neither as solid nor as strong as those methods; it has a life span comparable to contemporary frame construction in the USA, but there are examples at least 900 years old.

Rammed earth: Also known as *terre pisé*, this type is characterized by the use of forms (similar to those used in concrete construction) into which soil is poured and compacted; the technique is simple but requires either more workers or mechanized equipment, and perhaps for this reason it is less frequently used; it offers many design options and typically enjoys a life span of more than 200 years; it yields the strongest walls and produces the greatest interior comfort because its walls are very thick and dense; in some cases, massive fortifications have been constructed of rammed earth but without the use of forms.

Mud brick: The predominant form of modular construction, this type employs the same variety of construction methods as fired brick but offers a wider range of design possibilities; it predominates through time and place because it yields a strong and stable structure; a single person or a group of workers can erect a building, and less time is required if machinery for mixing, transporting, and pouring are used; mud-brick houses more than 200 years old are legion, and some nearly intact structures in Egypt are more than 4500 years old; interior comfort is excellent.

Within these major types of earthen construction are seemingly endless variations, whose numbers are apparently limited only by human imagination. On every trip that we made to investigate earthen buildings, we saw techniques that we had not seen before. Whether we were examining walls, roofs, floors, decorative design, or techniques for combating erosion and weathering, new methods came to light that likely had an extended local or regional history but which apparently had not spread to neighboring peoples.

No single method of construction is superior to the others in every respect; each has advantages and disadvantages. This chapter describes the construction method and characteristics of wattle-and-daub, its diversity, and its positive and negative aspects. The other three major types of earthen construction are treated similarly in subsequent chapters.

ANCIENT AND RECENT EXAMPLES OF WATTLE-AND-DAUB

Historically, wattle-and-daub has been widely used for house construction in Europe, Africa, the Near East, Asia, and America. In the Near East, it first appeared in the earliest settlement at Jericho, where a structure built of posts and mud in the late tenth millennium B.C. was discovered. Evidence from Jericho in the following two periods—the Epipaleolithic and the Pre-Pottery Neolithic A—indicates the continuing use of wattle-and-daub through the ninth millennium B.C. (Kenyon, 1981:272–274, pl. 51). In sections dating from the sixth millennium B.C., at Haçılar in Turkey, screen walls of wattle-and-daub were built to partially separate rooms (Mellaart, 1970a:11–14; 1970b: figs. 12a, 19a,b). In the lowest debris layers of the fourth millennium B.C. at Ur in Mesopotamia, fragments of baked mud (from a fire that destroyed a reed building) were found that were smooth on the outer surface but that retained impressions of a bundle of reeds on the inner surface (Woolley, 1961:45–48). Reed houses were common in marshy zones where reeds grew abundantly, as, for example, near the confluence of the Tigris and the Euphrates rivers in southern Iraq and in Egypt's Nile Delta. Such wattle structures were often heavily coated with mud, probably to increase their structural stability, to provide a more comfortable interior temperature, and to increase privacy.

As urban life and technological complexity increased in the Near East, the number of examples of wattle-and-daub structures declined and few appear in excavations. In the first century A.D., however, Pliny the Elder noted that this technique was still in use in Rome: "At all events everybody knows that party-walls can be made by coating hurdles with clay, and are thus built up as if with raw bricks" (Pliny the Elder, 1961 [translation]: book 35, ¶ 169). In subsequent centuries, continued use of wattle-and-daub seems to have retreated to regions in Asia where nomadic peoples and other transients required easily built, temporary shelter. Wattle-and-daub was known in Europe as early as the fifth millennium B.C.; its usage culminated during the Middle Ages, when it filled

Figure 6.1 Wattle-and-daub fence in southern Yemen (1991).

the spaces in half-timber buildings. It has disappeared from most regions of Europe and the Near East today; however, South Asia and East, Central, and West Africa remain as regions where it probably will continue in use for some time to come. In 1991, we saw an excellent example of wattle-and-daub fencing along the coastal road from Mukalla to Aden in southern Yemen (Figure 6.1). The ancient screen walls at Haçılar in Turkey during the sixth millennium B.C. must have looked like this.

We were anxious to find existing examples of wattle-and-daub houses and had the good fortune to see our first ones in 1990 in villages near Pondicherry, in Tamil Nadu, southern India (Figure 6.2). We photographed several inhabited rectangular houses, but unfortunately we were unable to study them in detail. In 1991, we discovered a number of circular wattle-and-daub houses in the villages of Sumara and Sumasar in Kutch, approximately 30–35 km north of Bhuj and some 390 km northwest of Ahmedabad, in Gujarat State, India. This extraordinarily flat land borders on Sind in Pakistan, with which it shares nearly identical topography and environmental conditions. Similar wattle-and-daub houses are likely to exist in Sind, which we were unable to visit because of political unrest at the time.

In Sumara, we investigated two compounds of an extended family of camel-herders, who tended to move back and forth across the Indian–Pakistan border as convenient. The compounds were separated by about 100 m with a common entrance lane between them. The easternmost compound consisted of a large, fired-brick platform about 30 cm high, finished with mud plaster on the surface. Two round houses were adjacent to the platform and opened onto it: one on the north side housed the family, and the other, on the east side, accommodated guests (Figure 6.3). A rectangular building stood on a separate platform to the west. We were unable to determine its function, although we speculated that it may have served as an isolation house for birth and recovery, as a chamber for newlyweds after the wedding, or for storage (Figure 6.4). The cooking area was situated south of the platform and the guest house. A low wall provided a wind break. Near the wall was a low, gabled hut of wattle, which provided storage, shade, and coolness during food preparation. Two small mud structures with a gabled roof and finished with mud plaster, each with a single entrance, housed pigeons. The entire compound was surrounded by waist-high thorn bushes for security.

The second compound consisted of three round houses standing on a fired-brick platform, which was also covered with mud plaster. A square building, a hen house, and the cooking area were situated northwest and southwest of the platform.

Figure 6.2   Rectangular house of wattle-and-daub with gabled, thatched roof, near Pondicherry, India (1990).

Figure 6.3   Compound of wattle-and-daub houses at Sumara in Kutch, Gujarat, India (1991).

In Sumasar, we investigated another group of three circular wattle-and-daub houses all in a row. They were empty, their owners having moved into a new four-room house that was built of concrete blocks just a few meters north of the vacated dwellings.

The round houses in Sumara and Sumasar were nearly identical in design and construction. Each was configured as a single room, and they ranged in diameter from 3.1 m in Sumasar to 3.8 m in Sumara. We chose compound 1 in Sumara as a typical example of wattle-and-daub construction in this region, and the descriptions in the section below are, in many cases, of the dwellings in compound 1. Differences seen in other examples of wattle-and-daub are also noted.

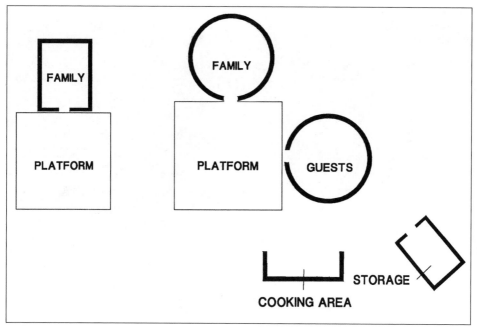

Figure 6.4   Ground plan of Sumara compound, Gujarat, India (1991).

FROM FENCE TO WALL TO DWELLING IN GUJARAT, INDIA

House construction began with a circular foundation trench excavated approximately 60 cm deep into which a number of poles, cut from relatively straight tree branches typically about 1.8 m long, were set vertically and spaced equally. Small limbs and twigs were then densely woven in and out around the vertical poles, producing a tight, basket-like circular fence roughly 1.4 m high at Sumara and about 1.2 m high in the dwellings at Sumasar. A gap was left in the wall for the only entrance.

The mud mixture typically used for wattle-and-daub consists of equal parts soil, straw, and manure, with just enough water added until it is stiff enough to minimize dripping and shrinkage once it is in place. With two people working inside and outside simultaneously, handfuls of the mud mixture are slapped against the fence and pressed sufficiently hard to squeeze the mud through the woven fence so that it bonds with the mud being pressed from the other side. More mud is compressed against the first coat until the desired thickness is reached. In Sumasar, the walls were about 15–18 cm thick (Figure 6.5). A mud wall of this thickness normally dries in two days in this region of India.

The top of a wattle-and-daub wall is usually rounded and smooth, and the entire wall is finished with mud plaster applied to both the inner and outer surfaces. The finished mud plaster may be painted. At Sumara, the inside was painted white, which lightened the interior of the otherwise dark room, but the outside was left unpainted, retaining the original brownish-buff color of the mud plaster. We saw two examples of decorative designs featuring crisscrossed lines and dots painted in red on the white

Figure 6.5   Close-up view of entrance to house shown in Figure 6.6, Sumasar, in Kutch, Gujarat, India (1991). Note thickness of wattle-and-daub wall.

inner surface of the wall. At Sumasar, the outside of the wall was painted light green with two vertical floral designs in reserve bordering the door (Figure 6.6).

Some of the circular wattle-and-daub houses of India were gaily decorated with mud designs in low relief or in paint. Although we did not have the opportunity to see any of them, the half-title page of Nora Fisher's (1993) *Mud, Mirror and Thread* shows three houses, all from Kutch, in vibrant color: one features an elaborate painted design; one is finished with mud plaster only; and one is decorated in low-relief designs.

Contributing to the darkness of the interior is the absence of windows in these round houses. Instead, there are usually four portholes, two each on opposing sides of the room and about equidistant from the doorway. At Sumara, each porthole was about 18 cm in diameter and about 40 cm above the floor. In floor cultures this height is convenient for anyone who wishes to look outside when sitting or sleeping on mats on the floor. In inclement weather, these holes can be closed quickly by filling them with wet mud. In one of the houses in compound 1, two of the apertures were plugged with mud when we visited in late October. All floors were of packed mud.

At Sumara, a white band was painted around each porthole on the mud-plastered outer wall (Figure 6.7). In many Near Eastern countries, painting a white ring around a window is believed to prevent the "evil eye" from entering the house, although we did not learn whether it had a similar symbolic meaning in India.

On round houses the roofs are typically conical in form, whereas they are gabled on rectangular structures. Most of those we saw were of thatch. Framing for a typical

Figure 6.6 The best preserved of three circular wattle-and-daub houses at Sumasar, India (1991). The outer walls are painted light green, with a floral design in reserve framing the entrance.

Figure 6.7 Wattle-and-daub house with whitewash encircling the windows in Sumara, India (1991). The design may have been intended to guard against the "evil eye."

conical roof consisted of about 14 poles, 6.0–7.5 cm in diameter, spaced equally around the top of the mud wall. A vertical wooden pole—sometimes carved—in the center of the room usually supported the roof frame by extending to the top of the conical roof. The poles were held rigidly in place by a series of seven or so horizontal rings of diminishing circumferences. The rings were made from limbs about 1 cm in diameter, spaced almost equally from the top of the wall to the peak of the roof, and tied tightly to the poles. This rigid framework carried the thatching, which was placed directly on it and bound to the framework by seven horizontal corded circles on the outside (Figure 6.8). We saw as many as 14 corded circles on other houses.

In the architectural section of the Ethnographic Museum in New Delhi, we saw a model of a slightly different wattle-and-daub house. The roof on this model consisted of a series of 38 horizontal ropes, about 30 vertical ropes, and two horizontal zigzag ropes reinforcing the spacing of the other ropes, to which the thatch was stitched (Figure 6.9).

These types of roofs typically lack any covering on the underside. In the climate prevailing in Kutch—hot days and warm nights during the entire year—relatively thin walls and thatched roofs are adequate. Indeed, thatched roofs prevail in such climates throughout most of Africa and Asia.

Directly opposite the doorway in the Sumara house, a mud bench was built against the wall, stacked with wooden boxes, bedding, and water pots. Above the

Figure 6.8 Detail of framing (underside view) of a conical thatched roof sheltering a circular wattle-and-daub house in Sumara, India (1991).

Figure 6.9 Model wattle-and-daub house in the Architectural Section of the Ethnographic Museum, New Delhi, India (1991).

bench were two shelves, one of which was decorated with geometric designs in mud relief and with Gujarati mirrors randomly set in the design (Figure 6.10). Both shelves displayed brass and ceramic vessels, as well as numerous condiment and medicine bottles. Immediately above, suspended from the roof framework were assorted cooking pots and bottles, a rifle, and a walking cane. Tied to two of the roof poles was a rope draped with clothes that served as a wardrobe or closet. This house was home to a family of 11 persons (Figure 6.11).

At the Sumasar house, shelves and a box were also built into the wall opposite the door. The box featured three mud partitions on the facade, which were decorated with zigzag edge designs and an elaborate, inverted, right-angled device on the right. The base border of the shelf was similarly decorated. A grinding stone and bowl stood on the floor beneath the shelf (Figure 6.12). Food was also prepared outside the house on a small, portable, U-shaped hearth (see Figure 13.27).

CHILDREN'S MODELS

While we were working in the second Sumara compound in India, we noticed a group of children playing and went to see what they were doing. To our delight, they were playing with small models of mud houses that they had made. Two of the models were round houses that almost exactly replicated the larger houses, except

Figure 6.10 Interior of circular wattle-and-daub house showing two portholes and storage shelving, in Sumara, India (1991). The porthole on the right is open, and one in the center is closed with packed mud.

Figure 6.11   Family of 11 persons living in the Sumara house, Gujarat, India (1991).

for the walls, which were built of flattened mud balls instead of wattle-and-daub. We suspected that weaving tiny twigs for the basket-like framework of wattle-and-daub was too difficult or time-consuming for children, who are often short on patience. Otherwise, each house had a single entrance, mud benches against a wall, two or more shelves on the wall displaying miniature plates, large and small bowls, pitchers and lamps all made of mud; there was also a cooking area consisting of three miniature bricks to support a pot above the fire, and a tiny handmade broom! These miniature houses were equipped with many more plates and vessels than are to be seen in full-size houses, suggesting that these items were the children's favorite objects to make. Outside, piled against one of the play houses was a neat pile of twigs and small limbs broken to about the same length, perhaps to be used for fuel or to build a wattle-and-daub fence to enclose their little compound. Lacking from the children's model houses were the roofs, which, of course, would inhibit their play activities.

Small mud animals shaped by hand were also arrayed outside; some had been broken, reminding us of the similar broken animal figurines recovered in our archaeological excavations at Tell Jemmeh. These children's figurines give credence to our long-standing view that many of our Jemmeh figurines were actually children's toys, rather than cultic objects intended to promote fertility in domestic animals, as often assumed by many archaeologists. It is characteristic of our profession that we look for the more profound meanings because we often lose touch with the common things of daily life.

These toy houses clearly define the concept of house in this region and their accoutrements. It verified our observations of the habitable houses we had seen, and

Figure 6.12   Grinding stone and bowl beneath shelf in Sumasar, India (1991).

fleshed out many details for us. For the children, their activities in building, furnishing, and playing with these toy houses represent their rehearsal for adult life.

MORE EXAMPLES OF WATTLE-AND-DAUB STRUCTURES

In 1977, while traveling in the Delta of Egypt (the heavily agricultural zone north of Cairo), we saw a roadside tea hut (Figure 6.13) built of reeds laid side-by-side and woven together with string similar to that of straw matting. The reed walls were placed upright and attached to wooden poles. A thin layer of mud pressed onto the exterior wall surfaces gave a total wall thickness of less than 5 cm.

The Museum of Folk Technology in Sibiu, Romania, rebuilt a number of structures representing traditional building styles and functions of the nation. Among these were two wattle-and-daub buildings, one a grape-pressing building with a cellar located in a vineyard in the village of Corni, Husi, in Vaslui County, near the eastern border with Moldova. Throughout history, this area has been known for its vineyard and wine industry, and these structures replicated those of the middle nineteenth century. The building was square in plan with walls constructed of "oak-forks driven into the ground at the four corners as well as along the walls. To reinforce the framework of the wall, vertical stakes [were] placed close together among [i.e., between] the forks ..." (Ruşdea, 1986:76–77) and were attached to the upper horizontal beam carried by the forks. The framework of the walls was covered on both sides with mud mixed with straw, finished with mud plaster—containing chaff—inside and out, and whitewashed. The hip roof sloped on all four sides from a central ridge beam. It was covered with reed thatching, and the reeds were secured on top with horizontal poles attached to battens by means of wooden nails.

Wattle-and-daub construction was also commonly used in houses in Bessarabia, according to Yosef Spivak (OVB's uncle), who lived in a wattle-and-daub house for several months sometime about 1940. The house was built with a wooden frame of posts, and a woven mat of limbs was attached to the posts with clamps. A mixture

Figure 6.13   Wattle-and-daub tea house in the Delta of Egypt (1977).

of soil, horse manure, and water was pressed on both sides, but it was thicker on the outside than on the inside of the framework. The roof consisted either of thatch or wooden shingles, both of which were in common use at the time. The house was painted with whitewash on the exterior walls and blue on the interior. The inner surface of the main wall had a niche for icons and an eternal light. The floor consisted of wood planks, and the room was furnished with an oval table, a chair at each end, and a bench on each side. A clay oven approximately 1.5 m wide and 2 m high was recessed below floor level with steps leading down to it.

INFILLING WITH WATTLE-AND-DAUB

In Europe, wattle-and-daub was widely used for infilling the walls of structures built with heavy wooden frames, as in the cruck cottages of England and the post-and-truss houses of England (Kahn, 1973), northern Europe, and eastern Europe (Figure 6.14). These massive timbers were attached to one another by wooden pegs that were driven into holes drilled a tiny fraction smaller than the diameter of the pegs. As the wood dried and shrank, the pegs were driven slightly deeper in the holes, and this practice continued over the years until the pegs were flush with the beam surface (see Figure 6.17).

The wattle-and-daub partitions in half-timber buildings essentially perform the same function as modern curtain walls made of cinder block, glass, or veneers of brick or stone, which form the outer skin of modern buildings with steel or concrete skeletons. On half-timber structures, the open square, rectangular, or triangular areas between the vertical posts and horizontal beams were closed-off to the weather in the following manner. In each open, panel-like area, three to five vertical staves or slats—pointed at the top and shaved at the bottom—were inserted into a tight hole drilled in the upper horizontal beam and into a groove cut in the lower horizontal beam. Wattle was commonly woven tightly in a basket weave technique between the staves. Daub, a mixture of mud, dung, horsehair, etc., was pressed into the woven material, finished smooth on both the inner and outer surfaces, and finally covered with mud, whitewash, or lime plaster (Figure 6.15). In some instances, mud brick (Figure 6.16) or fired brick (Figure 6.17) was used to infill between the timbers in addition to, or instead of, wattle-and-daub. Sometimes the timber frame was preserved by covering it with pitch, creating a striking color contrast between the black framing and white panels and adding beauty to the house (Brunskill, 1970). Wattle-and-daub walls shielded the interiors and provided important insulation to make rooms more comfortable, especially during European winters.

A number of wattle-and-daub cottages have survived in England and Germany (Oliver, 1987:8, 92–94) and elsewhere. Historic examples dating from the twelfth to the sixteenth centuries are still occupied (Figure 6.18), or have been moved and reconstructed in building museums to preserve them.

In the Lippe region of northwestern Germany, we visited several towns, including Detmold and its fascinating Open-Air Museum of historic buildings, Blomberg, and Lemgo, to see the design and construction characteristics of timber-framed or half-timber buildings (Figure 6.19). Also known as "Renaissance" houses, most were built between the fifteenth and nineteenth centuries A.D. They served a variety

Figure 6.14 Scale model of a timber-framed house illustrating both the massiveness of the beams and the many small openings left to close with wattle-and-daub, Weserrenaissance Museum in Brake Castle, Lemgo, Germany (1997).

of functions: farmhouses, barns, granaries, and other out-buildings; town houses, which often included both the barn and domestic quarters; town halls, churches, synagogues, and hotels. They accommodated virtually every type of business from banks to fast-food restaurants. Most buildings were renovated or restored in the nineteenth and twentieth centuries with considerable success, and many have been enhanced with products of modern technology, such as insulated-glass windows, in a suitable and attractive manner (Figure 6.20).

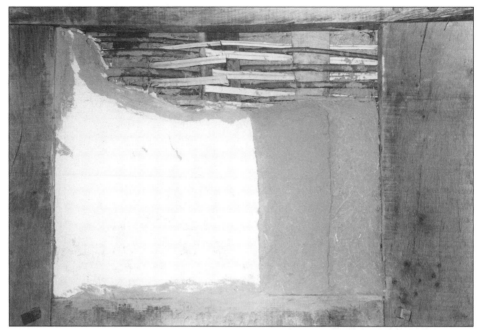

Figure 6.15 Reproduction of wattle-and-daub panel filled with vertical staves and woven limbs, covered with mud and white plaster, Weserrenaissance Museum in Brake Castle, Lemgo, Germany (1997). Note that the mud has pulled away from the beam on the right.

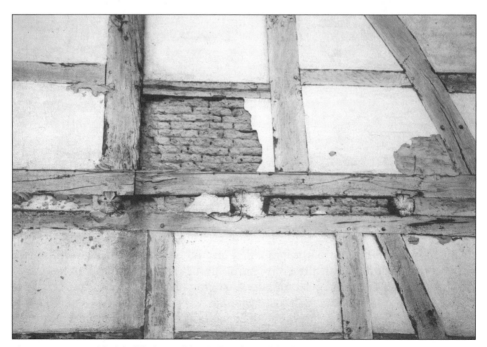

Figure 6.16   Mud-brick-filled panel in timber-framed building, Detmold, Germany (1997).

Figure 6.17 House with fired-brick panels laid in various attractive designs, Open-air Museum, Detmold, Germany (1997). Note the wooden pegs projecting from the wooden beams and the carved inscriptions on the two wooden beams above the windows.

Figure 6.18 Old timber-framed Renaissance house with wavy walls and roof, Detmold, Germany (1997).

The Renaissance houses generally ranged from three to six stories. They were roofed with heavy framing in gabled, hip, or mansard style, covered with red ceramic tile, occasionally with slate shingles or (rarely) with thatch. The facades are a delight for historical architects and archaeologists because the name of the builder (and often that of his wife) together with the date of construction—and sometimes a homily—were carved into a long horizontal beam between the first and second and/or second and third floors (i.e., in European nomenclature, between the ground

Figure 6.19 Renaissance houses in Detmold, Germany (1997).

and first floors or between the first and second floors), or sometimes immediately above the main entrance (Figure 6.21; see also Figure 6.17). When a house was renovated, the date of that event was often carved on the same beam. The exposed timber frame was also frequently decorated with a variety of painted designs, including fanciful animals, columns, half-rosettes, bands of leaves, guilloche, and elaborate floral displays.

How grand and beautiful are these towns where cobblestone streets are lined on both sides with Renaissance houses! (See Figure 6.22.) The sight of white plaster confined by dark massive beams, softly painted designs and carved gilded inscriptions, quaint finials, and red tile roofs—all clean and well maintained—is spellbinding. Almost every house holds a surprise that delights the eye and warms the soul.

ADVANTAGES AND DISADVANTAGES

Wattle-and-daub enjoys several advantages. Small structures are easy to build and nearly without cost, so this type of construction is ideally suited for people who cannot afford to purchase building materials and are accustomed or willing to build their own shelter. Such houses often serve as temporary structures, as in Afghanistan where they have been used seasonally for centuries by migrating peoples. More permanent houses built entirely of wattle-and-daub are generally restricted to more tropical environments where annual temperatures range from warm to hot. In these regions only minimal insulation is needed, and that provided by 15-cm thick, mud walls is adequate, while yielding even greater interior comfort than in houses built only of wattle.

Figure 6.20   Half-timber building built ca. 1570 in Detmold, Germany (1997). Originally the town brewery, it is now the Volkshochschule (adult evening institute) at Krumme Strasse 20.

Figure 6.21 Inscription carved above the door of a house built in 1606, Blomberg, Germany (1997). Note the various designs painted on the wooden beams.

Figure 6.22 Street lined with Renaissance houses in Blomberg, Germany (1997).

Another advantage is its structural flexibility that enables it to survive earth movements with less risk to human life than more rigid types of construction. A major earthquake occurred in Maharashtra State, India, on 30 September 1993. It struck just before 4:00 A.M. when people were sleeping, and most of the estimated 30,000 victims died when their houses collapsed. Molly Moore of *The Washington Post* (2 October 1993) reported:

> The earthquake struck in an erratic pattern, almost like a tornado—destroying some villages and leaving others unscathed. In some villages, casualties were higher in more prosperous neighborhoods, where houses were constructed of stone, while some of the poorer parts of town, where houses were built of straw and thatch, suffered fewer losses.

The stone houses referred to were probably built of rubble laid in mud mortar or, possibly, of fired brick with inferior concrete mortar, and they were easily shaken down. Most of the "straw and thatch" houses were almost certainly of wattle-and-daub, and they survived in greater numbers because the wattle frame is flexible, swaying and moving with the surface motion generated by the earthquake. Both the frame with thin mud walls and thatch roof are lighter in weight. If shaken off the wattle frame, the falling chunks of thin mud are too small and light to be life threatening.

Vitruvius was blunt in evaluating lightweight wattle-and-daub construction:

> I could wish that walls of wattlework had not been invented. For however advantageous they are in speed of erection and for increase of space, to that extent are they a public misfortune, because they are like torches ready for kindling.... [F]or these also make cracks in the plaster covering owing to the arrangement of the uprights and cross-pieces. For when the plaster is applied, they take up the moisture and swell, then when they dry they contract, and so they are rendered thin, and break the solidity of the plaster. But since haste, or lack of means, or partitions made over an open space, sometimes require this construction, we must proceed as follows. Let the foundation be laid high up, so that it is untouched by the rough stones of the pavement; for when they are fixed in these [in the paving stones], they become rotten in time; then they settle, and falling forward they break through the surface of the plaster. (Vitruvius Pollio, 1931: vol. 1, bk. 2, chap. 8, ¶ 20.)

Wattle-and-daub walls are thin and lightweight, and they have insufficient structural strength to carry heavy superstructures and mud roofs. This type of construction is less suitable, therefore, for harsher climates with cold temperatures and bone-chilling rain and snow. Only on timber-framed houses in which wattle-and-daub is used for the curtain walls, is it satisfactory in cold winter climates. In the course of time, however, the daub sometimes shrinks, pulling away from the timber beams. With the original seal broken, moisture and cold air enter the house so repairs have to be made from time to time to reseal the places where mud joins the beams.

The round and lightweight wattle-and-daub houses in Southwest Asia are difficult to expand, and adding rooms to such a house is rare. One cannot build a second floor or easily attach rooms onto the side of an existing round house. Perhaps two circular houses could be built close together and connected by a short, covered walkway, although we have not seen this done. These round wattle-and-daub houses are so cheap and easy to erect that, when the need for expansion arises, families increase their living space by simply building another circular house nearby, and it has become the tradition in this region. Attaching additional rooms to the square or rectangular timber-framed houses of Europe, however, is not difficult because of the greater stability of the timber frame that supports the wattle-and-daub curtain walls. These houses are proportionately so much more massive to begin with, that expanding by adding a room (or wing) is usually considered to be relatively simple construction.

Chapter 7

Layered Mud

Layered mud is often confused with form-built rammed earth or *terre pisé*. In nearly all Neolithic sites and in many later sites, walls described by researchers as rammed earth, *terre pisé*, or *tauf*, and in some instances *chineh*, were actually built by layering. Thus, in most archaeological journals and reports dealing with Near Eastern sites (chiefly in Iran, Iraq, Syria, Turkey, Israel, and Jordan), the term "layered mud" is a more accurate descriptive name for those instances where "rammed earth," *terre pisé*, *tauf*, and *chineh* appear. Only careful, on-site examination of each wall can determine how it was constructed, and even then the answer may be elusive.

Often, layered-mud construction is not readily distinguished from form-built, rammed-earth construction. For example, one occasionally sees references in the literature dealing with the residential architecture of southern Saudi Arabia and northern Yemen that describe the method of construction as "rammed earth," but these descriptions are incorrect; every structure that we examined in that region was built of uncompacted layered mud and without forms. Even Hans Wulff (1966), the ranking specialist in the traditional crafts of Iran, mistakenly described a wall being built of mud balls as *pisé*, or rammed earth, when neither compacting (apart from a slight flattening of the mud balls by hand when placed in the wall) nor the use of forms occurred (see also Chapter 5).

DIFFERENCES BETWEEN LAYERED-MUD AND RAMMED-EARTH WALLS

By examining wall areas where a sufficiently large portion (e.g., 1–2 m²) of plaster is missing, or the cross section of an unfinished or broken wall, one can see the characteristics that distinguish the two construction methods (Table 7.1).

Layered-mud walls are coarse and crude in appearance; the soil is not densely packed, lacks homogeneity, and generally contains a considerable amount of

Table 7.1 Summary of characteristics of layered-mud and rammed-earth construction, contrasted for easier identification.

Layered-mud walls	*Rammed-earth walls*
Thick, wet mixture of soil, straw (or sand/gravel), and water	Pile-dry soil; in antiquity, without additives
Constructed without use of forms	Wooden forms set in place as for poured concrete
Basic unit a thick slab of mud, as large as can be moved by a shovel	Soil poured into form and leveled to make a layer 10–12 cm thick
Soil compacted only by the weight of overlying slabs in the section	Soil systematically compacted by ramming tool, reducing depth of layer by half
Usually <50 cm	0.6–1.2 m or more thick
Rough, knobby appearance; random vertical cracks in each layer, some extend through several layers	Fine, homogeneous appearance with small pits and voids; two holes cut inwall on top of each block
Ideally, finished with one or two coats of mud or lime plaster and painted with whitewash or latex-based paint	Surface pits filled with soil; beaten with tool until smooth and with sheen; finished with lime or mud plaster or paint
Compacted strength (no data) probably 150–250 psi	Compacted strength 462–850 psi

straw and sometimes small rocks. For example, the unplastered rear wall of a men's guest house at Hanna, near Quetta, Pakistan, showed considerable gravel, some pieces as large as 4 cm in diameter (see Figure 5.5). Random vertical cracks occur in the layers, sometimes extending through several layers. The layers are typically 30–50 cm high and are seldom more than 50 cm wide. Horizontal or bedding joints are easily recognizable, but vertical or rising joints are often more difficult to define amid random vertical cracks of different sizes in each layer. Occasionally an oblique or S-curve joint may appear in a layer where a freshly laid layer joins one previously laid, which may be somewhat drier and lighter in color.

Rammed-earth walls consist of finer, homogeneous, dense soil. They are more finished in appearance because of the careful preparation of the soil and heavy compaction of the blocks. They rarely contain straw but may contain small rocks. In the USA, rammed-earth blocks are usually 6½ ft (1.2–2 m) long × 2–4 ft (0.6–1.2 m) or more high, and wall thickness is commonly 2–4 ft (0.6–1.2 m). Each block consists of many small compressed layers each 4–6 in (10–15 cm) high, which are easily recognizable when not covered with plaster. If the wall is relatively new, there may be imprints of wood boards on the wall face, similar to the striated and circular impressions of grain and knots on poured concrete that indicate the use of wooden forms. Bedding joints and rising joints are also easily recognized. In France these are emphasized by a thin layer of lime mortar in the joints. In Europe, rising joints in *pisé* may be either oblique or vertical. Random vertical cracks are rare in rammed-earth walls. Moreover, walls constructed this way are almost always more massive than layered-mud walls.

CONSTRUCTION

During our research, we observed six different layered-mud building projects in various stages of construction. Three were located in the vicinity of Quetta, Pakistan: a two-room customs office and two property walls. The other three projects were in the Arabian Peninsula: a house in Saudi Arabia and two houses at Marib, Yemen. All structures were being built by one or two experienced mud masons and a helper, with the exception of one north of Quetta, where two brothers—who could best be described as below-average "do-it-yourselfers,"—were engaged in constructing a new property wall along one side of their compound. As one might expect, the amateurs' project was quite instructive in illustrating what not to do, but at the same time it showed how forgiving layered mud can be of poor craftsmanship. The more professional projects showed how layered-mud construction should be done, with proper site preparation, advanced techniques for layer construction, clever devices for solving specific problems, quality workmanship, and realistic scheduling of construction phases.

At Marib, Yemen, we happened upon a multistory house being built for the son of a prosperous farming family (see Figures I.3, 3.51, 3.52). The house stood on a foundation of three courses of ashlar. The ground floor, occupying 85.5 m², was roughed in, the electrical wiring had been installed, and the walls were awaiting plaster. The walls of a second floor were under construction.

In the abandoned Marib Town on the nearby piggy-back tell (Figure 7.1), most of the tall houses had been built with walls of layered mud, except for some upper courses that were constructed of mud brick (Figure 7.2). A few houses were constructed entirely of mud brick, indicating that the Marib area was a transitional zone where layered-mud and mud-brick construction coexisted, offering a choice to local homeowners. In layered construction in Marib Town, mud layers varied in height from 34 to 45 cm and in thickness from 38 to 39 cm. As many as 26 layers were counted in the tall houses, with 25, 23, or 19 layers seen in other houses. As many as 30 courses of mud brick were also noted, usually in the roof rooms but sometimes in the floor below.

Building Layers

Construction of the layered-mud property wall enclosing the yard and house of the Mohsin Qazi family, our friends in Pishin near Quetta, Pakistan, serves as an

Figure 7.1   Ruins of Marib Town on the piggy-back tell of Islamic remains, which stands on the ancient, pre-Islamic tell that was once the capital city of Saba' (biblical Sheba), near Marib, Yemen (1991).

Figure 7.2 **Most of the houses in Marib Town, Yemen, were constructed primarily of layered mud (1991).**

example. A professional mason and his assistant, both refugees from Afghanistan although originally from Uzbekistan, built the walls with the occasional assistance of a third man. We witnessed all stages of construction, from destruction of the old layered-mud walls to completion of the topmost layer of the new walls. Fired-brick boundary walls already enclosed two sides of the property, so that only the layered-mud walls on the north and west sides required replacement. The north wall was to be 32 m long and the west wall 22.8 m long, for a combined length of 54.8 m. The planned height of the new wall was 2.8 m, and its thickness at the base was 45 cm. The demolition of the old walls (see Chapter 5) and the construction of the new ones required two weeks.

Layering began on a dry mud foundation (see Chapter 4). Taut strings, strung about 10 cm above the foundation, were used to center the wall on the wider foundation and to define its thickness. The mason trickled a powdery substance, in this instance wood ash, carefully on the foundation to mark the alignment of the strings, after which the strings were removed. To calculate the height of each layer, the projected height of the wall was divided by the number of planned layers. In this instance, the mason decided that because this wall was to be 2.8 m high, it would be built in four layers and each layer would measure 70 cm high.

Construction began at one end of the wall. The assistant, who worked in the mud pit, used a long-handled shovel to cut a slab of stiff mud about 30–35 cm long × 18–20 cm wide × 8–10 cm thick. He passed it on the shovel to the mason, who took it in both hands and slapped it down with its outer edge directly above the ashy line defining one face of the wall (Figure 7.3). Two other slabs were placed end-to-end along this line, with the three slabs having a combined length along one side of 90–100 cm and defining the length of this section of the layer. The next three slabs were similarly laid above the opposite ashy line marking the other wall face. Two or three slabs were thrown between the two outer rows of slabs (Figure 7.4). This process was repeated until the solid pile reached the planned height of the layer (70 cm). At this point, the length and width of one section of the layer was complete,

Figure 7.3 Professional mason and assistant (left) laying the first slabs of a new section in the second layer of a property wall for the Qazi house in Pishin, near Quetta, Baluchistan, Pakistan (1990). Note that the top of the first layer was not level, but this error would be corrected in the second layer.

Figure 7.4   A mason placing a slab of mud on a new section of the layered-mud wall at the Qazi property in Quetta, Pakistan (1990).

defining the length, width, and height of all other sections in the layer. In this wall, the section measured about 1 m long × 70 cm high × 45 cm wide. The mason then moved to the end of the newly laid section and began another section of the same size, abutting the end of the previous section. Section after section was built until the layer stretched from one end of the planned wall to the other.

Apart from slapping the slabs down on the wall, no attempt was made to compress the mud by beating or pressing it. (This is a primary characteristic that distinguishes layered mud from rammed earth!) The mason occasionally placed a foot or leaned his knuckles on the mud, but this was more to maintain his balance or to rest than to compact the mud in that place (Figure 7.5). Thus, nearly all compression that occurred in the wall was derived from the accumulated weight of wet slabs on the lower slabs in a given layer.

Some of the mud slabs on both faces of the wall protruded beyond the wall face. Sighting first along one wall face and then the other, the mason scraped off excess mud with the fingers of his cupped hand and used those handfuls to fill gaps and pits in the sides and upper surface of the completed section of the layer. Sometimes the mason trimmed the face of the wall with the shovel, leaving a series of wide and shallow parallel grooves on the surface (Figure 7.6).

This process of building a layer and allowing it to dry was repeated layer by layer until the wall reached its planned height. When a layer could not be completed during the workday, the mason finished the end of the section either by leaving its end with a vertical or near vertical face (Figure 7.7) or by bonding it to the next section where it joined the previous section. The latter was accomplished by laying mud slabs in the last section up to about two-thirds of its finished height and gradually sloping the remainder of the section with an S-curve profile. Later, when the section

Figure 7.5 The mason steps on a fresh mud slab for convenience, not to compact the layer in a new wall in Quetta, Pakistan (1990).

Figure 7.6 Wall surface partially trimmed with a shovel, leaving diagonal marks on layer 1 at the bottom and horizontal marks on layer 2 of the 4-layer wall under construction in Quetta, Pakistan (1990).

Figure 7.7 Sound section of the old wall trimmed slightly less than vertical to overhang the end of the abutting new layered-mud property wall under construction in Quetta, Pakistan (1990).

dried, new slabs were laid on the sloping curved area to bring the entire section up to the full height of the layer. The new section made using this method overlaid and slightly interlocked the partially dry previous section (Figure 7.8). If a mason used the first method of finishing a section and its vertical face had dried before a new section was added onto it, a vertical crack would occur between the two sections when the newer section dried, even if the mason attempted to press wet slabs of the new section against the finished section.

Drying Layers

Each layer must dry until it is sufficiently hard to withstand the weight of a new, wet layer without cracking or deforming—usually two to four days, depending on the weather and the layer's height and thickness. The greater the mass, the longer it takes to dry. In all regions, mud buildings are constructed during the driest periods of the year, when there is a minimal chance of rain or thunderstorms. Wetter and more humid environments require additional drying time. No time is wasted, however, waiting for a wall to dry. A house, having at least four exterior walls plus a number of interior walls, provides ample opportunities to work on other walls while one is drying.

When freshly laid, a layer is brown in color. After about three days of drying, it is a medium tan, and a new layer can be safely laid on top. After another three or four days, the first layer becomes a buff color (Figure 7.8). During the drying process, vertical cracks as long as 30–45 cm may appear within the sections, es-

Figure 7.8 An S-curve joint between a dried layer and a newly laid layer on a property wall near Quetta, Baluchistan, Pakistan (1990). Note the striking color differences between dry and drying layers.

pecially where they join. We saw one boundary wall in Baluchistan, Pakistan, in which almost every section of a seven-layer wall had cracked in many places during drying (Figure 7.9). Layered-mud multistory houses in Marib Town, Yemen, often showed vertical cracks running through several layers (Figure 7.2). Despite the aerial bombing of Marib Town in the 1960s and the subsequent earthquakes in 1982, neither concussion from bombs nor earth tremors caused all of the cracking we observed in these layered-mud houses, because neighboring mud-brick houses that were also badly damaged often did not show similar cracks. Some cracking always occurs during the drying process, but most cracking we saw in Marib Town likely resulted from the settling of houses during and after construction, and some was surely caused by erosion of the finishing coat of mud plaster that covered the walls.

Such cracks pose a threat to the layer laid immediately above because they tend to continue upward. To forestall this process, the mason would spread a mud pad about 5 cm thick on the top surface of the dried layer over the crack and then center a single fired brick on the mud pad. The top of the fired brick soon would be covered by mud as the laying of the next mud layer proceeded. The fired brick usually halted the upward spread of the crack into the layers above (Figure 7.10). It was not uncommon to see 10–12 fired bricks covering cracks in a completed layer, although the bricks eventually would be hidden when the wall was finished with a coat of mud plaster. In Baluchistan, cracks were frequently covered with *niru*, a sealer, which was immediately followed by the first coat of mud plaster. This is discussed in greater detail in Chapter 12.

Architectural Features and Variations

All mud walls more than 2 m high are gradually thinned as the wall rises from its base to its top. As a result of successively reduced weight through thinning, a wall resists the tendency to lean and collapse from top-heaviness. In the Near East, this

Figure 7.9   Cracks in drying mud layers of a boundary wall near Pishin, Baluchistan, Pakistan (1990).

empirical distribution of weight obviates the need for a structural framework of timber or other materials. In house walls, the tapering occurs on the outer surfaces throughout their height, and the inner surfaces are generally plumb from top to bottom. When finished, the layered-mud property walls at the Qazi house in Pishin gradually tapered in thickness from 45 cm at the base to 36 cm at the top, a batter of about 2%.

Many layered-mud walls feature rounded corners and tops. Rounding adds softness to structures, emphasized by the delightful play of moving sunlight and shade. Round corners are more attractive, massive, and damage resistant than square corners. The latter are very fragile and easily chipped by people, animals, or vehicles hitting their sharp edges. Rounded tops are protected from weathering by mud or lime plaster and sometimes by a layer of bundled straw or reeds that overhangs the wall on both sides to drip rainwater well away from the surfaces (see Figure 14.10). In many areas, the tops of property walls feature security devices—such as barbed wire strung along the surface or razor blades or jagged bits of broken glass set in mud or lime plaster—to discourage intruders from climbing over the walls.

Some property walls, as well as walls of lavish houses and fortresses, are finished flat, with two to four courses of fired brick laid on the tops to protect them from rain and snow. These capping bricks normally overhang the surfaces and drip water away from them. In New Mexico, fired-brick coping on mud walls is a characteristic of

Figure 7.10 Fired bricks centered over vertical cracks, which occurred during drying of a layer, to prevent their upward migration into a new layer being laid above in a property wall at the Qazi house in Pishin, near Quetta, Baluchistan (1990). Between layers 1 and 2, bricks stopped two cracks from spreading upwards, although this was not always successful in other layers. Between layers 4 and 5, the crack on the left bypassed the brick.

the elegant Territorial style of architecture, dating from the mid-nineteenth century to the present (see Figure 14.11).

The optimum height of a mud layer seems to be about 45–50 cm, yielding relatively square sections that make for sounder, more stable walls. In houses, layers are generally about 50 cm high. Thus, if walls are built to a height of about 2 m, only four layers are required; if they are to be 2.5 m high, five layers are used. Variations in layer size and composition abound depending on a builder's preferences and the soils available (e.g., layers in the new Qazi property wall were ~70 cm high), as well as on the thinning of layers in multistory buildings. In one house we saw, small layers ranged in height from 27 to 36 cm.

A notable characteristic of layered-mud walls in west central and southern Saudi Arabia is the convex shape of the outer face of each layer, resembling a long cushion or bolster. Some years ago, one of us (GVB) was privileged to see a mason building a layered-mud house with convex outer surfaces (Figure 7.11). The horizontal joint between each layer was sharply defined. These cushion-like layers added an attractive softness to the structure that was strikingly beautiful, similar to the effects of rounded corners. When asked how long this house would last, the mason replied without hesitation, "At least 200 years with care and maintenance!" The town wall and towers of Bishah, Saudi Arabia, are fine examples of major structures built of bolster-like mud layers. The uppermost course of the town wall is decorated with a row of small mud arches in relief just below the carinated parapet (Figure 7.12).

Figure 7.11 Convex outer surface of mud layers of a house under construction in Najran, Saudi Arabia (1968).

Figure 7.12 Bolster-style, layered-mud town wall of Bishah, Saudi Arabia (1968).

The Marib house under construction in northern Yemen exhibited a slightly different treatment of the outer surface of the layers that was becoming increasingly popular in that region. Each of the 14 layers of the 50 cm thick walls had a raked outer surface forming about a 5 cm overhang over the top edge of the layer below, resembling overlapping wood siding (Figure 7.13). In the ruined and abandoned Marib Town, we saw other examples of raked layers, indicating that this style must go back at least a century. In some instances this style of construction functions as a key to bond mud plaster, which is applied to create a smooth, vertical surface (see Figure 12.7).

A variation in style in many layered-mud buildings in the Asir and Najran regions of Saudi Arabia and in northern Yemen is for raised and rounded or pointed corners that extend above the parapet (Figure 7.14). To create this effect in houses with bolster-like mud layers about 50 cm high, for example, each corner of the base or first layer is given a rounded hump of mud reaching about midway to the planned height of the next layer—that is, about 17–25 cm higher than the rest of the 50 cm layer—and the additional mud is sufficient to maintain a slightly convex surface on each of the four humped corners (Figure 7.15). Each successive layer continues with these raised corner humps, including the topmost layer, so that the buildings appear to have horns thrusting upward from the earth.

Figure 7.13   Raked outer surface, resembling wood siding, on layers of a house under construction in Marib, Yemen (1991). The overhanging edges extend out about 5 cm.

Figure 7.14   Rounded, rising layers in the corners of a house in Najran, Saudi Arabia (1968).

These horn-like projections resemble the stylized "horns-of-the-altar" motif in ancient Israel, where it was commonly used on both communal and household altars (Figure 7.16). The altars typically featured corners protruding upward to a point, like horns; thus the "horns of the altar" were considered to be a place of sanctuary.[1] Perhaps the architectural device of horns on the corners of the house symbolically reflects the continuum of this ancient tradition, denoting that the house is a place of safety or sanctuary.

A unique type of construction appears in the mountains of the Asir region of south-western Saudi Arabia. Layered-mud houses are built with a row of shale or other thin stones between each mud layer from the ground to the roof (Figure 7.17). The mud layers are about 20 cm high, and the row of stones adds another 5 cm, so that each unit of mud layer plus stone row is about 25 cm high. The stone rows slope slightly downward and project about 15–20 cm beyond the outside wall face. The walls of some of these houses may have 20 or more layered-mud courses; 20 courses yield a wall about 5 m high. In this region of relatively high rainfall, the rows of stone serve as drip moldings to protect the integrity of the wall (see also Chapter 14). The rows of stones also strongly emphasize the horizontal aspect of the house.

GEOGRAPHICAL AND CHRONOLOGICAL DISTRIBUTION

Old World Sites

Layered-mud construction is dominant in many regions of the world, particularly in South and Central Asia and many countries of the Near East. Worldwide, it has remained second in popularity after mud brick during the twentieth century.

Figure 7.15   Corner detail of the bolster-like layers of house shown in Figure 7.11, Najran, Saudi Arabia (1968).

In Asia, it appears in Iraq, Iran, Afghanistan, Pakistan, and India and extends northward to Uzbekistan, Tajikistan, and probably into western China and adjacent regions. In the Near East, it is used from Saudi Arabia southward through the regions of Asir and Najran and into northern Yemen to a line about 83–125 km south of Sana`a, where it is replaced by mud brick as the preferred method of construction. Layered mud is also prevalent in Yemen eastward from Sana`a, including the region of Marib, to the Ramlat al Sabatein desert.

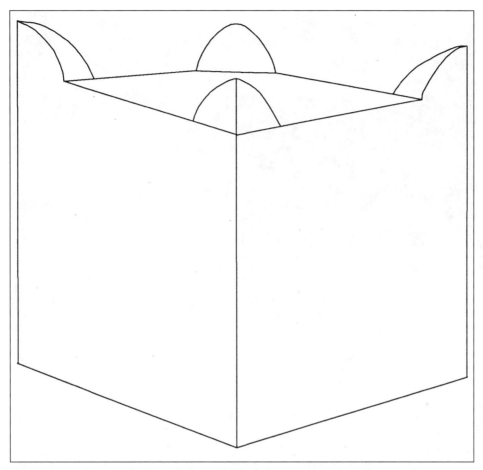

Figure 7.16   Diagram of a horned altar of biblical times common in ancient Israel.

This method of construction probably began no later than the seventh millennium B.C., and perhaps several centuries before, so that it ranks among the earlier methods employed for building with soil. It has been used for all types of structures: one-story to multistory houses; fortress houses; shops; government buildings; religious structures, including mosques and roadside prayer areas; property or boundary walls, including the perimeter walls of prisons; and fortifications of towns and cities (Figure 7.18). The most unusual structure we have seen is the tower house near Sana`a, Yemen, which is a truncated cone of layered mud with a square, fired-brick house built on top (Figure 7.19).

Historically, layered-mud construction is not as long-lasting as mud brick or rammed earth. In many places in the ancient Near East, there are superb examples of mud-brick walls 5000 years old or more. The greater compression of mud brick and rammed earth enables them to resist erosion better than layered mud. At the same time, mud brick, because of its modular aspect and density, survives in a state more easily recognizable than either layered mud or rammed earth, both of which might be mistaken for a natural ridge in the soil.

Figure 7.17   House with rows of thin stone slabs between mud layers, near Khamis Mushait, Asir, Saudi Arabia (1968). Note "horns" on several upper corners.

Few if any historical period sites in Southwest Asia, the Near East, or Arabia from ca. 3000 B.C. to ca. A.D. 1000 or later have yielded layered-mud walls. This suggests the existence of an enormous gap in the layered-mud sequence. It is difficult to assume that layered-mud construction was entirely replaced everywhere by mud brick, even though the latter certainly became the dominant mode of construction.

The apparent gap may be accounted for by two possible explanations. First, perhaps there is no gap at all. Layered-mud construction may have continued throughout the 4000-year period in some areas of Asia, although declining in popularity and eventually becoming little used. Or perhaps it was confined to villages and small towns in out-of-the-way places, which became minor archaeological sites long ago. If so, some examples may yet be found in these lesser-known regions and in poorly documented periods of human occupation, such as the first and second millennia A.D., which have been largely neglected by archaeologists. Even in a well-traveled country such as Iraq, perhaps an archaeologist or ethnologist observed layered-mud structures but thought them not sufficiently important to publish.[2] It is possible, too, that earlier archaeologists, who dug enormous areas in sites without careful excavating methods and sufficient staff to supervise 100 to 300 laborers adequately, inadvertently removed layered-mud walls without recognizing them. W. F. Albright (1949:10), the distinguished ancient Near Eastern archaeologist and scholar of the previous generation, described the situation thus: "More than one case is known where an excavator cleared away what he thought was a narrow room only to find that he had removed the wall, leaving rectangular masses of fallen brick in the space

Figure 7.18 The old city wall of Sana`a, Yemen, built of layered mud (1991). Most of this wall has been destroyed to make way for urban growth during the last 30 years.

previously occupied by Rooms!" Layered-mud walls would be much more easily missed than mud-brick walls. In addition, it is much more likely that walls in prehistoric Mesopotamian sites that have been described as rammed earth or *chineh* are actually layered mud. Then the gap largely disappears for Iraq, although it remains a conundrum for Pakistan, India, and Arabia.

Second, perhaps the gap is real. In this scenario, layered mud disappeared after giving way to mud brick around 3000 B.C. At some time within the past 1000 years or so, layered mud reappeared in Iraq, Iran, Afghanistan, Pakistan, India, and Arabia. This suggests that either (a) the concept of mud layering was reinvented by the same thought processes and experiments that were responsible for its earlier invention, or (b) it was discovered in some obscure area where it had survived and was reintroduced from there. Throughout human history, a number of technological processes have disappeared only to be reinvented at a later time or in another location. For example, in earthen construction, layered mud certainly was independently invented in North and South America before the Spanish Conquest, with no cultural input from the Old World.

Beyond the geographical focus of this monograph, layered-mud construction is also found in Ghana[3] and in forest areas of Africa (Courtney-Clarke, 1990:50, 159; Denyer, 1978:93).

Figure 7.19 Truncated conical tower house of layered mud with square, fired-brick house on top, near Sana`a, Yemen (1991).

New World Sites

Layered mud has also been used in the New World, where it is commonly known as "puddled mud." Near Coolidge, Arizona, the Hohokam community built structures of layered mud in the fourteenth century A.D. The most notable building, Casa Grande, has given its name to the site as a whole (Figure 7.20). This structure, ca. A.D. 1450, was originally four stories high and about 60 ft long × 35 ft wide (18.3 × 10.7 m). Its walls are about 4 ft (1.2 m) thick at the base, thinning as they ascend, and most layers are about 2 ft (61 cm) high although their heights vary (Figure 7.21).

Figure 7.20 Casa Grande Monument, ca. A.D. 1450, near Coolidge, Arizona, USA (1996). Originally four stories high, it was built of layered mud, known locally as puddled mud.

Abandoned in the fifteenth century, Casa Grande has survived almost 400 years of weathering and erosion, and it remains an excellent example of the durability of layered-mud construction. In 1892 it became the first archaeological preserve in the USA, and it is protected by a magnificent roof, which is also now a national monument. Now known as Casa Grande Ruins National Monument and under the excellent care of the National Park Service, it is a "must" visit for anyone interested in layered-mud construction. Still earlier (ca. A.D. 900), a large settlement featuring layered-mud buildings, known as Casas Grandes, was built in Chihuahua, Mexico (McHenry, 1984:32, fig. 2.57). To that same period belongs the original layered-mud construction of Taos Pueblo, Taos, New Mexico, one of the best known sites in the American Southwest (Figure 7.22). Several layered-mud structures belong to the Pueblo III (A.D. 1050–1300) period, and some were still occupied as recently as the beginning of the twentieth century, such as the Picuris Pueblo (Smith and Austin, 1989:10–11). Layered mud is still in use today in both Ecuador (Figure 7.23) and Peru, South America.

ADVANTAGES AND DISADVANTAGES

The widespread examples of layered-mud construction establish for it a secure place in mud architecture today, and one that will surely last well into the future. It is well suited for simple, functional structures.

This method joins mud-ball construction as the least expensive of all types of substantial mud construction. Except for rare cases in which soil must be quarried elsewhere and transported to the site, it costs nothing. Cost of the relatively small quantity of water required is negligible, unless it too is unavailable near the site and must be transported. The only other significant building materials that must be

Figure 7.21 Ora Van Beek and detail of Casa Grande layers, most of which are about 61 cm high, near Coolidge, Arizona, USA (1996).

Figure 7.22   Taos Pueblo, originally built of layered mud, Taos, New Mexico (1989).

Figure 7.23   Layered-mud house on a rubble foundation in Pinsagui, Imbabura, Ecuador. (Courtesy Paulina Ledergerber, Department of Anthropology, Smithsonian Institution; used with permission).

acquired are beams to support the roof, framing materials for windows and doors, and flooring materials if other than mud floors are desired.

Because layered-mud construction is labor intensive, the major costs are masons' salaries. Of course, for a committed do-it-yourselfer, no cash outlay is necessary to build walls. In Pakistan, as in many developing nations, most labor costs are very low, making it possible for persons with modest incomes to afford professional masons. We obtained cost figures for the boundary walls built around the Qazi house near Quetta by the Uzbek professional masons. They charged a total of 3,000 Pakistani rupees for their combined labor, which amounted to $139.21 at the exchange rate of 21.55 rupees = US$1.00 prevailing in late May 1990. Adding a small amount for the purchase of fired bricks (to stop cracks from spreading) would likely have brought the total cost of the walls to about $150.00. This costed out to $0.83/line-foot for a wall 2.8 m (9 ft) high and 45 cm (~18 in) thick! For purposes of comparison, we learned that the same walls, if built of fired brick, would have had a minimum cost of between 11,000 and 13,000 rupees ($510.44–$603.25)—about four times the price of the layered-mud wall.

The Customs Post at Beleli (see Figures 3.27, 3.28) with its two rooms and porch, built by two professional masons, cost Baluchistan's regional government 12,000 rupees, i.e., $556.84 at the prevailing exchange rate. For the amateurs we saw building a new property wall north of Quetta, it cost nothing except their time and energy. During our 1989 visit to Dudhian, a village near Harappa in Punjab, we asked our host-guide about the cost of a two-room house in the village. After consulting his brother, he replied, "About fifty dollars!" Unfortunately we had failed to ask whether the costs were for materials, labor, or both. Because many houses in the village had a steel I-beam and bamboo poles supporting the roof, we suspected the $50 included only materials, with labor provided by the family and friends.

Layered-mud construction is the easiest method for building substantial structures because it is simple, is easy to learn, and requires little or no experience. It is also forgiving of minor errors and sloppiness. These features make it ideal for amateur builders. Yet when carefully done it can produce buildings of considerable beauty that at the same time blend into and stand out from their setting. One person can excavate a trench, lay a foundation, and build a layered wall. Two or three workers vastly increase the efficiency and speed of wall construction, but no more than two people are required for any job with the exception of raising timber beams or a steel I-beam for the roof. With care and by employing some of the tricks used by the professionals we observed, conscientious amateurs can do almost as well as experienced masons.

Layered mud is also the fastest type of mud construction when measured by the quantity of line meters or feet of wall erected with minimal labor and without mechanical equipment. Professional masons mixed mud and laid a 70-cm high layer of wall at a rate of 1.77 m/h; a layer 62 cm high in a less massive wall built by amateurs was laid at a rate of 1.35 m/h. Although rammed earth is built faster per cubic meter or cubic yard of walling, it requires a large gang of laborers or the use of mechanical equipment (see Chapter 8).

This method of construction also produces sturdy walls that are stronger than many stone or fired-brick walls built locally in Southwest Asia for two reasons: (1) stone and fired-brick walls commonly lack sufficient cement mortar of good quality to bond these materials. For example, the bedding and rising joints of fired-brick structures, especially boundary walls and houses, are not consistently filled with good cement mortar (see Chapter 9). (2) Mud, when dried, becomes more like solid stone—in fact it is often referred to as "man-made stone"! It resists chisels, screwdrivers, knives, and even hand picks. From GVB's years of excavating, dressing, and cleaning mud brick, we can attest to the extraordinary difficulty of picking, scraping, and smoothing well-dried, dense mud layers. It is not surprising, therefore, that prison compounds in Pakistan are surrounded with walls of layered mud rather than of stone or fired brick. Consider again the four- and five-story houses of Marib Town in Yemen, many of which not only carried the heavy mass of mud layers above, but also survived the shock of nearby aerial bombing during the Civil War in the 1960s and of ground movements during the 1982 earthquakes. These examples surely provide the best evidence of the strength and sturdiness of layered-mud walls.

Another advantage of layered-mud construction is that it produces long-lasting structures. We learned from the mason in Najran, Saudi Arabia, that he was expecting the "bolster" house—with layers having a convex outer surface—to last 200 years with maintenance. Although abandoned, many of the residences in Marib Town were certainly more than 100 years old, and some were probably older than 200 years. In the southwestern USA and in Mexico, a number of layered-mud structures have survived for centuries (described earlier in this chapter). These houses have certainly survived longer than we might expect of many twentieth century American residences, whether condominiums, houses in tract developments, or custom-built residences. Even worse, many cities have public housing projects built of reinforced concrete, concrete blocks, or fired brick during the previous 30–50 years that, due to poor construction methods, neglect, and deterioration, have been destroyed or are abandoned and awaiting the wrecker's ball or dynamite.

Layered construction is not without disadvantages. It is more subject to cracking than mud brick. We have seen how cracks appear where sections of a layer imperfectly join, and how miscellaneous cracks occur during drying. This is due in part to the lower density and poor compression of layered-mud construction, and also in part to the faster, sometimes careless workmanship in building the layers.

From the point of view of design, layered mud is more difficult to work than mud brick because it lacks the convenience inherent in the small modular form of brick. Some specialized types of construction, such as domes and certain vaults, would have to be fully supported while drying if layered mud were used, which may be why we have not seen layered-mud examples of these. Moreover, decorative designs common in mud brick (e.g., recessed paneling, exotic columns with carved fluting, spiraled ridges, imitation palm trunks, various relief moldings) would be much more difficult if not impossible to render in layered mud because it lacks both fine grain and compression. Once layered mud is covered with mud plaster, however, the latter can be tooled and shaped into decorative designs.

NOTES

1. In biblical times, persons in danger could, in theory, flee to a sanctuary, grasp the horns of the altar, and be safe from harm so long as they remained there. Anyone clinging to the

horns was not supposed to be taken away or killed. See the following Bible passages for reference: For altar descriptions and purpose: Exodus 27:2, 37:25, 38:1–2; Leviticus 16:18; Ezekiel 43:15, 20. For fugitive sanctuary: I Kings 1:49–53 (respect of custom), 2:28–34 (violation of the custom).

2. Saggs (1967:276), however, includes a color photograph of property walls built of layered mud in a contemporary village near the ruins of ancient Babylon.

3. In one of Courtney-Clarke's (1990:50, 159) illustrations, a circular silo in the background shows layered walls finished around the top with mud plaster.

Chapter 8

Rammed Earth

Rammed earth or "beaten earth," also known by the French terms *"pisé de terre,"* *"terre pisé,"* or simply *"pisé,"* refers to soil that is compacted by tamping or ramming vigorously with any of several kinds of hand or power tools. There are two methods of building with rammed earth: without forms and with forms. Rammed-earth construction without forms was employed for building fortifications in China beginning about 2000 B.C. and in the Near East during the eighteenth to sixteenth centuries B.C. Rammed-earth construction with forms was used for building houses and other structures in China from about 1400 B.C., but this technique was apparently not known in the ancient Near East.

CONSTRUCTION WITHOUT FORMS

Revetments

Rammed-earth walls constructed without forms first appeared in a type of fortification known as a revetment[1] or glacis. An early example was built in the city of Ch'êng Tzû Yai in northeastern China during the last Neolithic period, between 2000 and 1600 B.C., by the people of the "Black-Pottery Culture." In the 1930s, sections of this fortification still stood 3.5 m high, more than 9.1 m thick at the base, and about 1.6 km long surrounding the city (Creel, 1937:48). The substantial thickness of the base suggests the fortification was a revetment.

In the Levantine countries (Syria, Lebanon, Israel, Jordan) and Egypt during the Middle Bronze IIB–C periods (ca. 1800–1550 B.C.), a new fortification system appeared, apparently introduced by a little-known group called the "Hyksos," in Egyptian inscriptions. The Hyksos' system consisted of a massive, sloping, earthen revetment, which was built along the perimeter of a site and crowned by a vertical wall. The cross section of the revetment had the form of either a truncated right triangle or a truncated isosceles triangle with a flat top. This flat top served as the base for a vertical wall—built of either layered mud, mud brick, or stone—that extended several meters upward. The lower slope of the revetment was faced either with stones, mud brick, lime plaster, or mud plaster. The natural height and sloping sides of a tell in these regions provided a good measure of natural defense. When a revetment and a vertical wall were constructed at the base of a large tell or on top of a low tell, the system provided great obstacles for an attacking army to overcome. A moat-like ditch increased the effective height of the revetment, making an attackers' climb longer and more difficult. Such a ditch also increased opportunities for the defenders to strike more severe blows from the top of the wall during the attackers' climb.

The best preserved revetment we know of is at Ashkelon, a coastal site in Israel. Director Lawrence Stager (1993) and his team discovered four successive building phases, in each of which the structure was modified. In the earliest phase, the earthen core was faced on the sloping surface by mud brick. The surfaces of the three later building phases, however, were finished with rubble and capped with a layer of soil about one meter thick (Figure 8.1). The outer surface of this revetment slopes at an angle between 35° and 40° and the wall is more than 30 m thick at the base. The structure stands about 15 m high and, in enclosing the ancient city, was probably about 2 km long! During the first two phases of its use, a mud-brick, radially arched gateway provided an entrance through the revetment (Stager, 1993:106).

A lime-plastered revetment at Jericho was 26 m thick, and 17 m high (Figure 8.2; Kenyon, 1976:562). At Tell Dan, Israel, a revetment was entered through an arched gateway like the one at Ashkelon—with radially laid mud brick (see Figure 11.11). Another example is the mud-plastered revetment at Tell Haror (Arabic: Hureireh)

Figure 8.1   Rammed-earth revetment with radial arched gateway, ca. eighteenth century B.C., Ashkelon, Israel (1996).

Figure 8.2 Cross-section of rammed-earth revetment at Jericho, ca. 1750–1650 B.C. (1971). The lime-plastered surface is the white oblique band. The highest point behind and to the left is an excavation dump, and the sloping surface above the lime plaster is later debris that accumulated after the revetment was no longer used.

in the western Negev of Israel, which had a preserved base thickness of about 20 m and a height of about 8–10 m (Figure 8.3; Oren, 1993a:582). The revetment systems at Ashkelon, Jericho, and Gezer, Israel, illustrate a high level of engineering and the vast manpower required to build them. Each must have provided a formidable defense against an attacking army.

By contrast, the revetment at Tell Jemmeh, Israel, seems to have been considerably smaller. Its fragmentary remains probably characterized the construction of the entire structure. The surface of the site was leveled and a thin layer of marly clay, only 1.0–1.5 cm deep, was spread over it and tamped down. On this base, a layer of sandy silt soil ranging in depth from about 20 to 28 cm was spread and tamped. This combination of distinctive layers was continually repeated as high as the revetment was preserved. The revetment was more than 6 m thick but was preserved only about 1.57 m high. After abandonment, the outer face eroded away and was cut repeatedly by pits. Unfortunately, in our limited excavation we were unable to reach the inner face to learn its thickness (Van Beek, 1992:4–9).

The attack strategies of besieging armies included (1) battering rams to smash the defensive wall, (2) tunneling beneath the defense system to undermine it, causing a portion to collapse or providing a means for troops to enter the city surreptitiously, and (3) all-out assaults on the revetment and wall by storm troops, archers, spear men, and slingshot throwers. The revetment system was designed to counter each of these strategies.

Figure 8.3   Remains of rammed-earth revetment, ca. seventeenth century B.C., at Tell Haror in the western Negev, Israel (1982). It was originally covered with thick mud plaster.

Because of a revetment's height and slope, a battering ram had to be dragged up the slope and stabilized. Because of the angle of the slope, a ram could strike only glancing blows, with less force and effectiveness, at the wall on top. Therefore a besieging army would need to construct a long, gradually sloping, earthen ramp on the revetment and a horizontal platform at or near the level of the wall to enable a ram to smash it with maximum force. (A level platform also helped prevent the ram from rolling downhill out of control.) Such a massive ramp and platform, of course, required many workers laboring under the most difficult circumstances, especially when constructing the upper sections within close range of the defenders' weapons. When the ramp and platform were finished, it was equally arduous to move a battering ram into position, secure it, and operate it when the defenders on the top of the wall were attempting to thwart these efforts.

The enormous thickness of a revetment made it extremely difficult for sappers to tunnel under it. Obstacles to overcome included the great length of the tunnel to dig, the vast amount of earth to be removed and disposed of, and the need for quiet during digging and removing earth, lest these efforts be detected by the inhabitants of the town, who could then initiate defensive countermeasures.

The sloping surface of a revetment was finished smooth without toeholds, making it very difficult for attacking soldiers to climb, especially when the defenders were unleashing volleys of missiles and weapons, such as stones, firebrands, arrows, and spears, in conjunction with pouring hot oil or water on attacking soldiers.

Ramps—built all or partly of rammed earth—were used for attacking revetment fortifications, and defensive counterramps were often erected against the inner face of the wall by the besieged. The Assyrian ramp at Lachish, Israel, is depicted among the Assyrian reliefs in the British Museum, London; the actual remains of both the ramp and counterramp were found in excavations at Lachish by David Ussishkin (Figure 8.4; Ussishkin, 1993:907–908). The reliefs show the battering ram standing on a very sharply angled slope of about 55°, punching at the wall at angles between 50° and 70°, and dislodging stones. The illustrations show the wheeled ram with no braking or locking devices, (e.g., wheel chocks or a combination of stakes and ropes) to keep it from rolling backwards down the slope. The Assyrian sculptor clearly exercised artistic license in failing to render these important details of operation; liberties were taken also with the angle of the slope, which was generally only 30° to 40°. Another example is the huge ramp constructed by the Romans to conquer Masada in Israel in A.D. 73 (Figure 8.5). This ramp was about 197 m long and about the same width at its broadest section. Reinforced with wooden posts, much of it still remains (Yadin, 1966:226–230).

However effective the rammed-earth revetment-and-vertical-wall fortification may have been, it ceased to be employed in the Near East about 1550 B.C. and never reappeared. The reason for its abandonment remains unknown. Ultimately, it may not have been cost effective, demanding too much time and physical effort of the local people to erect fortifications, which may have led them to employ defensive systems that were easier to build.

Sloping rammed-earth revetments were sometimes constructed using several types of soil, often with contrasting colors. Soils were transported directly from the quarry areas in any of a number of ways, singly or in combination—in straw baskets on the backs of asses or on the heads and hips of men, women, and children—to the building site where they were dumped to form piles. Alternately, soil taken from around the base of the site may have been moved on a drag-board drawn by a pair of oxen, asses, or other domestic animals.

Figure 8.4 Siege ramp at Lachish, Israel, built by the Assyrians in the reign of Sennacherib, ca. 701 B.C. (1987). The exposed part of the ramp is located between the parallel fence posts near the top of the tell.

Figure 8.5 Earthen siege ramp at Masada, Israel, built by the tenth Roman Legion, A.D. 73 (1996).

When soil arrived at the revetment site, it was poured out of the basket and roughly leveled. A workman tamped or rammed it until it was compacted into a dense earthen mass. The tamping tool was probably similar to that used in Morocco today in form-built rammed-earth structures (see Figure 8.30). A workman would raise the tamping tool with both hands and forcefully beat the soil many times in all directions until each basketful was compacted. This process continued until the compacted layer reached the desired thickness, which was commonly 25–50 cm.

Because little or no water was added to the soil, minimal drying time was needed for each layer, although a full cure might take days or weeks, depending on revetment density and thickness. Ideally the revetment would rise at about the same rate in its entire circuit, so that a work crew, having completed one layer, would move to an adjacent area and continue to add a layer of similar thickness to the structure. While construction proceeded elsewhere, inactivity in the completed area would allow time for that layer to dry. The major difference between drying individual layers and drying the entire revetment mass is that the latter may require several years for complete curing.

Generally each rammed-earth layer was finished with thick lime plaster (see Figure 8.2) extending 1–2 m from the sloping edge inward to where it gradually thinned and disappeared. At the front, it curved downward over the slope to join the plaster of the previously laid layer, producing a continuous cover of lime plaster on the revetment surface. Originally the lime plaster face was probably burnished, which brought the finer material to the surface and created a smooth, shiny surface. At Gezer in Israel, a revetment built of chalk ridges or dikes—triangular in section—to contain debris soil, was covered with a layer of lime plaster (Figure 8.6; Dever et al., 1970:42–43, pl. 5). Alternatively, the outer sloping surface was occasionally finished with stones, laid with their more flat and smooth surfaces facing outward. Sometimes the slope may have been covered only with mud plaster, as at Tell Haror. Any of these surface treatments on the revetment slope would be extraordinarily slippery when wet. During our excavations at Tell Jemmeh, the loess soil was as slippery as ice immediately after a rain, which made it almost impossible to climb the site, although the slope had a lesser angle than that of ancient revetments elsewhere.

The construction of rammed-earth revetments obviously required a large labor force for many months. Such a project would probably include, as minimum personnel for each crew, one tamper, five basket carriers, five quarrymen excavating the soil and loading it on asses, and one or two handling the pack animals, for a total of 12 or 13 workmen in a crew. A revetment project using 50 such teams would mean a workforce of 600 persons, a number that the average Near Eastern town would have found difficult to provide in antiquity, when the total population of most towns ranged between 500 and 1200 people. This type of project, involving most of the community, would have been undertaken either between planting and harvest or following harvest, which are the largest blocks of comparatively free time in agrarian societies. It would, of course, have required more than one year to complete. With these minimal numbers, one can begin to understand the labor intensive aspect of constructing rammed earthen revetments for the defense of towns.

Building Vertical Rammed-Earth Walls without Forms?

In earlier decades of Near Eastern archaeological research, excavators reported finding a much greater number of *terre pisé* walls than they do today. Based on our research and experience, nearly all of these reports were in error. When a wall was discovered in an excavation, archaeologists usually trenched along both of its sides, sometimes to its base, in order to define it and to draw its plan, after which they destroyed the wall to excavate deeper. Few archaeologists distinguished residual mud plaster from the core wall itself, and walls were seldom troweled or cleaned

Figure 8.6 Cross-section of lime plaster revetment at Gezer, Israel, ca. seventeenth century B.C. (1972). The revetment is constructed of a series of chalk dikes, with debris piled behind each dike and covered with lime plaster.

to expose layered courses, bonding patterns, or the bedding and rising joints of individual bricks. Failing to clean the earthen wall and to define layers or bricks, they wrongly assumed that the walls were built of *terre pisé* or rammed earth.[2] In the Levant and elsewhere in the Near East, house walls of rammed earth are not found today despite the fact that our excavating methodology is considerably advanced over that of our predecessors. It seems likely that *terre pisé* construction in the Levant is restricted to the Middle Bronze II period (1800–1550 B.C.).

Nevertheless it remains possible that some early buildings were constructed of rammed earth without forms. That they are not identified in excavation reports may be due to chance, to archaeologists' lack of experience or interest in details of earthen construction, or to the poor condition of walls. For example, in the Middle Bronze IIC period (ca. seventeenth century B.C.) at Tell Jemmeh, we found one wall (wall 6 in square J2 of field III) that was constructed either of rammed earth or layered mud (Figure 8.7). In a site where all buildings excavated were built of mud brick, this wall was special. Supervisor Egon Lass and GVB worked most of one afternoon, delicately scraping the wall surface and searching for bedding and rising joints that would help define layered mud courses or rammed earth blocks. While one person troweled, the other stood back to gain perspective and watch. We alternated roles every 10–15 minutes, yet it defied our best efforts to ascertain how it was constructed (see also Chapter 7 and Appendix B). Apart from a probable curving joint low on the wall, one certain horizontal joint midway in the preserved height, and a possible third horizontal joint above, we found no vertical joints.

Figure 8.7   Tell Jemmeh property or house wall (IIJ2, Wall 6) probably built of rammed earth, seen in cross-section in center of photograph. Note the debris layers on the left abutting the wall face. The cross-section of a mud-brick wall of a subsequent building phase appears at the top edge of the picture.

A possible explanation of this wall is as follows. The lowest section (6a) was built first. Through time it was eroded by wind and rain, so that the top of the wall curved downward, as can be seen in the cross-section shown in Figure 8.7. On the stub of section 6a, a slightly narrower wall (6b) was built. The latter, in turn, was reused for a third phase (6c), which may have been constructed with mud brick. This explanation is conjecture, and although it is by no means certain, it is the most attractive of those considered.

The soil of wall 6 was compacted more densely than that in any layered-mud walls seen by GVB, so it more closely resembled the quality of the rammed-earth revetment at Tell Jemmeh, described above. Thus rammed earth seemed more probable, but which of the two methods—without forms or with forms—was used? Against the use of form-built rammed earth are these facts: below the probable horizontal joints, there was no evidence of holes for the cross-members to support the forms during construction or of vertical joints between blocks. Despite these arguments, which suggest the wall may be a product of a quality layered-mud construction, we tentatively leave it as a "rammed-earth" wall built without forms.

Although we have never seen rammed-earth house or property walls being built without using forms, several procedures might make such construction possible. For example, a very small quantity of water might be added to dampen the soil. Slightly damp soil might hold together along the sides of the wall where one would expect the tamping of pile-dry soil to crumble along the edges of the wall causing soil to spall off, leaving irregular inner and outer wall faces. Possibly a builder might build the wall somewhat wider than its intended width and, immediately after ramming a layer, carefully trim the sides of the wall with a trowel, hand pick, hoe, or shovel back to the desired thickness. The trimmed surplus soil can be collected and reused elsewhere. These suggestions may or may not work, but they might be worth testing. Such a wall would have a density more comparable to a rammed-earth wall than to a layered-mud wall. Form-built walls, however, would always be the overwhelming choice, except where wood or other materials for making forms are absent or too expensive.

CONSTRUCTION USING FORMS

Moreover, are there not in Africa and Spain walls made of earth that are called framed walls, because they are made by packing in a frame enclosed between two boards, one on each side, and so are stuffed in rather than built, and do they not last for ages, undamaged by rain, wind, and fire, and stronger than any quarry-stone? (Pliny the Elder, 1961 [translation]: ¶ 169.)

The closest analogy to form-built rammed-earth construction is poured concrete, with which nearly every reader is likely to be familiar. The common element between concrete and rammed-earth construction is the form into which the building material was poured. In the case of rammed earth or *terre pisé*, the soil is poured in and compacted by ramming.

As in layered-mud construction, substantial foundations of stone, concrete, or mud are especially important to minimize the settling of rammed-earth structures because of the enormous weight of their walls. In many desert locations where the soil is packed hard, it is safe to build on the surface after leveling the building site, trimming the high places and filling the low places with well-tamped earth. In New Mexico, foundations of concrete predominate, although compacted gravel or crushed rock with sand are increasingly used with success (McHenry, 1984:138–140). The foundation is then capped by a reinforced concrete slab upon which the rammed-earth walls are built, usually set ~5 cm inside the edge of the slab.

Origins of Form-Built Rammed Earth

Although some researchers have assumed a Near Eastern or South Asian origin for form-built rammed earth, there is no evidence to support such a view. Indeed, the earliest evidence (known to GVB) in the Near East and adjacent regions is an illustration titled "Manual on Rammed Earth" that shows piles of soil, various types of rammers and other tools, and wooden forms with workmen ramming soil inside the forms (Figure 8.8). This painting was included in a record of crafts prepared in Kashmir in 1850 (Lewcock, 1978:113), and it illustrates the continuity of this Asian tradition.[3]

Form-built rammed earth certainly appeared in China in the second millennium B.C. and has continued in use there into the twenty-first century. This establishes the primacy of China as the ultimate place of origin of this method of construction, and from there it almost certainly spread to Nepal and Kashmir. But other occurrences of form-built rammed earth in places distant from China and in later times suggests the probability of independent discovery of the method elsewhere, especially in Europe, where it has figured prominently among construction methods during the last three centuries. Given the enormous geographical gap of rammed-earth structures between western Europe and China, contacts of the kind that would carry information about rammed earth between two such distant regions were probably minimal at best when rammed earth first appeared in Europe.

Our earliest literary evidence from Europe is the statement by Pliny the Elder, quoted at the beginning of the discussion of form-built rammed earth, which indicates that this method of construction was well-known in North Africa and Spain in the first century A.D. and possibly a century or so earlier. That the Spanish–North African tradition of rammed earth continued apparently in an unbroken sequence from Roman times to the present is supported by Ibn Khaldun, the distinguished Arab historian on the fourteenth and early fifteenth centuries A.D. Ibn Khaldun's familial roots had been in Spain for about 500 years before his parents moved to Tunis, where he was born in 1332. As an adult, he served in the government of Tunis and later in that of Spain, where he must have seen countless examples of rammed-earth construction, which he described:

> One builds walls with it [earth] by using two wooden boards, the measurements of which vary according to [local custom]. The average measurements are four cubits by two [approximately 170 × 85 cm]. They are set upon a foundation. The distance between them depends on the width of foundation the building considers appropriate. They are joined together with pieces of wood fastened with ropes and twine. Then, one puts earth mixed with quicklime into [this frame]. The earth and quicklime are pounded with special mixers … until everything is well mixed throughout. Earth is then added a second and third time, until the space between the two boards is filled. [Then] the earth

Figure 8.8 Mid-nineteenth century painting titled "Manual on Rammed Earth," showing rammed-earth tools and construction. It is from a record of crafts, prepared in Kashmir, India, 1850 (Lewcock, 1978:137).

and quicklime have combined and become one surface. Then, two other boards are set up in the same fashion, and [all] is treated in the same manner ... and then piece by piece, until the whole wall is set up and joined together as tightly as if it were of one piece. (Lewcock, 1978:137.)

Vitruvius Pollio, the dean of Roman architects, wrote ca. 27 B.C. the great treatise *On Architecture*, in which he commented,

Public statues do not allow a thickness of more than a foot and a half to be used for party walls.... Now brick walls of a foot and a half—not being two or three bricks thick—cannot sustain more than one story. Yet with this greatness of the city and the unlimited crowding of citizens, it is necessary to provide very numerous dwellings. Therefore since a level site could not receive such a multitude to dwell in the city, circumstances themselves have compelled the resort to raising the height of buildings. And so by means of stone pillars, walls of burnt brick, party walls of rubble, towers [apartment houses] have been raised, and these being joined together by frequent board floors produce upper stories with fine views over the city to the utmost advantage. Therefore walls are raised to a great height [limited to 21.3 m] through various stories.... Now, therefore, the reason is explained why, because of the limited space in the city, they do not allow walls to be of sun-dried bricks. (Vitruvius Pollio, 1931 [translation]: vol. 1, bk. 2, chap. 8, ¶ 17–18.)

This explanation of the prohibition against using mud brick possibly applied also to the construction of rammed-earth walls in Rome during and after the Augustan Period, although it is surprising that Vitruvius does not mention rammed earth at all. Outside the overcrowded capital, however, rammed earth seems to have been accepted in the Roman provinces. Hubert Guillaud noted, "These technologies ... were widely diffused by Roman colonists and progressively adapted by the Gauls. Several manifest clues of *pisé* construction have been discovered in the city of Lyon (Roman *Lugdunum*) and seem to correspond to the Gallo–Roman Age" (ca. 51 B.C.–A.D. 410; Guillaud, 1983:31). These suggestions in ancient literature and archaeology point to western Europe as a late, independent place of origin of form-built rammed earth.

Why there? The concept of using forms to contain the soil while being pounded into a compact mass may provide the answer. Unlike much of the Near East, the forests of Europe provided ample timber for making wooden forms. Such a bounty of good wood was essential, not only for withstanding the weight and vigorous beating of soil, but also for containing poured concrete during the drying process. Concrete was invented in Italy in the second century B.C., which may be about the time that form-built rammed earth appeared. Because both employ wooden forms and are roughly contemporary, it is tempting to see form-built rammed earth—like concrete—as a discovery of the Romans in the second century B.C.

It is, of course, possible that North Africa was the original home of rammed earth in the West, but apart from Pliny's statement and that of Ibn Khaldun quoted above, no corroborating archaeological evidence is known to us. Through Roman conquests in North Africa and Europe, Roman soldiers and colonists carried Roman political, economic, and cultural institutions, including technology and crafts, wherever they went. For example, many current farmsteads in Morocco—and we suspect elsewhere in North Africa as well—resemble Roman farmsteads in plan, design, and construction techniques.

Moreover, the subsequent distribution around the world of form-built rammed earth indicates a disseminating base in Europe rather than North Africa. Consider where form-built rammed earth has been significantly used during the last two centuries, apart from Europe, North America, South America, and Australia. These continents were heavily settled by European immigrants—English, French, German, Spanish, and Italian—during the seventeenth to nineteenth centuries at the same time that form-built rammed earth reached the zenith of its popularity in Europe. In the absence of substantive evidence to the contrary, we tentatively conclude that European form-built rammed earth was the source for its use in Australia and the Americas.

Geographical Distribution

It may come as a surprise to learn that rammed-earth construction has been used on five continents. Today it continues to be used in Australia, China, France, Germany, Morocco, South America, and is enjoying a modest revival in the USA. Rammed earth is still the preferred method of constructing with soil in Morocco, which is the country to visit if one wishes to see traditional methods of constructing walls for a variety of structures.

In France during the second half of the eighteenth century, *pisé* or rammed-earth construction blossomed as the rural architecture of choice, largely owing to both the buildings and writings of builder/architect François Cointeraux (1740–1830). The *pisé* methodology that he developed over thirty years was immediately influential in

Figure 8.9 Typical rammed-earth (*pisé*) house in Dauphiné, France (1997).

Europe and the USA, and it has continued to be the foundation of most rammed-earth technology.

Pisé construction in France extends from Brittany and the Paris region in the north to the Durance River valley east of Avignon in the south. However, the major zone for *pisé* is the region of Lyons between Mâcon on the north and Vienne on the south, and eastward between Bourg-en-Bresse and Grenoble, in the valleys of the Saône and Rhone Rivers and surrounding country (Guillaud, 1983:35–36). An astonishing array of different types of structures is found there, including farmhouses, barns and other out-buildings, churches, monasteries, chateaus, manor houses, residences (Figure 8.9), town halls, hotels, and shops. Notable buildings that we visited are the Manor of Peillet of the late eighteenth century (Figure 8.10), the town hall and school house ca. 1850 in Dolomieu (Figure 8.11), the church in Charancieu (Figure 8.12), the Hôtel de France in La Côte Saint-Andre, ca. 1850 (Figure 8.13), and the chateau of Montbrian in Messimy (Figure 8.14). The church in Charancieu and the chateau of Montbrian are probably of the nineteenth century.

Rammed-earth houses are scattered throughout Germany (Güntzel 1988). Our travels focused on the western region from Weilburg, northwest of Frankfurt am Main, to Idstein, Auerbach-Bensheim, and Tübingen, south of Stuttgart. Weilburg had 21 rammed-earth buildings (Figure 8.15), more than any other town in the region and the earliest of which was built in 1790. At least two of the houses were destroyed and replaced by new buildings of conventional construction in recent years. The most notable building was a six-story, rammed-earth apartment house with five

Figure 8.10 Manor of Peillet in Dolomieu, France, built of rammed earth (*pisé*) with ashlar quoins at the corners and stone enclosures of doors and windows, late eighteenth century (1997). The darker areas of the walls are rammed earth where plaster is missing.

Figure 8.11   Rammed-earth (*pisé*) town hall and school, ca. 1850, in Dolomieu, France (1997).

Figure 8.12   Rammed-earth (*pisé*) church with stone bell tower, Charancieu, France (1997).

Figure 8.13 Rammed-earth (*pisé*) Hotel de France, built ca. 1850, Côte de Saint-Andre, France (1997).

Figure 8.14 Rammed-earth (*pisé*) chateau of Montbrian, Messimy, France (1997). Small-stone construction appears in the corners, in the wall area to the right of the entrance, and in the stone enclosures around doors and windows. The building has been converted into an apartment house.

Figure 8.15 Bahnhofstrasse in Weilburg, Germany (1997). All buildings shown here were constructed of rammed earth between 1837 and 1842.

floors of dwellings, erected by the prolific German builder, Wilhelm Jakob Wimpf (Figure 8.16). Constructed in 1837 for his children (Schick, 1987), it was still in fine condition and fully occupied when we visited it in 1997. Of those 21 houses in Weilburg, only one was one story, eight were two stories, and 12 were three stories. All had high attics, many with dormer windows to accommodate storage, lines for laundry, or habitable space. At least eight of the buildings had a shop on the ground floor and apartments on the upper floors. The most attractive (to us) rammed-earth house in Weilburg, built ca. 1850, was 3½ stories plus a basement and finished in a pinkish-white color on the exterior (Figure 8.17).

At Idstein, several kilometers south of Weilburg, we saw a long farmhouse and barn of rammed earth built in 1812 with a driveway through it midway in its length (Figure 8.18). In Auerbach, adjacent to Bensheim, there is a magnificent park, the centerpiece of which is the Fürstenlager, the Prince's summer lodge, constructed in 1810–1811 (Figure 8.19). This house, probably the most beautiful rammed-earth building in Germany, features three floors with a hip roof and dormer windows. When we visited the house in late June 1997, it was being authentically and beautifully restored.

In South America, in the coastal area of Peru, the buildings of the city of Cajamarquilla in the Rimac Valley were all constructed of rammed earth and date as early as A.D. 700–1100 (Lumbreras, 1974 [translation]:178). Rammed-earth structures are still being built in the coastal zones where suitable stone is not found.

In northeastern China, form-built rammed earth is reported as early as the fourteenth century B.C. in the Shang city of Anyang. It continued to be employed in China

Figure 8.16 Six-story apartment house on Hainallee, Weilburg, Germany (1997). Built in 1837 by W. J. Wimpf, a major builder of rammed-earth structures, it is the tallest rammed-earth building in Europe. The right end of the upper three stories is covered with slate shingles to protect the wall from storms.

and was still in use during the 1930s (Creel, 1937:61, 70, 71). Creel cites a poem by a people contemporary with the Shang in which the construction method is described, leaving no doubt that rammed earth was used, as the following lines indicate:

> He called his superintendent of works;
>   He called his minister of instruction;
>   And charged them with the building of houses,
>   With the line they made everything straight;
>   They bound the frame tight, so that they should rise regularly.

Figure 8.17   Fine architectural details and a pinkish-white exterior make this house at 12 Limburgerstrasse, built ca. 1850, the most beautiful rammed-earth building in Weilburg (1997).

Crowds brought the earth in baskets;
They threw it with shouts into the frames;
They beat it with responsive blows;
They pared the walls repeatedly, and they sounded strong.
Five thousand cubits of them arose together.
So that the roll of the great drum did not overpower [the noise of the builders]. (Creel, 1937:64.)

Rammed-earth structures have also been used at least since the fifteenth century in the Himalayas of northern Nepal, in the valley of the Kali Gandaki region and the vicinity of upper Mustang. These structures include town walls, a palace, and two monumental temples: the three-story Jampa Lhakhang and the 49-pillared hall of Thubchen Lhakhang. In paintings by Robert Powell, these buildings are beautifully detailed in the rammed-earth construction, where even the support holes for the beams that carried the forms are represented and are enlivened by the brilliant colors with which many are decorated (Powell, 1999:38, 56).

Figure 8.18   Long, rammed-earth farmhouse and barn built 1812, Idstein, Germany (1997).

Figure 8.19   The rammed-earth Fürstenlager (Prince's summer house) built 1810–1811, Auer-bach-Bensheim, Germany (1997).

François Cointeraux's zeal for rammed earth is demonstrated by several letters and meetings with Thomas Jefferson, then Minister to France. The following letter regarding Cointeraux was sent by Jefferson (1990:634–635) to President George Washington, dated November 18, 1792:

> Th: Jefferson has the honor to inform the President that the papers from Monsr. Cointeraux of Paris contain some general ideas on his method of building houses of mud, he adds that he has a method of making incombustible roofs and cielings [sic], that his process for building is auxiliary to agriculture, that France owes him 66,000 livres, for

so much expended in experiments and models of his art, but that the city of Paris is unable to pay him 600. Livres decreed to him as a premium, that he is 51 years old has a family of seven persons, and asks of Congress the expences [sic]of their passage and a shop to work in.

Th: Jefferson saw M. Cointeraux at Paris, went often to examine some specimens of mudwalls which he erected there, and which appeared to be of the same kind generally built in the neighborhood of Lyons, which have stood perhaps for a century. Instead of moulding bricks, the whole wall is moulded at once, and suffered to dry in the sun, when it becomes like unburnt brick. This is the most serious view of his papers. He proceeds further to propose to build all our villages incombustible that the enemy may not be able to burn them, to fortify them all with his kind of walls impenetrable to their cannon, to erect a like wall across our whole frontier to keep of the Indians, observing it will cost us nothing but the building, &c, &c, &c.

The paper is not in the form of a petition, tho evidently intended for Congress, and making a proposition to them. It does not however merit a departure from the President's rule of not becoming the channel of petitions to that body, nor does it seem entitled to any particular answer.

Th: Jefferson

Among those impressed with Cointeraux's ideas and methodology was B. W. Johnson of New Brunswick, New Jersey, USA, who published *Rural Economy* in 1806. Cointeraux's and Johnson's books became the handbooks for enthusiasts in the mid-Atlantic states, among them Bushrod Washington, heir to the Mount Vernon estate. He built a number of rammed-earth structures at Mount Vernon, including two barns, two porter lodges measuring 12 × 14 ft square × 10 ft high (~3.7 × 4.3 × 3 m), an above-ground icehouse, and a greenhouse 50 × 18 × 10 ft (~15.25 × 5.5 × 3 m). The greenhouse burned in 1835, but the rammed-earth wall on one side remained standing until after 1869. Responding in 1814 to an inquiry from St. George Tucker of Williamsburg, Virginia, Bushrod Washington summarized some of the advantages of rammed-earth buildings:

> I wish to hear of these buildings becoming common in our state. They are so cheap to build that I make them sometimes in order to give employments to my carpenters and they must be comfortable for dwelling houses, being cool in summer and warm in winter. What houses can be better suited for the habitations of our Negroes?[4]

Elsewhere in Virginia, John Hartwell Cocke built five slave quarters and two garden walls of rammed earth at Bremo Plantation in Fluvanna County between 1815 and 1820. One of the houses has been restored. Each house was built of rammed earth with walls 20 in (0.5 m) thick, a gabled roof, central fireplace, and four rooms—two on the ground floor and two in the attic—each with a private entrance. These were slave quarters probably for household servants or skilled craftsmen (Miyagawa, 1985:21–23). Cocke may also have been responsible for the construction of the rammed-earth Manager's House and slave quarters on the Pea Hill Plantation in Brunswick County near Gasburg, ca. 1818, in view of marriage ties.

Among the early rammed-earth houses in the USA was "Hilltop House," built in 1773 in Maryland (in an area that is now in Washington, D.C.) by a German scientist and plantation owner. This two-story house, with walls 27 in (68.5 cm) thick, survived until after World War II (Figure 8.20). Some of the farm buildings constructed

Figure 8.20 "Hilltop House," Washington, D.C., built in 1773, destroyed ca. 1945–1960. (After A. B. Lee, 1937:6.)

by Thomas Jefferson at Monticello were also of rammed earth (Lee, 1937:6). The Church of the Holy Cross in Sumpter, South Carolina, was built of rammed earth in 1850–1852, and is still in service today. In Cabin John, a community near Bethesda, Maryland, H. B. Humphrey and his wife built a two-story Dutch colonial-style house of rammed earth with walls 18 in (46 cm) thick in 1922–1923. Known as "Oakmont," the house is an excellent example of the use of rammed earth in eastern American architecture. It is still inhabited, and it is now designated an historic site (Figure 8.21). During the Great Depression, the U.S. Farm Security Administration hired engineer Thomas Hibben to investigate rammed earth for a series of model homes. His research and enthusiasm ultimately led to the construction of 21 six-room, flat-roofed houses in Gardendale, Alabama, ca. 1936 (Lee, 1937:6). Post-World War II rammed-earth builders include Lydia and David Miller, who developed Rammed Earth International in Colorado, and David Easton, who founded Rammed Earth Works in Napa, California. In 1989, two rammed-earth construction companies operated in New Mexico (Smith and Austin, 1989:44–48) and several in Arizona. In 1995, we visited the late Stan Huston, founder of the Huston Construction Company, Edgewood, New Mexico. Stan was a leader in the mechanization of rammed-earth building methods with his imaginatively designed and efficient soil mixers and forms.

Form-Built Construction in Morocco and Elsewhere in the Old World

Form-built rammed earth is the most common type of mud construction in Morocco, with a tradition reaching back at least to the sixteenth and possibly to the twelfth century A.D. or even to Roman times. A variety of building types are still being erected. Rammed earth has been used for fortification walls defending cities and towns, good examples of which are the old city walls at Rabat and the nineteenth century wall surrounding Tiznit (see Appendix A, Map 4). It was also employed

Figure 8.21 "Oakmont," Cabin John, Montgomery County, Maryland. Built 1922–1923 and still occupied. (After A. B. Lee, 1937:7.)

for building the nineteenth century palaces and royal stables at Meknes. Private residences, farm houses, property walls, and shopping centers represent the variety of functions of form-built rammed-earth structures. A strip shopping center by the side of the road between Agadir and Goulimine displayed an unusual mixture of construction materials. All side, rear, and party walls of the shops were constructed of rammed earth, but the front arcade was reinforced concrete (Figure 8.22).

When we visited Morocco in September 1982 to investigate types of mud construction and building designs in northern Africa, we were baffled by the old Rabat city walls and structures mentioned above, never having seen form-built rammed earth before. We realized that we were dealing with walls of massive blocks of soil in layers with a series of spaced holes beneath each layer and cutting across the top of each block from one end of the wall to the other. The thick Rabat earthen fortification extended on both sides of a beautiful, indirect access gate of decorative fired brick (Figure 8.23). Last repaired in the eighteenth century, the rammed-earth walls still had a few areas of plaster intact, although the surfaces of most lower courses of blocks had lost their plaster (Figure 8.24). This fortification was constructed of layers about 92 cm high, with vertical joints at intervals of about 2 m and two spaced holes of 10–15 cm in diameter beneath the horizontal joints of each block in the layer (Figure 8.25). Were there not so many holes in every horizontal joint, one might interpret them as gun ports! Later we saw similar rows of holes in both abandoned and inhabited farmhouses between Agadir and Goulimine, but these were of smaller diameter, and some of them had been filled with stones (Figure 8.26). For more than a week we pondered the holes, hoping to see such walls being constructed. We saw none, and concluded that September was not the building season in Morocco.

Figure 8.22 New shopping center under construction, with rammed-earth walls and arcade of poured concrete, between Agadir and Goulimine, Morocco (1982).

Figure 8.23 Old rammed-earth city wall and fired-brick gateway, Rabat, Morocco (1982).

Although often dependent upon local guides and translators, archaeologists under-stand that most locals know very little about antiquities. They tend to memorize facts about the notable places visited by tourists but often know little else; in our experi-ence, many will bluff their way along by giving wrong answers to questions asked.

Figure 8.24 City wall with towers, Rabat, Morocco (1982). Plaster is partially preserved on the first tower in the area adjacent to the top of the wall.

Figure 8.25 Courses of rammed earthen blocks in the city wall, Rabat, Morocco, with transverse grooves cut in the top of the blocks (1982).

Figure 8.26 Ora Van Beek at wall of abandoned farm compound, with both empty and filled holes through the top of the blocks, near Goulimine, Morocco (1982).

Our guide in Rabat told us that the old city wall was built of a local stone, the name of which he did not know. Upon examining the wall, we could see potsherds, bits of china and glass, and fragments of animal bones embedded in the soil matrix. Like all archaeologists, we instantly recognized that it was built of soil probably taken from city dumps or possibly from habitation areas of the old city. (However, we had a very fine guide in Marrakesh. When he was unable to answer a question, he had the integrity to say that he did not know; he promised to try to find the answer in the evening and to share it with us the next morning, which he never failed to do.)

We found good fortune and clarity in Agadir. Taking a wrong turn while returning to our hotel, we became lost in a suburb of private residences. We suddenly came upon a rammed-earth project in progress: a form-built property wall that was replacing a hedge of cactus plants. Four workers were erecting the second course or layer of the wall. On the upper edge of the dry first course, one of the workers had cut two grooves, spaced about 1.2 m apart, across the wall with a pick (Figure 8.27). The grooves were sufficiently wide and deep to accommodate a galvanized pipe, about 4–5 cm in diameter, which was centered in each groove. The pipe was 1 m long, which was enough to extend at least 25 cm beyond each wall face, the thickness of the wall being 50 cm.

When we arrived, the builders were preparing to assemble three wooden forms on the wall. The side forms consisted of five boards laid side-by-side and held in place with a cleat (a board nailed at right angles on the outer surface and extending from top to bottom) on the end of the form that overlaps the previous block. Four or more cleats reinforced the end form. The two side forms measured about 1.7 m long × 1.1 m high, and the end forms were about 50 cm wide × 1.1 m high.[5]

Figure 8.27   Holes cut across rammed-earth blocks to carry pipes for supporting forms, Agadir, Morocco (1982).

The builders positioned the side forms upright on the two pipes so that the inner surface of each form slightly overlapped the edge of the upper face of the lower wall section and the sides of the previously laid block (Figure 8.28). On the other end, the builders placed the smaller end form on the top of the wall. Two vertical pipes were placed in pre-drilled holes in the horizontal pipes at each end. Thus secured at the base, they were tightly lashed together at the top and across the end form, rigidly supporting the forms to create a rectangular cavity or box that was open at the top (Figure 8.29) and ready for the soil to be added. The forms could be assembled by two persons, although three persons made assembly easier and more efficient.

When the forms were ready, a ladder was placed against one of the long sides, and the compactor—the person tamping the soil—climbed inside the box. A procession of two or three carriers, each with a basket of pile-dry soil on his head, climbed the ladder and dumped the contents of the basket into the rectangular box with the compactor's help (Figure 8.30). The compactor immediately pounded the soil from each basket as it was dumped until it became a homogeneous mass with the previously rammed soil.

The traditional tamping tool consists of a solid block of wood about 15–20 cm square and 20–25 cm high, with one flat end and a broomstick-like handle inserted into the other end reaching to about shoulder-height (see Figures 8.29, 8.31). The compactor used this tool to pound all soil dumped inside the form. Special care was taken to tamp the soil in the corners, along the sides of the forms, and against the end of the previous block to weld the blocks together for strength and for a continuous wall surface. This was a time-consuming activity, but thorough compacting is required to assure structural durability.

With many trips from the soil pile to the form, the level of the compacted soil inside the form gradually rose, and with it the compactor also. Eventually, the compactor stood on top of the block of compacted soil, level with the top edges of the

Figure 8.28 Assembling wooden forms for a rammed-earth wall, Agadir, Morocco (1982). The side forms are positioned on the vertical pipes.

forms (Figure 8.31). The ropes were then loosened and the forms removed, revealing a block of compacted soil standing alone. The two supporting pipes were then pulled out from below the base of the finished block, leaving two holes through the wall. The workmen next moved to the end of the new block and reassembled the forms for making the next block against the end of the one just finished.

In France, the ends of many blocks of *pisé* are constructed with oblique joints (Figure 8.32) instead of the universal vertical joints used elsewhere. The oblique joint is known as an *"equillade,"* which makes a strong, angled bond between the blocks in the same layer or course (Guillaud, 1983:38). Lime mortar is spread on the edge of an *equillade* before a new block is joined to it. A layer of lime mortar is also spread on the top edges of a finished block before the next course of blocks is made.

Most finished blocks we saw in Morocco measured about 76 cm high × 152 cm long, although blocks of various lengths—e.g., 114 cm and 76 cm—were also used to permit staggering the blocks so that they would end at doors and windows.

When the forms were removed the surface of a new rammed-earth block was riddled with pits of all shapes, ranging from as small as 2–3 cm to as large as 10–15 cm across, not unlike the pitted surface of poured concrete when its forms are removed. The new block was then finished on both the inner and outer surfaces by one or two workers while the next rammed-earth block was being constructed (Figure 8.33). Working with a basket of soil and a wooden mallet, the finisher put pinches of soil in each pit and then beat the soil with the mallet. Usually two or three fillings of

Figure 8.29   Assembled form ready for filling and tamping, Agadir, Morocco (1982). The end form is positioned just inside the two cleats on the side forms. The tamping tool stands on top of the previous block.

Figure 8.30   Pile-dry soil carried in baskets to the form, Agadir, Morocco (1982).

Figure 8.31 **The block is finished when the rammed soil in the form is level with the edges of the form and can be stood upon, Agadir, Morocco (1982).**

Figure 8.32 Oblique joints in a rammed-earth wall edged with lime plaster in Charancieu, France (1997). The holes are rectangular because squared wooden or metal members are used here instead of pipes to support the forms.

a pit were required to make the surface smooth, but both faces of the wall surface were beaten some more to bring the finest particles of the soil to the surface, which imparted a smooth, burnished-like sheen to the wall, similar to the way troweling concrete creates a smoothly finished surface (Figure 8.34).

When filling the pits, the finisher also filled the holes where the horizontal form supports had been, pounding the filled soil with the handle of the mallet from both sides. However, laws of physics dictated that the soil in the hole could not be rammed with as great a force as that applied during the vertical compacting in the form. Because these support holes are never as well compacted, the soil filling them eventually crumbles and falls out. This explains why we saw spaced rows of holes in the form-built rammed-earth walls.

In abandoned farm buildings not far north of Goulimine, stones of a diameter similar to that of the hole were sometimes pushed into the holes (see Figure 8.27). We were unable to determine if this was done when the wall was finished or later, after the earth filling the hole had dropped out. In Ecuador, both stones and soil are used to fill the holes left by the pipes or beams that supported the forms (Guillaud, 1983). In France, lime mortar is commonly used to fill these holes (see Figure 8.32).

Finishers also attempt to seal the very narrow joints between blocks by filling and beating. In this effort, they are only moderately successful. When the wall is finished with mud plaster the joints cannot be seen, but if the plaster is not well maintained, the vertical end joints of individual blocks usually appear in due course.

Figure 8.33 Workers filling surface pits of newly rammed, earthen block in Agadir, Morocco (1982). Filled holes for the support pipes can be seen in the top of the lower course at right beyond the workers.

When a wall is finished, it is covered with a coat of mud plaster. At that point the appearance of the wall is uniform; no holes or horizontal or vertical joints can be seen. Unless one knew how the wall was built, one might never guess because a well-built and well-plastered rammed-earth wall provides no clues except sometimes its thickness. Rammed-earth walls can also be finished with lime plaster, stucco, or whitewash and they can be painted with water-based or latex paint to add color and a protective coating.

Construction methods of rammed earth or *terre pisé* walls in Morocco have not changed over time. The rows of larger holes in the early city walls were made by large, round wooden beams that supported the forms. All of the walls were originally covered with mud plaster, which sometimes had a different coefficient of expansion from the *terre pisé* and showed shrinkage cracks, as in the city walls of Rabat and Tiznit. It may surprise some people that although essentially dry earth is used in the construction of these walls, they have remained standing and in good condition for several hundreds of years in a climate with an average annual rainfall of about 45 cm (16 in).

In multistory rammed-earth buildings, both exterior and interior walls are gradually thinned as they rise. This procedure reduces the weight of the upper walls, providing greater stability without reducing load-bearing capability. A six-story rammed-earth apartment house in Weilburg (see Figure 8.16), for example, has

Figure 8.34 Detail of rammed-earth block surface showing unfilled and filled areas, Agadir, Morocco (1982). After the pits are filled, the finisher continues to beat the surface with the club, which brings the finest soil particles to the surface and creates a smooth finish.

exterior walls that diminish in thickness as follows: first floor (above basement) 75 cm; second floor 70 cm; third floor 65 cm; fourth floor 55 cm; fifth floor 40 cm. The thickness of the interior walls also diminishes: first floor 65 cm; second floor also 65 cm; third floor 60 cm; fourth floor 50 cm; fifth floor 40 cm. Floor-to-ceiling heights mostly increase: first floor 2.05 m; second floor 2.3 m; third floor 2.95 m; fourth floor 2.9 m; fifth floor 2.7 m (Güntzel, 1988:271).

The astonishing similarities between form-built rammed earth and poured concrete are nowhere better illustrated than in the royal stable—or storage building—at Meknes, Morocco, which was built during the late seventeenth and early eighteenth centuries A.D. This enormous building has many aisles connected by arched doorways (Figures 8.35, 8.36). The walls and arches were all constructed with form-built rammed earth, which originally carried an upper terrace. Without mud plaster hiding details of their construction, the intrados, or inner surfaces, of the arches display impressions of the variously sized boards used in the forms. These impressions show how the boards overlapped and were skewed, leaving the inner surface of the arch broken into irregular, angular segments (Figure 8.37). Forms for the arches must have been supported either by heavy beams firmly based on the floor or by piles of loose stone or bricks filling the doorway to the underside of the forms themselves. The forms had to be especially strong and supported by something very solid below them to carry the weight of the soil and the compactor, as well as to withstand the considerable force of tamping. In the arch shown in Figure 8.37, long holes through the underside of the arched wall contain small-diameter pipes that may have been

Figure 8.35   Arched corridors crossing the aisles in the rammed-earth royal stable, ca. late seventeenth to eighteenth centuries, A.D., at Meknes, Morocco (1982).

Figure 8.36   One of the aisles in the royal stable at Meknes, Morocco (1982).

part of the forms that were used and reused to make identical arches. The roughly surfaced intrados of the arches originally must have been finished with one or more coats of mud plaster to smooth the surface.

Forms can be made of any material—wood, steel, other metals—that is sufficiently strong and rigid to withstand the jarring effect of tamping and the weight of the soil itself without bending or breaking. In western China, for example, small logs, about 5.0–6.5 cm in diameter are laid horizontally one on top of the other

Figure 8.37 Detail of an arch in Meknes, Morocco, showing the flat impressions of the framing boards (1982).

and held in place by poles driven into the ground. This stack serves as the outer side of a form, with the inner side constructed of boards. This type of form yields a rammed-earth wall with a corrugated outer surface and a smooth inner surface. In the Hadhramaut valley of Yemen, corrugated outer surfaces sometimes serve to key mud plaster. Without mud plaster, the long horizontal ridges might serve as drip moldings for a time, but they would eventually erode from wind and rain unless protected by a roof overhang.

Spring and autumn are traditionally the major seasons for building with rammed earth in France (and probably elsewhere as well). In both France and Germany, carpenters—rather than masons—are the craftspersons who build rammed-earth buildings, undoubtedly because of the need for good wooden forms. And once the walls are finished, carpenters also could frame the massive and complex gabled roofs. However, in some buildings in France, such as the Manor de Peillet in Dolomieu and the Chateau of Montbrian in Messimy, stone foundations and stone quoin construction in corners and around doors and windows would have required stone masons.

Form-Built Construction in North America and Australia

In the southwestern USA, rammed earth is enjoying a renaissance that will surely flourish in the future. Construction methods are similar to those of Morocco, except that experimentation has provided better materials, more diverse types of forms, and mechanical tools, which produce stronger and more beautiful walls that are easier and faster to build with fewer workers.

Throughout its history in the USA, wooden forms have been used for building rammed-earth walls, and there are as many variations as there are builders; for different types of forms, see references in Wolfskill et al. (1979:120). Wooden forms are commonly made of 5 cm thick boards for the sides and are typically 15 cm, 20 cm, or 25.5 cm wide laid horizontally, with 5×10 cm wooden cleats placed vertically and spaced every 61–91.5 cm apart. Or instead of 5 cm thick boards for the sides, 2.5 cm thick plywood is used with 5×10 cm vertical reinforcing boards spaced about every 46 cm. Bolts 1.3 cm in diameter or larger, threaded on one end and longer than the thickness of the wall, join the two side forms tightly through the cleats above the base and below the top of the form. Several 5×10 cm boards are cut to the thickness of the wall to serve as spacers along the top edge of the form to make the walls of uniform thickness.

End forms, constructed with boards of the same thickness, are made to fit inside the form and also serve to keep the side forms properly spaced. A vertical strip or a board with beveled sides extending from top to bottom is often attached in the center on the inner surface of the end form. This projecting board creates a groove on the end of the block; when the next block is rammed, the groove is filled with rammed earth, thus producing a projection that joins the blocks to form a tongue-and-groove, locking joint. When each vertical joint is reinforced in this manner, the structural unity and strength of the wall is increased. If wooden forms are oiled, they can be released from the soil more cleanly and easily, and they will not warp as quickly. Wooden forms can also be lined with metal sheeting or pressed board (Masonite) to make smoother wall faces.

Construction begins with an L-shaped form that makes a one-piece corner with no joint. This addresses the weakest points of earthen buildings, because the corners are where earthen walls are prone to split if poorly made. The corner form must be plumb to achieve verticality in the adjacent walls. When finished, the straight form on one side of the corner is then filled and rammed, continuing in the same direction, form after form. Blocks are staggered, as in laying brick, so that no joint falls over an earlier joint. Reinforcement against earthquakes and strong winds is required in many jurisdictions. It primarily consists of a reinforced concrete or wooden bond or tie beam on top of the rammed-earth walls, and reinforcement within the walls themselves, discussed in more detail in Chapter 14.

Wooden forms for windows are set in the main form and the soil is rammed around them. Wherever doors and windows are to be located, wooden blocks are also placed on the inner surface of the end forms at spaced vertical intervals as the earth is rammed. Door and window jambs are nailed or screwed to these wooden blocks during installation. Similarly, boards can be placed on the inner surface of the form at predetermined locations for attaching cabinets, shelving, paintings, etc. Electrical conduits are put in place before ramming the soil, and they are usually run through the top of the wall and bond beam for interconnections and to the service panel. The locations of outlet and switch boxes are represented by wooden blocks placed in the form before ramming and are replaced by metal boxes when forms are removed. Similarly, plumbing is run under the slab, under the ground floor in a house with a basement, or through the attic of a house with a raised roof. Pipes are placed in the forms before ramming, with wooden blocks marking the positions where they enter the kitchen, bath, laundry room, outside faucets, and other outlets.

An unusual wooden form commonly used for rammed earth in Australia features a steel roller at the bottom of one end and a second roller at the top of the other end, which permit two workers to move the form to its next position after a block has been finished. By using the rollers, the form can be moved in about eight minutes, in contrast to the dismantling and reassembly of the type of form described above, which often requires three workers and 30 minutes to an hour of labor (Miller and Miller, 1982:62ff.m appendix D).

In recent years Australian builders have developed a form made of interlocking steel frames lined with plywood panels. These forms are 2.44 m long by 0.61 m high and locked together by means of two rods on each end, one at the bottom and one at the top. The frames are attached to tall end boards that are externally braced to keep the boards plumb. When one row of horizontal forms has been tamped, another series of forms is set on top of them and tamped, and so on in 0.61 m increments. Such walls can reach a height of 5.5 m. The forms are left in place until the entire wall is finished (Easton, 1996:108).

In California, David Easton designed wooden forms without frames, instead using 4 × 8 ft (1.22 × 2.44 m) or 4 × 10 ft (1.22 × 3.05 m) HDO (high-density overlay) plywood. These sides are rigidly held in place on the outside by pipe clamps spaced 6–10 ft (1.83–3.05 m) apart horizontally and 15–24 in (3861 cm) apart vertically. Each pair of horizontal clamps supports a 2 × 10 in (5.08 × 25.4 cm) or 2 × 12 in (5.08 × 30.48 cm) horizontal plank—or waler—to reinforce and to align the plywood forms on the outside. They also serve as scaffolding and ladders for the form.

More importantly, the system obviates the need for the many cross-tying bolts that hold the forms together on other forming systems. Without the bolts, the interior of the form is open and unencumbered inside, making the tampers' work easier and more efficient (Easton, 1996:113). The Australian and Easton systems both accommodate continuous as well as panel wall construction.

Manual tamping tools usually feature steel or wooden blocks with a steel plate on the head, measuring 3–4 in (7.5–10 cm) square. Circular and rectangular shapes are also used. Each is equipped with a steel or wooden handle and weighs about 15–25 lb (6.8–11.4 kg) depending on size, with about 18 lb (8.2 kg) optimum. Enough soil to make a 4–6 in (10–15 cm) layer is poured into the form, raked level, and tamped with careful attention to the edges and corners. Tamping the layer continues until the dull thud of the tamper gives way to a sharp ring. Tests for soft spots are performed using a screwdriver or a knife blade, and if soft spots are found, that area is tamped again until the soil is hard (Wolfskill et al., 1979:120). Layer after layer of soil is added and tamped until the block is complete. Thick walls, which are created in more widely spaced forms, are easier to ram than thin walls, because there is more working space for the person doing the compacting.

Forms are disassembled by removing the bolts and end board. They are then set up against the end of the finished block to make a new block. The first tier of blocks is commonly laid before a second tier is begun, or one can leave the first tier of forms in place, erect a second tier on top, and construct the second tier immediately. Care must be exercised in removing the forms so that corners and edges of the blocks are not damaged. Rammed-earth walls require months or even years to cure fully, but this does not delay construction. Freshly built walls are sufficiently strong to install windows and doors, to carry the roof, to finish interior details, and even to be occupied.

In the southwestern USA, technological innovations in the form of new mechanical equipment are greatly reducing labor costs as well as increasing the quality of rammed-earth walls and the efficiency and speed of building them. We were introduced to some of these developments during a 1995 visit to the Huston Construction Company of Edgewood, New Mexico. The late Stan Huston, founder and builder, gave us a tour of two beautiful, rammed-earth homes, one of which was his residence (Figure 8.38). He also took us to inspect a house under construction and explained his procedures and equipment to us in detail.

Soils in the Edgewood, New Mexico, area produce grayish walls, which are not popular with clients. Huston therefore searched for other soils, particularly those with an attractive brownish color at crusher sites where the soil was screened through ⅜ in (1 cm) mesh. He noted that the finer the screened soil used, the more attractive the rammed-earth wall would be. Although he originally used soil alone, he began using stabilized soil, i.e., a mixture consisting of soil, 5% cement, and very little water, to make the mix slightly damp. Because of the difficulty in achieving a consistent mixture, Huston designed and built a machine to mix precise amounts of soil and cement in a ratio of 20:1 with a trickle of water. It featured a large hopper for soil, a small hopper for dry cement, and a series of nozzles to spray a little water to slightly dampen the mix. Mixing took place in a pug mill, a cylindrical chamber in which a series of angled paddles on a horizontal shaft slowly rotate. When thoroughly mixed, the mixture was ejected from one end and is ready to pour

Figure 8.38   Rammed-earth Huston house, Edgewood, New Mexico (1995).

into forms. A "Bobcat" (a small front-end loader) dumps the soil into the hopper of the mixer, transports the mixture, and pours it into the forms. It also mixes soil if needed and sets the forms in place.

Huston experimented with a number of form systems before settling on his present type, which consists of steel frames and smooth plywood panels that can be joined vertically and horizontally, without the use of metal straps or ties (Figures 8.39, 8.40). The latter are commonly used to hold the forms together, and they are left in the wall when the forms are removed. Forms range in size from 4 × 4 ft (1.22 × 1.22 m) to 4 × 10 ft (1.22 × 3.05 m), with the latter weighing about 600 lb (272.2 kg) each. The plywood panels could be changed quickly when they became damaged through use. Soil was dumped into a form to a depth of 6–8 in (15–20 cm) and was then compacted to a depth of 3–5 in (7.6–12.7 cm) using a pneumatic tamper powered by compressed air (Figure 8.41). Huston's exterior walls were commonly either 2 or 3 ft (61 or 91.5 cm thick (Figure 8.42), and interior walls were 16 in (40.6 cm) thick.

To achieve the rounded corners, he would cut a plastic pipe, about 8 in (20 cm) in diameter, longitudinally into quarters, and then place a quarter-piece vertically in the corner of the form, which, when the soil was rammed, created a convex surface on the outside corner (Figure 8.43). All corners, doorways, and window openings were shaped in this manner. Rounded corners are not only very attractive, in softening the lines of a building, but also resist chipping better than 90° corners.

In addition to inserting a plastic pipe for rounding the outer corner of a window, Huston would set a vertical board obliquely on each side of the planned window opening so that it would be wider on the inside than on the outside. These boards taper the opening at an angle of about 22°, increasing the amount of natural light that enters the room (Figure 8.44).

As part of the rammed-earth wall system, Huston also constructed the bond or tie beam of wood or reinforced concrete that capped the top of all earthen walls in New Mexico, as required by the state's building code (see Chapters 11, 14). The full curing time for a 2 ft (61 cm) thick wall is 1½–2 years, although the building would be ready for interior finishing and occupancy as soon as it was roofed. In the USA, builders of rammed-earth walls usually subcontract the roofing, installation of windows, doors, and other features to builders of conventional houses.

To build walls with the Huston equipment required only two persons. Huston and another worker could build a wall that was 20–30 ft (6.10–9.14 m) long, 8 ft

Figure 8.39   Forms designed by the late Stan Huston and finished rammed-earth walls, Edgewood, New Mexico (1995).

(2.44 m) high and 2 ft (0.61 m) thick in a day! He recounted how he and an associate had built a 3500 ft² (325.28 m²) house in three weeks for a client in Texas. Contrast this pace of construction with that of the Humphrey house at Cabin John near Bethesda, Maryland, where manual labor alone was used in 1922–1923. In a full day, three men built a wall section 6 ft (1.83 m) long × 6 ft (1.83 m) high and 18 in (46 cm) thick.

ADVANTAGES AND DISADVANTAGES

Although most rammed-earth structures built without forms are unsuited to present demands, form-built rammed earth offers many advantages. Only pile damp soil and sand are required; other materials, such as cement, are optional. If the soil is too dry, minimal quantities of water may be provided for dampening. The use of suitable soil from the site also saves funds because none need be purchased or transported to the site. Even if stabilized soil is used, the 5% of cement required is a relatively modest expense. The immediate pouring of soil into forms also eliminates the very time-consuming tasks of molding and drying mud bricks, transporting and stacking them at the site before construction begins, preparing the mud mortar, and laying the bricks.

Moreover, the prevailing practice of building thick rammed-earth walls in which soil is well compressed or compacted makes for extraordinarily strong, long-lasting walls. McHenry (1984) noted that rammed-earth walls have greater compressive strength than southwestern adobe brick walls. Rammed-earth samples ranged from 462 to 850 psi and the brick samples ranged from 260 to 439 psi (McHenry, 1984:174). Such walls are less fragile during curing, are more capable of supporting roof structures immediately, and withstand earthquakes better. In the Old World, their longevity is attested in the semiarid zones of Morocco and the temperate climates of Europe.

Figure 8.40 Inside the plywood-faced form. Note reinforcing rods, which are set in the concrete slab and eventually will be set in the concrete bond beam capping the wall for structural strength (1995).

Figure 8.41   Stan Huston with his pneumatic tamper powered by compressed air. Note electrical outlet boxes built into the wall behind him (1995).

In the southeastern United States, the rammed-earth church built during 1850–1852 at Sumpter, South Carolina, and still in use today, survived the Charleston earthquake of 1886, a three-day hurricane in 1895, and a cyclone in 1903 (Lee, 1937:5).

Rammed earth is even suitable for building load-bearing, free-standing decorative columns and for square or rectangular piers, either free-standing or engaged (i.e., built as part of the wall).

Rammed earth can produce buildings of extraordinary beauty, as some of the images in this chapter show. From the point of view of design, the thickness of rammed-earth walls creates exciting opportunities for charming interiors such as wide interior window seats that are sufficiently roomy for sitting and reading; large, deep niches in walls to accommodate built-in bookcases and display cabinets; and

Figure 8.42 Thickness of a solid rammed-earth wall, Huston house, Edgewood, New Mexico (1995).

Figure 8.43   Rounded corners, formed by inserting a longitudinally cut section of plastic pipe in the corners of the forms where outer corners of walls, doors, and windows are planned (1995).

stepped, recessed panels in interior and/or exterior walls to break the monotony of long, flat wall surfaces.

The massive walls of rammed-earth buildings are also psychologically comforting and assuring. David Easton observed in the introduction to his fine book, *The Rammed Earth House*:

> There is a certain magic to living in buildings with thick earth walls. It's hard to describe, but easy to notice. Just take a step inside on some warm summer day and you'll feel it immediately. It's cool, of course—everyone knows adobe houses are 'warm in winter and cool in summer'—but there's something else, too, a little harder to put your finger on. It's quiet, feels somehow incredibly solid and sturdy, very different from other houses, timeless even. I feel secure in here … it's almost as if I'm in some ancient building with centuries of its own secret stories to tell.… (Easton, 1996:xi).

If a rammed-earth building should fail or erode for whatever reason, and if no cement was used in the original mix for the wall, then the soil from which it was made can be dissolved in a pond of water, dried, and reused in making new walls, as in other types of earthen buildings. Nothing could be more environmentally friendly.

As all methods of construction, rammed earth is not without its disadvantages. In spite of savings on materials and transport, in the Old World it is labor intensive, requiring form installers, compactors, finishers, and a horde of basket carriers. If labor is expensive, a rammed-earth building would be far more costly than a layered-mud structure and about the same cost as a comparable mud-brick building. Yet in Germany, rammed earth seems to have been more prevalent in times when the economy was depressed, only to be forgotten during periods of prosperity. Modern mechanization as seen in New Mexico can reduce the number of workers to as few as two, which is less than commonly needed for mud brick construction.

Figure 8.44   Interior window openings at the Huston house, Edgewood, New Mexico, are angled to be wider on the inner face of the wall to distribute more daylight in the room (1995).

Rammed earth is more limiting than mud brick in the ability to produce specialized design features. Although arches can be built of rammed earth, as at Meknes, Morocco, could one erect a vault or dome of rammed earth? It would be much more difficult given the need for adequate centering for support during construction. However, the construction of domes and vaults on rammed-earth walls would be easier—as well as exceptionally attractive—if constructed of mud brick. Such beautiful roof structures have a very long history in the Near East (see Chapter 12).

As a basic, straight-forward method of construction, rammed earth is at its best in massive structures such as manufacturing plants, houses, shops, and theaters. For these and similar buildings it is worthy of consideration, and it is our favorite type of earthen wall construction.

NOTES

1. The term 'revetment' as used herein and by other archaeologists refers to the entire structure of the embankment barricade or fortification wall (as given in *Merriam-Webster's Collegiate Dictionary,* 11th edition, definition 2; and *The American Heritage College Dictionary,* third edition, definition 2), not solely the facing to sustain the embankment.

2. An exception was Sir Flinders Petrie (GVB's predecessor at Tell Jemmeh). Although he rarely defined all bricks in a wall, he cleaned enough sample areas to provide us with a series of measurements of bricks from different buildings of each strata. Such series of measurements are very useful for reconstructing technological (and potentially cultural) change through successive historical periods.

3. We are indebted to Hugo Houben of CRATerre for bringing this painting and article to GVB's attention.

4. Letter from Bushrod Washington to St. George Tucker, 13 August 1814. Photocopy of document in the Collection of the Mount Vernon Ladies Association, Mount Vernon, Virginia.

5. Similar forms are used in Ecuador, where they range in length from 1.5 to 1.8 m, in height from 0.9 to 1.2 m, and in thickness from 40 to 50 cm (de Sutter, 1984:16).

Chapter 9

Mud Brick

The use of mud brick in construction is found almost everywhere in the world because it is made of readily available materials, relatively easy to make, baked by the sun, and, therefore, inexpensive. It also can be used for all sorts of structures: houses of all shapes and sizes, from one-room dwellings to multistory buildings reaching as high as eight stories; shops, shopping centers, and cinemas; industrial structures such as pottery kilns, furnaces, manufacturing plants, shopping malls, garages, and service stations; religious buildings such as temples, churches, mosques, monasteries, and their associated support buildings; tombs and memorial monuments; privacy or property walls; and fortresses and city fortifications. Mud brick is modular (i.e., it can be produced in a variety of shapes and sizes, by hand or using forms), so it is an extraordinarily flexible medium that adapts to almost any conceivable architectural design.

Hand-formed shapes are described in both the Introduction and Chapter 5. Techniques for making, drying, and stacking mud bricks made in standardized forms are also detailed in Chapter 5. This chapter focuses on the construction and use of walls made with form-molded bricks.

BRIEF HISTORY

Mud brick has been the favored material for building mud walls throughout human history, and it remains the dominant type of earthen construction today. If we include in this category all types of mud modules (e.g., balls and elongated plano-convex brick shaped like Italian bread—see Figure 5.18), then mud brick first appeared about 11,000 years ago. By about 5000 years ago, brick as we know it—i.e., made in standard-sized molds with sharp edges and squared corners—came into use in the Mediterranean region and the Near East, and its use has continued to the present. It was from mold-made mud brick that the concept and form of fired brick was derived.

Mud brick was the overwhelming favorite form of mud construction in antiquity in the Near East. Fired brick predominated in the Indus Valley culture, although sun-dried mud brick was employed in constructing bases or foundation platforms for the massive fired-brick buildings. All buildings in Egypt, including the royal palaces, were built of mud brick; only the houses of the gods and human souls—the temples, tombs, and mortuary temples—were built of stone because they were believed to shelter life for eternity. There, and in Syria, Mesopotamia, and Persia, mud brick also provided palaces, temples, shops, industrial installations, storage facilities, residential housing, and defenses for towns and cities.

Most of these nations were centered in plains or on valley floors where soil was abundant, trees were relatively few or non-existent, and building stone was often far away. However, archaeologists often have found evidence of mud-brick construction in Israel, Jordan, Turkey, Greece, and Italy, usually associated with rubble foundations and with industrial structures such as furnaces and kilns. Those researchers often assumed superstructures of mud brick in their reconstructions. Where the terrain is flat and local sources of good building stone do not exist (e.g., Tell Jemmeh, Ashdod, and Ashkelon in coastal Israel; Jericho and Tell Rehov in the Jordan Valley), all or most buildings are of mud brick.

In some nations, mud-brick construction continues to be used for most buildings; in others it is chiefly limited to residential housing; and in still others, the urge to become modern is overpowering the traditional building crafts and it is rapidly disappearing. Foremost among countries where mud architecture persists is Yemen with its traditional tall (or "skyscraper") houses, which are now witnessing considerable growth in the affluent suburbs of the Hadhramaut, with new and attractive three- to five-story houses. Representative of the countries where considerable residential housing is of mud brick are Syria, with its "beehive" houses and its pillow-like roofs, and the southwestern USA. Typical of the countries where the urge for modernism prevails are Egypt and India, where concrete block and fired brick are replacing traditional mud construction.

CONSTRUCTION WITH FORM-MOLDED BRICK

Brick Shapes and Sizes

In antiquity, brick shapes seem to have been determined primarily by ethnic or geographic considerations, and once a choice was made, it became a tradition that persisted through time. For example, rectangular brick prevailed in ancient Egypt and Palestine, whereas square brick dominated in northern Syria, Mesopotamia, and Iran. This does not mean that square bricks were never used in the southern regions, or that rectangular bricks were never employed in the northern regions, because both shapes fulfilled specific construction needs. Through time, rectangular and square bricks (whether made by hand or by machine) provided more than 90% of all modular mud construction for floors, walls, domes, arches, and vaults.

Brick shapes were also determined by structural design, which sometimes required their modification and the creation of specialized forms. An example is the use of rectangular bricks in the floor of the ovoid, Philistine pottery kiln of the twelfth century B.C. at Tell Jemmeh. These bricks were carried by four radial arches spaced about 70 cm on center, and they spanned from one arch to another. Such bricks had to be enormous to span between the arches, and they probably belong in

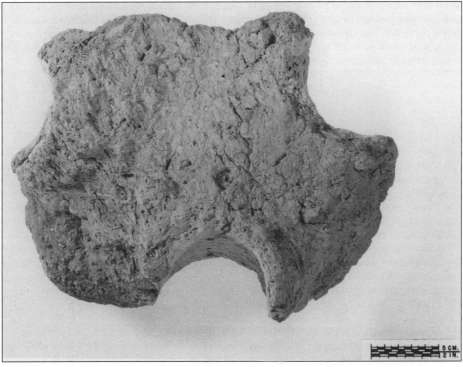

Figure 9.1   Fragment of a floor brick from the twelfth century B.C. Philistine kiln at Tell Jemmeh, Israel. Holes in the brick, three of which are partially preserved here, permitted heat to reach the baking chamber directly above the fire box.

the size range of rectangular brick common in the Late Bronze II period (thirteenth century B.C.). To permit the direct transmission of heat from the fire box below the floor to the baking chamber above it, holes measuring 10–12 cm in diameter and probably numbering 9 or 10 per brick were cut through each brick after it had set up but before it was dry. The largest fragment of one of these floor bricks that survived represents about 30% of a whole brick and preserves portions of three holes (Figure 9.1). In the Hadhramaut in 1991, we observed square bricks being modified by a mason, who trimmed opposite sides of each brick to give it a keystone shape for closing a radial vault (see Figures 11.51, 11.52).

Special bricks were also created for many other different applications. A triangle-shaped brick was molded to function as a springer to force or establish the arc of a radial arch in the Philistine pottery kiln at Tell Jemmeh (see Figure 11.31). The invention of rib vaulting in Iran was based on the creation of long, relatively thin, curved bricks resembling the shape of a mammalian rib, which were surprisingly strong and stable (see Figures 11.45, 11.46). Perhaps the most amazing of all was the custom-made series of segment bricks used to form the structurally complex, engaged columns of the nineteenth century B.C. Tell al-Rimah temple (see Figure 12.30). Finally, bricks for radial (see Figure 11.5) and pitched-brick (see Figures 11.6–11.8) vaults were shaped to resemble bundles of reeds in tombs of the Fourth Dynasty (ca. twenty-fifth to twenty-fourth centuries B.C.) in Egypt.

Table 9.1 Size and weight of mud bricks, by shape, from various regions and periods, roughly ordered from smallest to largest by country group. Dimensions are given as length (L) × width (W) × depth (D); except for mass in metric, all measurements and calculations are rounded to the nearest whole number. Weights cited for modern bricks in Egypt and New Mexico, USA, are actual weights; all other weights of individual bricks are approximate.[a]

| | Size (L × W × D) : volume : mass or weight | |
Locality and period	cm : cm³ : kg	in : in³ : lb
Rectangular Brick		
Egypt		
Modern	23 × 11 × 8 : 2,024 : 4.09	9 × 4 × 3 : 124 : 09
Ramses	33 × 20 × 5 : 3,300 : 6.63	13 × 8 × 2 : 201 : 15
Elephantine	33 × 20 × 8 : 5,280 : 10.61	13 × 8 × 3 : 322 : 23
Akhenaten	36 × 16 × 10 : 5,760 : 11.58	14 × 6 × 4 : 351 : 25
Iraq, Tepe Gawra	36 × 18 × 10 : 6,480 : 13.03	14 × 7 × 4 : 395 : 29
Yemen		
Marib, Modern	38 × 24 × 8 : 7,296 : 14.67	15 × 9 × 3 : 445 : 32
Hadhramaut, Modern	46 × 33 × 5 : 7,590 : 15.26	18 × 13 × 2 : 463 : 34
Hadhramaut, Modern	55 × 38 × 5 : 10,450 : 21.01	22 × 15 × 2 : 638 : 46
Turkey		
Carchemish, Early Hittite	48 × 20 × 10 : 9,600 : 19.30	19 × 8 × 4 : 586 : 42
Carchemish, Middle Hittite	43 × 20 × 13 : 11,180 : 22.47	17 × 8 × 5 : 682 : 49
Israel		
Arad, Early Bronze	56 × 28 × 10 : 15,680 : 31.52	22 × 11 × 4 : 957 : 69
Tell Jemmeh, Middle Bronze	53 × 35 × 13 : 24,115 : 48.48	21 × 14 × 5 : 1,471 : 107
Tell Jemmeh, Late Bronze	69 × 41 × 13 : 36,777 : 73.93	27 × 16 × 5 : 2,244 : 163
Tell Jemmeh, Philistine	56 × 36 × 13 : 26,208 : 52.68	22 × 14 × 5 : 1,599 : 116
Tell Jemmeh, tenth century B.C.	54 × 37 × 12 : 23,976 : 48.08	21 × 15 × 5 : 1,463 : 106
Tell Jemmeh, ninth century B.C.	53 × 35 × 12 : 22,260 : 44.45	21 × 14 × 5 : 1,358 : 98
Tell Jemmeh, eighth century B.C.	52 × 38 × 11 : 21,736 : 43.55	20 × 15 × 4 : 1,326 : 96
Tell Jemmeh, seventh century B.C.	48 × 24 × 12 : 13,824 : 27.79	19 × 9 × 5 : 843 : 61
Syria, Modern	46 × 25 × 8 : 9,200 : 18.49	18 × 10 × 3 : 561 : 41
USA, New Mexico, Modern	36 × 25 × 10 : 9,000 : 18.09	14 × 10 × 4 : 549 : 40
Square Brick		
Iran		
Modern	20 × 20 × 5 : 2,000 : 4.02	8 × 8 × 2 : 122 : 09
Persepolis	33 × 33 × 13 : 14,157 : 28.46	13 × 13 × 5 : 864 : 63
Yemen		
Marib, Modern	24 × 24 × 8 : 4,608 : 9.26	9 × 9 × 3 : 281 : 20
Hadhramaut, Modern	36 × 34 × 8 : 9,792 : 19.68	14 × 13 × 3 : 597 : 43
Israel, Jemmeh, Hellenistic	33 × 33 × 11 : 11,979 : 24.08	13 × 13 × 4 : 731 : 53
Iraq		
Tell al-Rimah	33 × 33 × 10 : 10,890 : 21.89	13 × 13 × 4 : 664 : 48
Nimrud, Ancient	44 × 44 × 10 : 19,360 : 38.92	17 × 17 × 4 : 1,181 : 86

[a] Weight estimates calculated by multiplying average density value of Tell Jemmeh bricks (1.16 oz/in³) by volume.

Like shape, brick size varied considerably, depending on intended structural use and prevailing traditions in specific regions at given times in history. The data in Table 9.1 illustrate the considerable size variability of ancient and contemporary mud brick. Because we could obtain actual weights only for modern bricks in Egypt and the USA, we estimated the weights for all other bricks in the table based on the average density of Tell Jemmeh bricks (1.16 oz/in³). Despite the weight estimations, these data probably encompass the major size ranges of most of the world's mud brick, although still larger bricks have been used, as in ancient Iran where curving, ribbed-vault mud bricks are about 1.2 m long! Apart from special applications requiring bricks of extreme size or custom shape, in some regions it was common practice to use mud bricks of different sizes in the same structure, as exemplified in the tall houses of the Hadhramaut. Vitruvius described ancient Greek brick sizes thus:

> Now there are three kinds of bricks: one which in Greek is called *Lydion*, that is the one which we use [in Rome], a foot and a half long, a foot wide [thus rectangular]. Greek buildings are constructed with the other two. Of these, one is called *pentadoron*, the other *tetradoron*. Now the Greeks call the palm *doron*.... Thus the brick that is of five palms every way is called pentadoron; of four palms, tetradoron [both are obviously square bricks]. Public buildings are erected with the former; private buildings with the latter. (Vitruvius Pollio, 1931 [translation]: vol. 1, bk. 2, chap. 3, ¶ 3.)

What is the optimum size of a mud brick? It depends on the application, on the number and physical strength of masons and helpers, and to a degree on the tastes of the homeowner and builder. There are advantages and disadvantages to all sizes.

Fewer large bricks are required to construct a building than small bricks. A wall can be built faster with large bricks if there are a sufficient number of workers to carry them to the mason and to mix and carry mud mortar. All of the larger Tell Jemmeh bricks from the Middle Bronze period onward into the Iron II period (seventeenth to seventh centuries B.C.) were laid as headers (i.e., the long axis of the brick is perpendicular to the line of the wall), so the length of the brick defined the width of the wall.

In a Philistine period (eleventh century B.C.) wall where bricks measured 56 × 36 × 13 cm, only 10 bricks—plus a small allowance for narrow rising joints—would be required to lay a course in a wall 3.66 m long and 56 cm thick. If this wall was 2.44 m high, it would probably have 16 courses of 10 bricks each, or 160 bricks. By contrast, if the wall were built of bricks of the same size as those from Tepe Gawra, Iraq, measuring 36 × 18 × 10 cm, it would be necessary to lay them in English bond—with headers along one side of the course and stretchers on the other side, alternating positions in successive courses—to make the wall about 56 cm thick. This would require 580 bricks, more than three and a half times as many as the number of larger Philistine bricks to build the same wall.

There is, however, a major disadvantage in using such large bricks: their weight, which is far more than one would think. Each Philistine brick from Tell Jemmeh used in the above example weighed about 52.7 kg; the largest brick in Table 9.1 is a Late Bronze Age brick from Tell Jemmeh, which measured 69 × 41 × 13 cm and weighed 73.93 kg! Most of us could not carry one of these bricks from the brick stack to the mason even once, much less 30 to 40 of them during a working day. In the Near East, however, bearers are a permanent institution in the older cities, where narrow, stepped streets make vehicular transport impossible. An experienced bearer can carry from one to four such bricks at a time all day long with an occasional rest period. It was difficult for two researchers with normal strength to carry a single brick of the Philistine period on a piece of ¾ in (~2 cm) plywood at Tell

Jemmeh. Two helpers would be needed to lift such a brick carefully and place it on the mortar bed. Moreover, if a single large brick is dropped, it represents a much greater loss than if a small brick is accidentally broken. Although its pieces can be returned to the mud pit and made into a new brick, the drying takes a longer time than for a smaller brick. If a stockpile of large bricks is not maintained, breakage would certainly slow construction.

Small bricks are also more adaptable to special architectural configurations. The largest bricks we saw being used in building vaulted roofs in the Hadhramaut were about 55 × 38 × 5 cm and weighed 21.01 kg. Their thinness and added straw temper resulted in their reduced weight. Hod carriers regularly carried four to six such bricks on their backs or heads, generally supporting them with one hand. These bricks were easily trimmed to special shapes with a machete; we watched a mason trim a rectangular brick to a keystone or voussoir shape with two quick slashes, one along each edge, while another workman held the brick upright. The major disadvantages of these bricks are that (1) they are somewhat poorly formed, thinning toward the edges and lacking sharply defined corners, and (2) they are quite fragile, much more so than the bricks at Tell Jemmeh. Even the smallest Tell Jemmeh bricks, such as those used in the Assyrian vaulted building, are perfectly formed with sharp edges and corners, proving that smallness does not necessarily mean poor quality. Small bricks are also more adaptable to different bonding patterns, coursing designs, and relief decorations. Serpentine walls, recessed niches in several stages or levels, and fancy engaged columns are applications that require smaller brick.

Brick shapes and sizes depend in a large part on changing building traditions through time. Consider the size variation at Tell Jemmeh throughout 1500 years of continuous occupation (Figure 9.2). In the Middle Bronze IIC period (ca. 1700–1550 B.C.), rectangular bricks commonly measured about 53 × 35 × 13 cm

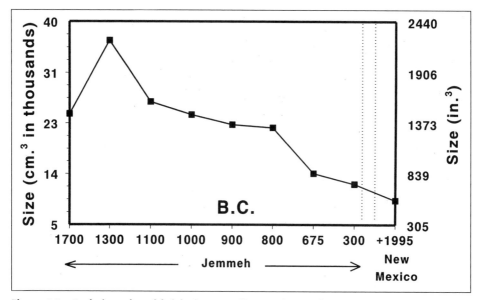

Figure 9.2 Evolution of mud brick sizes at Tell Jemmeh, Israel, through time. Contemporary mud brick from the southwestern USA is included for comparison.

or 24,115 cm³. During the Late Bronze period (ca. 1550–1200 B.C.), the standard rectangular brick notably increased in size to about 69 × 41 × 13 cm or 36,777 cm³, a volume almost 50% larger than Middle Bronze bricks. Brick sizes peaked during the Late Bronze period, and gradually became smaller in the Iron Age (1200–600 B.C.). In the eleventh century B.C. (Philistine period), bricks measured 56 × 36 × 13 cm or 26,208 cm³. From the tenth through the eighth centuries B.C., brick sizes stabilized in a near plateau, visible in Figure 9.2, changing only from 23,976 cm³ to 21,736 cm³. In the seventh century B.C., brick sizes abruptly decreased by about one-third; the rectangular bricks in the walls of the vaulted building measured 48 × 24 × 12 cm or 13,824 cm³. Finally, in the late Persian and early Hellenistic periods (ca. 450–200 B.C.), square bricks averaging 33 × 33 × 11 cm or 11,979 cm³ were employed, although half-bricks (i.e., rectangular in shape) were also used when required for bonding.

How do we explain these variations? Do they represent different building traditions of different ethnic or national groups? During the Middle and Late Bronze periods, when sizes of rectangular brick were increasing, the region of modern Israel was dominated by Canaanites, who are thought to have been the indigenous Semites in the southern Levant. At the beginning of the Iron Age, Israelites entered the area after the exodus from Egypt, and Philistines infiltrated or invaded the region from the Mediterranean Sea. The Israelites occupied the hilly areas, and the Philistines settled on the coastal plain, which includes the Tell Jemmeh area. At Jemmeh, the size of rectangular brick began to decrease from that of the Late Bronze or Canaanite period. The trend continued into the seventh century B.C. when the Philistine town was conquered by the Assyrians from northern Mesopotamia, who built a forward military base on the site, using their own building plans, construction techniques, and brick sizes.[1] In the late Persian period and continuing into early Hellenistic times, square brick replaced rectangular brick at Jemmeh, perhaps under the influence of either the Persians, who presumably continued their preference for square brick, or of local builders who developed a new bonding pattern. Many more suites of measured bricks from sites in this and other regions and of different time periods are needed to determine whether changing traditions reflect the preferences of different groups of peoples who controlled the site, as suggested here by our analysis.

Alternately, we may be documenting a functional evolution in the sizing of mold-made mud bricks. From this point of view, the process began with relatively small bricks (56 × 28 × 10 cm or 15,680 cm³), as were produced at Arad, Israel, in the third millennium B.C. Dimensions gradually increased until the fourteenth to thirteenth centuries B.C., then slowly decreased, eventually stabilizing in smaller bricks. Perhaps the largest bricks of the Late Bronze period became so unwieldy that masons decided to make smaller bricks that would be faster drying, more easily and safely transportable and maneuverable, and that, if accidentally broken, would represent a smaller immediate loss than larger ones. Once down-sizing had begun, the process seems to have accelerated until bricks achieved an optimum range of small sizes. The Assyrian bricks of the seventh century B.C. at Tell Jemmeh, weighing 28.09 kg—just over one-third the weight of a Late Bronze brick—may represent a major step in the trend toward significantly smaller size that culminated in the twentieth-century bricks that weigh from 3.30 kg to a maximum of about 16.11 kg. This evolution may have occurred everywhere because small bricks appear to be almost universally used today. Of these two potential explanations, it is possible that both are working simultaneously, although in the long run, the latter seems more likely.

Wall Thickness

Without benefit of a structural framework of wood or steel, walls of multistory houses carry an extremely heavy load of mud brick, as well as anchoring the successive floors. To prevent a wall from toppling, its thickness (and thus weight) is reduced as it goes higher. The outer face of the wall slopes inward, and the inner face of the wall remains vertical; the wall then becomes thinner as it rises floor by floor, and the load of each additional story is correspondingly reduced. Table 9.2 describes a specific example of this: a seven-story house in Shibam, Hadhramaut, in which the thickness of the outer wall gradually decreased at each level from the base to the top. To achieve the different wall thicknesses, five sizes of mud brick were used in different combinations and bonding patterns. The largest brick size[2] was 50.5 × 32.75 × 5 cm, one of the intermediate sizes was 42.5 × 30.5 × 5 cm, and the smallest was 25.5 × 23 × 5 cm.

Wall thickness may depend also on prevailing building traditions, as well as on the function and design of the building. Walls of one-brick thickness may suffice if the bricks are sufficiently large. The walls of a palace or house of a noble from the Late Bronze II occupation at Tell Jemmeh (fourteenth to thirteenth centuries B.C.) were built of rectangular bricks 69 cm long that were laid as headers, making the wall 69 cm thick without mud plaster. This wall thickness provided both structural stability and an extraordinarily comfortable interior temperature. These walls have nearly the same thickness as that of the Assyrian vaulted building (75 cm), which was built with smaller bricks laid in English bond. As another example, the late Persian–early Hellenistic walls built of two side-by-side square bricks bordered on both sides by a row of rectangular bricks have a total thickness of about 123 cm; these probably served as compound or house walls.

Walls are sometimes built thicker than stability and function demand. To our knowledge, the thickest mud-brick walls in the world were built in ancient Egypt. The mud-brick fortification wall of Tanis, a city in the Delta, erected by the Nineteenth Dynasty ruler Ramses II (the reigning Pharaoh during the Israelite exodus led by Moses), was 24.4 m thick, and 13.73 m high (Clarke and Engelbach, 1930:211). Building such massive walls, of course, creates problems: (1) how to dry or cure the interior to prevent cracking and shrinking, and (2) how to prevent them from settling after the annual Nile floods, when the ground sometimes softened. Several devices were employed to speed drying. A series of air passages, two bricks high and half a brick wide, were built extending through the entire thickness of the wall. In the great wall at Karnak, these passages occur every 13 courses (i.e., about every 1.83 m vertically) and are spaced 84 cm apart within the same course (Clarke and Engelbach, 1930:210). Another method involved laying woven mats of reeds, grass, or rushes between the brick courses at intervals of three to seven courses; examples of this are known from the Old Kingdom to recent times (Figure 9.3). Also, wooden grids were occasionally placed in the wall about every five courses, presumably to hasten the drying process (Clarke and Engelbach, 1930:210).

Table 9.2 **Reduction in wall thickness in a seven-story building in Shibam, Yemen, as documented by Lewcock (1986:98).**

| | Wall thickness at base of level | |
Level	*(cm)*	*(in)*[a]
Ground	86	34
Second	69	27
Third	57	22.5
Fourth	46	18
Fifth	34.5	13.5
Sixth	28.5	11
Seventh	23	9

[a] Data converted into English units are rounded to the nearest whole or half inch.

Figure 9.3 **Reed mats laid between courses of mud brick, third millennium B.C., Saqqara, Egypt (1977).**

The explanation for such apparent excesses in constructing very thick walls is perhaps to be sought in perceived needs for the greater security provided by increased mass, in aesthetic considerations that unfortunately escape us, or possibly in a more subtle psychological aspect of size relationships. With regard to the latter, it seems that the size of buildings and rooms and the thickness of their walls often relate to the size of the settlement—whether it is a village, town, or city—and to its perceived importance. The walls of major buildings from the Middle Bronze II period at Lachish (Ussishkin, 1983:105–106), an important city in Israel, were about 150 cm thick. This was more than twice as thick as contemporary walls of comparable structures in the smaller town at Jemmeh (53 cm thick) but for no apparent structural reason.

Both were sufficiently thick to have carried at least two or three stories, and to judge from the tall houses of Shibam, the very thick walls of the Lachish palace suggest that the structure may have conservatively reached five or six stories.

Bonding Patterns

"Bonding" refers to the arrangement of bricks relative to one another in successive courses, so that vertical joints between bricks in a given course never fall directly above the joints in the course below. Straight joints are those that correspond in successive courses. The most common, and also the most extreme, straight joints are those between two sections of walling that abut yet are structurally independent of each other. Typical examples are two walls that come together at a corner, or a later addition whose bricks are not bonded—or interlocked—into the earlier wall. Because of the weakness of straight joints, walls often settle, crack, and separate with time, ultimately resulting in their collapse. The purpose of bonding, therefore, is to lock all bricks together, thereby making the structure as solid and strong as possible.

There are many different bonding patterns, and those most commonly used in mud-brick construction are briefly discussed below. Bricks are optimally bonded by centering them over the rising joints of the bricks in the course below; however, depending on the bricks and bonding pattern, perfect centering is not always possible in practice, and a minimum overlap of one-quarter of the length of a brick is permissible.

Rectangular bricks lend themselves to a variety of bonding patterns, and any pattern that can be used with fired brick can also be used with mud brick. Two commonly used masonry terms that apply to rectangular brick are (1) header, meaning the short edge of a brick, and (2) stretcher, the long edge of a brick. Square bricks were often cut in half, and the resulting rectangular half-bricks made possible many types of bonding arrangements. Vitruvius (1931 [translation]: vol. 1, bk. 2, chap. 3, ¶ 3) noted this practice among the Greeks.

When all bricks in the courses of a wall are laid as stretchers, with half-bricks used at corners and ends of walls to create an even surface, the bonding pattern is called running bond (Figure 9.4). Square bricks are almost always laid in this pattern, and of course it is also possible to lay rectangular bricks in running bond.

Another popular bonding pattern is English bond (Figure 9.5), in which the positions of headers and stretchers alternate in successive courses of a wall. Thus a course consisting of a row of stretchers is laid along the outer face of the wall, and a companion row of headers along the inner face. In the next course, the positions reverse with the row of headers set along the outer face and the row of stretchers along the inner face. This type of bonding appears in all walls of the seventh century B.C. vaulted building at Tell Jemmeh, and it was widely popular in antiquity as it is today. A good example can be seen in the walls of the most prominent house (II 201, from ca. first century B.C. to A.D. first century) at Soknopaiou Nesos in the Fayum region of Egypt (Boak, 1935:5).

A variation on this pattern was sometimes employed in the walls of the vaulted mud-brick storerooms of the Ramesseum, the mortuary temple of Ramses II (1296–1224 B.C.) at Luxor, Egypt (Figure 9.6). Headers were set on edge or turned on their long axis 90°. To distinguish this type of bonding, we refer to it as Egyptian bond. In

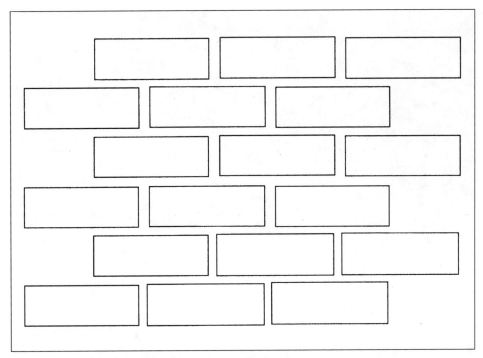

Figure 9.4 Brick-laying pattern known as running bond.

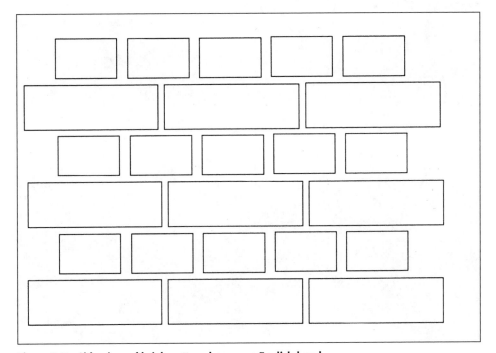

Figure 9.5 Side view of brick pattern known as English bond.

Figure 9.6   Egyptian bond, Ramesseum storeroom, Luxor, Egypt (1977).

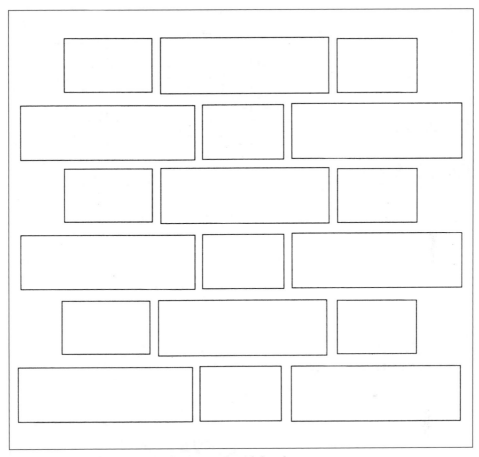

Figure 9.7   **Brick-laying pattern known as Flemish bond.**

Egypt, rectangular bricks were frequently laid as headers in the core of thicker walls, and the wall faces were constructed with alternate courses of headers and stretchers, i.e., English bond (Clarke and Engelbach, 1930:211).

We have seen no instance where Flemish bond or Dutch bond (also sometimes referred to as English cross bond) has been employed in mud-brick construction, but there is no reason why it cannot be used. In a given course in Flemish bond, one or two stretchers are placed side-by-side followed by a header, then comes another single or pair of stretchers again followed by a header. In the next course the header is centered over the one or two stretchers of the previous course, and the next stretcher or pair of stretchers is centered over the header of the previous course (Figure 9.7). Flemish bond is also characterized by a stretcher course whose rising joints are separated from an identical stretcher course by three intervening courses consisting of two header courses and one stretcher course; rising joints never correspond with the lower and the upper stretcher courses. Flemish bond is easier to use if the brick module is half as wide as it is long, including half the width of the mortar joint. Bricks of this size can easily be made in appropriately sized molds. If

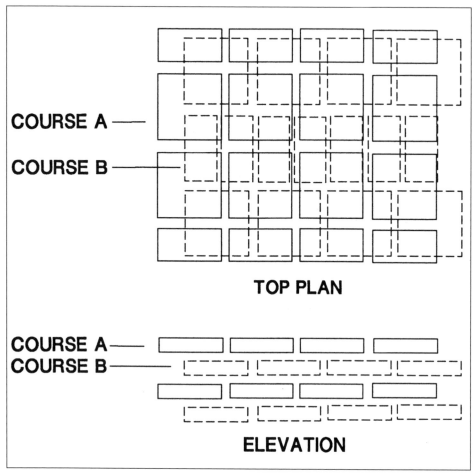

Figure 9.8 Square and rectangular bond used at Tell Jemmeh, Israel, fifth to fourth centuries B.C.

spacing does not exactly suit the plan, a half or quarter of a brick is inserted where needed to restore the spacing arrangement.

A bonding pattern common at Tell Jemmeh during the Persian period (fifth to fourth centuries B.C.) (Figure 9.8), which also occurs at Ashkelon, Israel, consists of two rows (occasionally one row) of square bricks laid side-by-side and bordered on the outer edges of the wall by a row of rectangular bricks (half the width of the square brick) laid as stretchers. In the next course, three rows of square bricks are laid side-by-side, or two rows of square bricks form the borders with one or two rows of rectangular bricks centered between the borders. This pattern and its several variations are seen where square brick predominates, such as in Iran, Iraq, and Syria. For strong bonding and for terminal wall areas such as doors and windows, rectangular bricks about half the width of square bricks are used. Apart from residential walls, this style of bonding was also used in the springers of a large, radially arched, mud-brick wall supporting the roof of the circular mud-brick granary of the third

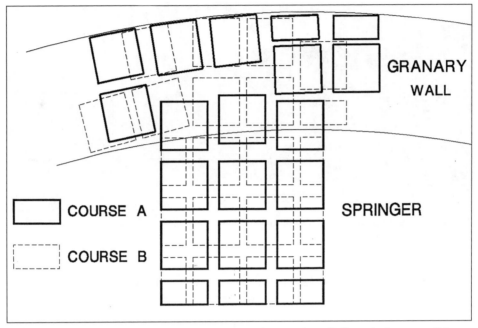

Figure 9.9 Square and rectangular bond in the springers of a radially arched cross-wall in a granary at Tell Jemmeh, Israel, late fourth to third centuries B.C.

century B.C. at Tell Jemmeh (Figure 9.9). An earlier example occurs in a major building—probably a palace—at Hammam et-Turkman in northern Syria, dating in the Late Bronze I period (ca. 1500 B.C.) (Van Hafften, 1988:129–139, pl. 52).

Curiously, the ancient Egyptians sometimes deliberately built mud-brick walls with courses that were not horizontal; if this seems to defy conventional wisdom, these walls were sufficiently sound to survive for as much as 3500 years. During the New Kingdom (fifteenth to twelfth centuries B.C.), walls were occasionally erected in relatively short sections, one section with concave courses (high at the ends and low in the middle) and the next section with either convex courses (low at the ends and high in the middle) or horizontal courses, alternating throughout the length of the wall. Each section was offset from its adjacent sections by up to 60 cm, and the coursing of each section might or might not correspond to those of abutting sections (Figure 9.10). This type of construction continued into the Roman and Coptic (Christian) periods. Apart from possible aesthetic relief afforded by the curving courses, which might be seen as a welcome contrast to the horizontal and vertical lines of the Egyptian landscape, no satisfactory functional explanation for this type of wall design has been suggested.

Another unusual wall design is the serpentine or undulating wall that curves in and out through its length. In ancient Egypt, half-bricks were used exclusively to achieve smoother curving surfaces (Clarke and Engelbach, 1930:213). Egyptian walls of this type functioned as property or privacy walls. Apparently some were also used as retaining walls to hold back the sand when tombs were being dug. Because these walls were only half a brick thick, each small undulation was made with

Figure 9.10 Wall built with of alternating sections of concave and convex mud-brick courses in Egypt (1977).

about six of these small bricks. More massive, wavy walls as much as 1.06 m thick, were also built, an example being the wall enclosing the compound of the Middle Kingdom pyramid at Mazghuneh.

Archaeologically, there is still much to learn about ancient mud-brick construction. Specifically, surprisingly little data exist on the dimensions of the mud bricks and the variety of bonding patterns that would establish specific characteristics of brick-making and construction details of each occupation period in a site. Such information would be extremely useful in intra-regional and cross-cultural studies.

Structural Decoration of Walls

One of the most attractive features of earthen buildings is the possibility of decorating walls with recessed niches, panels, and engaged columns, all constructed with mud bricks. These decorative devices are, of course, planned before construction is begun. When completed and finished with plaster for a smooth surface, they must have aroused awe and admiration for their beauty in their time, and they still do today.

Many Egyptian and Mesopotamian structures are decorated with recessed panels and niches. An example of each illustrates their complexity. During the First and Second Dynasties in Egypt (ca. 3100–2700 B.C.), palace facades (Emery, 1961: fig. 103) and exterior walls of *mastabas* (bench-like tomb structures) in Egypt were built with alternating offset and inset sections. Typically each section was decorated with two-stage recessed niches in groups of three. Offset, or projecting, areas featured three identical recessed niches. Insets, or recessed areas, were set deeper in the wall by lengthening (or deepening) the outer, first stage of the end recesses; and centered in its rear surface was a two-stage niche larger than in the others (Figure 9.11; Emery, 1961: fig. 80).

At Persepolis in Iran, the enclosure wall around the Treasury complex built by king Darius ca. 520 B.C., which averaged about 2.5 m thick and probably reached a height of about 11 m, was constructed with recessed niches. They featured a four-stage recess, the first or outermost of which was deeper than the others, and each recessed

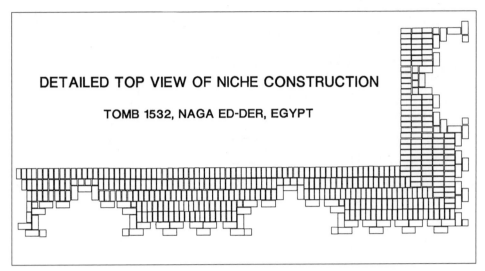

DETAILED TOP VIEW OF NICHE CONSTRUCTION

TOMB 1532, NAGA ED-DER, EGYPT

Figure 9.11 Schematic sketch of the two-stage recessed walls of a *mastaba* at Naga-ed-der, Egypt. (Drawing based on Emery, 1961: fig. 80.)

niche was about 2.5 m wide and spaced about 2.5 m apart. Centered on the wall between each niche was a narrow, vertical slot (Schmidt, 1939:17, fig. 11).

Among the best and most complex examples of recessed decoration in mud brick are Temple III and the ziggurat of the nineteenth century B.C. at Tell al-Rimah in northern Iraq. The exposed outer walls of the ziggurat, the outer walls of the Temple, and the inner surface of the walls surrounding its interior courtyard had a combined length of about 246 m, and featured recessed panels that were either 9 or 12.5 m high as reconstructed. The designs are characterized by two features: recessed sections of the wall surface, and a prolific use of engaged half-columns designed with different motifs, the construction of which is examined in Chapter 12.

An entrance is centered in each wall on three sides of the Temple (Figure 9.12), and the corner of each jamb is cut back in three steps. On both sides of the entrances, walls diminish in thickness in three deep stages from about 4 m to 2.5 m to 1.9 m. Each of the identical north and south facades has these features: (1) on its 4-m section, a panel of seven half-columns bordered by a niche on each side with a larger column; (2) on the 2.5 m section, another panel of seven half-columns bordered by a two-step narrow recess on each side; and (3) on the 1.9 m section, still another seven half-columns panel, but without niches or recesses.

Both walls of the east facade are identically decorated. The first section (nearest the entrance) features a four-step niche filled with a large engaged, composite column consisting of two large, opposed spiral columns and two smaller diamond-pattern palm columns (Figure 9.13). This niche is bordered by two large, scale-pattern palm columns in a one-step recess. The second section has a three-step recess niche with a scale-pattern palm column bordered on each side by a diamond-pattern palm column of equal diameter. The third section features a one-step niche with a diamond-pattern palm flanked by opposed spiral columns. This temple surely illustrates the possibilities of mud architecture far beyond anything we would

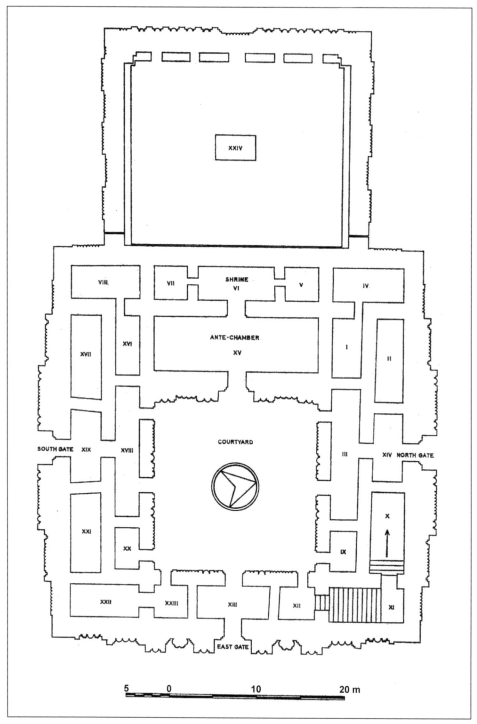

Figure 9.12   Plan of Tell al-Rimah temple, Iraq, ca. 1900 B.C. (After Oates, 1967: pl. 30; used with permission).

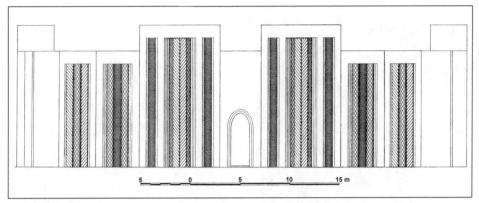

Figure 9.13   Reconstruction of the east façade of temple at Tell al-Rimah, with enlarged detail of the outer face of the wall. (After Oates, 1967: pl. 36; used with permission)

conceivably design today. For all of its complexity, we can hardly imagine how beautiful it must have been when it was newly covered with plaster, and when sunlight danced from surface to surface (Oates, 1967:84, pls. 30, 32a,b, 33a,b, 36).

Near Dhardhar, Pakistan, we saw the remains of a once-magnificent mud-brick octagonal tower that served as a nobleman's tomb. The inner surface of the wall was divided into seven panels, each of which is decorated with a four-stage recessed panel surmounted by a corbelled arch and two wall niches (Figure 9.14). The structure is believed to date from the twelfth century A.D. Its former grandeur could be seen in the domed roof (see Figure 11.1). Unfortunately the river bank on which the tower stood was rapidly eroding in 1990, placing this monument in grave peril; it may no longer exist today.

In Seiyun, Hadhramaut, we saw an attractive, mud-brick property wall enclosing a newly constructed house. Built in sections between reinforcing piers painted dark blue with diamond-shaped medallions, each section featured a simple, centered framed panel with concave corners painted in light blue (Figure 9.15).

Mud Mortar

Mud mortar is universally employed in laying mud brick, with few exceptions. It is a mixture composed of the same materials used in making mud brick. Although it is better to screen all soil used in both bricks and mortar, "dirty" bricks with inclusions of small artifacts and stones were sometimes used (Figure 9.16). In mud mortar, however, only very small flat artifacts occasionally have been left in the plaster mix, because mortar joints are at most only 1.5 cm thick after a brick is laid. If the same screened soil and proportions of ingredients in the mixture are used throughout, bricks and mortar will "fit" perfectly, having the same expansion and contraction ratios. Cement should never be added to the mixture for use with plain, unstabilized mud bricks, because they are not compatible. If stabilized bricks are employed, mortar and plaster should contain similar proportions of the same stabilizing agent for compatibility. Lime can be mixed with sand and water to produce a strong, compatible mortar for use with mud brick, but it is expensive and not essential.

Figure 9.14   Interior recessed panels of mud-brick tower near Dhardhar, Pakistan (1990).

Figure 9.15 Newly constructed mud-brick property wall with a small, light blue vertical panel centered in each section, surrounding a new house in Seiyun, Hadhramaut, Yemen (1991).

Figure 9.16 An example of "dirty" mud mortar containing a potsherd still adhering to a rectangular mud brick, from Tell Jemmeh, Israel.

In the Near East, mortar is mixed by treading soil, temper, and water in a shallow pit until it is a homogeneous mass (Figure 9.17), similar to mixing mud for bricks. For convenience and efficiency, the pit should be located as near the building site as possible. Mortar must be sufficiently liquid to allow some of its water to be absorbed by the dry surfaces of the brick, but not so wet that much of the mortar is squeezed out of the joint by the weight of the brick. Water is sprinkled on the bedding surface before the mortar is spread to reduce the amount absorbed from the mortar mix. The sequence of dampening the previous course of brick before spreading mortar continues in the laying of all brick. It is not necessary to "butter" the end of each brick with mortar as is done in laying fired brick, because some of the mud mortar will fall in the rising joints, and whatever gaps are left in the vertical joints provide excellent keys for securing plaster on the wall surface later.

Occasionally mud brick is laid without using mud mortar. A notable instance occurred at Tell Jemmeh in the walls of the seventh century B.C. buildings erected during the Assyrian occupation. These walls were constructed with a silty sand in place of mortar in both the bedding and rising joints. The sand had to have been laid wet because dry sand would have fallen out immediately during and after the laying of bricks. While the sand mortar was still damp, both wall surfaces were quickly covered with a thick layer of mud plaster to prevent the sand from flowing out. The reasons for this type of construction are discussed in Chapter 14.

Laying Mud Brick

In nearly all masonry construction, whether concrete, stone, brick, or mud, great care is taken to keep courses and layers horizontal and the wall surfaces vertical

Figure 9.17 Mortar mixing pit used for construction of mud-brick vaulting, Hauta, Hadhramaut, Yemen (1991).

and at right angles. Walls built with irregular or uneven courses and walls out of plumb are structurally unsound in varying degrees. The horizontal coursing can be achieved with a tightly drawn, leveled string attached to tall stakes, which are driven into the ground adjacent to the ends of the walls and reach the projected height of the wall; the string can be moved upward as each course is laid. McHenry (1985) recommended a "story pole" as a convenient method of assuring the string is at the right height each time it is moved up to define the level of another course. Before beginning to lay brick, one can mark the leveled stakes at the end of the walls to show exactly where each mortar course and each brick course should be, allowing ¾ in (1.9 cm) for each mortar joint, plus the measured thickness of the brick course. Thus, if the bricks to be used are 4 in (10 cm) thick, one should measure up from the top of a slab or stem ¾ in (1.9 cm) for the first mortar bed, then 4¾ in (12.07 cm) for the second brick course and mortar joint, repeating the 4¾ in (12.07 cm) spacing to the top of the wall. The string is moved up each interval and becomes a guideline for each mortar bed and brick course (McHenry, 1985:55–56). In addition, the courses should be checked frequently with a 4 ft (1.22 m) long spirit level. In ancient times string was similarly used; it was leveled by measuring from a level surface, sighting by an experienced mason, or by any of several simple devices. Verticality was checked by suspending a weighted string, using a stone or other heavy object that would serve as a plumb bob. As today, a square was used to maintain right angles, wooden examples of which have been found in Egypt. These common techniques have been used by professional masons throughout time, and they are absolutely necessary for the occasional "do-it-yourself" builder.

Unless the brick stacking area is adjacent to the building site, bricks should be carried and restacked as near to the site as possible. Laying mud brick is similar to laying fired brick. Mud walls begin on a level foundation or base, whether soil, sand, stone, concrete, or fired brick. This is a primary principle in building mud-brick walls. If they are not level, or are badly uneven at any point, corrections can be made by cutting off the high places or increasing the thickness of mud mortar in the low areas.

An excellent example of such a correction was discovered when architect David Sheehan drew the bricks of the circular granary of the late fourth to third century B.C. at Tell Jemmeh. In one area between the third and fourth courses above the floor, we noted a course of varying thickness—either a sloping course of added bricks or a very thick bedding joint of mortar—about 3.1 m long. The site architect and GVB spent two hours taking turns lightly troweling and brushing this area and studying the results from six to eight feet away. If bricks had been especially made or trimmed to level the coursing at this point, we should have found rising joints between bricks. Finding no such joints, we realized that a homogeneous bed of mud mortar had been spread to provide a level base for the fourth course.

When building walls, every wall is defined by its ends. Each wall end is called a "lead," or a major dividing point, and all leads are treated identically. A doorway is also a lead, so that one wall extends from the corner lead to a door jamb lead. Rough door frames should be placed according to plan, plumbed, and held rigidly in place with braces. The first course of the mud-brick wall should be raised on a stem no less than 15 cm above ground level (to protect it from run-off water) and should extend from lead to lead. The leads at the corners and door frames should be built up with two or three step-like courses in advance by laying four bricks of the second course, three bricks of the third course, and two bricks of the fourth course, after which each successive course is then filled in, and the procedure is continued. No more than four courses should be laid in a day to permit the mortar to dry; otherwise the weight of the additional courses will squeeze out too much of the mud mortar of the lower courses. Rough window frames are set in at the desired height, plumbed, and braced, and they are also leads, further dividing areas of the wall into smaller lengths.

Because solid earthen construction does not take nails or screws well, as the wall advances, wooden blocks (or nailers) are inserted into the brick coursing at the end adjacent to the opening and between every four courses to which door and window frames will be attached by screws or nails. Ideally the blocks should be of the same thickness as the mud brick, and they can be substituted for one or two bricks in the course. Whenever cabinets will be attached to kitchen and bathroom walls, or fixtures such as wall-mounted bookcases, shelving, framed pictures, and hangings are planned, boards for attaching them should be built into the brick wall during construction. One or more 2.5 cm boards, which actually measure ~2 cm thick, 10 cm wide, and of the desired length can replace the 2 cm thick mortar.

Because of the weight of the mud wall above openings, heavy lintel beams are required. These beams must be somewhat longer than the opening so that they will be well anchored in the wall. The beams, which may be of wood, reinforced concrete, or stone, should be squared to provide good support for the heavy brick courses above them. If the building is to have a flat roof, the roofing beams are laid before the top of the wall is reached, and then followed by several courses of brick between the beams to bring the wall above and over the top of the beams. In the southwestern USA, building codes now require mud-brick walls to be capped by a bond or tie beam of wood or reinforced concrete to stabilize and to strengthen them against cracking and settling due to erosion, construction deficiencies, and damage by natural disasters. Traditionally in both the Old World and the New World, these problems have been countered with massive buttresses. The bond beam is discussed in greater detail in connection with earthquakes in Chapter 14.

Nogging

Nogging means the use of bricks to fill spaces in frame buildings, as for example, laying bricks between studs of the outer walls of a frame house. In heavy timber-framed houses in England, wattle-and-daub infilling was sometimes replaced with nogging; the bricks were laid horizontally, on edge, or diagonally, and often finished with whitewash (Brunskill, 1970). A different type of nogging occurs in old Damascus, Syria, where the walls are built with spaced wooden studs, and every interstice between studs is filled with mud bricks laid with minimal mud mortar in a herringbone-like stack from floor to ceiling (Figure 9.18). Nogging, of course, also provides some insulation from extreme temperatures.

ADVANTAGES AND DISADVANTAGES

The comparative costs of the different types of mud construction depends on a number of factors: availability and price of necessary supplies and equipment;

Figure 9.18 Nogging discovered in a house being torn down in Damascus, Syria (1994). The bricks are stacked loosely in a herringbone pattern between wooden studs.

availability of local labor; labor costs; extent to which construction is done as a communal project or as a "do-it-yourself" effort; degree of mechanization in all aspects of building. These factors combine in many different ways. Mud brick is much cheaper to build with than wood, concrete, or fired brick in the Old World. This applies especially to countries where timber and cement must be imported, which is extremely expensive at the family level and devastates the hard currency reserves at the national level. Even in the USA with our abundance of lumber, mud brick is cost competitive with frame construction. However, mud brick is more expensive than layered construction because it requires a series of extra steps, namely the molding, drying, transporting, and careful laying of the brick. It is also much more time-consuming than layered mud. In the Old World, mud brick is less expensive than rammed earth, where many laborers are required. In the New World, mud-brick construction appears to be more expensive than mechanized form-built rammed earth.

While comparing costs of construction between different materials used in building walls, one should also compare the interior temperature range of these materials. Here, mud brick is much superior to fired brick, stone, or timber-framed walls in providing comfort and in saving money spent on central heating and air conditioning.

For sizing, shaping, and handling, modular mud brick stands above all other methods of construction. Because the units are comparatively easy to make and to handle, construction can be interrupted and resumed at a later date. It is an excellent method of construction for individuals who do-it-yourself. It is certainly possible for one person to build the walls of a mud structure, but it is slow, time-consuming, hard work. Ideally, there should be at least three workers for a modest, efficient operation: one mason to lay brick, one to carry bricks to the mason, and one to mix and to carry mud mortar. However, a do-it-yourselfer, spouse, and children, or two or three friends working as a team, can build quite satisfactory house walls at a good pace.

Common practice in the West is to "butter" bricks, or at the very least to lay a continuous bead of mortar on the edges to give the wall an attractive, solid appearance. In Southwest Asia, however, only a dab or a small pedestal of mortar is placed on the two inner corners, and perhaps another dab midway along the edge of the bedding joint on the inner face, a continuous bead on the outer edge, and little if any in the rising joints. As a result, large stretches of the brick surfaces are not joined or supported by mortar at all. Small sections of mortar with too little cement in the mixture easily crumble, break, or can be pried out with a dinner knife or a nail by anyone wishing to remove a brick or bricks, or to make a hole in the wall. Thus, to ensure structural stability and longevity in building with mud brick, sufficient mortar must be used.

Mud-brick construction lends itself to group or communal projects, such as the Cornerstones Community Partnerships in New Mexico that advises and provides expertise to communities interested in restoring and maintaining historic structures. During the Adobe Workshop in 1995, our group of 20 or so spent one day replacing disintegrated adobe bricks with new ones and pulling up chancel floorboards for later reuse in the Virgin Delores Church in Tecolote, New Mexico, built in 1844. The members of our workshop group and the townspeople involved were all infused with a strong communal spirit, and this rewarding experience suggested how such projects can transform urban neighborhoods and engender pride in group accomplishments at the same time.

Mud brick is extraordinarily durable even when it receives little care and maintenance. For example, the precincts of the Ramesseum at Luxor, Egypt, include vaulted mud-brick storerooms built about 3300 years ago, with substantial sections of vaulting still standing. San Simeon, a Coptic monastery at Aswan, Egypt, built in the seventh century A.D. and abandoned in the thirteenth century A.D., is in remarkable condition having survived the past 700 years without occupants.

In Pakistan, a number of examples exist of mud brick more than 4000 years old, but we know of no instances of layered-mud walls surviving more than about 250–300 years. Several more recently built mud-brick structures are still standing. An elaborate cylindrical tower near Dhardhar had, in 1990, about one-third of its corbelled dome intact. This dome was elaborately finished with lime plaster covering ribs in relief and resembling an umbrella (see Figure 11.1). It is remarkably beautiful, and it probably dates from about the twelfth century A.D. A large fort, known as Mid Chakar Khan Rind, is variously reported to have been built between the thirteenth and sixteenth centuries A.D. The fortification wall about 4 m thick encloses a very large square area. We observed two large hemispherical structures on its east side said to have served as guest rooms for distinguished visitors. Both were roofed with corbelled domes, one of which had a circular staircase that wound around the outside to the top, possibly to an observation point or to an upper room. So far as we could see, none of these remarkable structures had received any maintenance in recent centuries.

NOTES

1. Tell Jemmeh, located in southwestern Israel on the southern border of ancient Canaan, later Israel and Philistia, was captured by the Assyrian king Esarhaddon in the year 679 B.C. He apparently evicted the townspeople and converted the former town into a forward military base for his projected conquest of Egypt. Esarhaddon fortified the top perimeter of the site with a mud-brick casemate wall, a system consisting of two parallel walls tied together at intervals by bonded cross walls. He constructed a series of buildings, most employing a basic Assyrian plan with a number of variations, probably completing most or all of the construction during a five-year period. With the major building phase presumably finished, he launched his first campaign against Egypt in 674 B.C.

2. The local unit of measure for length in the Hadhramaut is the *dhira*, which is about 48.5 cm; brick sizes are calculated in number of *dhira* and fractions thereof.

Part IV

ROOF CONSTRUCTION

Chapter 10

Flat and Raised-Frame Roofs

Whether walls are built of wattle-and-daub, layered mud, rammed earth, or mud brick, they must be covered with a roof as soon as possible to prevent the onset of wall erosion. As with stone, fired brick, and concrete buildings, nearly all kinds of roofs can be used on mud structures: flat, shed, gabled, conical, domed, and vaulted. Worldwide, the flat roof is far and away the most common type of roof throughout history for mud brick or adobe buildings. Its popularity stems from the ease of construction and from the added floor space that a well-built flat roof provides for all sorts of family activities. A distant second in popularity might be gabled roofs, third would be conical, followed by domes and vaults.

In Pakistan, most mud roofs are flat, although 500–700 years ago, domes built of mud brick enjoyed popularity for specific types of structures such as guest houses, ice houses, and tombs. Gabled roofs are becoming increasingly popular, especially among more affluent people in mountainous areas of Baluchistan, where snowfall is frequent and often heavy in the winter. Eastward in India, gabled and conical roofs with thatch covering and gabled roofs with ceramic tiles seem to be more popular than flat roofs. Their popularity is probably due to (1) the discovery that higher roofs make for cooler interior temperature (hot air has more vertical space to rise and to collect at a higher level than in houses with flat roofs), and (2) sloping roofs provide better drainage during the monsoon rains and winter snows. Westward in Afghanistan, the flat mud roof is common today, but mud domes and vaults are preferred in some regions. In parts of Iran and Iraq, houses are sheltered by flat roofs, but vaults and domes also appeared in tombs and temples of the third millennium B.C. and continued in occasional use well into the first millennium A.D.

In southern Saudi Arabia and both northern and southern Yemen, flat mud roofs prevail except for a few domed tombs. Flat roofs probably always predominated in Egypt, but from the late fourth millennium B.C. to the present, vaulted mud roofs have been used frequently on tombs, houses, monasteries, churches, and warehouses. Flat roofs apparently prevailed throughout the Levant—Syria, Lebanon, Israel, and Jordan—and westward across North Africa to Morocco. At some time in the past, mud domes on houses, stables, and granaries appeared in the Aleppo region of Syria, where they continue to be used. In Europe and much of central and eastern North America, the raised-frame roof has always predominated. By contrast, in the southwestern USA, both the flat and gabled roofs are extensively used, but the former style predominates.

This distribution of roof types suggests that in very warm regions without a great deal of rainfall or snow, the flat roof is the roof of choice. Where monsoon-like rains and heavy snows prevail, and summers experience intense heat, sharply sloping roofs—i.e., gabled, conical, domed, and vaulted roofs of mud or thatch—are preferred because of their ability to shed moisture quickly and to add vertical space into which hot air can collect above the height of the inhabitants' heads.

Construction techniques for each of the major roof types are described below and evaluated in terms of environmental suitability, aesthetic characteristics, functional usefulness, and costs.

FLAT-ROOF CONSTRUCTION TECHNIQUES

Primary Beams

Before the wall reaches its finished height, the construction of a flat roof begins with the heavy primary beams that will carry the weight of the roof itself and of both people and things that may use it as an activity area. In the case of a multistory building, beams are required for the ceiling and floor of each story. Most beams are wood, either tree trunks or large limbs from which the bark has been removed (Figure 10.1). The beam is cut to the length of the span including the thickness of both walls, plus an additional 1–2 ft (~30–60 cm) longer on each end if the builder decides that it should project beyond the wall surface. This is a hallmark of the pueblo style in the North American southwest. The difficulty presented by unmilled tree parts is that trunks and limbs taper and may not be as straight as one would wish. The tapering can be advantageous, however, if the beams are laid so that the larger diameter ends are all set on one wall and the smaller diameter ends on the other wall, which creates a slightly sloping, flat roof with natural drainage. Squared wooden beams are rare in the Old World except in houses of the wealthy. In the New World, such beams are available at lower costs and are more widespread. In some Near Eastern houses, steel I-beams are now being used by people who can afford them because they are straight, carry heavier loads, and are more rigid, thereby reducing movement of the roof components, which can cause leaks (Figure 10.2). They are certainly less attractive than wooden beams; although it is possible to frame them in with wood and finish them to resemble wooden beams, we have not seen this done in the region.

In the Old World, long straight trunks and limbs are often difficult or impossible to find, and builders make do with bent saplings and limbs that yield crooked beams. If a sapling or limb is relatively straight except for a bend in one direction, it will be laid so that the bend is positioned flat or horizontal rather than vertical or oblique. With several such crooked beams, the ceiling resembles a stage where the individual beams seem to have danced freely and then suddenly were frozen at

Figure 10.1   Round primary roof beam supported by interior pier on left, secondary cross beams, and bamboo poles tying reeds together, north refugee camp, abandoned June 1967 near Jericho in the Jordan Valley (1978).

Figure 10.2   Primary steel I-beam and milled wooden secondary beams with reed mats on top, Dudhian, near Harappa, Punjab, Pakistan (1989).

Figure 10.3   Irregular beams of different shapes and sizes (for the ceiling of a lower room) carrying the mud floor of an upper room Marib Town, Marib, Yemen (1991).

a moment of time (Figure 10.3). Crooked beams are sometimes hewn to make a square or rectangular primary beam, which is much more elegant than a series of bowed or twisted beams. Almost anything that is strong can be used. In the four-story mud house in Wadi Beihan, Yemen, which served as the expedition house in 1950–1951, the ceiling of the dining room on the third floor had among its crooked wooden beams the metal rib of an airplane wing salvaged from the wreckage of a crash in the area! It proved to be an adequate support as well as a fascinating conversation piece, no matter how incongruous!

Beam size varies with the type of wood as well as whether it is round or trimmed square or rectangular. In the Near East, the choice is governed more by what is available than by what is ideal, and therefore a wide range of sizes prevail. Log beams ranging about 14–18 cm in diameter predominate, whereas saplings and boughs range about 10–14 cm in diameter, and trimmed beams about 12–16 cm wide are found in square or rectangular shape. McHenry (1985:80) provides a general guide to recommended ratios between diameters and maximum spans (Table 10.1). The word "general" is stressed here because there are so many variables that only engineering studies or a builder experienced in working with available materials would provide the most reliable guide.

Beams are placed on the walls spanning the narrowest dimension of the building. Their spacing depends on their size and perceived strength. In the Near East, if beams are large and straight they may be spaced at intervals up to 1.22 m, but if they are smaller they will be set closer to one another, perhaps at intervals of about 50 cm. In the customs post at Beleli in Baluchistan, for example, two beams were used to span each of the two rooms, which measured 3.66 m in length and width (Figure 10.4; also Figure 3.28). If smaller beams had been used, at least three and possibly four beams would have been needed over each room. After beams are in place, wall construction continues to the parapet, which surrounds and locks the beams in place.

In the southwestern USA, flat mud roofs were traditionally constructed in much the same way as those in the Old World. Both *vigas* (the round beams) and trimmed square or rectangular beams have long histories. In New Mexico, USA, if a wooden bond beam is used, the state building code requires that *vigas* be attached to it with large nails or screws. If the bond beam is concrete, *vigas* are fastened to it by means of a metal plate or metal straps set in the concrete when poured (Smith and Austin, 1989:53).

Table 10.1 General guide for maximum ceiling beam span for various diameters or depths of round or hewn beams, respectively, after McHenry (1985:80). (Metric data were converted from McHenry's data in English units.)

Type of beam	Diameter	Depth	Maximum span
Vigas (log-like beams)	15 cm (6 in)	—	3.05 m (10 ft)
	20 cm (8 in)	—	4.88 m (16 ft)
	25 cm (10 in)	—	6.02 m (20 ft)
Hewn beams 10–15 cm	—	15 cm (6 in)	3.05 m (10 ft)
(4–6 in) wide	—	20 cm (8 in)	4.88 m (16 ft)
	—	25.5–30.5 cm (10–12 in)	6.02 m (20 ft)

Figure 10.4 Roof under construction, with primary wooden beams and secondary bamboo poles, in the customs post at Beleli, Baluchistan, Pakistan (1990).

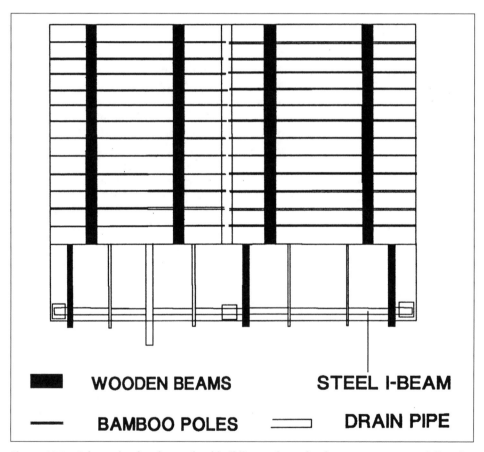

WOODEN BEAMS   **STEEL I-BEAM**

BAMBOO POLES   **DRAIN PIPE**

Figure 10.5 Schematic plan for roofs of building and porch of customs post at Beleli, Baluchistan, Pakistan (1990).

Secondary Beams: Bamboo Poles and Branches

In the Old World, bamboo poles or medium-thick branches are laid side-by-side at a right angle to and across the top of the primary beams. If the builder can afford them, bamboo poles with a diameter of 5–7 cm are preferred. In the Beleli customs post, bamboo poles were spaced about 30 cm apart (Figures 10.4, 10.5; also 10.6). In another house we saw, two layers of spaced bamboo poles were laid, the upper layer at a right angle to the lower one.

Lining: Woven Mats and Reeds

A layer of straw or reed mats, sewn with string or fastened together by sewing with flexible wire, is placed over the bamboo poles or secondary branches (Figure 10.6). In the house we saw, in which two layers of bamboo poles were used, the mats were tied to the intersections of the bamboo poles to prevent movement. In debris of houses of the seventeenth to sixteenth centuries B.C. at Tell Jemmeh, Israel, we found a number of large fragments of mud roofs with impressions of reeds on one surface. The thickness of the fragments ranged from 54 to 62 mm, and the reeds, with diameters of 9–14 mm, were spaced no more than 2–3 mm apart, indicating that

Figure 10.6   Woven mats over the bamboo poles of customs post ceiling at Beleli, Baluchistan, Pakistan (1990).

Figure 10.7   Reed impressions on the underside of mud roof fragments, Tell Jemmeh, Israel, seventeenth to sixteenth centuries B.C.

they must have been portions of woven mats (Figure 10.7). At Tuleilat el-Ghassul in the eastern Jordan Valley north of the Dead Sea, late Neolithic–Chalcolithic houses were roofed with a similar combination of reeds and mud (Lee, 1978:1208). In a house with a pillow-shaped flat roof at Beir al-Helu in northeastern Syria, sheets of tin were used on the primary beams instead of mats. The mats, reeds, or metal sheets act as a liner to prevent bits of twigs, straw, and mud from falling through cracks and openings into the room below.

Insulation: Branches and Straw

Selected small branches, twigs, or tufts of straw are spread densely over the mats and laid as flat as possible to form a layer about 15–30 cm thick (see Figure 10.17). In Pakistan, the branches and twigs are woven together and are known as *kerra*. This layer locks in a reservoir of air that provides insulation for the interior of the house.

Compressed Mud

Layers of mud are spread over the insulating layer of branches, which is somewhat compressed by the additional weight. When each mud layer is almost dry, it also is compressed with a stone roller that is run over it back and forth, side to side, and diagonally, corner to corner. The rolling stone presses the mud into the interstices between branches and reeds, keying the mud layer (see Figure 10.7). This process is repeated until the thickness of all the mud layers combined totals about 10 cm, although some builders prefer thicker roofs. The finished roof is usually inspected a number of times throughout the year, especially after each hard rain during the rainy seasons. If cracks or leaks develop, they are sealed with additional mud, which when almost dry is also compressed with a roller.

Stone roof rollers in the Near East are commonly cylindrical, although sometimes they taper slightly toward one or both ends; they are seldom more than 60 cm long or 20 cm in diameter. Many have a hole or deep recess in the center of each end into which a wooden or metal frame, serving as a handle, is attached to permit the roller to be pushed by a person. Some with no holes or recesses for a handle are rolled back and forth by hand while on one's knees. These rollers can also be used to pack the earthen floor inside the house. During the 1950s, almost every house with a mud roof in Jordanian villages had a roof roller.

Such stones are occasionally found in archaeological excavations in the Near East. Near the turn of the twentieth century, some archaeologists described them as "cult objects," believing them to be symbols of gods. Some may have had cultic significance; but to demonstrate cultic use in antiquity, these cylindrical stones should also be found in a religious context, in temples, or in regions where thatched roofs and flagstone floors prevailed (i.e., where cylindrical stones were not needed to compact roofs or floors). Until a number of such discoveries are made, their purely functional use as roof rollers is far more probable than their supposed religious symbolism.

Finish

Flat mud roofs are not waterproof. They may become completely waterproof and even longer lasting when protected with a final coat of lime plaster (see also Chapter 12). Lime plaster is laid on top of the compressed mud or mud plaster roof and the mud parapets, covering all exposed surfaces and corners. Mud roofs sometimes extend beyond the walls and terminate in a rounded overhang that curves back to the wall face, serving as a drip molding to prevent water from touching the wall surface below. For ideal drainage, the roof must be laid with a slight slope either from a slightly raised center downward to the parapets or from one slightly elevated side of the roof downward to the other. One or more channels or openings are cut through each parapet wall, and are thoroughly coated with lime plaster. Sometimes long drain spouts are set inside the channel to pitch the water away from the wall (Figure 10.8). In other instances, a vertical channel 25–38 cm wide is built against or into the wall extending downward from the parapet drain hole to the ground. The channel is bordered on both sides by ridges to keep the flow within the channel. Such channels are always surfaced with lime plaster to prevent erosion of the wall (Figure 10.9).

Figure 10.8 Drain spouts and pipes, all piercing the wall of the roof activity area, which is finished with lime plaster, in Shibam, Hadhramaut, Yemen (1991). An area on the left is awaiting repair of the lime plaster.

Figure 10.9 Hadhrami Bedouin Legion performing in Seiyun, Hadhramaut, before a large audience on New Year's Day, 1962. Note that the mud-plastered building to the right has two wide drainage channels finished with lime plaster that continue over the wall buttress to the ground (1962).

The wooden roof structure is often finished on the under side with varnish, paint, or carving, any of which adds considerable beauty and refinement to the rooms beneath (see Figure 1.7). It is also possible to build a ceiling below the beams that hides the roof structure. An example is the dropped ceiling of milled boards in the rooms of the upper, mud-brick story of the Qazi house in Pishin, near Quetta, Baluchistan (Figure 10.10).

In the southwestern USA, some of the intermediate layers (secondary beams, reed mats) are skipped in creating an attractive ceiling for the room below. A deck, traditionally consisting of peeled aspen poles—*latillas*—or split cedar poles—*cedros*—that are 1¾–2 in (4–5 cm) in diameter, was laid directly over the *vigas* (primary beams). The *latillas* or *cedros* were nailed to the beams at right angles or in a herringbone pattern (Figure 10.11). Boards are generally used today, often joined to one another by tongue-and-groove. Sometimes individual boards are cut and laid to make a herringbone pattern, with the boards oriented from the upper left corner to the lower right corner over the space between one pair of beams, and from the lower left corner to the upper right corner over the space between the next pair of beams, alternating orientation across the room. Such a deck would add stability to the roof, give a more finished appearance to the ceiling, and prevent bits of straw, twigs, and soil from falling into the room.

This calls to mind an annoyance common to flat mud roofs in the Near East, where wooden deck ceilings are not typically available. Debris and dust from the settling roof tend to fall down into the room, but this has an imaginative, low cost remedy. In the men's house in a family compound at Hanna, near Quetta, Baluchistan, the owner had tacked up a red fabric decorated with a print of tiny flowers under the ceiling, primarily to catch any disintegrating roof materials from falling

Figure 10.10 Varnished, dropped ceiling of milled boards in upper floor of the Qazi house in Pishin, near Quetta, Baluchistan, Pakistan (1991). Note heavy structural beams and corrugated metal roof panels above.

Figure 10.11 Split poles laid in herringbone arrangement, Huston house, Edgewood, New Mexico, USA (1995).

on the heads of the inhabitants or guests; this also created a pleasant surprise in adding color and design to an otherwise drab room.

New World Innovations

Creative ideas and new technologies have produced new materials and methods for constructing flat roofs that dominate office buildings, shopping malls, stores, and residences in the twentieth century. These materials are perfectly suited to flat roofs on mud houses, and they have replaced limbs, twigs, and straw capped with compressed mud throughout much of the American Southwest. Two or more sheets of rigid insulating board may be laid on top of the wooden deck over the *vigas*; alternatively, a wooden frame 6–10 in (15–25 cm) high can be filled with a soft insulation such as fiberglass and covered with a second deck. The latter option not only provides better insulation, but also makes it easier to run and repair wiring and pipes in the roof.

A built-up roof is laid on top of the insulation. It consists of several layers of roofing felt (asphalt-impregnated paper available in different weights). A triangle-shaped board is affixed where the roof meets the vertical wall so that the felt is backed and can be bent upward without cracking, thus sealing the joint of the roof and parapet wall. The joint is then sealed with thick, hot asphalt and a layer of gravel that partially embeds itself in the asphalt. Flashing of either very heavy felt or metal is bent over to cover both the inside edge of the layered felt and the top of the mud brick parapet, where it is sealed by exterior plaster or stucco. If properly laid, such roofs last 10–20 years, depending on the number of felt layers and their weight. As McHenry (1985:112) observes, "Surprisingly enough, the roof will last just about that period of time.... If a ten-year roof has been in place for ten years, you can count on trouble at any time." Built-up roofs assure the owner that minimal repairs, if any, will be required during the life of the roof, which is, of course, much more convenient than having to check a conventional flat mud roof for cracks several times a year.

RAISED-FRAME ROOFS

Raised-frame roofs can be built in a number of different styles: shed, gable, hip, mansard, and gambrel, and there are many variations within each style, most of which are aesthetically quite pleasing. Common to raised-frame roofs is an angle or slope, which provides rapid run-off of rain and melting snow, abundant room for insulation, and, if high enough, additional floor space for habitation or storage. They also permit the use of a wide choice of covering materials. Because gabled is the most common style of raised-frame roof, it is emphasized here; however, much of what is described could be applicable to other styles.

Raised-frame roofs are not indigenous to the ancient Near East, and those that exist today are chiefly in India, northern Pakistan, northern Iran (Wulff, 1966:113), and Turkey. Most examples date from the last few centuries, and they may represent influence from eastern Asia or derive from European architectural examples imitated locally during colonial periods. Gabled roofs on mud houses in India are generally covered with thatch or ceramic tile, and both gabled and hip roofs in the mountains north and northeast of Quetta in Baluchistan are increasingly finished with metal sheeting. Both thatch and sheet-metal roofs occur in the old refugee camps on the north and south sides of Jericho in the southern Levant's Jordan Valley. Mud houses with gabled roofs and ceramic tiles are common in Cyprus, Turkey, and elsewhere around the Mediterranean, and identical roofs are also ubiquitous on buildings of stone or fired brick. All of the raised-frame roof styles occur in England, France, and Germany, and may be covered with any kind of material, including thatch, shingles of wood or slate, or ceramic tile.

The reasons for the general dearth of raised-frame roofs in the Near East are several. (1) Timber sources were not readily available, and to import or transport suitable framing members would cost a considerable sum of money. Most of the region already consisted of nearly treeless landscapes in antiquity, so there was comparatively little good lumber to be had. Even now, a lot of framing consists of patched-together pieces of scrap lumber, chiefly obtained from shipping crates and boxes arriving by ocean freight. Boards from these boxes are cobbled together to make joists of poor quality and dubious strength.[1] (2) The strength of the flat-roof tradition is rooted in centuries of experience in construction and use. (3) Mud cannot be used on sharply angled roofs even if well-compressed because it cannot survive fast-flowing run-off water. Low-angled, gabled mud roofs are used in Baluchistan and in rainless regions such as the Jericho area.

Framing

The framing of gabled roofs generally resembles construction methods common in Europe and North America, and therefore may be somewhat familiar to most homeowners in the West. Briefly, in gabled roofs, the slope of the sides is based on triangle-shaped assemblies, having a bottom member or chord with two top chords that are attached at each end of the bottom chord and join together at the top. Each assembled unit requires internal bracing—of which there are many types—to distribute the weight of the roof. Such a unit is known as a truss, and when a number of trusses are set at specified intervals, they provide the supporting framework for the roof. Trusses can be custom-made at the building site or mass-produced in a factory, from which they can be purchased and transported to the site. Trusses must be securely fastened to the walls or to a concrete or wooden bond beam. Below the bases of the trusses are the ceiling joists, on the underside of which the finished ceiling is attached, and over the top of the bottom chord an attic floor can be laid. On top of the triangular-shaped trusses, a decking of heavy boards or plywood is fastened, which carries most finished roofing materials, such as ceramic tiles, metal sheeting, or shingles. Thatch requires narrower boards for easy attachment of the bundles.

Many Near Eastern gabled roofs have a simpler framework. The edges of the mud-brick end walls begin to taper inward about 1.8–2.4 m above the floor, forming a triangle at each end—the gable ends. A ridge pole rests on the apex of each gable end wall or is built into the end walls just below their apexes (Figure 10.12). In some instances, a smaller ridge pole is augmented by two matching poles paralleling it equidistant down the slope between the ridge and the side walls. This is particularly important when the roof slope is long and needs additional support (Figure 10.13), as for example when the ridge bisects the long axis of a building (i.e., the "side" walls are actually the front and rear walls of a house, and the gable ends are the long sides). Smaller poles extend from each side wall to the ridge pole, sometimes braced by a few crude purlins beneath them, providing the supporting frame for

Figure 10.12   Gabled roof of a political party headquarters building, with a large projecting ridge pole, Hanna Valley, Baluchistan, Pakistan (1990).

Figure 10.13 Typical lateral support pole between ridge pole and side wall, Charada, Gujarat State, India (1991).

Figure 10.14 Wooden brace used to support a broken roof beam, Charada, Gujarat State, India (1991).

reed mats, loose reeds, small branches, or leaves. As in flat roofs, mud is sometimes laid on this structure if the angle of the gable is low. Surprisingly, we have never seen a lime-plaster coating on mud roofs of gabled houses, although we have no reason to doubt that they exist.

If a room is unusually wide along the same axis in which the ridge pole lies, a heavier beam is used for the ridge pole, and it is carried not only by the end wall but also by a pier or buttress against the inner face of each end wall (see Figure 10.1). If heavy ceramic tiles are used, or if inferior beams are incorporated in the framing, one or more beams may break. In a house in Charada, India, two wooden stands were employed to brace a broken beam (Figure 10.14), and in the road-side market building at Kuchlagh, Baluchistan, a beam supporting the mud porch roof broke and was awaiting replacement (see Figure 3.31).

The strongest and most massive roof framing in earthen architecture exists in the rammed-earth structures of the eighteenth and nineteenth centuries in Europe. This framing used squared wooden beams of various sizes, e.g., 30 cm, 20 cm, and 15 cm in width and depth. Custom designs in bracing the frame illustrate the creativity and determination of the carpenters to erect strong, durable roofs (Figure 10.15; see also Figure 8.10). That the framing still supports roofs after 150–200 years of use testifies to the knowledge and success of the builders. Wooden framing for the half-timber houses in Europe (see Figure 6.14) is more regular in design than that for rammed-earth buildings. The hip, mansard, and gambrel roofs, however, are variations of the basic gabled roof that require special framing designs.

The cathedral ceiling, a popular roofing option in the southwestern USA, opens the living space from the floor up to the decking on the underside of the roof. It is

Figure 10.15   A small section of the roof framing in the Manor of Peillet, from the late eighteenth century A.D., Dolomieu, France (1997).

constructed with a heavy central ridge beam supported by a series of widely spaced, opposed pairs of heavy support beams that are anchored to the concrete or wooden bond beam at the top of each side wall. Laid on top of these support beams parallel to the ridge beam and spaced at intervals from the ridge downward are purlins, heavy boards to which the decking is attached. Cathedral ceilings require considerable insulation for a pleasant interior temperature.

Covering Materials

Thatch

When we mention "thatch," we usually think of northern Europe and England, where lovely houses and cottages are finished with soft, often decoratively trimmed thatched roofs. Thatch for roofing is obtained from a number of different plants. In the Near East, it is chiefly straw from wheat or barley, and reeds (for examples, see Figures 10.12, 6.2, 6.6, 6.9). In botanically lush England in early times, thatch was from "reeds, rushes, broom, heather, and even bracken … [and in more recent times] cultivated barley, wheat, and rye straw" (West, 1971:112). Of these, the marsh reed of Norfolk, combed wheat (sometimes called Devon reed), and long straw have expected service lives of at least 100, 50, and 35 years, respectively (West, 1971:113–114).

Thatched roofs require a frame that includes a series of equally spaced, horizontal battens to which the thatch is attached one horizontal row at a time. Starting at the eve, it extends beyond the lowest batten to overhang the walls and form a drip edge. A bunch of thatch is spread, flattened, and combed—reeds are combed with upward strokes, straw with downward strokes—to produce an even surface. The thatch is then sewed to the battens in long stitches with a tarred cord and a special stitching needle (West, 1971:112). The second layer overlaps the first layer and its stitches for about two-thirds of its length, and it is sewed to the next higher batten. The third layer overlaps the first layer about one-third of its length and the second layer by two-thirds of its length; it is sewed to the third batten from the bottom. Thus each row of thatch is sewed to three battens for security.

Application of the thatching progresses in this manner to the ridge. The angle of the roof combined with the overlap of the thatch assures a waterproof roof. During earlier centuries in England before battens were used, wattle provided the base for thatch; some examples of this have survived to the present, such as Apple Tree Cottage in Quarley, Hampshire (West, 1971:114, fig. 19). A rather inelegant but functional method of securing thatch was frequently used in Ireland. Householders employed a series of horizontal ropes laid at intervals on top of the thatch, each weighed down by a stone tied to each end and overhanging the end walls. After the horizontal ropes were in place, another series of ropes with stones at each end was laid vertically at intervals over the ridge from eve to eve. This crisscross combination held the thatch in place even against heavy winds. For still other methods and illustrations of attaching thatch, see *Shelter* (Kahn, 1973:76–77) and *The Thatcher's Craft* (Anonymous, 1960). If properly installed, a thatched roof is light in weight, has good insulating characteristics, and is waterproof and biodegradable. The most obvious disadvantage of thatched roofs is the danger of fire.

Ceramic Tiles

Ceramic roof tiles seem to have appeared first in Greece during the third millennium B.C., in a round building on the acropolis at Tiryns (Robertson, 1969:4, 24). From the seventh century B.C. onwards, temples with gabled roofs were roofed with tiles. Some tiles were semicylindrical and laid with the concave surface of the lower tiles facing up and the concave surface of the upper tiles facing down to fit over the top edges of the lower tiles, locking them in place. This style continues to the present with a number of variations. Such semicylindrical tile prevails in India (see Figures 3.38, 3.40). Other tiles were flat with a raised ridge on each side, which overlapped and locked in a number of imaginative ways, such as narrow tiles covering the joints of adjacent tiles, and were often finished like small gabled structures (Robertson, 1969:49).

Ceramic tiles are very heavy, and therefore require strong, well-constructed framing with good timber that provides a minimum of movement. They are also fireproof and long-lasting. Ceramic tiles are strikingly beautiful, as anyone who has visited the Mediterranean region, especially the Greek Islands would attest.

Metal

Metal roofs of iron, steel, tin, or copper have been used for centuries, and aluminum has become increasingly popular in recent years. In many regions of Southwest Asia, metal is gradually replacing the 1 × 2 m corrugated asbestos panel in use for decades; the latter is still to be seen in Pakistan (Figure 10.16), and is commonly used in Israel. Flat metal panels joined and sealed on the two long sides—like traditional terneplate and copper roofs—are gaining acceptance in the southwestern USA. Many now available are finished with factory-baked paints in a variety of colors, such as red, brown, and blue, which make the house roof more attractive than shiny steel or aluminum panels. Metal roofs are the choice of the more affluent fruit growers and farmers in the mountains north of Quetta, Pakistan, at elevations of 2134–2438 m. Figure 4.13 shows a new layered-mud house with a well-designed and attractive aluminum hip roof on the left side of the photo.

Such roofs make excellent shed and gabled roofs that turn away both rain and snow much better than mud roofs. To protect the mud walls of the building, they are usually designed with long overhangs to discharge runoff water and snow from the walls. In a house built by young amateurs in northern California, a tin roof was installed overhanging the walls by 4 ft (1.22 m) to protect the mud brick walls in an environment with about 70 in (1750 mm) of rainfall annually (Kahn, 1973:67). Metal roofs are also lightweight, largely maintenance free, long-lasting, and relatively inexpensive. Unfortunately, they transmit heat and cold, requiring considerable insulation above the ceiling for a comfortable interior.

A porch at the entrance to a house provides welcome shade in sunny, hot countries. As a result, it serves as a major activity area where family chores are done, children play, and family and friends gather to pass the time. Porches are common in India, Pakistan, and the refugee camps at Jericho, but are rare elsewhere in the Levant, Arabia, Egypt, and across North Africa. The chief characteristic of most porches is the roof. A porch roof may be an extension of the house roof, continuing its line

Figure 10.16 Corrugated asbestos roofing panels on the men's house, Hanna Valley, Baluchistan, Pakistan (1990).

and angle (see Figures 3.36, 3.40); a separate roof attached to a wall (see Figure 3.30); or built within the basic house (see Figure 3.48).

When a porch projects from the front of the building, beams spanning the width of the rooms may be extended to carry the porch roof. Wooden beams of this length are generally rare in the Near East, so another series of beams usually rests on, or is set in, the front wall on one side and is attached to a beam supported by piers or columns on the other side. The porch of the customs post at Beleli (Figure 10.17; see also Figures 3.27, 3.28) was carried on the outer side by three square piers of fired brick supporting a lightweight metal I-beam. By contrast, the long porch at Kuchlagh in Baluchistan (see Figures 3.29, 3.30) was supported by wooden beams. The three fired-brick piers of the Beleli customs post were covered with mud plaster to make their appearance harmonious with the mud-plaster walls of the building. The mud roof of the porch was built exactly like the flat mud roof over the main building, and a galvanized pipe was set in the mud of the porch roof to drain water from the roof of the building.

Snow is frequent during the severe winters at higher elevations in Baluchistan. It must be removed immediately from flat or low-gabled mud roofs because (a) it softens the mud as it melts, and (b) build-up of heavy snow may break the supporting

Figure 10.17 Detail of porch roof, showing metal I-beam, woven mat, insulation layer of tree limbs, mud layer, and drain pipe for the Beleli customs post near Quetta, Pakistan (1991).

beams. In New Mexico, many houses have a homemade ladder leaning against the roof to serve both as access for roof maintenance and as a characteristic decorative feature of the Pueblo style. We were surprised, therefore, to see no ladders in this mountainous area of Pakistan. Instead we saw a device that provided access to the roof for snow removal that was permanently installed on one wall of the building. This consisted of a log (two thick, roughly trimmed boards nailed together would serve equally well) with one end anchored in the higher ground about 3 m from the base of the wall and the other end attached to the coping of the building (Figure 10.18). A series of shallow crude steps had been cut in the sloping upper surface of the log to serve as a stairway to the roof. This enabled the resident to get on the roof quickly during or after a winter storm to remove snow before damage occurred. Similar "ladders" cut from heavy tree limbs are used in many places in West Africa (Courtney-Clarke, 1990:47, 58, 61) to gain roof access for inspecting and repairing the mud surface.

ADVANTAGES AND DISADVANTAGES

Flat roofs have many uses. Best suited for arid and semi-arid climates, and often with raised walls to shield the occupants from public view, flat roofs provide work areas for a variety of household activities such as food preparation, washing and drying clothes, and sewing. They also provide a play area for children, a spacious area for wedding parties and other social functions, and a sleeping area if one wishes to sleep outdoors (Figure 10.19). Sometimes the roof provides space for an additional enclosed room for a family member or guest. This could even be a honeymoon room where newlyweds stay after the wedding if their own house was

Figure 10.18 Permanently mounted pole bridge or "ladder" for reaching the roof, near Katch and Ziarat, Baluchistan, Pakistan (1990).

Figure 10.19 The flat roofs of Seiyun, Hadhramaut, Yemen, with house walls extending up to enclose rooftop activity areas (1963).

not yet built (Figure 10.20). Virtually all roofs also serve as safe storage areas for foodstuffs, wood, manure pads (for cooking fuel), furniture, bicycles, and assorted junk. In short, it is an all-purpose area that functions as a courtyard, patio, attic, and basement in houses more familiar to many in the West. We urge everyone who visits Near Eastern cities to find a high spot—the top of a building, a minaret, or a nearby hill—and look down on the flat roofs of houses and apartment buildings

Figure 10.20 "Honeymoon" roof room of the family home on the right, next to the Marib house under construction on the left, Marib, Yemen (1991).

on all sides. If you can watch what is happening for a half-hour or so, you will be surprised at what you see!

Flat mud roofs provide good service if kept in good repair, but this requires frequent inspection and renewal. With periodic maintenance, these roofs last a decade or more. Raised-frame roofs are more expensive than flat mud roofs because of the cost of materials and labor in constructing them. As we have learned, the quality of materials and workmanship determine whether it is a 10-, 15-, or 20-year roof (plus a few years of additional service with increasingly frequent repairs). If flat roofs are covered with lime plaster, however, they can survive for several decades if regularly inspected and repaired. Their only disadvantage is the higher initial cost of the plaster (see Chapter 12).

Raised-frame roofs can be impractical in many regions of the world where there is a dearth of forests. Because of the limitations of the physical environment and increasing depredations by animals and human beings, the Near East, northern Asia, North Africa, and the southwestern USA are among the regions where suitable trees for timber are few or non-existent. Sometimes it can be a challenge to find sufficient timber for even the few support beams required for a flat roof. On the plains of northern and eastern Syria, for example, one can drive for miles without seeing a tree. The Arabian Peninsula, Egypt, Iraq, Iran, Afghanistan, and parts of Pakistan, and India share an overall deficiency of timber. The few surviving trees are often small, deformed, weakened by leaf-eating animals, and/or scavenged by people who break off limbs for firewood, fences, and sticks. This situation has been exacerbated in the twentieth century because of the burgeoning populations of these countries, which has led to further shrinkage of forests, and the subsequent imposition of severe restrictions on the trimming and removal of trees by many governments. As a result, much of the wood used for building is imported and very expensive. In fact, throughout the Near East and Southwest Asia where mud construction is commonly used, many of the beams are old and reused, acquired illegally, or brought from a great distance. The remaining "beams" are marginal and makeshift—either crudely assembled from pieces of salvaged crates and boxes or bent or curving tree limbs. The latter, of course, must be placed with the curving portion in a horizontal position so that they do not curve upward or downward to protrude above or below the finished roof.

No flat roof, regardless of its construction, can rival the varied family of gabled roofs in drainage efficiency, which means longer lasting roofs and, with long roof overhangs, good protection for all types of earthen walls. The cost of framing gabled roofs is greater than for flat roofs, and simple gabled roofs are less expensive to build than hip or mansard roofs. Gable framing is also lighter in weight when covered by thatch, wood shingles, asphalt shingles, or metal roofs. Framing is heavier and more costly when heavy ceramic tile roofs are used. As for covering materials for gabled roofs, thatch requires much more maintenance than ceramic tiles or metal roofs. In terms of safety, thatch and wooden roofing are subject to fires, both inside and outside. Mud, ceramic tile, and metal roofs are fireproof, but are, of course, vulnerable to fires originating inside the house that destroy the wooden framing.

Aesthetic considerations of roofs are quite personal. Although we doubt that broad agreement could be achieved, perhaps most people would regard the flat roof as homey, as belonging to the earth from which it rises, and as compatible with the horizontal lines and planes of the landscape. Thatch-covered, gabled-roof cottages seem warm, quaint, country, and delightfully frilly, especially if the thatch is laid and trimmed in one of the attractive English styles. Metal roofs with their simple clean lines suggest modernity, efficiency, and brightness in the variety of their colors. Red ceramic tile roofs bespeak continuity through time, security, and stability while adding brilliant colors to the landscape. All styles of roofing can make a house interesting and beautiful; all depend on the climate, the traditions of the place, the tastes of the owner, and the maintenance they receive.

NOTE

1. Ceramic tiles are extraordinarily heavy, and joists often bend or break under their weight, creating wavy roofs with one or more low places. India is a land of wavy roofs (see Figure 3.36), and while they may be as enchanting as a fairy tale, they evoke fear for what might happen to those under the roof if beams were to give way and a large section of heavy ceramic tiles fell.

Chapter 11

Curved Roofs: Domes, Arches, and Vaults

Curved roofs, either domed or vaulted, provide an alternative to flat or raised-frame roofs. They may be essential or at least highly desirable, depending on roofing material availability, environmental conditions, building traditions, and individual taste.

The primary reason for the invention of the various types of curving roofs was the lack of suitable timber to carry flat or framed roofs. The dearth of local wood resources and the prohibitive costs of importing timber make domes and vaults the preferred choice for roofing in many regions because they limit the requirements for structural wood to finishing applications, such as door and window frames. Arching roofs also add even more interior comfort to the already superior comfort derived from mud construction. Most of the treeless regions of the world are characterized by scorching hot summers. The higher ceilings of domes and vaults create an increased holding area for room heat well above the heads of the inhabitants. If ventilating holes or windows are built into the dome or the end walls just below the apex of the vault, the rising heat will be dissipated by the slightest breeze (see also Chapter 13).

All evidence indicates that the mud arch, vault, and dome were invented in the Near East about 5000 years ago. Egypt, Iraq, and Iran played formative roles in the invention and development of these forms of roofing, which were subsequently distributed far and wide. In these regions, domes and vaults have been used successfully in diverse applications ranging from churches, mosques, and schools to private homes, shops, and ice houses, and they have long been an accepted feature of the community.

TERMINOLOGY

Because the terminology of these types of structures is technical and not always transparent in meaning, the definition of a few terms employed in this chapter may be useful.

311

Dome: An arch rotated around its vertical axis, creating a hemispherical structure—like half of a ball—that rests on a circular or square building. When
erected on a circular building such as the Pantheon in Rome (second century
A.D.), the weight and thrust of the dome are carried by the continuous circular
wall beneath it. When built over a square room, the circular base of the dome
rests on a small stretch midway in the length of each side wall, and the rest of
its base is supported by squinches or pendentives.

Squinch: A triangular-shaped curving fan of brick that extends upward and inward
from the corner of a square room to support one of the four curving segments
of the base of the dome that do not rest directly on the straight side walls (compare with pendentive).

Pendentive: A curving, triangular-shaped fan of brick that arises between arches
instead from a room corner; together with the apex of the arches, it carries
the base of a dome. Structurally, both squinches and pendentives transfer the
weight of the dome via the curving segments to the side walls at the corners.

Vault: An elongated or continuous arch forming a half-cylinder set on top of
parallel walls. It is primarily suited for rectangular rooms that are long and
relatively narrow, but it is also used with relatively small square rooms.

Cross vault: An intersection of two vaults, usually at right angles, common in
Gothic churches.

Composite arch: Composed of two or more types of arch construction. In ancient
Egypt during the second and first millennia B.C., composite arches were erected
by laying one or two courses of pitched brick followed by several courses of
radial brick on top.

Intrados: Inner surface or underside of a dome, arch, or vault.

Extrados: Outer surface or topside of a dome, arch, or vault.

Springer: The base or the starting point of an arch, vault, or dome. Sometimes a special, wedge-shaped brick or stone is used to force the initial curve of the arch.

HISTORY OF DOMES

The history of the dome is more obscure than that of the arch and vault because few
early examples have been found in archaeological excavations. Known early dome
structures tend to be relatively small in size, such as those of the Old Kingdom in
Egypt (third millennium B.C.) that covered square shafts giving access to underground tombs, pottery kilns, and other small chambers (Clarke and Engelbach,
1930:185–186). All were constructed of corbelled rings of mud bricks, the first of
two methods of erecting domes to be invented. During the same time period, large
circular huts—7.63–7.93 m in diameter—roofed with corbelled, mud-brick domes
appeared in Greece at Orchomenus in Boetia and at Sesklo in Thessaly (Dinsmoor,
1950:5–6).

The most notable ancient domed structures are the *tholos* or "beehive" tombs
of Mycenae, Greece. Donald Robertson (1885–1961), a distinguished historian of
classical architecture, described them as "the most impressive of all of the remains
of prehistoric Greece" (Robertson, 1969:32). The most famous of these—featured

on every tour itinerary to Greece—is the "Treasury of Atreus," ca. 1350 B.C. Built in a hillside, this circular structure constructed of limestone blocks has an inside diameter of 14.64 m and a corbelled dome rising to a height of 13.12 m. Surfaces of the blocks were trimmed to produce smooth horizontal and vertical curves. When finished, the tomb was entirely covered with soil.

Although a few earlier domes are known from the ancient Near East, they were apparently not common before the first century A.D.; after the discovery of concrete by the Romans, however, they became increasingly popular. The Pantheon in Rome, built during the second century A.D., is the oldest intact, domed building in the world. Constructed of concrete and faced with fired brick, it has an interior diameter of 43 m (Robertson, 1969:246–251). Byzantine, Muslim, and later Christian masons developed new construction techniques in succeeding centuries and were responsible for the plethora of domes in a variety of shapes, such as hemispherical, elliptical, and onion-shaped, that serve all kinds of structures in Europe, around the Mediterranean Sea, and across the northern tier of Islamic countries from the Balkans, through Turkey, Iraq, Iran, Afghanistan, Pakistan, to India, and northward in southern Asia.

There are, however, many gaps in the history of the application of the dome to different structures. We have little firm evidence apart from those still standing, because archaeologists have been less concerned with late or recent cultures in the Near East. For example, we know neither when the traditions of domed mud-brick houses in Syria and Iran began nor the stages in their structural development. They may go back to pre-Christian centuries or be as recent as 1000 years ago.

Mud-brick domes continue in use to the present in Iran, where entire villages are roofed with hemispherical domes (Wulff, 1966:105). In Pakistan, three large circular structures with magnificent corbelled domes reflect designs of earlier centuries of this millennium. One, built in the twelfth century A.D. according to villagers of Par Hawaja Ibrahim du Pasi, near Dhardhar, was an elaborate cylindrical tower marking the tomb of a nobleman (Figure 11.1). The inner walls were divided into seven vertical panels with four stages of recessing (see Figure 9.14). Two corbelled arches further divided each vertical panel into two sections, reminiscent of wall paneling of Mesopotamia and Iran. The corbelled dome was covered with a fine lime plaster divided at intervals by ribs so that it resembled an open umbrella. In 1990, this beautiful tomb was within 2 m of the edge of a rapidly eroding river bank, and by now it may have been destroyed. A large fort at Sibi known as Mid Chakar Khan Rind, said to have been built between the thirteenth and sixteenth centuries A.D., is now largely in ruins. It featured two circular mud-brick towers on its east side with walls 2.93 m thick and interior diameters of about 5.6 m, making the exterior diameters about 11.46 m. Both towers were roofed with enormous corbelled domes (Figures 11.2, 11.3), and a circular stairway wound around the outside wall to the top of the dome of the better preserved tower (see also Chapter 9's discussion of advantages of mud brick).

Farther eastward on the Changthang plain in northern Tibet, circular mud-brick houses roofed with ogee-shaped, mud-brick domes are still built by nomadic tribes as winter homes in this region, where freezing temperatures are said to prevail 280 days of the year. Explorer Michel Peissel suggested that they may represent a long tradition of contact with ancient Persia stemming from pre-Buddhist times before the seventh century B.C. (Thomas, 1998:A3).

Figure 11.1 Mud-brick domed tower of a nobleman's tomb, ca. twelfth century A.D., near Dhardhar, Pakistan (1990).

It is surprising that we do not have more examples illustrating the use of domes, especially in ancient houses from the third millennium B.C. onward. The explanation chiefly lies in the fact that so few ancient buildings have survived in most

Figure 11.2   Domed guest house, ca. thirteenth to sixteenth centuries A.D., with exterior stairway winding upward, at fort Mid Chakar Khan Rind, in Sibi, Pakistan (1990).

Figure 11.3   Interior of broken corbelled dome of guest house at Mid Chakar Khan Rind, Sibi, Pakistan (1990).

archaeological sites, and diagnostic debris is either very limited or non-existent. Mud-brick walls standing 20–60 cm high are typical, and finding any preserved to 1 m or more is a bonus in many sites. Although corbelling may begin with the lowest courses of bricks, it is sometimes difficult to determine if an excavated wall is intentionally curved inward or is simply out of plumb, and difficult also to distinguish between deliberate and accidental overlapping of courses.

Corbelling is normally built on vertical supporting walls usually beginning at a level one to two meters high, which in most instances is higher than ancient walls are preserved. If a corbelled dome were built over a square room, one might find no indication of it, with the possible exception of the lowest courses of squinches in the corners of the room. The only type of debris that could indicate a building had once been covered with a corbelled dome would be a section of a dome that fell inside the room and remained substantially intact, i.e., with the bricks still joined by mud mortar. In such a chunk of debris, if horizontal curvature in the brick courses was visible, as well as vertical curvature in which each course slightly overhung the one below, one could conclude that it was a section of the corbelled dome.

The bricks used in dome construction are generally similar in size and weight to those used in building regular walls, although circular structures of a small diameter require smaller bricks. The small domed structures serving as storage areas in Syria that are built of smaller bricks are an example. Before ca. 3200 B.C., when plano-convex bricks were used, corbelling probably could not have been employed in substantial buildings because the rounded tops of the bricks would have made corbelled walls and domes unstable.

HISTORY OF ARCHES AND VAULTS

Curved roofs have a long history in the Near East dating to at least 3300 B.C. Many surviving examples illustrate different designs and methods of construction. From the archaeological evidence currently available, vaults were far more common in antiquity than domes.

In prehistoric times, the Egyptians and Mesopotamians, who lived near shallow, perennial bodies of water where reeds grew, dwelt in curved-roof structures built of bundles of reeds bent and tied together at the top to form supporting arches for a covering of reed mats. In the twentieth century, vaulted buildings of reeds probably reached the zenith of design in the hands of the Marsh Arabs in southern Iraq (Figure 11.4). These magnificent structures range about 7.7–31.1 m in length, about 3.04–4.57 m in width, and are supported by 7–17 arches. They serve as community centers where justice is meted out, weddings and funerals take place, and men observe the ceremony of drinking coffee (Salim, 1962:72–73). Their considerable height permits heat to rise, leaving those on the floor much cooler in that extraordinarily hot, steamy environment.

Perhaps the high arching roofs of reeds led some imaginative individuals from the surrounding dry regions where reeds did not grow to think about substituting mud, their local building material, because a vaulted mud house would be much more permanent and comfortable inside. This may have led those early masons to experiment with erecting mud vaulting, probably during the middle centuries of the

Figure 11.4 Sketch of typical vaulted reed building of the Marsh Arabs in southern Iraq.

fourth millennium B.C. Of the three early methods—corbelled, radial, and pitched-brick vaulting—corbelling was the simplest and was probably developed first. Through trial-and-error, the more complex problems involved in the construction of both radial and pitched-brick vaulting were solved by about 3100 B.C.

The oldest corbelled vault known to us, dating in the Early Dynastic I period, ca. 2900 B.C., was excavated at Tell Razuk, Iraq, by McGuire Gibson (1980:19–28). The circular building had a central court surrounded by a single row of vaulted rooms. In a typical room, the corbelled vault measured 3 m wide and extended from the floor to just over 3 m high. Surprisingly, of the three earliest vaults known, two—one at Tepe Gawra in Iraq and the other at Helwan in Egypt—featured radial vaults, and the latter also had a pitched-brick vault; neither was of corbelled construction (Speiser, 1935:36–37, pls. 13, 24a; Emery, 1961:152–153, fig. 90). These indicate that the late fourth millennium B.C. was a time of considerable innovation in the development of vaulting. The radial vault at Tepe Gawra was no small structure; it measured 8.5 m long, 3.25 m wide, and 2.1 m high. The Helwan example of the First Dynasty, ca. 3100 B.C., was a tomb of the artisan or servant class; it had a pitched-brick vault that supported a thick layer of sand and was capped by a radial vaulted roof.

The origin of mud-brick vaulting in "reed" construction is confirmed in Egypt. During the Third and Fourth Dynasties of the Old Kingdom, in the Pyramid Age (ca. twenty-seventh–twenty-fifth centuries B.C.), tombs were often designed with both radial and pitched-brick vaulting in imitation of arching bundles of reeds. This was an exciting age of experimentation in many facets of Egyptian culture including architecture. In vaulting, all sorts of bricks and combinations of bricks were created and tried, and even now we can identify with what must have been a sense of wonder and delight at their inventions. When transferring the reed bundle design to mud construction, masons made several different shapes of brick in special molds that, when assembled, created solid, rounded ridges of mud in high relief. After being plastered, these mud ridges were painted reddish-brown to resemble the color of bundles of reeds (Fisher, 1924:15).

Most of these vaults covered the offering rooms in tombs of the *mastaba* type, which resembled a mud bench in form. All of the tombs mentioned here are located in the Giza Necropolis, near the Great Pyramid of Khufu (Cheops). A typical "reed-shaped" radial vault was found in the Mastaba of Neferi (Figure 11.5; Abu-Bakr, 1953:131, fig. 106). One long edge of each vault brick had two deep scallops, which appeared as two reed-like bundles when combined with identical bricks in the courses above and below.

Pitched-brick vaults were also shaped to simulate reed bundles in different types of construction. In one style, found in Mastaba G3003, the lower edge of the brick was rounded to a semicircle, so that the assembled courses represented a bundle of reeds (Figure 11.6; Fisher, 1924:105–106, fig. 96). In Mastaba G2098, the tomb of Ruwz, a larger "reed bundle" was created by putting two bricks together, the bottom edge of each brick having been shaped in a quarter-round, which, when joined together, formed a half-round molding (Figure 11.7; Fisher, 1924:63–67, fig. 52). But the most remarkable of all were the interlocking pitched bricks (Figure 11.8). Two projections—one extending from the upper right corner and the other from the lower left corner—fit into corresponding cut-outs on adjacent bricks. Each interlocking brick also had a quarter-round base on one side, opposed to the quarter-round on the other brick, and the interlocking pairs joined together formed a single imitation reed bundle (Fisher, 1924:14–16, figs. 107, 108, pls. 17, 18). Also dating from the Fourth Dynasty, this experimental design was apparently abandoned after Mastaba G3033 (the tomb of Sabef) was built, because no other example has been found. Evidence that mud-brick arches and vaults continued through the end of the third millennium B.C. in Egypt appears in a number of mud house models—"soul houses"—at Rifeh, which were placed over graves and were eventually covered by encroaching gravel (Petrie, 1977:18–19, pls. 18:101, 20:64,160).

In Mesopotamia during the First Dynasty of Ur, about 2500 B.C., the drains of the buildings on the ziggurat terrace were covered with radial vaults, and a radial arched, mud-brick doorway, dated about 200 years later, was found at Tell Taya (Reade, 1968:252). At Ur, Sir Leonard Woolley found the royal tombs of King Abargi and Queen Shubad roofed with radial barrel vaults of fired brick. Evidence of straw adhering to the mud-mortar-filled joints on the intrados indicated that during construction the radial vaults were supported by a pile of soil or loose mud bricks covered with a bed of straw that served as centering while the mortar of the vault dried (Woolley, 1963:62, 65, 89).

Radial arches and vaults burgeoned in Mesopotamia during the second millennium B.C. Tell al-Rimah, located about 60 km west of Mosul, Iraq, is the type site for vaulting in the Near East between ca. 2000 and 1250 B.C. More examples of radial and pitched-brick vaults were recorded in the temple complex at Tell al-Rimah than in any other site excavated to date. No less than 12 applications of radial arches and vaults and about an equal number of pitched-brick vaults and domical vaults belong to this period. Among radial vault constructions are the following: the barrel vault of a temple that spanned 3.8 m; a stairway supported by eight arches, each

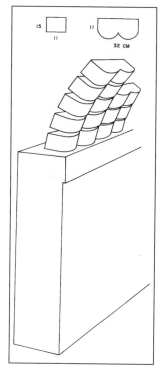

Figure 11.5   End view, top view, and placement diagram of radial bricks with two scallops on one edge to imitate two bundles of reeds, from the Mastaba of Neferi, Giza Necropolis, Egypt. (Brick dimensions in cm; drawing by G. Robert Lewis, after Abu-Bakr, 1953: fig. 106.)

one progressively higher than the one before; three vaulted passageways through a monumental entrance ramp connecting two terraces; and two arched doorways, a vaulted tomb chamber, and a series of arches on two levels supporting a terrace or possibly a building (Oates, 1968:120–121).

Turning to pitched-brick vaulting, mention must be made of the pitched-brick, domical vault built of mud brick, which is similar in form to the domical vaults of fired brick at Ur but different in construction method. Both examples are roughly contemporary, dating ca. 2000 B.C. Altogether, eight domical vaults on walls surrounding rectangular spaces were excavated at Rimah. In some places domical vaults stood only about 1m above the floor, with a second domical vault directly above, creating a chamber between them 1.7 m high. Fan-like structures, curving diagonally upward over the corners and resembling squinches, created an octagonal space in which rings of pitched-brick vaulting were laid simultaneously from both ends of the building, meeting in the middle of the space, the remainder of which was then filled with smaller rings until the hole became so small that it was closed with a single brick. David Oates gave a superb description of the construction of these vaults (Oates, 1970:20–23). The evidence from Rimah and Ur suggests that the development of domical vaults—roofing rectangular space with domes by means of special squinch-like structures—occurred during the late centuries of the third millennium B.C. This development was a milestone in architecture.

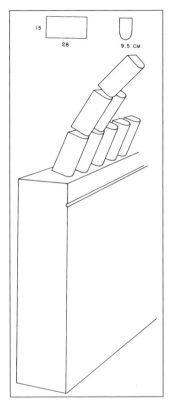

Figure 11.6   Side view, end view, and placement diagram of pitched bricks shaped to represent bundles of reeds, found in Mastaba G3003, Giza Necropolis, Egypt. (Dimensions in cm; drawing by G. Robert Lewis, after C. S. Fisher, 1924: fig. 96.)

Among the best preserved, major pitched-brick vaulted structures surviving from antiquity is the Ramesseum at Luxor, Egypt, built by Ramses II of the thirteenth century B.C. as his mortuary temple. The central structure is a beautiful, small stone temple, similar in style and detail to the much larger and more impressive Karnak Temple. Also within the compound and surrounding the stone temple are blocks of mud-brick storerooms fronting on both sides of each street (Figure 11.9). These structures once held provisions for the king's afterlife, and many of them still retain substantial sections of their original pitched vaulted roofs. Built in blocks, each vaulted chamber shares its supporting walls with its neighboring chamber (Figure 11.10; Van Beek, 1987).

If you visit Luxor in the course of a tour in Egypt, leave the tour group for an hour or two and take a west bank taxi to the Ramesseum. If time is short, forget the stone temple, because you will certainly spend time in the grander example at Karnak. Instead, tour the compound and examine in detail these remarkable structures that once numbered more than 100, about 60 of which are of the size shown in Figure 11.10 and are still standing after 3300 years! You will come away with a much better understanding of ancient Egyptian architecture, which was always predominantly of mud brick, than if you had seen only the eternal stone temples and tombs. These

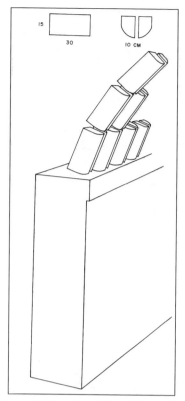

Figure 11.7 Side and end views and placement diagram for two pitched bricks joined to imitate a single reed bundle, from Mastaba G2098, Giza Necropolis, Egypt. (Dimensions in cm; drawing by G. Robert Lewis, after Fisher, 1924: fig. 52.)

vaults not only will show you the type of storage structures the Israelites built at Pithom and Ramses for the Pharoah Ramses II (see Bible passages in Exodus 1:7–11; 5:6–19), but will also speak to you about the durability and the design possibilities of pitched-brick vaulting in mud brick.

In the Levant at Tell Atchana (ancient Alalakh) north of Antioch (now Antakya) in southern Turkey, bricks from collapsed vaults were found scattered on the floors of the palace, dating about 2000 B.C. (Woolley, 1953:58). At Tell Dan in northern Israel, access through the rampart fortification was gained by means of a triple-arched gateway with a span of 2.4 m, built of three courses of radial-arch brick during the eighteenth century B.C. (Figure 11.11; Biran, 1984). At about the same time, a radial-arch gateway was also constructed through the massive revetment at Ashkelon on the southern coast of Israel (see Figure 8.1). Later, in the twelfth century B.C. at Tell Jemmeh, Israel, a series of four radial arches 1.05 m high supported the perforated mud-brick floor of a large ovoid pottery kiln built by the Philistines (Figure 11.12; Van Beek, 1984:688–690).

Few examples of any type of vaulting from the first millennium B.C. have been found in Mesopotamia, and those known are chiefly part of sewer conduits. This is surely accidental in view of the extensive use of arches and vaulted roofs of mud

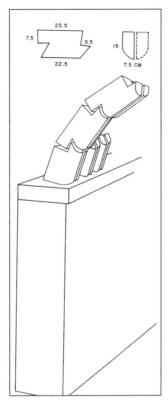

Figure 11.8 Side and end views and placement diagram for interlocking pitched bricks, paired to imitate a single reed bundle, from Mastaba G3033, Giza Necropolis, Egypt. (Dimensions in cm; drawing by G. Robert Lewis, after Fisher 1924: figs. 107–108.)

Figure 11.9 Blocks of pitched-brick vaulted storerooms in the Ramesseum compound, thirteenth century B.C., Luxor, Egypt (1977).

brick in the preceding millennia as well as the number of later structures in the early centuries A.D. The gap in continuity is likely due to (1) massive rebuilding of towns and cities, which destroyed the earlier remains, (2) abandonment of many old urban centers in the late centuries of the first millennium B.C., and/or (3) plowing and cultivation of ancient sites during the past 2000 years. Domes, arches, and vaults cannot survive more than minimal destruction of a site because these roof structures,

Figure 11.10   Five partially preserved vaulted chambers sharing party walls in the Rames-seum, Luxor, Egypt (1977).

Figure 11.11   Radial arched gateway, ca. eighteenth century B.C., Tell Dan, Israel (1988). Most of the fill in the gate remains to provide continuing support for the structure.

being at the very top of buildings, are most exposed. Indeed, leveling a site for new construction, 2500 years of plowing, and natural erosion by wind and rain ensure removal of not only the upper parts of buildings—destroying all evidence of roofing systems—but often entire structures. This is surely what happened in Mesopotamia, because both radial and pitched-brick vaulting must have been extensively used during the Assyrian and Babylonian empires of the first millennium B.C.

Moreover, a pitched-brick vaulted building at Tell Jemmeh built at the beginning of the second quarter of the seventh century B.C. by Assyrian masons almost certainly was erected with the assistance of Persian masons conscripted into the

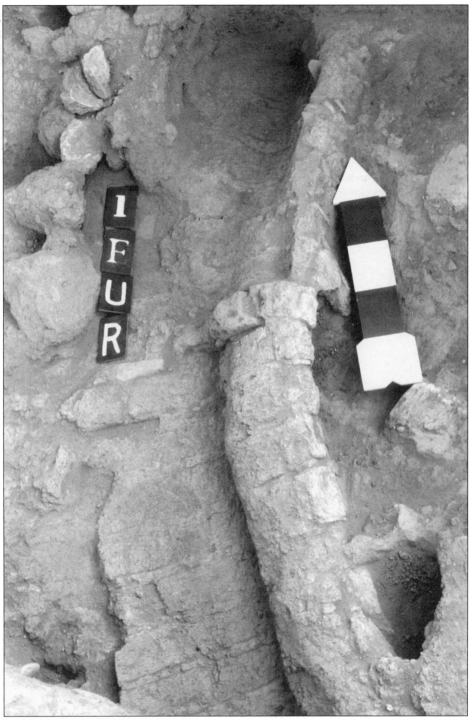

Figure 11.12   One of four radial arches that supported the perforated mud-brick floor of the twelfth century B.C. Philistine pottery kiln, as found fallen on its side, at Tell Jemmeh, Israel.

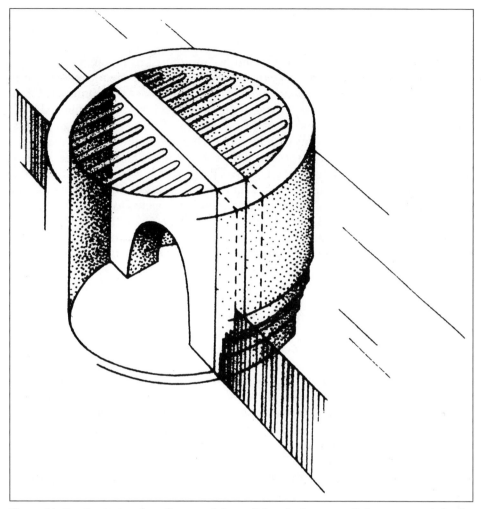

Figure 11.13 Reconstruction diagram of the radial-arched cross wall that supported the flat roof of the granary, from the late fourth to third centuries B.C., Tell Jemmeh, Israel.

Assyrian army. This unique building provides superb evidence of the ongoing development in the use of curved roofs in the Mesopotamian homeland through the first millennium B.C.

Radial arch and vault construction continued elsewhere. In Iran, at a site known as Nush-i Jan during the late eighth to early seventh centuries B.C., the Western Temple was reconstructed with a high, radial vault spanning about 3 m. The most prevalent vaulting at the site, however, is ribbed—or strut—vaulting, which was apparently invented in western Iran early in the first millennium B.C. At Tell Jemmeh, the larger circular mud-brick granary of the Ptolemaic occupation (late fourth to third centuries B.C.) featured a huge radial-arched cross wall that supported the flat roof of the structure (Figure 11.13). Two massive, composite arches of the first millennium B.C. have survived in Egypt. One is the pylon or gateway built by Shishak at Dra` Abu el-Naga (or Dira Abu el-Naga) at Thebes in the tenth century B.C., and the second is the archway at el-Asasif at Thebes, probably of the seventh to sixth centuries B.C.

In the early Roman period and continuing into the Christian and Islamic eras, fired brick gradually replaced mud brick for arch and vault construction of monumental structures in many affluent communities in Egypt, Mesopotamia, and Iran. However, at Soknopaiou Nesos, a town in the Fayum region of Egypt, pitched-brick vaulting of mud brick continued in use from the first century B.C. through the first century A.D. in basement rooms with high ceilings carrying the floors of the rooms above (Boak, 1935:12, plan 16). At about the same time at Karanis, another town in the Fayum region, many houses and granaries had pitched-brick vaults of fired brick for roofs (Boak and Peterson, 1931:23–24, figs. 24, 25, 27, 28). In Mesopotamia, the radially vaulted tomb at Tel Umar (largest mound at ancient city of Seleucia), Iraq, from Level II, is dated A.D. 43–118 (Waterman, 1933:49–51, pl. 18, fig. 8).

The greatest variety of vaulting occurs in the Coptic monastery of San Simeon on the west side of the Nile at Aswan, Egypt. Built during the sixth to seventh centuries A.D. and abandoned in the thirteenth century, the basilica was roofed with three parallel pitched-brick vaults, with a cross vault in the nave, surmounted by a dome (Figure 11.14). A monastery of at least three stories housed the monks, whose cells opened off a central corridor. Each corridor floor was supported by a single course of pitched-brick vaulting. An ingenious system of small secondary vaults occupying the space between the main vault and the side walls served two functions (Figure 11.15): (1) it greatly lightened the weight load on the vault by reducing the number of bricks otherwise needed to fill the space between the extrados of the main vault and the side walls to support the floor above; (2) it also served as ducts or wind tunnels to conduct the cool night desert air collected by an outside wind tower into the building, where it was distributed to each of the cells by means of vertical ducts inside the walls (Van Beek, 1987:102). Pitched-brick vaults of catenary form are prolific on Elephantine Island in the Nile at Aswan, and at Medinet Habu, across the Nile from Luxor in all sorts of buildings of the Coptic period.

In Mesopotamia, radial and pitched-brick vaults in tombs were discovered at Tel Umar (Seleucia) dating from the first and second centuries A.D. (Waterman, 1933:51, pl. 20:1,2, fig. 9). And both radial arches and pitched-brick vaults supporting the substructures of the Great Palace of Byzantium in Constantinople were identified (Rice, 1962:80, pl. 10). The most spectacular pitched-brick vault in the world is the one covering the reception hall of the winter palace of the Sassanian kings at Ctesiphon in Iraq (Figure 11.16). Built of fired brick, probably late in the third century A.D., it remains the largest unreinforced single-span vault in the world, reaching a height of 28.4 m, spanning 25.5 m, and preserved for a length of about 48 m.

Corbelled, radial, and pitched-brick construction persisted and spread widely from their developmental homeland in the Near East. At Nalanda, a Buddhist University of the ninth century A.D., southeast of Patna in Bihar State of northern India, a small one-room building in one of the courts was roofed with a pitched-brick vault built of fired bricks. In Nubia, the region south of Aswan, pitched-brick vaulting continued apparently without interruption as the major form of roofing in vernacular architecture. It was brought to the attention of the archaeological community by

Figure 11.14 Three parallel pitched-brick vaults in the nave of the church, seventh to thirteenth centuries A.D., at San Simeon monastery, Aswan, Egypt (1977). The position and arch of the cross vault appear on the wall at center right, which intersected the three parallel vaults.

Figure 11.15 Corridor floors in the San Simeon monastery supported by pitched-brick vaulting and by secondary vaulting between primary vaults and walls, Aswan, Egypt (1977).

Woolley at Karanog in 1907 (Woolley and Randall-Maciver, 1910:18–19, pl. 111), but apparently had little or no immediate effect on contemporary architecture and archaeology. In 1941, Egyptian architect and urban planner Hassan Fathy was searching for a method of erecting mud vaulting without centering, and he visited this region based on information provided by his brother. He hired two masons and

Figure 11.16 Pitched-brick vault of fired brick, ca. late third century A.D., Ctesiphon, Iraq. It is the largest unreinforced single-span vault in the world. (After Sarre and Herzfeld, 1911: pl. 39.)

brought them back to the Delta, where they built a pitched-brick vault in a day and a half! Having learned from them, Fathy designed and built a variety of beautiful structures throughout the Near East (Fathy, 1973:6–11) and also in New Mexico, where he designed and constructed a large mud-brick Islamic complex at Abiquiu known as Dar al-Islam in 1980. The complex includes a mosque (see Figure 2.10), boys' school, girls' school, and administrative offices (Figure 11.17). Inside is a corridor covered with a vaulted ceiling and a series of radial arches (Figure 11.18).

In Pakistan, radial arches built between the thirteenth and sixteenth centuries A.D. can still be seen in the large fort, Mid Chakar Khan Rind, in Sibi. On the fortification wall of the west side is a two-room building with radially arched windows and niches. On the east side of the fortification, one of the circular towers (Figure 11.2) is entered through a radially arched doorway, and the inner wall surfaces are decorated with a series of 14 radially arched niches (see Figure 9.14).

CHARACTERISTICS OF CURVED ROOFS

Shapes

Domes, arches, and vaults are built in a variety of shapes. Domes may be conical, hemispherical, or onion-shaped. Arches may be round, basket-handle, horseshoe, flat, as well as exotic styles in Islamic and Gothic structures, such as keyhole, trefoil, ogee, and lancet. Vaults may be barrel, parabolic, catenary, basket-handle, or flattened. The choice of style is based on load-bearing characteristics, tradition, and personal choice, or a combination of these factors. All domes, arches, and vaults must be planned in advance so that special molds can be made for unusual brick shapes or routines can be developed for subsequent modification of brick shapes by cutting.

Figure 11.17 The schools of Dar al-Islam built by Hassan Fathy in Abiquiu, New Mexico, USA (1989).

Figure 11.18 Vaulted corridor with radial mud-brick arches in Dar al-Islam, Abiquiu, New Mexico, USA (1989).

Brick Sizes

Mud bricks used in curved roofs are not always the same size as those employed in building walls. Vault bricks may be slightly smaller and sometimes considerably larger, depending on the type of construction and local building traditions. Bricks in domes, corbelled vaults, and in many radial vaults are often identical in size to those used in walls. For example, the bricks used for both walls and radial vaults at Tell al-Rimah, Iraq, measured 34 × 34 × 8 cm or 35 × 35 × 9 cm. Similarly, bricks used for the radially arched cross wall in the larger of the two granaries at Tell Jemmeh (late fourth to third centuries B.C.), Israel, were also the same size as those of the circular wall, 33 × 33 × 11 cm.

In pitched-brick vaulting, however, bricks are generally smaller and thus lighter in weight than those in the walls of buildings (see Figure 11.36). Weight reduction is also achieved by increasing the amount of straw in the mud-brick mix. At Tell al-Rimah, pitched vault bricks were 24 × 24 × 4 cm, somewhat smaller than the wall bricks (Oates, 1970:22). The wall bricks of the vaulted Assyrian building of the seventh century B.C. were 48 × 24 × 12 cm, about 12.5% larger than the voussoir (keystone-shaped) vault bricks, which ranged from 37 × 30 × 12 cm to 37 × 24.5 × 12 cm. On the other hand, an Egyptian *mastaba* tomb of the Fourth Dynasty was constructed with wall bricks measuring 25 × 13 × 9 cm and pitched bricks in the vault measuring 28 × 15 × 9.5 cm, nearly 27% larger. In New Gourna, the town built by Hassan Fathy on the west bank of the Nile River at Luxor, bricks used in the pitched-brick vaults were also 25 × 15 × 5 cm, 18% larger than those of the walls, which measured 23 × 11 × 7 cm (Fathy, 1973:209).

Wall Requirements

Curved mud roofs are extraordinarily heavy, and their weight must be borne by sturdy walls. The walls, therefore, stand on deeper foundations and must be well built, plumb, and level so that the roof and walls will not collapse before or after the building is finished. The walls are also thicker and more massive than those required for flat roofs, typically ranging from 61 to 91.5 cm and sometimes even thicker. The corbelled domes of the guest houses in fort Mid Chakar Khan Rind at Sibi, Pakistan, are carried by circular walls 2.93 m thick. Although I know of no actual examples in the Old World, rammed-earth walls with their greater density and size should be ideal for domed and vaulted buildings.

TECHNIQUES OF ERECTING DOMES, ARCHES, AND VAULTS

Corbel Construction

Although corbelling is chiefly used for building domes, it is also used for constructing arches and vaults. In erecting corbelled structures, arching may begin at ground level so that the walls incline inward in a gradual curve, as in the domed guest house at fort Mid Chakar Khan Rind in Pakistan; there is no clear division between side walls and dome. Most corbelled structures, however, have vertical walls on each side, which are built to a planned height where arching begins. A basic characteristic of corbelled structures is that all courses of brick from the base to the apex of the curved roof are horizontal, near horizontal, or tilted slightly—i.e., they are not increasingly tilted from the outer edge to the inner edge as the dome, arch, or vault is erected. On the inner edge, the end of the last brick in each horizontal course is extended 2–4 cm over the end of the brick in the course below. Eventually the size of the opening becomes so small that a single brick can cap the opening, closing the arch or dome. Limiting the projection of each course to a few centimeters produces a dome, arch, or vault that is structurally sound, with a smooth, attractive curve that lends itself to great variety in design. The jagged line forming the arch is attractive in its own right, good examples of which are the inner surfaces of the domes in the Syrian "beehive" houses (see Figures 11.26, 11.27). By varying the amount of the overhang of each corbelled course, differently shaped arches can be formed: conical, catenary, hemispherical, keyhole, and pointed. The shape of the arch and the varying amounts of overhang required can be planned in advance by drawing in scale on graph paper. In building a corbelled vault, one applies the same method used in erecting corbelled arches except that the courses are bonded so that rising joints do not correspond to those in adjacent courses.

If a corbelled dome is erected on a circular wall, the process is straightforward, as in the domical guest house at the fort Mid Chakar Khan Rind (see Figure 11.2), in the beehive house at Fah, Syria (see Figure 1.1), and in the mud-brick houses in northern Tibet. But if the room is square, squinches must be built in each corner of the room, rising and fanning out in an arc to support the curving segments of the base of the dome unsupported by the walls of the room. Squinches are built as high and curving as is required to make the base of the dome a true circle. Their function is to transfer the weight of the otherwise unsupported portions of the dome to the walls and their corners. Squinches are bonded into the corner walls and corbelled as they rise to meet the circular base of the dome (Figure 11.19).

Corbelled domes of the beehive houses of northern Syria are typically built by three men, one mixing the mud, one laying the walls of the square room, and one building the dome. In the division of labor, women often serve as brick and mortar carriers, and they traditionally do all mud plastering both inside and out. A 4.5-m-square house with a corbelled dome requires from one to two months to build and uses some 4000 bricks. The mud bricks were rectangular, measuring 43 × 22 × 8 cm or 46 × 24 × 10 cm in houses, but in smaller structures such as granaries, smaller bricks were used, measuring 33 × 21 × 6 cm.

The mud-brick walls forming the square are 65–75 cm in thickness and commonly reach a height of 2.56–2.77 m. Dome bricks are laid at right angles to the radius of the circle and are set in thick mud mortar (Figure 11.20). Because rectangular bricks are used to form a circle, the rising joints between bricks are narrower on the inside and wider on the outside. Lumps of mud mortar fill the wider, triangle-shaped interstices between the spreading bricks. Some squinches are built into the corners of the room beginning between 65 and 120 cm above the floor, usually with a steel rod, wooden pole, or tree limb anchored in both walls and crossing the corner obliquely to provide support for the base of the squinch (see Figure 11.19). When the squinches and walls reach their full height, the corbelling of the base of the dome begins with a near perfect circle about 2.5 m in diameter. Each corbelled course of the circle is laid to extend 4–5 cm inward over the course below it to create a conical, or occasionally a hemispherical, dome. The number of courses required varies with the amount of overhang used in each course, the desired height of the dome, and the diameter of the base of the dome. We saw domes with 22, 25, 26, 27, 30, 31, 33, 36, and 47 courses of corbelled brick; Table 11.1 shows estimated dome and building heights for each, assuming a uniform brick thickness of 10 cm plus

Figure 11.19   A squinch in an abandoned domed storage building in Fah, Syria (1994). It is the fan-shaped, unplastered brick area in the corner (defined by the dash lines) with a horizontal reinforcing rod at its base.

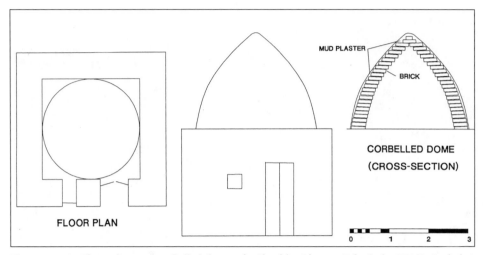

Figure 11.20   Floor plan and corbelled dome of a "beehive" house, Fah, Syria (1994). Scale bar is in meters.

Table 11.1   Estimated heights for a corbelled dome and an entire building (rounded to the nearest 0.1 m and ¼ or ⅓ ft) for varying number of brick courses actually seen. Estimates assume uniform brick thickness of 10 cm (4 in), mortar thickness of 1 cm, and wall height of 2.5 m (~8¼ ft) to base of dome.

	Approximate dome height		Approximate total building height	
Number of courses in dome	*(m)*	*(ft)*	*(m)*	*(ft)*
22	2.4	8	4.9	16¼
25	2.8	9	5.3	17¼
26	2.9	9⅓	5.4	17½
27	3.0	9⅔	5.5	18
30	3.3	10¾	5.8	19
31	3.4	11¼	5.9	19⅓
33	3.6	12½	6.1	20
36	4.0	13	6.5	21¼
47	5.2	17	7.7	25¼

1 cm of mud mortar. The heights are approximate, not measured figures, because they assume all brick and mortar joints are the same size, which of course seldom occurs. The small hole at the top, remaining after the final course is laid, is covered with one or two flat bricks and possibly a quarter brick on top.

We saw a few domes with two rows of flagstones projecting from the outer surface, spaced horizontally about 60–70 cm apart with the upper row 1.22 m above the lower one (Figure 11.21). Each stone projected about 20 cm from the outer surface of the dome. These stones were inserted when the dome was erected to provide permanent, convenient steps for workers to stand on when applying mud plaster to the dome surface, a process that is repeated annually. Paul Copeland noted that sections of tree trunks about 10 cm in diameter were sometimes inserted in the dome at different places when it was being built and manually twisted several times while

Figure 11.21   Stepping stones projecting from corbelled domes in Fah, Syria (1994).

the dome was drying so that they would be loose enough to be removed during the summer (Figure 11.22). The holes then provided airflow and ventilation, allowing heat collected in the dome to escape during the hot weather (Copeland, 1955:23).

At Vivin, Syria, a structure described by the villagers as being at least 200 years old provided a fine example of mud brick combined with stone—in this instance the use of mud-brick domes on ashlar stone walls and arches (Figure 11.23). The building was about 15 m square, divided into nine "rooms" arranged in three rows of three, and each room was roofed with its own mud-brick corbelled dome (Figure 11.24). The rooms were open to one another because all interior walls consisted of broad, pointed arches. (The word "room" here denotes spatial divisions in which broad arches replace virtually all of each wall.) Each of the 12 pointed arches was constructed of one course of ashlar with mud-brick pendentives in between (Figure 11.25). Each pendentive was composed of 30 courses of mud brick to reach the base of the dome at the level of the top of the pointed arches, and to carry its weight. The domes were built with 47 courses of corbelled brick for a height of about 5.17 m; adding about 3.6 m for the height of the outer stone walls yields a total height of about 8.77 m (Figure 11.26).

If the outer surface of the dome is not regularly inspected for cracks and the beginning of channels cut by rain and run-off water, and if it is not seasonally maintained by an additional coat of mud plaster, the top of the dome often cracks severely, sometimes beyond repair. In several domes we saw, the damaged top section, consisting of as many as five or six courses, had been removed to the level of a sound course, giving the dome the shape of a truncated cone (Figure 11.27). The resulting hole had been covered by a sheet of flat or corrugated metal that was supported by eight or so tree limbs set in the mud brick. Such rooms are commonly used as indoor kitchens. In some instances, it seems likely that the dome was originally built truncated for a kitchen.

Figure 11.22 Logs set in dome for ventilation when necessary, Fah, Syria (1994).

Figure 11.23 Turkish structure, probably a military stable, with ashlar walls and nine mud-brick corbelled domes, ca. eighteenth century A.D., Vivin, Syria (1994).

The outer surface of all vaults and domes exposed to the weather must be covered with lime or mud plaster to fill in the "steps" created by the offsets of corbelled bricks as well as all visible cracks and low places. Otherwise, rain will collect and

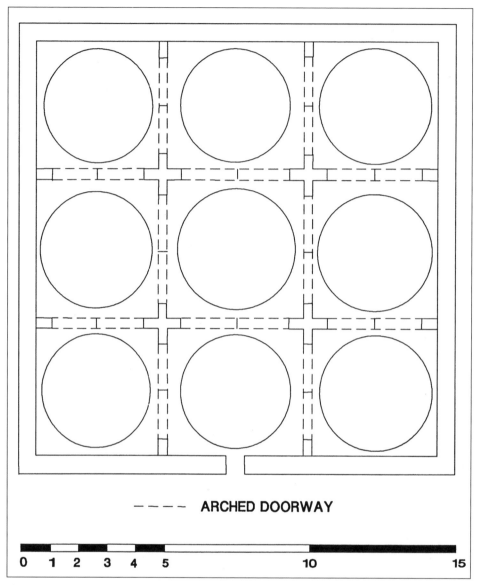

Figure 11.24 Plan of nine-dome building in Vivin, Syria (1994). Scale bar is in meters.

erode the brick and mortar. In Syria, mud plaster is commonly used on the outer surface, but some domes are painted inside and out with whitewash (Figure 11.28). In the more modest houses we visited, the inner surface of the dome was rarely finished with mud plaster, leaving the "step" pattern of the corbelling to create an interesting, if busy pattern. In more affluent, well-maintained homes, the interior of the dome was filled with plaster and whitewashed, which greatly lightened and brightened the room (Figure 11.29). In a few instances, we saw that wetter mud mortar had been used in laying the dome, as it had been squeezed out of the joints

Figure 11.25   Ashlar-pointed arches and mud-brick pendentives, Vivin, Syria (1994).

Figure 11.26 Interior of domes with mud-brick pendentives reaching to the top of the pointed arches, Vivin, Syria (1994).

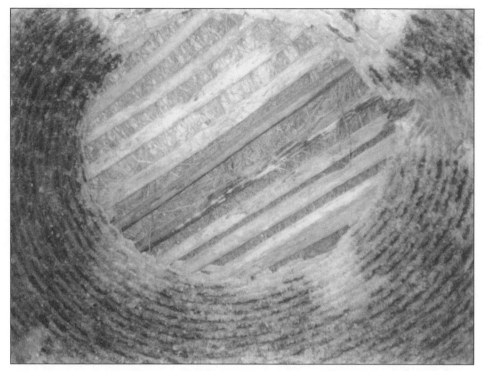

Figure 11.27   Truncated dome covered with boards and metal sheeting, Vivin, Syria (1994).

to form small stalactites on the edges of the bricks. Although we never saw an example, it should be possible to achieve smooth surfaces on both the inside and outside of corbelled domes by forming bricks, whose longitudinal cross sections are parallelograms, in special molds with sloping parallel ends. Alternatively, it might be possible to trim the ends of bricks early in the drying process, as soon as any danger of the brick sagging or slumping is past. Such bricks should minimize rough "steps" or offsets on the inner and outer surfaces.

Radial Construction

In radial construction, the side walls of the room are built to the height where the vault will begin. The hallmark of radial vaulting is the orientation of the vault bricks: they are laid with their large surfaces—i.e., the top and bottom—aligned with the radius of the vault's curve, and with their narrow end surfaces perpendicular to the vault's radius (Figure 11.30). Their gradual advance from a horizontal position on the wall to a near-vertical position at the apex of the vault contrasts markedly with that of bricks in corbelled construction, which remain in a horizontal position throughout. In a radial vault, the first course is set on top of the wall in a bed of stiff mud mortar. Several small stones or potsherds are placed in the mud mortar under the outer edges of the bricks while the inner edges are carefully aligned with those of the bricks immediately below to create a smooth intrados.

Figure 11.28   Mud-plastered domes on right and whitewashed dome on left, Syria (1994).

Figure 11.29   Whitewashed, smooth interior of domed house in Syria (1994). Behind the cradle where the corner line ends is the beginning of the squinch.

Figure 11.30 Schematic drawing of radial vault construction with side and top view of square bricks. (Dimensions in cm; drawing by G. Robert Lewis.)

An alternate method of raising the first brick on both sides of a radial arch or vault was discovered in our excavations of the pottery kiln of the twelfth century B.C. at Tell Jemmeh. A specially molded, triangular, mud brick was used as a springer to cant the first course of radial brick at the same angle. This mud brick measured 24 cm long × 11 cm wide × 13.5 cm high at the back, tapering to about 2.5 cm high at the front or inner end, creating surface-to-base angles of 11° and 15°. The springer was laid on one of its angled surfaces so that the base of the triangle (the brick's back, or high, end) defined the extrados, and its apex (front or inner end) the intrados of the arch (Figure 11.31). The brick springer transfers the load of the arch with more stability than the mud and stone or sherd packing beneath the outer edge of regular brick. It was especially suited for building flatter radial arches because it provided greater stability under heavy loads. The Tell Jemmeh mud-brick springer, like the radial-arch bricks of the kiln, had been secondarily baked during the many firings of the kiln. Mud bricks repeatedly baked during use are much more friable than those that are simply sun-baked.

In the next course of the arch or vault, stones or sherds are again set in the mortar under the outer end, tilting the brick even more. This process continues until the bricks, each canted at an increasingly steeper angle, form an arch, which can be closed at the apex with one or two bricks positioned vertically. Thus it is the rows of stones or sherds—or the mud-brick springer—that forces the bricks into an arc.

Figure 11.31   Springer brick for canting bricks of a radial arch, Tell Jemmeh, Israel.

In radial arches the bricks are laid directly on one another, but in long radial vaults, bricks in successive courses are bonded by staggering the rising joints, requiring several rings to be under construction at the same time and progressively beginning new rings to make interlocking possible (see Figure 11.30).

Centering must be erected for radial arches and vaults because the bricks have to be supported when laid and while the mortar is drying to prevent them from sliding out of position and collapsing the vault. Centering may be constructed of any material that can securely support the weight of the curing roof. For example, it may consist of a wooden or steel frame carrying a series of arcing templates or forms; heavy wooden beams carrying stacked boards; stones or bricks piled and possibly covered with a cushion of soil and straw, the top of which is shaped like the curve of the intended arch or vault. In a vaulted tomb we saw at Ur that was built of rubble and mud mortar nearly 5000 years ago, the centering consisted of a fill of earth shaped to the curvature of the desired vault and covered with a layer of straw to cushion the vault bricks when laid and while drying. Remnants of the straw that stuck to the wet mud mortar when the vault was laid were found when the tomb was excavated (Woolley, 1934:233). Perhaps the easiest and quickest centering to assemble and disassemble consists of loose mud bricks piled inside the room, with variously sized fragments of broken bricks used to fill irregularities on the rounded top of the pile (Figure 11.32). When the arch or vault laid on this centering has dried, the pile of loose bricks is easily removed, and is ready to be stored or used in other projects.

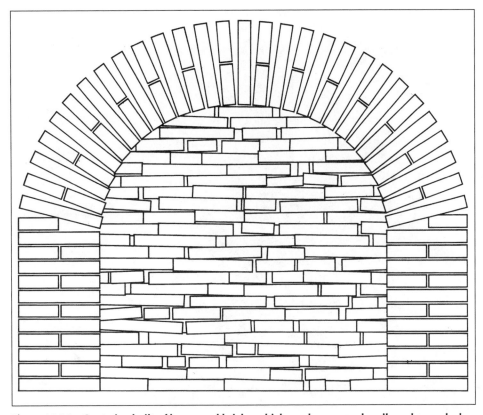

Figure 11.32 Centering built of loose mud bricks, which can be removed easily and reused when the radial arch or vault is dry. (Drawing by G. Robert Lewis.)

Centering of this type is still used for building arched doorways in northern Syria (Figure 11.33; Sweet, 1960:268, fig. 30).

Radial arches are often used in cross walls and in narrow heavy structures. At Tell Jemmeh, for example, when the region was under the control of Ptolemaic Egypt (ca. 310–198 B.C.), the site was converted from a typical functioning town to a centralized tax collection center with storage granaries replacing houses, shops, and other buildings characteristic of typical settlements. Evidence from the field immediately south of the site suggests that citizens of the town lived around the base of the site instead of on the hilltop during this period. Sir Flinders Petrie and GVB excavated 12 such granaries scattered over the site, which were built in three sizes, large, medium, and small. The Smithsonian research team completely excavated one middle-sized granary and partially cleared one small granary. The middle-sized granary measured 6.1 m in interior diameter and was bisected by a large, radially arched cross wall, 6 m high as reconstructed, with the arch 1.12 m thick and spanning 4.2 m (see Figure 11.13). The flat top of the cross wall and the granary wall carried the roofing beams. Near the ends of the cross wall, single beams could reach from granary wall to cross wall to opposite granary wall; but through most of the length of the cross wall, two beams would be used, each extending from the granary wall to the cross

Figure 11.33 Ora Van Beek standing at a radial-arch entrance to a "beehive" building that was subsequently modified with mud-brick fill, wooden lintel, and door frame, in northern Syria (1994).

wall where they met. This arrangement was necessary because there was no timber available that could span the interior diameter of the granary plus the additional length needed for embedding in the walls, a distance of 6.5–7.0 m.

The cross wall was superbly bonded into the circular wall on both sides and constructed with a very effective bonding pattern consisting of two alternating arrangements of brick courses (see Figure 9.9): Course A bonding pattern consisted of three rows of square bricks with a row of rectangular bricks at the intrados end. Course B featured two rows of square bricks bordered by a row of rectangular half-bricks on each side. From its base, the brick courses of the cross wall sloped slightly downward from the circular wall to the intrados of the arch, and the angle of declination gradually increased in successive courses. During excavation, we probed for evidence of settling by the springer of the arch, and found no cracks or indications of movement; it was as tightly attached to the circular wall as when it was constructed (Van Beek, 1983:18–19).

Radial-arch construction is employed in erecting composite arches. The two Theban examples cited earlier—the Shishak pylon at Dra` Abu el-Naga of the tenth century B.C. and the archway at el-Asasif of the seventh to sixth centuries B.C.—share a similar method of construction that may have been developed in Egypt. It consists of one course of pitched brick that supports and serves as the centering for the six or so courses of radial brick laid above it, each of which is anchored in the successive courses of the wall on either side (Clarke and Engelbach, 1930:183, fig. 216).

In the Ptolemaic period and continuing into the Christian and Islamic eras, fired brick replaced mud brick for arch and vault construction in affluent communities and in monumental structures in Egypt, Mesopotamia, and Iran. An example is the radially vaulted tomb at Tel Umar (Seleucia), Iraq, from Level II (A.D. 43–118). In Egypt, radial arches of both fired bricks and mud bricks were extensively used at two Fayum towns, Dimê and Karanis. Radial arches and vaults of mud bricks can be seen today in the Medinet Habu compound at Luxor. Although the main structures belong to the time of Ramses III in the twelfth century B.C., the radially arched rooms near the older compound walls are dated as late as the ninth century A.D.

Pitched-Brick Construction

Pitched-brick vaulting has been in use for more than 5000 years! Here we must honor those nameless, extraordinarily talented masons whose imagination and experimentation led to the invention of this magnificent, unique building technique. It remains the best method of vaulting a room and, with modifications, of erecting a domical vault. Pitched-brick vaults were favored through time because they are the easiest to build, they are strong, and they permit the greatest flexibility in scheduling the work.

What makes the construction of pitched-brick vaults different? (1) No internal support or centering is required. (2) Construction requires only two masons. (3) Pitched-brick vaults are exceptionally strong even before they are finished. When the mud mortar is still wet, one can stand on a new vault when as little as 45 cm of vaulting has been erected. (4) Work can be stopped at any time after a ring is complete, whether it is the first, sixth, or nineteenth. The freedom to stop work at intervals can be very convenient when circumstances halt construction—i.e., when the weather suddenly changes for the worse, fatigue or illness overtakes the builders, or the builders need to stop in order to finish another job. (The latter problem constantly occurs in the USA!) These characteristics make pitched-brick vaulting the most desirable type for mud construction at all levels from private residences and shops to cinemas and houses of worship.

Pitched-brick vaulting provides a choice of shapes. The most popular design is a catenary vault. A catenary is the inverted arc formed by a cord or chain when freely suspended between two points. The catenary is a natural curve, and it not only is strong but sheds rain more quickly than any other shape. Examples include the great vault at Ctesiphon of the third century A.D. (see Figure 11.16), one or two of the Ramesseum storage buildings of the thirteenth century B.C. (see Figure 11.39), and the parallel vaults of the San Simeon Church of the seventh century A.D. The barrel or semicircular pitched-brick vault is only slightly less popular in mud architecture than the catenary (see Figure 2.9). The flatter vault, describing an arc with a radius that is longer horizontally than vertically, is adaptable to a variety of construction needs. For the semicircular and flatter vaults, voussoirs—keystone-shaped mud bricks—provide still greater design possibilities, strength, and stability to the structure. Sometimes vaults with different arcs are employed in the same building, as in the seventh century B.C., pitched-brick vaulted building at Tell Jemmeh, where one semicircular and two flatter vaults were used.

Pitched-brick vaulting uses bricks different from those used in other types of vault construction. When still wet in the molds, each brick is deeply scored on the undersurface—i.e., on the lower face that leans backward into the mud mortar—with grooves made by fingers or a tool. The Tell Jemmeh voussoirs have four or five deep and broad vertical grooves on the undersurface (Figure 11.34). In Egypt, sometimes both the upper and lower surfaces were scored, as on the rectangular vault bricks used in the Ramasseum. In other Egyptian vaults, four or five deep horizontal or oblique grooves were scored, but bricks at Aswan were scored with deep concentric circular grooves (Figure 11.35). These grooves increase the surface area of the bricks and create a suction with the thick, wet mud mortar, which aids in holding the brick in place while it dries.

This type of vaulting also represents a considerable departure from the corbelled and radial schemes. Recall that in both corbelled and radial vault construction, bricks are laid with their edges aligned with the long axis of the vault and with their larger surfaces down in the mud mortar. In pitched-brick vaulting, bricks are laid with their faces at right angles to the axis of the vault and leaning back from the vertical.

The side walls are erected to the height from which the vault will spring. At Tell Jemmeh, the pitched-brick vault began when the side walls reached a height of 1.22 m. The end walls are built to a point above the planned height of the vault, because the vault must lean against one or both end walls.

Construction proceeds in the following manner. Only two masons are needed to build a pitched-brick vault. They prepare a working platform that spans from wall to wall, usually of loose boards placed on top of the side walls. They divide the work equally: one builds the left half of the vault, the other the right half, and they meet in the center. First, they spread a layer of thick mud mortar on the end wall in an arc corresponding to the planned curvature, height, width, and thickness of the vault. The mortar layer thus defines the lines of the extrados and the intrados of the vault. Next, they spread a bed of mud mortar on top of each side wall to receive the first ring of bricks. Each mason then presses the lower edge of a brick—here we will assume a half-brick to start the first course—into the mortar on the side wall and leans it back into the mortar on the end wall. It provides support for the first brick of the next ring and establishes the angle for leaning subsequent rings of bricks.

As in radial-arch construction, bricks are raised by setting potsherds or stones in the mud mortar under their outer edge to cant them upward. Mud mortar is also slapped on the face of the leaning brick and a small wedge of bedding mortar is placed on the side wall. The second ring begins with a full-sized brick, which is laid on the side wall and also raised on its outer edge by a row of potsherds or small stones in the mortar. It is then pressed against the leaning half brick previously laid. A third brick—or a half-brick—is set on the upper edge of the full-sized brick of the second ring and leaned against the mortar on the end wall, thus starting a second course (Figure 11.36). This second-course brick must also be canted upward by the insertion of sherds and small stones under its outer edge so that it slopes more inward than the brick in the course below. At this point, each ring has begun to form an arc when viewed from the opposite end of the room (Figure 11.37).

0 .5 I 2 3 4 5 6 7 8 9 10 CM

Figure 11.34 Lower surface of a mud voussoir fragment with deep, parallel grooves from pitched-brick vaulted building of seventh century B.C., Tell Jemmeh, Israel.

This process continues with the laying of successive rings until a ring closes the top of the vault against the end wall; usually this occurs in the fourth to sixth ring, depending on the height of the vault and the sizes of bricks used. Thereafter, successive rings are laid until the base of the vault reaches the opposite end wall (Figure 11.37). The resulting triangular space is gradually filled by laying increasingly

Figure 11.35   Mud bricks in a pitched-brick vault, with concentric grooves on both their upper and lower surfaces, at Aswan, Egypt (1977).

smaller rings between the vault and the end wall or by stacking bricks in large amounts of mud mortar (Figure 11.38). Finally, the very top of the vault is closed by mud mortar and a single brick or brick fragments.

A second course is often laid on top of the first course of rings, increasing vault thickness, load-carrying capacity, and insulating capabilities of the vault. In ancient Mesopotamia, where square bricks were employed in pitched-brick vaulting, vaults were usually built with two courses of bricks, making the total thickness of the vault about 48 cm. At the same time in Egypt, where rectangular bricks were used, as many as four or more courses were laid to make a thick vault. In the storerooms of the Ramesseum at Luxor, the vaults spring from a base consisting of four or five courses of corbelled brick (Figure 11.39). Successive courses of rectangular brick were laid leaning against opposite end walls—i.e., the first course against the rear end wall, the second course leaning in the opposite direction against the front end wall, and this alternating pattern continuing for the remaining courses (Figure 11.40). The resulting vault was about the same thickness as the two-coursed Mesopotamian vaults, but the boustrophedon pattern of the successive courses of the Egyptian vault made a well-bonded, strong vault.

Some vaults were built simultaneously from both end walls so that the two sections met midway in a V-shaped gap. Partial rings were laid on both sides of the "V," with the rings becoming increasingly smaller as the gap filled with bricks until only a hole—often almond-shaped—remained at the top. It was closed with one or two bricks and brick fragments set in thick mud mortar. Examples from the second millennium B.C. were found at Tell al-Rimah in northwestern Iraq (Oates, 1970:14,

Figure 11.36 Courses of pitched-brick vaulting, above a side wall, at the Ramesseum, Luxor, Egypt (1977). Note the use of half-bricks and whole bricks and the thinness of the vault brick when compared with wall bricks

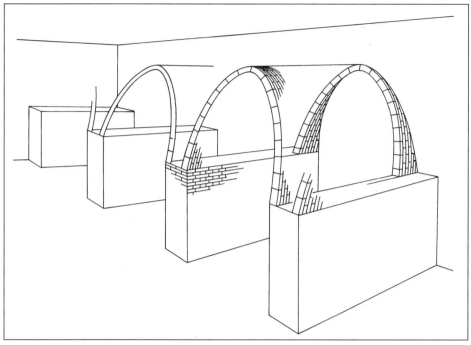

Figure 11.37 Pitched-brick vault construction, showing how the courses lean against the end wall and gradually cant inward to form an arc. (Drawing by G. Robert Lewis.)

pl. 5a) and from the second to third centuries A.D. at Karanis (ancient Kom Ausham) in the Fayum region, Egypt.

A technological improvement to the square-vault-brick tradition of Mesopotamia appeared in the vaulted building at Tell Jemmeh with the introduction of voussoirs in the pitched-brick vaulting. This is the first-known (and thus far only) appearance of mud voussoirs in vaulted buildings in the ancient Near East, a variation likely introduced by the Assyrians in the early seventh century B.C.

The Assyrian vaulted building excavated at Tell Jemmeh measured 11.81 m long by 10.16 m wide, but it was originally at least 5 m longer, the front or western end having been either destroyed by erosion or cut off in earlier excavations. The basic arrangement consisted of three long, parallel rooms side-by-side (Figure 11.41), built with different widths according to a preconceived scheme: the widest room (B) was in the middle, with the room of medium width (A) on its left and the narrowest room (C) on its right.

In some of the Assyrian buildings there was a transverse room crossing the width of the building on one or both ends. Often these transverse rooms were divided into three small rooms corresponding in width to the adjacent long rooms, as in our excavated building at Tell Jemmeh. Each of the small end rooms was 3.13 m long and was connected to its adjacent long parallel room by an arched doorway. All rooms were floored with mud bricks laid on sand. The building was preserved to a height of 2.68 m. Above the intersection of the long wall (separating rooms A and F from rooms B and E) with the cross wall (separating rooms A and B from rooms E and F),

Figure 11.38   Nearly horizontal brick filling between the end of a pitched-brick vault and the end wall in a covered family compound gateway, in Nush-i Jan, Iran (1974).

Figure 11.39 Four or five corbelled-brick courses as a base for the springing of pitched-brick vaulting courses, Ramesseum, Luxor, Egypt (1977).

Figure 11.40 Egyptian pitched-brick vaulting laid in alternating courses, one leaning on the rear wall and the second on the front wall, at the Ramesseum, Luxor, Egypt (1977).

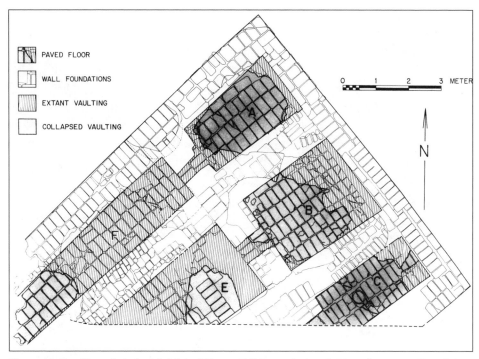

Figure 11.41   Plan of pitched-brick building at Tell Jemmeh, Israel. Note that rooms B and E are widest, A and F are slightly narrower, and C is the narrowest.

we discovered an area of floor bricks belonging to an upper floor. It is possible that originally there was a third floor, given the strong structure of the building.

All rooms were roofed with voussoir pitched-brick vaults, which varied in the amount surviving over each of the five remaining rooms. The longest stretch of vaulting was that of room F, which was essentially intact for a distance of 4.75 m (Figure 11.42). At some time in the past, most of the room F vault broke and dropped about 50 cm, where it miraculously caught on the side walls, held, and remained intact. We excavated the rooms with the preserved vaulting from the west end, shoring the vault like miners as we progressed.

The voussoirs were commonly 37 cm high, 30 cm wide at the top (extrados side), tapering to 24 cm wide at the bottom (intrados side), and 12 cm thick; an example is visible in the excavated vault arch in Figure 11.43. The dimensions and angles of the voussoirs in each vault varied, however, depending on the curvatures of the vaults over the rooms, which were all of different widths. The shape and size of the voussoirs indicated that they derived from square Mesopotamian bricks, rather than from the rectangular Egyptian bricks. Because such forms were foreign to local construction methods in ancient Israel and Philistia, they were surely introduced by Assyrian masons, who were part of the supporting entourage traveling with the Assyrian army. Thus it was possible that voussoirs were already in use in Assyria by the late eighth century B.C. or perhaps even earlier.

In this building, the pitched vaults were one and two-thirds bricks thick, for a total thickness of 61.67 cm. They were built by starting the first ring with a shorter

Figure 11.42 Room F of pitched-brick building at the end of excavation, Tell Jemmeh, Israel. Note remains of two courses of mud voussoirs in the end of the vault. Author GVB and excavators are in the room celebrating the breakthrough of the arched doorway to room A.

Figure 11.43 Voussoirs in room C of pitched-brick building at Tell Jemmeh, Israel, with original, thick mud plaster beneath on the intrados of the vault. The piers of debris under the vault and to the left remained unexcavated to support the vault, which had broken in antiquity.

brick (two-thirds of a full-size brick) 24.67 cm high and laying a full-sized brick, 37 cm high, over it for the second course. In the second ring, positions were reversed, with the full-size brick set first and a short brick set on the top edge of the full brick (see room C in Figure 11.44). Thus the shorter and taller bricks alternated in successive rings at the base of the vault throughout its length, and this bonding pattern added strength and stability to the vault. Indeed, the sides of each voussoir were in full contact with adjacent voussoirs, creating tremendous compression and squeezing out most of the mud mortar placed between them, such that the average joint between voussoirs measured less than 5 mm thick. The rings leaned at an angle of about 72° toward the end wall.

One of the advantages of voussoirs is that stones or sherds are not needed to force them into the desired arc; their sloping sides automatically cant successive bricks properly. Fitting voussoirs to a vault of a given arc and length is not as difficult as

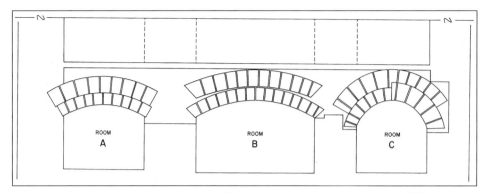

Figure 11.44 Cross section of the vaulted building at Tell Jemmeh, Israel. The different room widths required different arcs in vaulting so the upper floor could be level without requiring many courses of bricks above.

one might imagine. To lay out a voussoir vault, one need only measure the width of the room and then determine the vault's desired height and thickness. With these dimensions, the plan of the vault can be drawn anywhere—even in the soil—circumscribing the curvature of the top (extrados) and bottom (intrados) of the vault with a centered peg and an attached string (which, given its fixed length, acts as the radius of a circle), and then dividing the parallel arcs of the extrados and intrados into equal segments to establish the size and shape of the voussoir bricks required. Wooden molds can then be built for the size and shape needed for bricks of each vault, irrespective of their varying arcs. Alternatively, square bricks could be molded, and after they had begun to set up, the mold could be removed and two parallel sides could be carefully trimmed to the specific dimensions required. (The former method would be ideal if the vault's arch was a uniform arc; the latter would be better if custom sizing was needed for the voussoir bricks.)

Voussoirs enable a builder to design rooms of varying widths and to accommodate them with vaults of varying arcs. This customization was required in the Tell Jemmeh building, where the vaults over the rooms of different widths carried an upper floor (Figure 11.44). If all three rooms had semicircular vaults like that over room C, the vault over room B (the widest room) would have been much higher than the vaults over rooms A and C. Building a level second floor above these vaults of different heights requires either (1) laying several additional courses of mud brick over the vaults of rooms A and C to be level with the room B vault, which would have placed an enormous weight load on the shorter vaults; (2) constructing secondary vaults over the semicircular vaults of rooms A and C to carry the upper floor; or (3) flattening the arcs of the vaults over rooms A and B to bring them down to the level of the room C vault. The builders chose the third option, and by employing voussoirs specially made for the arc of each vault, they were able to achieve very strong vaults with flatter curvatures. The use of voussoirs, therefore, gave the builder greater freedom and flexibility in designing a building than would have been possible with either square or rectangular vault brick.

Apparently, voussoir pitched-brick vaulting did not catch on in the ancient Near East, even though it brought a significant advance in the technology of mud-brick vaulting. Only one other example of the use of mud voussoirs in vaulting is known—the north gateway of a Roman frontier fort at Ain Sinu in northern Iraq, built in the late years of the second century A.D. (Oates and Oates, 1959). Voussoir bricks, measuring 28 cm × 24 cm tapering to 21 cm wide × 3 cm thick, and conventional bricks were combined in the structure. For anyone willing to take the extra time to make voussoir bricks, vaulting constructed with such bricks pays handsome dividends by allowing more flexible floor plans, sturdy construction without an overload of excessive bricks, and beautiful roofs with greater strength and insulating qualities.

Ribbed Construction

Ribbed or strut vaults of mud brick seem to have been little known in the ancient Near East. Like voussoirs, ribbed vaulting probably represents a late development, perhaps not going back more than one or two centuries before the eighth century B.C. Ribbed vaulting is a type of construction in which two long, curving bricks were set, one on each side wall, and they leaned over the central space until they met. Such an arch was used to reduce the width of the entrance to a room opposite the throne room suite at Fort Shalmaneser in Nimrud, Iraq (Mallowan, 1966:434, fig. 360).

Ribbed vaulting that employed curving mud bricks was probably developed in the western mountains of Iran. Thus far, all known examples, with two exceptions, are found there and eastward in Iran. One exception is the Fort Shalmaneser example mentioned above. The other is found hundreds of miles westward at Tell Jemmeh, where ribbed construction was employed to arch the doorways of the pitched-brick, vaulted building. It seems likely that the Assyrian army included both Assyrian masons from Mesopotamia who built the voussoir-vaulted structures at Tell Jemmeh, and Median masons from northwestern Iran, who built the arched doorways of ribbed bricks.

The unique feature of ribbed vaulting is not so much the technique of laying bricks as it is the ribbed brick themselves. The bricks, rectangular in section, are molded in a curve with a convex upper surface (extrados) and a concave inner surface (intrados), and are surprisingly long. At Nush-i Jan, an eighth to seventh century B.C. site in Iran excavated by David Stronach, the tall storerooms of a fort and rooms of the western temple were roofed with ribbed vaults whose bricks measured 1.5 m long × 20 cm high × 12 cm thick, and weighed about 60 kg each. The vaults of the storerooms were set on the side walls 4.8 m above the floor (Figure 11.45; Roaf and Stronach, 1973). Because of their length, the ribbed vault bricks appear to be extremely fragile. One wonders how they could have been laid without breaking and how they could carry their own weight. Yet they did just that and more—they supported an upper floor over at least one room (room 18 in Stronach et al., 1978:1–11). There is also evidence that at least some of the rooms had load-bearing corbelled vaults above the ribbed vaults, suggesting that the latter may have been primarily decorative in some instances (Stronach, 1969).

At a site known as Qumis close by the Elburz Mountains in north central Iran, three square, somewhat cruciform buildings were excavated that shared similar vaulting. These included stepped vaults beneath a staircase, each one constructed with three pairs of slightly curving, ribbed, mud bricks set more upright on end, to form a

Figure 11.45 Ribbed vaulting at Nush-i Jan, Iran, eighth to seventh centuries B.C., Iran. (After Roaf and Stronach, 1973: pl. Va.)

series of pointed vaults. Each vault rose one step higher than the one before. Another interesting variation at this site—noteworthy because it is the earliest example of its type known—is a barrel vault erected with three ribbed-vault bricks, laid end-to-end, spanning a room 2.3 m wide. These structures may have served a religious function in Zoroastrian worship during the late first century B.C. A fourth building also featured pointed vaults of ribbed bricks (Hansman and Stronach, 1979).

The arched doorways connecting the long and short rooms in the Assyrian vaulted building at Tell Jemmeh were each constructed with six pairs of ribbed-vault bricks measuring 52 cm long at the top (extrados), tapering to 42 cm long at the base (intrados), 20 cm high, and 12 cm thick, and weighing about 19 kg each (Figure 11.46). Note that the height and thickness of these bricks are identical to those of Nush-i Jan, Iran; only their lengths are different. Bricks of this size are better proportioned than longer ones and are probably less likely to break under stress. Indeed, the two surviving arched doorways at Tell Jemmeh—one found intact and one poorly repaired in antiquity—carried the upper courses of the wall and the floor of the upper story with its accompanying traffic.

Ribbed-vault bricks were set in mud mortar on the side walls and inclined inward over the open space until their inner edges met. The resulting triangular spaces formed by each brick where it rested on the side wall and at the top where the two bricks met were filled with mud mortar loaded with potsherds, stones, and

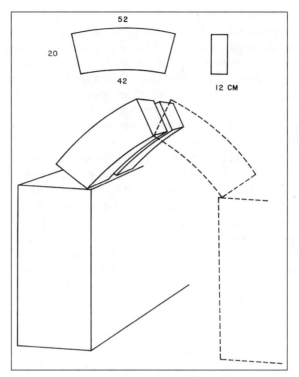

Figure 11.46 Side and end views of rib bricks, and placement diagram for the ribbed-vaulted doorways between rooms A–F and B–E, Tell Jemmeh, Israel. (Dimensions in cm; drawing by G. Robert Lewis.)

sometimes mud brick fragments. It seems as if it should have been possible to shape the ends of the ribbed brick at an angle that would have enabled them to rest squarely on the side walls and to meet vertically with their end surfaces touching at the top of the vault. However, a smooth joint might permit the ribbed brick to slide outward and fall, so it is possible that the thick mass of mud mortar in the triangular interstices added strength and stability to the vault. This type of arch and vault construction—like pitched-brick vaulting—is also erected without the centering needed for radial construction.

Radial, Timber-reinforced Domical Vault

While passing through Hauta en route from Shibam to Seiyun in the Hadhramaut valley of southern Yemen, we noticed men in the distance constructing a large, square mud-brick building. We immediately investigated and were surprised to see a type of vault construction that we had not seen before. In plan, the house featured a broad central hall, with a second hall crossing the central hall at right angles. The four quarters of the house were thus divided on the east–west axis by the central hall and on the north–south axis by the cross hall. Basic construction of the first floor was complete—i.e., all walls and ceilings were roughly finished but the house still lacked mud plaster, window frames, door frames, and utilities. Looking up from the first floor, we could see 16 large, rectangular openings piercing the ceiling: three were oriented north–south over each of the four quarters, and four slightly shorter openings were aligned on an east–west axis over the crossing hallway. The 12 larger rectangles were 3 m long × 1 m wide, and the four smaller ones were 2 × 1 m, each of which was edged on the topside with three courses of mud bricks resembling a ledge, which served as the base for the springing of a vault.

Many vaults were already finished when we arrived. During our two-hour visit we saw the final 30% of a vault in the extreme southwest corner completed and 80% of one of the easternmost vaults erected. Between the two, we were able to observe the entire construction process. Both of these were the large vaults, and they required one hour to build. Immediately after a vault was finished—even while the mortar was still wet—one could stand on top of it without fear of collapse. We know this first-hand because GVB was invited to climb up and walk on the southwestern vault immediately after the last brick was inserted; it was sound and rigid.

Each vault was built as a team effort. The team consisted of fifteen persons: a master mason, six assisting masons, three mud-mortar carriers, three mud-brick carriers, and two mortar mixers. The mud bricks used in the vaulting measured 47 × 25 × 6 cm, and each brick carrier transported up to five or six bricks on the top of his head at a time (Figure 11.47). In mixing the mud mortar, water was permitted to pond in the mud, a layer of straw was strewn over it, and all was then mixed thoroughly. When the mix was ready, it was loaded in straw baskets and carried on the head or hip of the mortar carrier into the hallway and up the stairs to the construction site.

The construction method for these vaults began with a bed of mud mortar about 3 cm thick being spread over the bricks edging the rectangular opening. The next steps could be described as corbelling a radial vault. A course of bricks was laid with the bricks oriented as stretchers (longest edge paralleling the long axis of the opening) overhanging the edge of the bricks below by about 3 cm. The back edges of these bricks were raised by adding more mortar there, causing the front edges to slope downward and begin the radial vault. Two additional courses were similarly laid—i.e., each with front edges each extending 3 cm further over the opening and canted at an increasingly greater angle, which imparted a rounded shape to the vault when viewed in cross-section. Identical courses were also laid on the narrow ends of each vault so the curvature of the ends was the same as that of the long sides, forming an elongated domical vault.

Three pre-cut tree limbs—as straight as were available locally but all with slight curves, and about 7–8 cm in diameter—were placed diagonally across the opening and anchored in the corbelled bricks. Each limb was turned so that its curve arched upward. Anchoring was achieved by cutting out a small area of the brick where the limb was to rest, placing the end of the limb in the niche, and covering it with mud mortar (Figure 11.48). Three slightly smaller limbs were then placed end-to-end and centered on top of the diagonal framework, aligned with the vault's long axis to serve as a ridge pole (in three segments). The two ends were similarly set in niches cut in the corbelled bricks of the narrow ends of the domical vault. On top of this framework, still smaller limbs about 2.5 cm (1 in) in diameter were laid with their lower ends anchored in the fourth course of corbelled bricks and their upper ends resting on the ridge pole but not fastened to it (Figure 11.49).

Figure 11.47   Brick carriers loading vault bricks on their heads in Hauta, Hadhramaut valley, Yemen (1991).

Figure 11.48   Three major beams laid obliquely, with ridge pole on top, to support domical vault under construction in Hauta, Hadhramaut, Yemen (1991).

Bricks and brick fragments were balanced on these limbs to weigh down and hold them in place. After the fourth course, subsequent courses were laid only radially, so the bricks and fragments also served as space-fillers in the timber framework. The in-

Figure 11.49 Small limbs anchored in fresh mud in the fourth course of corbelled brick but resting loosely on the supporting timber framework of a vault in Hauta, Hadhramaut, Yemen (1991).

ner edges of the successive radial bricks rested lightly on them, and they eventually supported the lower edges of bricks used to close the vault (Figure 11.50).

After nine courses of corbelled and radial bricks were completed, a long keystone-shaped hole extending from one end of the vault to the other remained open at the top. Rectangular mud bricks were trimmed with a machete on their parallel long edges to narrow the base of the bricks converting them to voussoirs (Figure 11.51). Working from both ends of the domical vault, masons set these bricks leaning obliquely against the mortar-covered face of the last radial brick at each end of the remaining hole. The trimmed voussoir-shaped bricks continued to be laid from both ends of the vault until only a small hole was left in the middle. This hole was then filled with small fragments of bricks and mud mortar until the vault was completely closed. The final closing of the vaults with nearly vertical bricks was reminiscent of the gap-closing techniques in pitched-brick domical construction that appeared at Tell al-Rimah in northern Iraq at the beginning of the second millennium B.C.

Once completed, a mason climbed on top of the vault and walked from end to end to make certain it was structurally sound (Figure 11.52). It was surprising how quickly the mud mortar dried, because the mortar mixture was quite wet when applied. But the seemingly excessive amount of water in the mortar quickly evaporated into the dry air and was also absorbed by the dry bricks. The areas between the 16 finished vaults (Figure 11.53) were eventually going to be filled in with bricks to the level of the tops of the vaults to support a second floor.

Looking up from the room on the first floor, we saw a deeply coffered ceiling that would surely be spectacular when finished inside. The intrados of a similarly

Figure 11.50   Bricks laid radially on the framework, of a domical vault in Hauta, Hadhramaut, Yemen (1991). Note brick fragments weighing down small limbs in timber framework. A pile of mud mortar is in the foreground.

Figure 11.51   Worker on extreme left uses a long, heavy knife to trim sides of square bricks so that they will have voussoir bricks to fit the remaining hole in the vault, Hauta, Hadhramant, Yemen (1991).

Figure 11.52   Masons testing the soundness of the newly finished vault at Hauta, Hadhramaut, Yemen (1991).

Figure 11.53   Finished domical vaults ready for additional bricks to fill remaining spaces level with the tops of the vaults for supporting the second floor of the structure, Hauta, Hadhramaut, Yemen (1991).

constructed gateway of a family compound we saw in Seiyun, Hadhramaut, had been left unfinished (see Figures 13.21, 13.22); however, given the size and certain elegance of the Hauta house, the deeply coffered ceiling likely would be finished with plaster (or possibly with wood) and perhaps painted.

There are surely other ways of erecting domes, arches, and vaults in addition to those discussed here. Previously unknown methods of curved-roof construction are sometimes discovered in archaeological excavations and occasionally during careful observation of buildings with a practiced eye. All of us who deal with mud architecture are constantly amazed by the range of human creativity in finding imaginative and practical solutions to construction problems.

ADVANTAGES AND DISADVANTAGES

Curved roofs have a number of advantages. Domes, arches, and vaults are as easy to build as flat roofs, especially if the pitched-brick method of vault construction is used, which does not require centering. Domes and vaults also provide superior environmental conditions inside the roofed area. The sun's rays strike curved surfaces obliquely and are less direct and intense than on flat surfaces. Both domes and vaults are almost always thicker than flat roofs, thus they provide better insulation. Ancient mud-brick vaults, at Tell Jemmeh for example, are 61.67 cm thick, but most flat roofs in the Near East seldom exceed 10–15 cm in thickness. Furthermore, a curved roof rises higher over the living space than does a flat roof, thereby creating a larger storage area for rising heat, which then also permits the cooler air near the floor to rise higher in the room. In the warm, humid climates of the tropics, as well as in much of the USA before the days of air-conditioning, buildings were constructed with ceilings 50%–100% higher than the seven- or eight-foot (2.13 or 2.44 m) ceilings of most contemporary houses. Higher ceilings provide more comfortable interiors. It is also possible to obtain cross ventilation in vaults by placing one or more openings in each end wall just below the intrados so that even a slight breeze will remove accumulated hot air without creating drafts at floor level. Such openings in the Near East are often finished with grilles formed by bricks (see Chapter 13). Curved roofs also provide speedy and more efficient drainage than flat surfaces, where standing water may collect in hairline cracks and shallow depressions and eventually will begin to dissolve the flat mud roof.

The curving lines and surfaces of arches, vaults, and domes treat us to visual surprises and at the same time relieve us of the stark, straight lines of typical modern buildings. Today, our cities of office buildings, shopping malls, and houses tend to be a monotony of discordant angles as Western architects and builders attempt to create interior space that is both functional and cheap. We have employed post-and-beam to the point of boredom and pre-cast concrete and glass to the state of numbness in post-World War II construction in every city in the world, much of which looks the same. Hassan Fathy said that there are no straight lines in nature, yet we defy the natural order with our use of straight lines in their diverse combinations. Often when architects employ curves in buildings, they do so with such timidity and insincerity that the result is tawdry at best. A typical example, which has gained popularity among builders during the last decade or so, is the single, thin, non-functional arch that "decorates" the tops of commercial and office building entrances, often hiding glass roofs over an atrium behind. Such a tiny arch is unattractive simply because it does not fit the huge rectangular box under it in size or design. Domes and vaults are more sensuous and beautiful than flat or angular, gabled roofs. They seem more natural, probably because nature itself is almost entirely structured with curving lines, yielding soft surfaces resembling those of the human body. They remind us also of rolling countryside, hills, and mountains, and they provide endless movement and change to the architectural landscape in their form and through the ever-changing interplay of light and shadow, restoring visual beauty to our lives. Both domes and vaults add a softness to the urban skyline, in contrast to the sharp boxes and rectangular slabs that jaggedly stab the skies of modern cities. For those of us who spend our lives surrounded only by buildings of straight lines and assorted angles, curving domes and vaults are a true delight.

Such roofs are not without disadvantages, although they are relatively few and minor. Most domes and vaults require more time to build than flat roofs. The one clear exception is the radial, timber-reinforced, domical vault described last, but the construction of many such vaults would consume as much or more time as the laying of a flat roof. Curved roofs are more difficult to maintain than flat roofs. To repair cracks and renew either mud or lime plaster on large domes or high conical domes requires agility in climbing and maintaining balance when using ladders, steps, or scaffolding. Curved roofs also deprive inhabitants of the useful activity space provided by a flat roof. In severe winters, more space heating is required to maintain a comfortable interior temperature at floor level, compared with a lower flat roof, owing to the greater interior volume created by the curved roof. But with a little added space heating, a room with a curved roof is far more comfortable in the winter. Without air conditioners, it is infinitely more comfortable in the summer than a concrete room with a flat roof.

Part V

FINISHING DETAILS AND SOLUTIONS

Chapter 12

Walls, Columns, and Stairways

WALLS

Plaster

When mud walls are dry, they require one or more coatings of smooth plaster over the outer surfaces if they are to survive and to be attractive. Without plaster, earthen walls of every type—wattle-and-daub, mud balls, layered mud, rammed earth, or mud brick—whether their surfaces are even and smooth or uneven and rough textured, will erode when exposed to water and wind, although an uneven and rough surface erodes faster than others. Whether in the form of rain, groundwater run-off, or wastewater from household activities, water seeks and inevitably finds low places in wall surfaces. It immediately settles into hairline cracks, tiny pits, and low places, where it begins dissolving the mud. Left unrepaired, these cracks and pits increase in size during subsequent wetting and drying cycles, culminating in holes in the roof, splitting of walls, and eventual collapse of a building. Even if such damage to a wall is repaired, it is never as strong as when first built. For this reason, structures are coated with plaster as soon as possible.

Plaster makes the wall surface smooth so there will be fewer cracks, depressions, or runnels where water might pool and start the process of erosion. In some structures—especially revetments of rammed earth, some layered-mud buildings, and walls with sand as mortar—each layer or course was plastered immediately after it was laid. In the walls of the Assyrian vaulted building at Tell Jemmeh, Israel, in which the mortar consisted of a considerable amount of wet sand, mud plaster was applied to both wall surfaces before the sand could dry and trickle from the joints, which, had it occurred, would have left the bricks unstable and ultimately led to wall collapse.

Plaster also unifies and hides the disparate elements of construction into a smoothly surfaced, unified whole. Often we cannot know what type of materials and construction techniques were employed in a building because of the plaster. This coating, no matter what color is used, adds enormously to the appearance of the building. The hodgepodge shapes of mud balls, the rough surface and uneven joint lines of layered mud, the joint lines of rammed earth, and mud brick with its ubiquitous bedding and rising mortar joints are useful for learning how structures are built, but make it harder to see the entire structure as a unit. In a visit to Larnaca, Cyprus, we assumed that the plastered buildings in a row near our hotel were all built of stone. Imagine our surprise when we saw that a small area of plaster was missing from the end wall of one of the buildings, disclosing that the wall was built of mud brick!

A lack of plaster on a building could be compared with looking at a human body with bones, organs, muscles, and tendons exposed, lacking its covering of skin. Plaster is, in fact, the skin of mud buildings, and it greatly enhances their unity (Figure 12.1). The rounded top of a mud wall or the rounded corner of a mud house never attracts as much attention as when hidden beneath a unifying coat of plaster. The smooth finish of the plaster provides a stage for the ever-changing light on architectural features, and it greatly adds to the unique beauty of well-designed mud buildings.

In the Old World, three types of plaster are commonly used—mud, lime, or gypsum. Mud plaster is less expensive and more traditional; the latter two are more waterproof, more durable, and more expensive. Historically, mud plaster predominated in Central and South America and in the North American Southwest. In the twentieth century, stucco on mud buildings has been used almost exclusively on exterior wall surfaces in the American Southwest. Indeed, its use is mandated by

Figure 12.1   A deteriorating house in Seiyun, Hadhramaut valley, Yemen, with worn mud plaster above, eroded brick on both sides, lime plaster below, and decoration in relief under two windows, on left (1962).

the New Mexico [USA] Administrative Code, although mud plaster is widely used also for interior walls. Paul Graham McHenry, Jr., recommended a modification to the Code that would permit the use of mud plaster on the exterior surface if it is of the same basic composition as the wall and if the building is located where there is no danger of flooding (McHenry, 1984:204–205). Below we examine mud, lime, and gypsum plasters, with a discussion also of stucco in the interest of completeness, although it has not traditionally been used in those regions of the Old World covered in this book.

Mud Plaster

Whereas lime plaster is easily recognized, archaeologists may fail to see remnants of ancient mud plaster on walls unless they clean the mud-brick walls carefully. There are several possible explanations for such failures. Perhaps they do not consider mud plaster as important as cleaned mud brick with well-defined mortar joints; possibly they are lacking in curiosity; maybe they are so eager to move on to the next phase of excavation that they become careless in their digging. Whatever the reason, the tragedy is that we have lost, and continue to lose, much information about ancient mud construction, which not only is valuable for understanding ancient craftsmanship at a site but is also extremely useful for intraregional and cross-cultural studies.

Mud plaster predominated throughout the world in antiquity. Generally a simple application of one or two coats was used, but in some instances, a more complex application was employed in which a series of several coats of different soils was used. At Tell Jemmeh, we saw occasional bits of mud plaster on buildings of different occupation periods, but none of those findings prepared us for the extent to which original mud plaster was preserved inside the pitched-brick vaulted Assyrian building described in Chapter 11. We found large, intact patches of mud plaster 1.5–2.0 cm thick on most of the inner surfaces of walls, and in one instance (in room B) the inner face of the south wall was almost entirely covered (Figure 12.2). The late Yigael Yadin (1917–1984), a leading Israeli archaeologist, upon seeing the extant plaster in room B, asked if GVB had plastered the wall!

Mud plaster at Tell Jemmeh was purely functional; it lacked the elegance of the fine plasters used at Tell al-Rimah in the Assyrian region of northern Mesopotamia, where plastering involved an elaborate process. Consider the number and colors of coats of plaster found by David Oates in the excavation of the antechamber of the temple of the nineteenth century B.C.: (1) A thin coat of reddish-brown plaster; (2) a heavy coat of gray plaster 6 cm thick; (3) a coat of red-brown plaster 2–3 cm thick; (4) a thin coat of fine green plaster; and (5) a black finishing coat, the black color being derived from mixing finely ground charcoal with mud (Oates, 1967:72). Traces of plaster were also found on the half-columns in recessed panels on both the interior and exterior wall surfaces. At Khorsabad, the Assyrian capital built by Sargon II in the eighth century B.C., the walls of Gate 7 and adjoining walls were coated with mud plaster and painted with whitewash (Loud, 1936:1, 3, fig. 3). A mud-brick temple of the late Assyrian period at Tell al-Rimah, ca. seventh century B.C., was also finished with mud plaster (Oates, 1968:122). This suggests that in times of political and economic decline, the government reverted to using mud for

Figure 12.2   Original mud plaster on wall of room B, in the pitched-brick vaulted Assyrian building, ca. 675 B.C., Tell Jemmeh, Israel.

plaster and floors because it was less expensive. For private dwellings, mud plaster was used throughout time.

Mud plaster is composed of the same materials as mud brick: soil, water, straw, and sometimes cow manure. In Egypt, India, and perhaps elsewhere, the proportions of ingredients are one-third soil, one-third straw, one-third cow dung, and enough water to create the desired consistency. Straw and cow manure are added to the mixture to make the plaster more flexible and to forestall cracking and spalling. Indeed, Egyptian masons believe that the addition of dung to the plaster renders it more waterproof, although the precise nature of the chemical and mechanical actions responsible for retarding water erosion are not understood and require scientific investigation (Fathy, 1973:224–225).

The process of mixing and applying mud plaster is straightforward. In the Old World, just as in preparing the mixture for mud balls, layered mud, or mud bricks for walls, the plaster is mixed with a hoe or by treading the ingredients in a shallow pit (see Figure 5.7). At the Customs Post at Beleli, Baluchistan, Pakistan (see Figure 3.27), straw was spread over the soil in the mixing pit (Figure 12.3), water was poured over the straw and soil (Figure 12.4), then the contents were thoroughly mixed by treading (Figure 12.5). The plaster mixture is thinner than that used for making mud layers or mud brick, and straw is often omitted in the final coat for a smoother, more homogeneous finish (see Figure 12.8).

While the mud plaster is being mixed, the wall should be cleaned by scraping it lightly with a trowel and then gently brushing it with a soft brush. A section of the wall about 1 m² should be painted or sprinkled with water immediately before the

Figure 12.3 **Preparing mud plaster: spreading straw over mixing pit at Customs Post, at Beleli, near Quetta, Baluchistan, Pakistan (1990).**

Figure 12.4 **Preparing mud plaster: adding water to soil and straw in pit at the Customs Post, Beleli, Pakistan (1990).**

Figure 12.5   Preparing mud plaster: mixing mud plaster by treading, at Customs Post, Beleli, Pakistan (1990).

plaster is applied to reduce absorption of water from the plaster mixture. A handful of plaster is spread quickly with an upward motion of the hand or trowel, pressing it into joints, pits, and other low places (Figure 12.6). Whenever the plaster does not stick to the wall surface, the area must be dampened again and replastered. If the rising joints in mud-brick walls are left partly free of mortar when laid, these cavities will serve as keys for securing mud plaster to the wall surface. After setting for 20 to 30 minutes, the plaster can be smoothed with a wet paint brush or trowel, or as in New Mexico, USA, interiors, with a dampened sheepskin.

With experienced masons, the plaster goes on quickly. At the two-room Customs Post in Beleli, two professional masons prepared the mix and plastered a coat on both the exterior and interior of all walls of the building (totaling about 45 m²) in eight hours. Not all plasterers are men. In some contemporary villages in the Near East—for example, Tell Toqaan in Syria—the traditional division of family labor assigns the building of mud-brick structures to men and the task of mud plastering to women. McHenry (1985:115) noted that Native American women were said to do most of the plastering of their pueblo houses.

In Baluchistan, all cracks are sealed by painting the wall with *niru*, a mixture consisting of black soil thinned with water until it is liquid, before mud plaster is troweled on the surface. *Niru* serves as a bonding agent to improve the adherence of mud plaster, especially if the wall has dried so thoroughly that mud plaster will not stick to it. Sometimes by the third day of drying, cracks appear in the plaster, usually caused by too much clay in the mixture; such cracks are repaired with *niru* followed by an additional layer of mud plaster.

Figure 12.6 Applying first coat of mud plaster to the layered-mud Customs Post at Beleli, Pakistan (1990).

Near the house under construction in Marib, Yemen, we visited another layered-mud house that was being finished with mud plaster. The coat averaged about 7 mm in thickness at the lower edge of the sloping layer and about 35 mm thick at the top of the layer (Figure 12.7). The darker colored, still-damp plaster had been spread two to three hours before we arrived. Each coat of mud plaster typically requires about 48 hours to dry thoroughly, depending upon the weather.

Usually two coats of mud plaster are applied for longer wear and a better appearance. The layered-mud houses of the Najran region in Saudi Arabia, whose layers are convex on the exterior surface, are finished in this manner. The first coat contains a great deal of straw, but the second, finishing coat consists of only the finest soil screened to remove unwanted foreign matter (Figure 12.8).

In New Mexico, USA, imaginative architects and builders search for soils of different colors for interior mud plaster, which enable them to finish rooms with walls of slightly different colors. Ranging from white through many shades of beige to light brown, the colors create an exciting variety of hues, providing contrasts of increased or decreased light reflection and absorption, while adding warmth and coziness. McHenry reported that once he had found five different colors of soil along a 10-mile (16 km) stretch of highway, proving that various colors can be found if one searches the land for them (Paul Graham McHenry, Jr., personal communication to GVB).

Relief sculpturing of mud plaster is occasionally used to decorate the exterior walls of layered-mud structures. Attractive examples are the relief designs on the immaculate courtyard buildings and courtyard wall of a compound in Punjab, Pakistan (Figure 12.9; see also Figure 3.6). In Seiyun in the Hadhramaut valley of south-

Figure 12.7   First coat of mud plaster nearly complete and drying, on house being built in Marib, Yemen, with mixing pit in foreground (1991).

ern Yemen, a projecting panel is decorated with a keyhole arch and three levels of recessing (Figure 12.10). On the third or deepest recessed surface are two additional niches—a longer one in the lower section with five recessed steps, and a shorter one in the arched area with three recessed steps—of essentially the same design as

Figure 12.8　Convex layered-mud house under construction and receiving second coat of mud plaster after first coat had dried, in Najran, Saudi Arabia (1968). Note straw visible in dry first coat is omitted in second coat for a smooth finish.

the outer frame. Two small, engaged columns feature upward spirals in their lower halves and downward spirals in their upper halves. This interesting design is bordered on each side by harmonious recessed panels on the house wall.

The main entrance to the fortress house at Qila Skarnah in Baluchistan, Pakistan, is also embellished by a pilaster with capital on either side of the doorway; above the doorway is an arch in relief; still higher on the wall is a framed rectangular area where a plaque or other decorative device was once attached (see Figure 3.20).

In north-central and western India, especially in Gujarat and Rajasthan, walls are plastered and often replastered to purify the house. The mixture used is known as

Figure 12.9   Relief sculpture and finial in the courtyard of a house in Punjab, Pakistan (1989).

Figure 12.10   Projecting recessed panel and walls elaborately decorated with carved mud plaster in Seiyun, Hadhramaut Valley, Yemen (1991).

gobar-mitti, which consists of one-third mud, one-third cow dung, and one-third straw, with enough water added to achieve the consistency of wet dough. Huyler (1993:174) explains,

> Hindu philosophy divides the world into two realms: the pure, *pakka,* and the impure, *kaccha....* *Pakka* refers to articles of permanent substance, such as stone or metal, which can be cleaned and purified. *Kaccha* refers to absorptive materials, such as clay and dirt whose porousness makes cleansing difficult.

Because cleansing a mud surface is not possible without some damage to the material, the custom has evolved to achieve purification by simply resurfacing it with a new coat of plaster.

The walls and floors of houses in these regions also serve as a stage for designs in low relief and in paint that sometimes change daily for ceremonial occasions. Those in relief generally consist of geometric forms, but sometimes they include floral designs and images of the gods, using a mud-plaster mix of equal parts soil and dung. Coils, small balls, and wedges of the mix are used, and sometimes straight or curved sticks or small pieces of bamboo are attached to the wall to serve as bases for ridges of mud. These sculptured and painted designs decorate the interior walls of houses, partitions, doorways, large storage chests, and bins built of mud (Figure 12.11). Small pieces of mirrors are often set in the mud plaster and become points of light in the relief work. Most designs reflect textile motifs, and many are awe-inspiring in their intricacy and beauty (Figure 12.12).[1]

In regions where mud plaster is common, householders examine exterior plastered surfaces several times during the rainy season for pits and tiny cracks where erosion might begin. The most likely places are flat or curved roofs, parapets of a flat roof, areas around drainage channels and spouts, window ledges, and along the base of the exterior walls. If surface defects are found, they are repaired by mixing a small quantity of mud plaster, filling the imperfections, and smoothing the surface. Plaster is much simpler to repair than a mud wall. In fact, it is even less difficult than spackling a small area of a gypsum plaster or dry wall board.

Figure 12.11 On left, mud-plastered, large mud chest with painted design; center, wife and grandmother are turning a churn; Modhera, Gujarat, India (1991).

Figure 12.12 Mud plaster with relief designs and mirrors in a fine house in Bhuj, Gujarat, India (1991). Depicted in the design are two women turning a churn, as in Figure 12.11.

In 1974, we visited Hasanlu, a site of many mud-brick structures excavated by Robert Dyson in western Iran. Because the excavations were extending over a number of years, Dyson was determined to preserve the mud-brick walls he had exposed. He coated the walls with mud plaster to protect them during the winter rains and snows. This was the only viable method of preservation, because the only other solution—roofing the enormous area of excavation—would have been too costly. If the excavation staff wanted to remeasure bricks or to examine the bonding pattern of walls exposed in previous field seasons, they simply tapped on the plaster coat of the selected area until it cracked and fell off, laying bare the mud brick behind it. They investigated, photographed, or drew as needed, then replastered the area to continue protecting the wall. Was it effective? The mud plaster worked wonders at virtually no cost. We saw several walls covered with mud plaster that had been excavated more than 10 years earlier, and all were in fine condition despite annual exposure to strong winds, rain, and snow. This story is not finished, however. During one field season, the Iranian site inspector assigned to Dyson's excavation by the Department of Antiquities of Iran described the plastering of excavated walls to his superior in the Department as destruction of the site. The Director of Antiquities then came to see for himself, quite possibly intending to terminate the excavations. Dyson convinced him that plastering the exposed walls was conservation rather than destruction.

Supposedly knowledgeable antiquities officials—especially conservators and monument specialists—in the more westernized governments of Near Eastern countries often deliberately ignore the evidence of excellent preservation of exposed mud buildings provided by traditional mud plaster on both exposed and buried walls. Some examples have survived for decades, centuries, and even millennia, which surely provides sufficient proof of the durability and longevity of mud plaster. Worse yet, these officials show absolutely no interest in experimenting with mud plaster on mud buildings. When archaeologists and archaeological architects propose to conserve exposed mud structures with mud plaster, numerous conservators inevitably respond either with blank stares or with declarations that they are waiting for experimental data on new complex, sophisticated products under development by conservation institutes and chemical industries. All sorts of new compounds produced by joint archaeological–chemical projects have been tried with little or no success in the twentieth century, and none have been sufficiently effective, practical, and economical to warrant use. No conservator of ancient monuments is worth his salt if he lacks interest in and knowledge of the ancient technologies that produced and preserved the very monuments in the first place and are now regrettably in his charge. It is quite astonishing how ignorance can reinforce arrogance!

With respect to the durability of mud plaster, two twentieth century examples are worth noting. At Beth-shan, a site at the junction of the Valley of Jezreel and the Jordan Valley in Israel, the original excavators, Fitzgerald and Rowe, covered their mud-brick walls, which they excavated in the 1930s, with mud plaster. When Amihai Mazar undertook major excavations there in 1989, the mud plaster had protected the mud-brick walls so well during the 59-year interval that he could identify each wall in Fitzgerald and Rowe's original site plans (A. Mazar, Institute of Archaeology, Hebrew University of Jerusalem, Israel, personal communication). Not bad for a single coat of mud plaster!

When the excavations of Tell Jemmeh began in 1970, there were two mud-brick buildings in the field south of the tell that had been abandoned by their Arab owners in 1948, 22 years earlier. Both were covered with mud plaster, and the plaster on one was in surprisingly good condition although its flat roof had long since fallen and dissolved. In 1975, one of the archaeologists on the Tell Jemmeh team, Jerome Schaefer, removed a vertical strip of the mud plaster about 1 m wide to investigate the bonding pattern of the underlying mud brick, because the exterior plaster was mostly intact (Figure 12.13) despite 27 years of exposure to wind, rain, hot summers, and cold winters and of abandonment without maintenance. By contrast, during the same time interval in the USA, every frame or concrete house would have required two or more coats of paint; adobe houses would have been restuccoed at least twice; and the joints of most stone and fired-brick residences would have been ready to point.

Whereas mud plaster is cheap and easy to apply, erecting a roof over a monument provides effective protection while permitting access to it. The roof may be very expensive and an aesthetic disaster, but if the monument is worth preserving for ongoing study and as an important cultural artifact for people to see, it is generally the ideal solution. Perhaps we need committed architects, construction engineers, and landscape architects with a flair for experimentation to design inexpensive, attractive, lightweight structures with translucent roofing that will protect monuments and at the same time require minimum maintenance. Until that time comes, mud plaster remains the easiest, cheapest, and best all-around material for preserving mud structures.

Lime and Gypsum Plasters

Both lime and gypsum plasters were used in the ancient Near East. They have rarely been clearly distinguished by archaeologists, and identification in the literature

Figure 12.13 Original mud plaster on house abandoned for 27 years near Tell Jemmeh, Israel (1976). The 1-m wide strip of plaster had been removed by archaeologist Jerome Schaefer (pictured) during the previous year to allow study of the underlying mud-brick bonding pattern.

is not always reliable because they look much the same and have about the same useful life. In Iran they are separate crafts, but in rural areas a family may use the same kiln to prepare both lime and gypsum for plasters on different days (Wulff, 1966:126). There were environmental factors, however, that influenced ancient choices so that one type or the other tended to dominate in a region. Apart from local deposits of limestone and gypsum, forests are the most important factor. Lime burning requires much higher temperatures, about 880°C (1616°F), than gypsum, about 160°C (320°F), and therefore lime consumes considerably more fuel, which in antiquity was furnished by trees and other plants. Thus in well-forested regions, such as Italy for example, the use of lime predominated in Roman times, while gypsum was more common in the northern Near Eastern countries, Syria, Iraq, and Iran. Today, however, lime kilns are often fired in semi-arid regions, such as southern Yemen, with tumbleweeds and scrub for fuel (Figure 12.14).

Apparently lime plaster was an early invention in the eastern Mediterranean and Near East regions. During the Pottery Neolithic A period (sixth millennium B.C.) in Turkey, walls were covered with white plaster, sometimes 3–4 cm thick (Mellaart, 1970a:3–11). Probably gypsum plaster also goes back to early times in Mesopotamia and Iran. In any case, at Tell Jemmeh we found fragments of lime plaster from the seventeenth to the third centuries B.C. Most of the places where it was found intact were on the walls and floors of rooms, such as bathrooms, that were subject to damage by splashed or running water.

In Pakistan, lime plaster was the premier finish for mud walls until about 1930, when production began to slow and eventually stopped. During late 1980s considerable interest in lime plaster revived because it is superior to other materials suitable for mud structures, and it provided a means of rebuilding the household industry that manufactured it to improve economic conditions for rural and semi-rural families.

We know of no region in the world where lime plaster has been so commonly employed as in the Hadhramaut of Yemen. An example is the city gate of Shibam, which was finished with mud plaster when photographed in 1962 (Figure 12.15). Between then and our visit in 1991, the gate was refurbished by replacing pediments with consoles, rectangular window panels with arches in relief, and the plain arch over the main entrance with a scalloped one, and by covering the structure with lime plaster (Figure 12.16). Most of the processes, costs, and applications described below are based on practices in the Hadhramaut.

To fully cover a building with lime plaster costs about two-thirds as much as its basic construction, as we learned from masons building the grand mud-brick, vaulted-ceiling house in Hauta, east of Shibam in the Hadhramaut (see Chapter 1). Because lime plaster is very expensive, traditionally it has been an index of family wealth in the Hadhramaut, measured by the extent of lime-plaster coverage on the mud-brick house. In Seiyun, no more than about 10% of the houses are entirely covered with lime plaster; this small group includes the Sultan's palace, reflecting his considerable financial resources during his rule (see Figure 3.60). A second group (about 30% of all buildings) consists of town and suburban houses; these are partially covered with lime plaster. The remaining structures are finished only with mud plaster.

The first and third groups are easily understood, but the second group requires further explanation, although it, too, is a function of financial resources. In this

Figure 12.14 **Lime-burning kiln in operation in the Hadhramaut valley, Yemen (1991).**

group, lime plaster is reserved for the flat roof, the parapets, the drainage channels that carry wastewater from inside the house, and the lowest 1–2 m of the wall immediately above its junction with the ground. These are the most vulnerable areas that must be protected from erosion and leaks. When additional funds become available, the lime plaster is extended from the parapet downward as far as possible, especially on those sides of the building that face the prevailing wind and rain.

Interiors of wealthy homes are also finished with lime plaster, covering walls, ceilings, and floors in all important rooms. An abandoned, once-palatial house built in 1939 in Terim, Hadhramaut, was offered by the al-Kaf family to the Smithsonian research team in 1961 as a base for our archaeological survey while the team worked in the surrounding area. The field camp was set up in the large salon on the ground

Figure 12.15 Mud-plastered city gate in Shibam, Hadhramaut Valley, Yemen (1962).

Figure 12.16 Same gate in Figure 12.15 finished with lime plaster and new, more elaborate decorative designs and devices (1991).

floor, which we shared with birds and bats for several weeks. The fluted columns in this room were finished with lime plaster (see Figure 1.7). This once magnificent house was renovated since then and is now a hotel (see Figure 1.6)! In more modest houses, floors and stairways are surfaced with lime plaster if the owner's finances make it possible.

Lime plaster is expensive because of the number of operations involved in its production: quarrying limestone,[2] transporting it, crushing it, burning it in a kiln, and final processing. In Iran, lime burners are built of layered mud. They typically consist of a firing chamber, sometimes dug into a slope; a cylindrical or truncated conical baking chamber about 2.4 m in diameter; and a perforated floor between the two chambers. Rocks about 38 cm in diameter at most are spread over the floor, with smaller sizes grading down to about 4 cm in diameter loosely filling the kiln to the top, so that combustion gases may easily pass between them. Vast quantities of tree scraps and desert shrubs are gathered to fire the kiln, and they are constantly fed to the fire box below the floor for 12 to 24 hours. When finished, the stones are sometimes covered with about 30 cm of soil; after the kiln has cooled, the powdered lime (quicklime) is removed (Figure 12.14; Wulff, 1966:125–127).

The procedure for preparing lime plaster involves several steps. Powdered lime is mixed with water in a pit or trench and is beaten with sticks (in the Hadhramaut, by 10–20 men alternating their strokes) so that any remaining lumps are smashed and dissolved. During this process, the lime expands, and beating continues until expansion is complete, creating slacked lime. The plaster mix consists of one part slacked lime, five parts washed fine sand, and one part screened soil, with water added until the consistency is wet enough for spreading on the wall with a trowel (McHenry, 1984:113).

In the late first century A.D., Vitruvius described the mixture of lime plaster as follows: "When [lime] is slaked, then let it be mingled with the sand in such a way that if it is pit sand, three of sand and one of lime is poured in; but if the sand is from the river or sea, two of sand and one of lime is thrown together" (Vitruvius Pollio, 1931 [translation]: vol. 1, bk. 2, chap. 5, ¶ 1). He also noted that in ancient Greece, lime was mixed with sand and then beaten: "The Greek plasterers ... make a mortar trough with lime and sand mixed, and a gang of men beat the mortar with wooden staves, and they use the mortar thus worked up in the pit" (Vitruvius Pollio, 1934 [translation]: vol. 2, bk. 7, chap. 3, ¶ 10). At Tell Jemmeh, seashells were sometimes smashed and added to the mix, which was troweled when spread to bring the finer materials to the surface. In the Hadhramaut of Yemen, wood ash is sometimes added to the plaster mix; this mixture is known locally as *ramad,* and it provides exceptional strength in foundations and in the structure of stairway piers, as well as excellent waterproofing. Many Hadhramis added egg whites as a binding agent for increasing sheen, and they would boast about the number of eggs used in plastering a house (Lewcock, 1986:100).

Generally, a base coat of mud plaster with straw is applied to the walls. In Baluchistan, camel or goat hair is often added to the mixture (Farooqi, 1986:C-6). This forms an even base that covers the horizontal joints in layered construction and the bedding and rising joints of mud brick. Any straw protruding from the mud plaster also serves to key the lime plaster. The plasterer piles the mixed lime plaster on a board and applies it with a trowel (Figure 12.17). Flat trowels of different sizes and shapes are used for spreading plaster and may be of steel or wood, the latter of which is used in the Hadhramaut. The plasterer trowels the plaster smooth and sometimes burnishes interior surfaces with a smooth chert or flint stone until they shine like marble.

Lime plaster is durable because its coefficient of expansion closely matches that of earthen construction, so no cracking is caused by the expansion and contraction characteristics of these materials. Lime plaster also provides the best waterproofing for mud construction. The former Sultan's Palace in Seiyun was already more than 80 years old in 1962 when the photo for Figure 3.60 was taken, illustrating that when lime plaster is well maintained it will last for a hundred years or more.

In antiquity, no less so than today, mud-brick interior walls were protected by lime plaster, especially vulnerable areas such as bathroom walls, floors, and the drainage channels passing through the walls. Two bathrooms of the Late Bronze II period (thirteenth century B.C.) at Tell Jemmeh had lime-plastered floors and walls with rounded, "hospital" corners and plastered drains extending through the mud-brick walls to dry wells or sumps (see Figure 14.17).

Lime plaster was called "stucco" by the Romans and was used extensively in many sites, especially in the well-preserved buildings of Pompeii and Herculaneum, where it added great beauty to the walls of villas. For a fresco, the plaster base required considerable preparation. A rough, coarse coat was spread on the walls; when this was nearly dry, it was smoothed, corners were squared, and walls plumbed. The second and third rough coats were applied to provide a stable and lasting base. This was followed by a complex finish consisting of three coats of plaster with powdered

Figure 12.17   Applying lime plaster in Shibam, Hadhramaut valley, Yemen (1950).

marble added to the mix: the first marble coat was spread thickly; while it was dry-ing, a second, thin coat was applied; and while the second coat was still wet, a third, finer coat was spread. The many layers of lime plaster prevented cracks and other faults from developing. When the final coat was still wet, the artist painted the scene with his palette of colors. According to Vitruvius (1934 [translation]: vol. 2, bk. 7, chap. 3, ¶7),

> When the colours are carefully laid upon the wet plaster, they do not fail but are perma-nently durable, because the lime has its moisture removed in the kilns, and becoming attenuated and porous, is compelled by its dryness to seize upon whatever happens to present itself.

Paint

Painting mud-plaster walls, both in solid colors and multicolored designs, has a long history in the Near East and there are many early examples. In the Pre-Pottery Neolithic B (ca. 7000 B.C.) at Haçılar in Turkey, Mellaart found fragments of cream-colored plaster with traces of a geometric design in red, which, given their fine state of preservation, had probably fallen from the upper areas of the wall (Mellaart, 1970a:4). In the late sixth to early fifth millennia at Tuleilat el-Ghassul in the Jordan Valley near the north end of the Dead Sea, the remains of frescoes in black, yellow, white, red, and brown were found painted on lime-plastered, mud-brick walls. They featured an elaborate eight-point star about 1.8 m in diameter, peculiar masks, a bird, and geometric forms (MacLeish, 1967:90–91; Levy, 1993).

About 3000 B.C., at Warka in Mesopotamia, interior walls were painted with geo-metric designs in tempera. Between ca. 2900 and 2700 B.C., life-size human figures were painted in color on the walls at Tell Uqair in Mesopotamia (Woolley, 1961:61). In Sargon's Palace at Khorsabad (eighth century B.C.), remains of painted mud plas-ter that had fallen from the ceilings (and probably the upper walls) carried designs of rows of circles, concentric circles, rosettes, and hexagons in red, white, and blue (Loud, 1936:23, fig. 27, pl. I). In Fort Shalmaneser at Nimrud (ancient Calah in Mesopotamia), Mallowan found a mural about 3.7 m high painted on the mud-plastered walls of the throne room of the Palace, The mural featured two registers: a lower one showing a procession of attendants advancing to the right, and an upper one of equal size consisting of 5 bands. Bands 1 and 5 were floral borders, bands 2 and 4 each had three lines of rosettes, and band 3 had a single row of large rosettes alternating with rectangles having concave sides (Mallowan, 1966:379–380, figs. 307, 308). In the Treasury at Persepolis, Iran, of the late sixth century B.C., doorways in the Court of Reception and in suites of rooms were enhanced with a painted border above and on both sides. The border design was painted in blue, red, and white and consisted of a single row of rosettes, formed of two concentric circles with a centered dot, enclosed on both the inner and outer edges by a narrow band of small, equilateral triangles. The triangles were touching one another at their bases, with their apexes pointing away from the door in the outer band and toward the door in the inner band (Schmidt, 1939:19, fig. 17).

Examples of wall painting in Egypt were found in Soknopaiou Nesos, a town in the Fayum region. Two houses dating between the first century B.C. and the first century A.D. contained mural fragments. In House 202, a rider standing with the head of his horse behind him was painted on white plaster; in House 204, a niche finished with white plaster featured a man and woman making offerings with their right hands to identical horned incense burners. The walls adjacent to the niche were covered with yellow mud plaster, upon which were painted a human figure with a crocodile-shaped head—the god Sobek, presumably to whom the offering was made—a palm tree, a chariot, a bull, and other symbols (Boak, 1935:9–10, figs. 4, 6, 7).

The most common paint finish for mud buildings worldwide is whitewash, which is composed of lime and water and applied with a brush. It generally lasts about a year, so to maintain a good finish it must be reapplied annually. It is the most inexpensive material for obtaining a fresh, white building. For an exterior painted finish that is longer-lasting, the mud wall should be primed with a sealer that is followed by two or three coats of paint. Mud plaster can be successfully painted with water-based, latex paints when applied after the proper prime coat. This yields an attractive and durable coating.

A method of painting that was probably developed during the 1930s in the USA makes use of ordinary oil-based house paint. A coat of raw linseed oil was thoroughly brushed into a clean, well-swept mud wall at the ratio of 3.45 qt (3.26 L) per 100 ft^2 (9.28 m^2) of wall. Three days later, a priming coat of the house paint was brushed on at the ratio of 2.9 qt (2.75 l) per 100 ft^2 (9.28 m^2). When dry, a second coat of house paint was applied. This finish was reported to have survived perfectly for two years with no indications of problems (Lee, 1937:26).

In Baluchistan, Pakistan, road-side restaurants, village buildings housing political parties, and some houses are commonly painted on the front walls, less frequently on the end walls, and rarely on the back wall. The favorite color is white. On political party buildings, the white base is used as a background for slogans and logos painted in various shades of green, red, or black, and in various calligraphic styles. On the white front and end walls of the buildings of one political party, attractive stylized trees are painted with foliage rendered in various shades of green to create depth (Figure 12.18).

In many areas of Pakistan and elsewhere in Southwest Asia, some houses appear to be covered with badly deteriorating white paint. A householder will find his house gradually turning white because many soils used in construction contain salts. In the course of weathering, the salts migrate to the surface, leaving a white deposit. Sometimes the salt so completely covers the surface that it can be mistaken for old paint.

The walls of both modest and affluent houses as well as shops in Baluchistan are commonly painted inside. White walls predominate, but other colors are also used. In many houses, walls are sometimes painted with one color on the wainscot—the lower third of the wall—and with a different color on the upper two-thirds. Common color combinations include blue wainscot with white above, and pink wainscot with green above. On the white upper walls of a house in Hanna, just above the wainscot, a row of red, tulip-like flowers with green leaves and stems had been painted. On an end wall immediately above the band of flowers, a green floral wreath with red flowers crowned the band of flowers. In another house, previously hand-painted stars, flowers, and plants in blue were partially covered over with a

Figure 12.18 Stylized trees, symbols of a political party, painted on the meeting house, in Hanna, Baluchistan, Pakistan (1990).

Figure 12.19 Wall painted with blue designs subsequently covered with color pictures from calendars or magazines at Hanna, Baluchistan, Pakistan (1990).

row of posters of people and landscapes taken from magazines, calendars, or travel posters and affixed to the walls (Figure 12.19).

The men's house in the same compound at Hanna was elaborately, if modestly, decorated with coordinated colors and may serve as an example of local taste. The wainscot was painted pink. Above the wainscot, the walls were finished in white, which terminated in a carved mud decoration consisting of four spaced bars, or square-section ridges, in relief; the bars were painted green and the wall surface between each bar was painted pink. Immediately above this band was an unbroken row of landscape pictures from around the world on calendars mounted with thin wooden strips. Above this display, the ceiling was covered with printed cotton fabric featuring small pink flowers and green leaves on a maroon background; the cloth extended down about 15 cm below the ceiling on all four walls to which it was tacked. This tacked cloth also collected bits of twigs and crumbled mud from the mud roof, preventing them from falling on the floor and the heads of guests.

In the al-Kaf house in Terim, Hadhramaut, Yemen, where the Smithsonian team camped in 1961, there were molded medallions in high relief on the ceiling between each wooden structural beam. Each medallion featured a frame with curving concave sides painted green and edges painted white. In its center was a circular disk painted black. At each end of the frame was a black crown-like form, and on both long sides within the concave areas was a curving vine design, also in black (see Figure 1.7).

A common feature of mud houses in India are designs painted on mud plaster that are frequently renewed to satisfy ritual requirements, although exterior walls are generally left unpainted. At Sumasar, Kutch, in Gujarat, India, a round wattle-and-daub house featured an exterior wall surface painted green with a vine-and-leaf design surrounding the doorway in reserve—i.e., in the natural brown of the mud plaster without paint (see Figure 6.6). Occasionally a house will be painted white using a rice paste. On either the natural mud-plastered or white-painted walls and floors, traditional painted designs commemorate festivals and major events in life, and magic diagrams, often confined within a sacred area, communicate divine power (Figure 12.20). Subjects of drawings are infinitely varied: floral designs, geometric patterns, symbolic animals, and textile motifs (Figure 12.21). The paintings and diagrams differ by regions, areas, and families. Even to Westerners unfamiliar with their meanings, many are charming. Color pigments are made from natural substances and, more recently, from chemical dyes: white from rice paste, chalk, or lime; red from mercuric sulfide; yellow from turmeric; blue from flowers of the nightshade family; black from coal dust or burnt coconut shells. They are applied by spreading with the hands and fingers, trickling paint, sponging with a cloth, or stenciling (Huyler, 1993:178–180).

No discussion of painting mud structures would be complete without calling attention to the West African custom of house painting by women of the family. Using traditional as well as commercial pigments, and painting with their hands, they create exciting geometric and stylized figures of animals and humans. Designs reflect tribal traditions, symbolism, and individual creativity. Although further discussion is beyond the scope of this book, anyone interested in West African culture as expressed in mud architecture would enjoy Margaret Courtney-Clarke's (1990) book, *African Canvas*.

Stucco

Unlike the lime plaster called "stucco" by the Romans, cement stucco has been little used for wall plaster in the Near East and Southwest Asia because it does not

Figure 12.20 Village house in Bihar, India, with painted design on exterior wall behind shrine (1989).

Figure 12.21 Building with an elaborately painted motif at the Architectural Section of the Ethnographic Museum in New Delhi, India (1991).

adhere well to mud and it is very expensive. Moreover, cement does not breathe like lime plaster, the latter of which hastens drying and is of great importance in mud construction. As a result, cement stucco cannot compete with mud plaster and lime plaster as a suitable wall finish. This may change, however, as affluence increases in these regions, which makes the required wire mesh, cement, and paints more affordable. However, we visited a beehive house in the village of Susiyan, Syria, in which a thin layer of concrete had recently been applied directly on the mud-brick walls from the floor upwards to a height of about 85 cm above the floor. We observed no cracking in the coat, but the test would be how well it held up after a year or two.

In American usage, stucco means a mixture of cement, sand, and water. As such it has different properties and requires a different method of application. Cement-based materials and mud have different coefficients of expansion, which is why cement stucco does not adhere well to mud walls. Cement stucco, therefore, is applied to wire mesh attached to the wall rather than to the wall itself. In the USA, building codes require that exterior mud wall surfaces be covered with 17-gauge galvanized mesh called "stucco netting," which has a hexagonal pattern of 1.5 in (4 cm), although 20-gauge "poultry netting" with an identical pattern of 1 in (2.5 cm) is also in common use (McHenry, 1984:126–127). The mesh is stretched over the wall and nailed to it at intervals of 18 in (46 cm) with nails sufficiently long to hold fast in the mud walls.

Three coats of cement plaster having a combined thickness of ¾ in (2 cm) are used on exterior surfaces. First is the scratch coat, so called because it is scratched before it is dry with any of a number of tools to provide keying for the next coat. Second is the brown coat, applied to level and smooth the surface. After it has thoroughly cured for a week or so, a thin color coat is third, to finish the process. For stuccoing interior wall surfaces, the mesh and the scratch coat are not required; the final coat can be either finished smooth by troweling or textured by wet sponging before the stucco is dry (McHenry, 1985:115–116, 118). The unattractive gray color of concrete is then painted—usually to resemble the color of adobe! Because of the materials and the added manual labor required, stucco in the USA is expensive.

Mosaics

Among the oldest decorative devices for walls and columns are mosaics, designs composed of elongated baked-clay cones about 9 cm long × 1.5 cm in diameter. The pointed end of each cone was set deeply in the mud wall, and the circular base—left plain or colored with red, black, or cream paint—was flush with or slightly projected from the wall surface. Such mosaic cones were found at Warka in Mesopotamia, where they formed colorful designs including rows of triangles (which formed other triangles in the vertical courses), lozenges, and zigzag patterns on massive engaged, mud-brick columns and walls dating from ca. 3200 B.C. These cone mosaics have been reconstructed and are on permanent exhibition in the Berlin Museum (Figure 12.22). During the excavation of the ziggurat terrace at Ur, Woolley (1963:38–39, pl. 3) found thousands of clay cones on the floor dating from the twenty-ninth to twenty-seventh centuries B.C. Mosaic cones from the same general period were also found far to the northwest at Tell Brak in Syria. These examples seem to indicate that cone mosaics were common throughout Mesopotamia for at least 400–500 years, but they apparently ceased to be used as wall decoration by the middle of the third millennium B.C. and never appeared again.

Figure 12.22 Mosaics composed of multicolored flat heads of ceramic cones as found at and reconstructed from Warka, Iraq (Courtesy Berlin Museum, Berlin, Germany).

Orthostats

An orthostat is a stone slab generally about 1–2 m high, which, in the context of mud construction, is set vertically on a stone base or on the ground against the outer surface of a mud wall. In the ancient Near East, these slabs were placed side-by-side, generally on a projecting stone base, to form a continuous surface on the fronts of city gate towers and on facades of palaces. Their function was (1) to protect the mud wall from damage by people, animals, and carts striking or rubbing against them, and (2) to prevent erosion by deflecting both run-off water and direct rainfall away from the base of mud walls. This type of construction, featuring polished basalt slabs, was apparently invented in Asia Minor (ancient Anatolia) probably late in the third millennium B.C. By the eighteenth century B.C. it had spread to the northern Levant where it appeared at Alalakh in the palace of Yarim-Lim. At Hazor in northern Israel, a temple and a mud-brick palace of the fourteenth to thirteenth centuries B.C. yielded orthostats of dressed polished basalt that protected the base and lower courses of the walls (Yadin, 1993:597–600). This discovery indicated influence from the Syro–Hittite-culture region in northern Syria and eastern Turkey. Woolley (1961:130–131) related that in a private house of the fourteenth century B.C., the mud-brick walls were finished with a fresco featuring paintings of polished basalt slabs with cedar beams above them. The painted fresco anticipated the much later Roman frescoes, just as orthostats seem to have anticipated Roman veneers. The latter was the origin of the use of veneers in nearly all residential and most commercial construction in Europe and North America today.

Between the fifteenth and thirteenth centuries B.C., the Hittites began sculpting or-thostats in low relief (Figure 12.23). By the ninth century B.C., the Assyrians adopted the orthostat to face both the inside and outside of most palace walls in every capital city; Nineveh, Dur Sharrukin, and Calah. Made of gypsum (a softer stone yielding greater detail in carving), the Assyrian orthostats featured a considerable variety of subject matter in designs and motifs, as well as inscriptions: e.g., magical scenes with genii (Figure 12.24); the investiture of the king by the god; and narratives il-lustrating the king's wars and conquests, including gory views of dying and impaled captives, glimpses of the king's cooking tent in the field, scenes of pleasure featuring the hunt, and relaxing moments in the garden (Mallowan, 1966:96–103).

Orthostats continued in use into the Persian period (late sixth century B.C.), when mud-brick walls of the southern and eastern porticos of the Court of Reception at Persepolis were lined with a single, repeating scene reversed in orientation on oppo-site walls. Beautifully sculptured in relief on limestone slabs, the scene featured King Darius seated on a throne with his son, Xerxes, standing behind him as he receives a dignitary from Media whose attendants are standing by (Schmidt, 1939:21, fig. 14).

Glazed Brick

Beginning in the ninth century B.C., glazed bricks were employed by the Assyrians, Babylonians, and Persians to create multicolored designs, often with figures in low relief, on both outside and inside walls of important structures. Although glazed bricks were fired, they decorated the core walls of mud brick, so can be considered a decorative device. Chiefly featured on monumental entrances, these dramatic and beautiful surfaces must have delighted and awed both citizens and visitors to the ancient cities, as they do museum visitors today. At Fort Shalmaneser in ancient Assyria (present-day Nimrud, Iraq), a magnificent, glazed-brick decoration above the doorway to an antechamber (providing the only entrance to the Throne Room from the south) had collapsed to the courtyard floor. Julian Reade painstakingly reconstructed the panel with the somewhat elliptical shape of an arched gateway. The panel itself was 4.07 m high by 2.91 m wide, and had been installed on the wall above the door; its top reached about 8 m above the floor. Constructed of 38 courses of bricks, it featured a blue background and motifs in white, green, black, and yel-low colors, each brick individually glazed to suit the design. The center panel shows King Shalmaneser III (ninth century B.C.) under the winged disk of the god Assur, with an inscription separating it from an upper scene of a sacred tree behind two rampant bulls, all surrounded by five border designs gradually increasing in width from the center panel to the outer edge (Mallowan, 1966:452–454, pl. 373). Other early examples include Asshur-nasir-apal's scene of prisoners (ninth century B.C.), and Sargon II's use of a blue background and yellow figures at Khorsabad (ancient Dur-Sharrukin) in the eighth century B.C.

The largest and most spectacular use of glazed bricks found was in the proces-sional street of the god Marduk in Babylon, built by Nebuchadnezzar II (605–561 B.C.). It extended some 250 m connecting the Ishtar gate and the facade of the throne room. The mud walls along this street were covered with glazed bricks and featured a procession of lions in low relief, with three identical borders above and below the lions. The gate structure consisted of two towers flanking an arched

Figure 12.23 Replica of a Syro–Hittite orthostat from Zinjerli, Syria, featuring the god of hunting holding a rabbit, at the National Museum of Natural History (catalog no. A158200), Smithsonian Institution, Washington, D.C. Dimensions are 37 × 47 in (~91 × 105 cm).

entrance measuring 4.5 m wide and 14.73 m high. The vertical surfaces of the towers and gate featured vertical rows of individual animals—bulls and dragons—also in low relief. An estimated 575 such animals were originally represented on these structures (Jakob-Rost et al., 1987). An example of the Persian use of enameled

Figure 12.24 Replica of Assyrian orthostat featuring a genie, at the National Museum of Natural History, Smithsonian Institution, Washington, D.C.

bricks is the scene of palace guards at Susa from the time of Darius I, ca. 500 B.C. (Jakob-Rost et al., 1987:108, fig. 130).

Ceramic Tiles

The earliest ceramic tiles (known by GVB) in the ancient Near East are from the eighth century B.C. at Pazarli in Anatolia (Turkey), where the Phrygians nailed a row of tiles decorated with painted figures in low relief to form a frieze near the top of the wall just below the eaves. Some featured geometric designs, others marching warriors, griffins, and goats heraldically facing a tree. As Woolley (1961:149, 166) noted, the style "looks remarkably Greek" and certainly reflected Aegean influence.

From Spain and Morocco across North Africa to Egypt, as well as in the northern tier of Muslim countries from Turkey through Iran, interior walls have been traditionally finished with ceramic tiles, beginning in the thirteenth century A.D. Walls in halls and rooms were typically covered with tiles from the floor to a height of about 2 m and sometimes to the ceiling. Most designs were geometric or floral. In the northern Muslim countries, scenes of paradise, featuring lush gardens and predator animals and their prey, and scenes of men hunting were frequently used in series of individual panels surrounded with floral or geometric borders. The tiles were hand-painted in blues, greens, yellows, and reds, creating a colorful and lively ambience. Imagine how these scenes must have lifted human spirits during the drab, cold rainy days of winter.

Today, the finest tile panels and murals that we have seen are those painted by Marie Balian of Jerusalem; they decorate finer homes, such as the residence of the President of Israel, and were featured in exhibitions at the Smithsonian Institution, Washington, D.C., in 1992, in Jerusalem in 1999, and in the Haaretz Museum in Tel Aviv, Israel, in 2000. In Europe and in the USA, ceramic tiles are usually employed for floors and walls of kitchens and baths, with a wide range of solid colors plus white and black,[3] although most are in pastel or earthy colors with a matching or contrasting border. In the southwestern USA, plain and painted tiles made locally or in Mexico with traditional motifs are especially popular for kitchens and bathrooms of adobe homes.

Tile panels and murals are used in buildings constructed of all types of materials, but they are especially suited to mud buildings with interiors of mud plaster. Ideally they should be recessed in the wall to be flush with the wall surface. With mud-brick walls, an allowance of 1 cm can be made by inserting a board of that thickness on one long side of the brick mold, and earmarking those bricks for courses behind the wall panel areas. If the wall is built of rammed earth, a plywood sheet cut to the overall dimensions of the planned tile panel, and as thick as the panel plus tiles, can be set in the proper place in the form before ramming is done. When forms and plywood sheet are removed, there will be a recess in the wall to accommodate the installation of the tile panel. Alternatively, a tile panel can be placed on the deepest surface of a stepped niche. The wall should be sized before installing the tile. Because each tile in a hand-painted panel is different, care must be used in handling during layout and installation to avoid breaking them. If hand-painted tile has to be cut, only a diamond-blade saw should be used.

Wood Paneling

Literary evidence informs us that wood paneling was occasionally employed to decorate the interior of buildings in antiquity. One of the clearest examples is in the Temple of Solomon as described in the Bible (I Kings 6:14–15): "So Solomon built the house [i.e., the Temple] on the inside with boards of cedar; from the floor of the house to the rafters of the ceiling, he covered them on the inside with wood; and he covered the floor of the house with boards of cypress." Because wood has rarely survived from ancient sites, we tend to assume that it was little used, and then only for certain applications and types of objects. Archaeological excavations, however, sometimes yield wooden beams preserved in situ as well as other pieces in a fragmentary state. At Alalakh in the northern Levant for example, Woolley (1953:159) discovered the remnants of wooden paneling that had lined a recess in the rear wall of the sanctuary of a mud-brick temple in the thirteenth century B.C. In the Ptolemaic period (ca. early first century B.C.) at Soknopaiou Nesos in the Fayum region of Egypt, wooden paneling was found in excellent condition in the second level of house 201. Constructed of finely dressed timber 12–15 cm square, it was preserved to a height of ~1.45 m (although the paneling probably reached the ceiling when built) and a thickness of 20 cm. It was secured to the wall by wooden blocks set in the brickwork, and to which the paneling was attached with wooden pegs (Boak, 1935:11–12, plan 15).

Other Decorations of Walls

A rare type of decoration locally important in some regions of Southwest Asia is the mounting of animal horns on the parapet of mud walls, usually on the top of privacy or property walls. In Quetta, Baluchistan, bull horns were mounted on the tops of gateways and property walls of private residences. In the Hadhramaut of Yemen, walls around houses of renowned hunters were decorated with one or more sets of ibex horns to illustrate the prowess of the man of the house (Figure 12.25).

Thus, a vast range of possibilities for finishing and decorating mud walls have been created by masons, artisans, and householders throughout history. When combined with designs built into mud-brick walls, such as recessed niches and panels, the number of available choices is almost overwhelming. Certainly some of these options—glazed fired brick, orthostats, or cone mosaics—are not likely to be used in our time as mud architecture increases in popularity. They do not fit our present idioms in building design and are more expensive than governments, businesses, and home owners are likely to bear. But all are possible, and from what we have seen, many would prove attractive to those with imagination and the necessary funds.

COLUMNS

Wooden posts made from the trunks of trees provided the first load-bearing columns. In antiquity in the arid and semi-arid Near East, the palm tree was most frequently used because of its considerable height and straightness, but other trees including poplar, pine, cedar, and `ilb (jujube tree) were used according to their

Figure 12.25 Ibex horns set along the tops of the property walls of two houses in Terim, Hadhramaut, Yemen (1961).

availability. Wooden posts or columns do not survive in archaeological sites unless they have been burned and quickly covered by debris, which is relatively rare. Archaeologists generally infer their presence from post holes, circular marks on the floor, impressions of beams in the debris, or column bases not accompanied by column fragments of mud brick, fired brick, or stone.

Apart from removing the bark, most wooden posts were probably left in their natural state, decorated with carved designs, or covered with oil or whitewash. Today in most of the tall houses of the Hadhramaut, wooden columns support the beams in the middle of the room that carry upper floors. Some are plain, but many are carved with simple rosettes and grooves, which are usually seen in finer houses (Figure 12.26). Although specific identifications of the woods used are lacking, we suspect that most of the carved posts in the Hadhramaut are of `ilb wood.

Wooden posts sometimes formed the core of finely finished columns. At Persepolis in Iran, Darius the Great began construction of his great fortified palace compound circa 520 B.C. Successive kings added other palaces and structures to it, all of which were burned by the troops of Alexander the Great in 331 B.C. In Darius's treasury, the roof was supported by 99 columns, each of which was based on a torus, a pillow-like block of stone, which rested on a square base. Many fragments of

Figure 12.26   Wooden column and capital inside Beit Jarhum, with traces of white-washed mud plaster and small decorative motif, in Shibam, Hadhramaut, Yemen (1991). Note the damage done to the ceiling and column by a water leak from the floor above.

gypsum plaster with painted designs on the outer surface and rough impressions on the inner surface were recovered by archaeologists. When carefully reconstructed, the fragments showed that each column consisted of a wooden post wrapped continuously from bottom to top with rope made of reeds to key the plaster. Gypsum plaster was then applied, shaped, and painted with a highly stylized wave pattern in red, blue, and white (Schmidt, 1939:19, fig. 33).

True, or free-standing, columns commonly support porches and beams that carry upper floors and roofs. Depending on the length of a room, there may be one or two columns or posts in a line to support the major wooden beam carrying the ceiling or upper floor structure (Figure 12.26); if the room is very wide, two or more rows of columns may be required. The free-standing mud-brick columns in the northern Levant at Alalakh, in the excavations of level XII of the Early Dynastic period, circa twenty-ninth to twenty-seventh centuries B.C., may be the earliest. These columns were solid and massive, measuring about 2 m in diameter and finished with mud plaster. They stood in a line, probably forming a colonnade before a heavy mud-brick wall about 2.35 m thick in front of a high platform upon which the royal palace stood (Woolley, 1953:51, fig. 7, pl. 4). Similarly constructed columns dating to about the same time were found in the hypostyle hall at Kish, near the Euphrates River south of Baghdad in Iraq. Later, circa 2000 B.C., a free-standing mud-brick column in a temple at Ur was constructed of six or so mold-made, curving mud bricks that formed the perimeter around the solid core interior of bricks (Woolley, 1963:142, pl. 22b).

In the Hadhramaut, free-standing columns are used in larger salons to carry load-bearing beams and to support porch roofs on the front side of the house and gateways. Incidentally, between 1962 and 1991, a new house design appeared that featured porches supported by exterior free-standing columns. Interior columns, which had been used for several centuries, were apparently so successful that homeowners and builders decided to try them outside. These columns are commonly constructed of 12–18 small drums of roughly dressed limestone, each about 15 cm in diameter and 10 cm high. These drums are joined together by either mud mortar, limed mud mortar, or (more recently) cement mortar. When dry, the rough stone column is either left plain or covered with mud or lime plaster, the latter of which is sometimes carved with flutes resembling Greek or Roman columns and painted (see Figure 1.7). In a new, three-story house in Seiyun, Hadhramaut, which was not yet finished in 1991, columns on the upper floor showed bare stone drums in place. Each stone drum was about 16 cm in diameter and 10 cm high. Columns on the top floor in the center were covered with a base coat of mud plaster. Those on the lower floor were finished with white lime plaster (Figure 12.27). On such a large house, these columns were proportionately too thin and spindly; for a more pleasing balance, the stone drums should have been of a larger diameter, but the added weight might have created a load too heavy for the structure as designed. Identical columns, not yet plastered, flanked the gateway of an enclosure wall (Figure 12.28). Another new house of three stories in Seiyun had columned porches on the adjoining west and south sides (Figure 12.29). Here the columns reached a diameter of about 45 cm, creating a better balance with the massive proportions of the house.

An engaged column is one that is bonded or attached to a wall—i.e., not free-standing. In ancient Mesopotamia, engaged columns have been found at a number

Figure 12.27 Unfinished house with slender columns in various stages of completion in Seiyun, Hadhramaut, Yemen (1991).

of sites. At Uruk (Warka) in the late fourth millennium B.C., the facade of the temple courtyard was constructed with massive side-by-side engaged columns about 2.74 m in diameter, built with molded curving bricks and covered with a layer of mud plaster about 10 cm thick. As mentioned above, the columns were finished with mosaics made of ceramic cones whose flat heads were painted in red, black, or cream and whose pointed ends were pressed into the wet mud plaster to form various geometric designs (see Figure 12.22; Woolley, 1961:42, 51, 61).

In the magnificent temple and ziggurat of the nineteenth century B.C. at Tell al-Rimah, Iraq (see Figure 9.13), there are mud-brick, engaged, spiral columns, and other columns decorated with two different features of the trunks of palm trees. Here can be seen an attempt to reproduce the textured bark of the palm tree and the surface scars left by pruning the fronds. These remarkable columns are made with a series of individually designed mud bricks to achieve the desired relief ornamentation and to provide structural stability by bonding mud bricks with one another and between the column and wall. The planning of both of these highly complex patterns required considerable skill and patience. Archaeologist David Oates is to be congratulated for his careful analysis of these columns; he has described the process in considerable detail:

> Each column, whether palm trunk or spiral, was built with mud-bricks bearing on their outer face patterns in relief, which, by repetition in a standard sequence, produced the required motif. The basic shape of brick employed was a 60° sector of a circle of radius c. 29 cm (11½").... To produce the correct outline, either in making a mould or in cutting

Figure 12.28 Slender columns of small stone drums not yet plastered, in Seiyun, Hadhramaut, Yemen (1991).

the brick, a 60° angle could easily be defined by drawing the 29 cm circle and then intersecting the circumference with an arc of the same radius. The ornament was then carved on the curved surface. In the 'scale' palm trunk the motif was only one course high and each brick bore three scales; the 'diamond', being four courses high, required four different patterns of brick.

The cutting of the component bricks in spiral columns presented a slightly more complex problem in geometry.... Each bore on its outer face parts of two adjacent strands of the spiral separated by a slanting groove, the angle of which determined the twist of the spiral [Figure 12.30].... The radius of the individual strands was approximately half that of the sector brick and their centres were 15° off the line of the sides of the brick, to right or left according to whether a right-hand or left-hand spiral was required. The angle of the groove to be cut on the outer face was established by shifting the position of the centres on the under surface of the brick through an arc of 15°, again to right or left as required.... The actual method of cutting them was probably less sophisticated than the theory. The use of templates would have been an obvious labour-saving device, but we cannot show that they were used and in one instance that we can show that they were not. On one brick we found that the centre of the strand on the upper surface was marked by a circular depression such as might be made by rotating a man's thumb, and the radius was approximately the span between thumb and forefinger, which apparently served as a primitive pair of compasses.... The use of these bricks alone would have produced half-columns of the required patterns, provided that they were laid with an axial twist of 15° in successive courses so that the position of the groove on the top of one brick corresponded with that on the bottom of the brick immediately above. But there would then have been no satisfactory bond between the half-column and the wall behind it. This difficulty was overcome by using the complete sector bricks only in alternate courses, interspersed with bonding bricks of horse-shoe shape which overlay the points of the sector bricks and penetrated to a depth of half a brick into the wall face. The profile of the spiral was continued by cutting smaller pieces of brick in the shape of the missing segments of individual strands and setting them around the circumference of the horse-shoe. The top course consisted of four sector bricks.... These completed an arc of 240°, and a half of each of the two lateral bricks was set into the wall face. In the second course was a horse-shoe bonding brick with three segments of strands set around its circumference. The bonding brick overlay the points of three sector bricks in the course beneath, which formed a semi-circle and thus made a straight joint with the wall face. The fourth course consisted of a horseshoe brick surrounded by four segments of strands forming an arc of 240°, so that half of each lateral segment was inset in the wall. The gaps between the bricks were filled with brick fragments and mortar.... This arrangement produced vertical joints one half brick behind the wall face in the first, second and fourth courses of the sequence, and a joint on the line of the face in the third course. The column was therefore locked together by a bonding brick in every second course, and every second bonding brick was overlaid by a square brick penetrating a full 35 cm (13¾") into the wall. (Oates, 1967:88–89.)

Figure 12.29 New three-story house with heavier columns supporting porches and roofs in Seiyun, Hadhramaut, Yemen (1991).

Oates also called attention to the only other example of a similar column known, which was found by Woolley at Ur in southern Mesopotamia, some 750 air kilometers southeast of Tell al-Rimah. The mud-brick column at the entrance to the bastion of Warad-Sin is decorated with the same 'diamond' pattern used in the Tell al-Rimah temple and was similarly constructed. Oates also noted that spiral columns were rendered on square fired bricks, with a full cross-section on each brick at Aqar Quf in the Kassite period (ca. 1600–1150 B.C.), but this was not comparable to the elaborate design of the Tell al-Rimah spiral columns (Oates, 1967:90).

Pilasters are typically square or rectangular in cross-section and usually bonded into a wall. In addition to providing increased structural support by projecting beyond the wall surface, they break the plain wall into a series of sections or panels, which are often individually decorated. Today, many property walls in the Hadhramaut are constructed with pilasters, and some are attractively finished with relief and paint (see Figure 9.15). Pillars, or piers, are also square or rectangular in cross-section but are free-standing; although they are fairly common in stone, they were less frequently used in mud architecture.

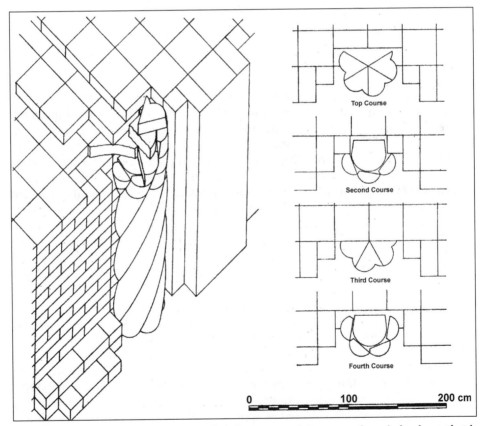

Figure 12.30 Detail of brick shapes and their sequence in courses of a spiral column that is bonded into the temple wall, nineteenth century B.C., Tell al-Rimah, Iraq. (From Oates, 1967, figs. 32a,b and 40; used with permission).

STAIRWAYS

Archaeologists know comparatively little about stairways of mud buildings in ancient times because few have survived human and natural agencies of destruction. We often recover the beginning of a flight of stairs, but only few steps are preserved, and these seldom take us even to the first landing. A stairway supported by a central pier was discovered in a side room of Gate 7 at Khorsabad, built by Sargon II (Loud, 1936:5). Today in mud buildings of two stories or more, stairways commonly wind around a massive central pier built of ashlar, generally with two landings between each floor, a design that conserves floor space, as in the house we studied at Marib, Yemen, (see Figure 3.52). We realize that thick mud walls in nearly all mud structures may indicate several stories, but most archaeologists have been timid in estimating the original number of stories or the height of the building. At Alalakh in the northern Levant, Woolley discovered a temple built by the ruler Yarim-Lim in the eighteenth century B.C., with walls 3.96 m thick, which he suggested was at least two stories high and possibly more (Woolley, 1953:77). As we discussed in Chapter 9, a solid mud-brick wall 86 cm thick has served a seven-story house in Shibam, Hadhramaut, for more than 400 years. Given the carrying capacity of solid mud-brick walls as shown by this example, Woolley would have been well within the limits of possibility if he had suggested a height of 10–15 stories! Yet Woolley is among the few archaeologists who relate thickness of mud walls to building height, and he is to be commended for his keen observation of details and his architectural reconstructions.

Among the best surviving examples of stairways in an ancient building are those at Tell al-Rimah in Iraq. In the magnificent mud-brick temple of the nineteenth century B.C., a stairway ascended northward to a landing in the northeast corner of the structure, and then turned westward to continue its ascent over room X to room XIV (Figure 12.31). Taken together, they indicate that the stairway reached a height of about 7.56 m above the ground floor in a building whose facade was about 11.34 m high. The first flight of steps was apparently supported by a fill of mud brick; each step consisted of two courses of mud bricks and was one and one-half bricks wide, for a total interior stairway width of about 53 cm with a riser height of 21 cm. All steps were overlaid with plaster. The mud-brick landing was not bonded into the temple wall; instead it was supported only by a mud-brick pier, which had settled slightly. The second flight of steps was carried by a series of eight radial vaults—each one three bricks long—and the apex of each vault was four courses of wall brick higher than the apex of the previous vault. Each vault was sufficiently deep to carry two steps, for a total of 16 steps in the second flight, and each step was constructed of two courses of bricks, as in the first flight. The bricks of the steps were in relatively good condition, indicating that the stairway had been roofed (Oates, 1967:80–81).

A long stairway of the same period was discovered also at Tell al-Rimah, reaching from the level of the town at its lower end to the upper terrace of the temple complex. Built on a mud-brick foundation and enclosed by side walls, the stairway was about 34 m long and consisted of approximately 44 steps, each step two bricks high, about 17.5 cm, and two bricks long, about 73 cm. The bricks of the steps were all baked, indicating that this stairway was always without roof and open to the sky. Almost midway in the length of the ramp were three radial vaults of increasing

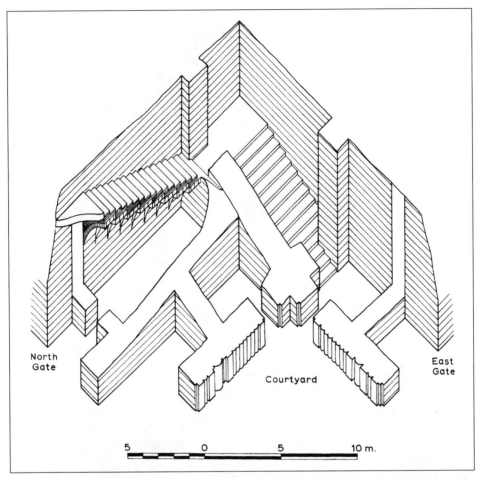

North Gate

East Gate

Courtyard

5   0   5   10 m.

Figure 12.31   Detail of temple stairway, the upper section of which was supported by eight radial vaults, nineteenth century B.C., Tell al-Rimah, Iraq. (From Oates, 1967, fig. 34; used with permission.)

height, in keeping with the slope, that provided tunnels extending through the ramp to connect the two sides of the terrace (Oates, 1968:120–121, figs. 30, 31).

Baked-brick steps also appeared in the apartment of *rab ekalli*, a high official at Fort Shalmaneser at Nimrud in the middle ninth century B.C. These steps led, in two flights at right angles to one another, to an upper floor (Mallowan, 1966:420, fig. 348).

At Alalakh, near the forested mountains of northwestern Syria, wood figured more prominently in construction, and it is not surprising, therefore, that indoor stairs frequently were made of wood. For example, in a sixteenth century B.C. temple (possibly dedicated to the worship of Mithras) with an entrance chamber below ground level, a flight of wooden steps led down to the worship center, complete with a fire altar and a mud bench around the room (Woolley, 1953:95).

All of the above-mentioned stairways resembled modern staircases in the regularity of the risers—i.e., all steps were vertically spaced the same distance apart. This

Figure 12.32   Construction detail of stairway winding around a central ashlar pier (now mostly fallen) in a ruined layered-mud house, twentieth century A.D., Marib Town, near Marib, Yemen (1991).

was due to the standardized brick modules and construction technique consistently employed in each instance. In the southern Arabian Peninsula, on the other hand, stair risers tended to vary considerably, so much so that it seemed incomprehensible why anyone would build a flight of steps with varying heights, which would force a person to watch every tread carefully when ascending and descending. We only discovered the reason when I visited Marib Town in Yemen.

Figure 12.33 Curving flight of narrow steps at Taos Pueblo, Taos, New Mexico, USA (1989).

This now-abandoned town, as mentioned earlier, was severely damaged by aerial bombing during the civil war beginning in 1962, and again substantially destroyed by two earthquakes in 1982. Some houses remained relatively intact, while many others were entirely destroyed. A few were split open, with one half falling to the ground and the other half still standing. The standing halves provided us a rare opportunity to study building design and construction methods in cross section. Here too, stairways were built around a central pier (Figure 12.32), which was often constructed of ashlar masonry quarried from the pre-Islamic ruins adjacent to the "piggy-back" tell, on which the town was built. In the standing half of this four-story house, we could see that a single, transverse heavy log had been set in the house wall on one side and in the pier on the other, midway between each landing. On top of these large logs, and spanning the diagonal between the load-bearing logs of the landing below and those of the landing above, were smaller logs laid tightly side-by-side, running the length of the flight of stairs. The steps were constructed on the resulting irregular sloping surfaces. The logs, of course, were of different diameters, and it was the varying diameters of these logs that determined the differing heights of the risers in southern Arabia.

In the six-story Beit Jarhum in Shibam, Hadhramaut (see Figures 3.55, 3.56), the stairwell occupies the northwest corner of the house. It consists of a solid, massive, rectangular pier that supports a flight of steps on three of its sides, each flight separated by two small landings, for each floor of the house. The stairway winds upward in this fashion to the fifth floor, where the stairwell is moved slightly to the west; after the fourth floor, it is constructed with one landing between two straight flights between each floor up to the sixth-floor roof. A single window on each of the second, third, and fourth floors provides a modest amount of light to the stairwell.

East of Shibam, the plan of the grand mud-brick house (with the ceiling of 16 coffered vaults) under construction in Hauta featured two intersecting central halls, one oriented east–west and the other north–south. The main, north–south hall was enhanced by two stairways leading to the second floor—one from near the front door on the north and the other from near the rear door on the south. Each stairway began at about one-third the length of the hall from the door it was nearest, one ascending to a landing against the front wall and the second to a landing against the rear wall; from the landings they both proceeded to the upper floor, creating a grand design. These well-designed stairways featured small, equally spaced risers and comfortably long treads of the mud-brick steps.

The most amusing and dangerous flight of steps we have ever seen, however, was in Taos Pueblo, near Taos, New Mexico, USA. It was only one brick wide and curved as it ascended, without side walls or railings, around an outdoor oven or *horno* (Figure 12.33). One would need to be quite steady and sure-footed to climb this stairway, especially on a dark night!

NOTES

1. This work is now often done by professional craftswomen, but traditionally it was the responsibility of young unmarried daughters of the family, who were required by *vratas*—direct petitions to deities—to honor the spirits of ancestors, or as "supplications for fertility and success in marriage" (Huyler, 1993:172–188).

2. Seashells may also be used, but they were not readily available where we observed lime plaster being produced.

3. GVB once saw a bathroom completely tiled in black, including floor and ceiling!

Chapter 13

Floors, Windows, Doors, Ceilings, and Utilities

FLOORS

Mud construction accommodates all types of flooring. Most of the factors that determine the type of building we construct—environment, local tradition, cost, and personal taste—also determine our choice of floors. For example, wooden floors are seldom seen in houses located in arid and semiarid lands, primarily because of the scarcity of good wood. In the Near East and Southwest Asia, the major types of floors in mud buildings include earth, lime plaster, mud brick, stone of many kinds, fired brick, ceramic tile, and concrete. A few other types can be found in other regions.

Earth

Throughout the Old World the vast majority of floors in mud buildings have always been beaten earth. For example, the floors and courtyards of most private houses at Tell Jemmeh, in Israel through 1500 years of occupations were packed earth. In Mesopotamia, such floors were common in the workshops and storage structures in Fort Shalmaneser at Nimrud (ancient Calah) from between the ninth and seventh centuries B.C. (Mallowan, 1966:404, 407). In the northern Levant at al-Mina, the port downriver from ancient Alalakh in present-day Turkey (eighth-fourth centuries B.C.), beaten-earth floors in the warehouses were laid on a layer of pebbles to reduce dampness in lower areas, but earth floors at higher elevations were laid without the pebble base (Woolley, 1953:167). Anyone who has camped for a week or so in a tent without a sewed-in floor understands how quickly soil turns to dust with foot traffic. Dampening and tamping the soil once or twice daily develops a smooth, somewhat traffic-resistant surface. In successive tent camps of the Smithsonian's expedition in the Hadhramaut of Yemen during the winter of 1961–1962, a crew member leveled and smoothed the wadi soil of the cook tent, sprinkled it with water the first two days and thereafter once a day, with each sprinkling followed by a drying period. This procedure, with variations, was and still is the most common type of floor preparation used from prehistoric times to the present throughout the Near East and Southwest Asia.

A better earth floor can be prepared by removing all top soil containing organic matter to a depth of about 15–18 cm. The base is then smoothed and tamped. A 10 cm thick layer of sand or gravel is spread on this base and tamped. This is followed with a 5 cm thick layer of slightly damp soil (it should be about the same moisture as soil used in constructing rammed earth), which is also leveled and tamped. The floor should cure for several days until it is hard (Wolfskill et al., 1979:134).

Clay also makes a fine floor, especially if it is burnished with a trowel or smooth stone when still damp, making it shiny and nearly water resistant. During the 1952 excavations at Jericho, we found that the 9000-year-old Pre-Pottery Neolithic A clay floor of a mud-brick room had been finished in this manner; it was still so impervious that, after a rain storm, it held water for a week until the water finally evaporated. If an earth floor is well maintained, additional fine soil can be gradually added to its surface so that it becomes thicker through time. In one house in the destroyed and abandoned Marib Town in Yemen, we saw a mud floor that had built up gradually until it was 15 cm thick.

Ancient builders eventually learned that an application of oil made earth floors last longer with less maintenance. In the southern Levant, Arabs traditionally poured a 5-gallon (18.9 L) tin of olive oil on an earth floor after a thorough tamping. After a few days, the oil was gradually absorbed and the floor hardened. Oil also seals the floor sufficiently to prevent some of the damp and cold from entering the room. In New Mexico, USA, Native Americans and Spaniards often prepared earth floors by mixing animal blood with ashes to harden the earth and make the floor more water resistant (Bunting, 1964:8).

In the Taos and Santa Cruz areas of New Mexico, some earth floors are made by mixing screened soil and water and spreading a layer of the mixture 4–6 in (10–15 cm) thick on leveled, dampened earth. The amount mixed and poured should be enough to finish the entire floor of a room in one day. (If two or more mixtures are poured over two or three days to cover a single room, the interruptions in pouring will cause the formation of perceptible joints.) The mixture should be distributed equally to all areas of the room, and the surface leveled and finished with trowels. Once poured, the floor should dry for about 10 days before it is walked on.

If cracks appear during drying, they can be filled with slip—a mixture of soil and water with the thickness of cream—using a vessel with a pouring spout to control the flow. After three or four days when the slip is dry, the floor can be painted with a coat of boiled linseed oil and permitted to dry for about a week. A second coat is then applied, consisting of boiled linseed oil thinned with turpentine (one part turpentine to four parts linseed oil), which causes the floor to dry more quickly. When it is dry, the floor should be finished with several coats of paste wax—a step that should be repeated from time to time—which will give it a rich, satin-like, deep brown color. Such a floor is durable and will last for decades. If cracks develop with time, the floor is easily repaired by again filling them with slip and treating the filled area with linseed oil. If an area becomes damaged, it can be cut out, filled with mud, and finished by repeating this procedure (Southwick, 1965:8).

Another method of preparing an earth floor is to mix the mud with linseed oil, lay the floor 15–20 cm deep, and when it is dry, pour polyurethane varnish on it.

This produces a hard, shiny floor that withstands heavy traffic; such a floor is more comfortable to stand on than one of concrete, stone, fired brick, or ceramic tile. The beautiful black floor in one of the galleries in the Coronado State Monument at Bernalillo, near Albuquerque, New Mexico, which was built in 1940 is this type (Figure 13.1); it withstands the traffic of about 40,000 visitors annually! These floors—like all others except those made of ceramic tile, fired brick, and stone—can be damaged

Figure 13.1 Mud floor finished with polyurethane, at Coronado State Monument, Bernalillo, New Mexico, USA (1995).

by the stiletto-like heels of women's shoes, athletic shoes with metal spikes, and hob-nail boots, but they can be repaired by repeating the procedures with which they were laid and finished.

Earth floors are not confined to building interiors; they are also frequently used for courtyards. In Niamtougou, Togo, West Africa, the family compound is prepared by the women. In preparing the courtyard 'floor,' they dig up the surface, then repack it by tamping with their hands until it is smooth. They make rounded, or hospital, corners where the floor and walls meet to prevent run-off water from eroding the base of the walls. The women slope the surface and contour it so that water drains down the middle of the compound and outside through prepared holes in the base of the perimeter walls of the settlement. Finally, to make a long-lasting surface, they rub on it a watery red oil made from the outer shell of the fruit of a tree known as *merre,* which acts as a hardening agent (Morris, 1973).

In Jadar, Gujarat, India, mud plaster (*gobar-mitti)* is primarily mixed by women and commonly applied by hand to the ground immediately before the front entrance of the house to invoke the goddess Lakshmi to protect the home from malevolent spirits and trouble. The size of the plastered area generally is about 1–2 m². The mud mixture is spread over an area of about 45 × 30 cm, with a uniform thickness of 2 cm. Lightly placing her hand flat on the mud and using the heel of the palm as a pivot point, the woman sweeps the palm and fingers in an arc to create semi-circular grooves, each set off by a low ridge above and below (Figure 13.2). The plasterer then moves her hand down, so that the lower ridge becomes the upper ridge, and makes another series of semi-circular grooves, repeating this process until there is a column of grooves. Moving to the top of the column just completed, she begins another column beside it, repeating the design in column after column until the freshly applied mud plaster is completely covered with the pattern. The spreading and decorating of the mud plaster progresses quickly, with each column requiring little more than two minutes. Alternatively, if she pivots her hand in a counterclockwise direction, she produces a design half as wide as the one made with a clockwise motion.

When dry, the plaster forms a hard surface that typically survives use and wear for as much as one month. This surface is renewed many times during the year for ceremonial occasions by adding another coat of mud plaster and repeating the decorative process. In this region, such decorated mud plaster is used not only for entrance areas, courtyards, and porch floors, but also on the plastered exterior wall surfaces and occasionally on interior surfaces of both mud- and fired-brick walls.

Lime Plaster

The use of lime plaster for floors also has a very long history in the ancient Near East. In the Pre-Pottery Neolithic B period at Haçılar, Turkey (ca. 7000 B.C.), the floors of important rooms were laid on a bed of small stones or pebbles and covered with lime plaster, which was often stained with red ocher and burnished. In one instance, a floor had a circular depression decorated with red paint, leaving a broad cream-colored band in reserve. Subsequently during the Pottery Neolithic A period (sixth millenium B.C.), earthen floors with added lime were beautifully smoothed and off-white in color (Mellaart, 1970a:3–11). At Alalakh in the northern Levant,

Figure 13.2 Woman applying a swirled groove pattern to newly laid mud plaster on courtyard floor in Jadar, Gujarat, India (1991).

the major inner court and bathrooms of the palace were paved with lime plaster (fifteenth to fourteenth centuries B.C.), as was the courtyard of the temple built by the Hittite king Suppiluliuma in the mid-fourteenth century B.C. (Woolley, 1953:105, 135). At Tell Jemmeh, the floors and walls of all bathrooms were paved with lime plaster (see Figure 14.17). Many small fragments were also found in all occupation periods except the Chalcolithic of the late fourth millennium B.C., but our area of excavation in that period was so small that it does not represent a viable sample of the material culture. In the Treasury at Persepolis, built by Darius in the late sixth century B.C., the floors were of white gypsum plaster (or possibly lime plaster) and colored red (Schmidt, 1939:20).

The more expensive contemporary mud houses and important public buildings in Iran, Pakistan, and Yemen have lime-plaster floors. Areas most vulnerable to water damage (kitchens and bathrooms) and areas most subject to wear from heavy traffic (floors and stair treads) are finished with lime plaster first, before the interior walls and ceilings. Lime-plaster floors become smooth and shiny when burnished; they are also waterproof and easy to wash for maximum cleanliness. We have been in many houses where the floors might be characterized by the widely used compliment, "one can eat off the floors"!

Sadly, use of lime plaster has decreased in recent decades partly because of its costs, which have risen as the household industry of lime burning has declined, but primarily because of the increasing availability of cement in the Old World. In the New World, lime plaster is still used in Mexico, but has long since disappeared from floors in the southwestern USA. However, Santa Fe, New Mexico, architect Robert Nestor told us that lime-plaster technology was being revived in New Mexico, thanks to Cornerstones Community Partnerships. This organization, dedicated to helping communities restore their historic churches and other structures, brought a group of Mexican craftspersons to New Mexico to teach local groups and builders how to make lime plaster and apply it. Nestor also said that during a tour in Mexico, he examined cathedrals roofed with lime plaster because of its waterproofing characteristics. He now believes lime plaster should be used for more applications because of its advantages, such as its greater flexibility and softness, over Portland-cement-based products.

Mud Brick

Structures occasionally have mud-brick floors, and these are quite serviceable given normal traffic and footwear as long as water is not permitted to pond or run on them. Mud bricks can be laid on leveled soil or, preferably, on sand without mortar, which permits one or more mud bricks to be easily lifted and replaced with new ones as needed. At Tell al-Rimah in northern Iraq, as early as the nineteenth century B.C., mud-brick floors were finished with a black mud plaster by adding charcoal to the mixture (Oates, 1966:127–128). All kinds of floors were used at Nimrud (ancient Calah), one of the capitals of the Neo-Assyrian kingdom in the first half of the first millennium B.C. Mud-brick platforms or daises were used to elevate the royal throne in palaces, but mud-brick floors seem to have been largely confined to private, wealthy houses in the seventh century B.C. (Mallowan, 1966:186, 202, 239).

The floors of the Assyrian vaulted building at Tell Jemmeh consisted of rectangular bricks laid as stretchers between the side walls of the room in regular courses on a bedding of sand. A layer of sand varying 1–3 cm in thickness was found on each floor during excavation, but this may have fallen from the bedding and rising joints in the walls when the mud plaster on them deteriorated. On the other hand, specks of lime plaster on the surface of floor bricks suggest that sand may have served to level the floor as a base for a lime-plaster surface, although it seems unlikely that the entire lime-plaster surface would have disintegrated to flakes. The orientation of the bricks changed in the connecting doorways to headers between the jambs (see Figure 11.41).

In the circular granary of the late fourth to third century B.C. at Tell Jemmeh, we found two successive floors, both of square mud bricks. The lowest, earliest floor was laid in straight neat courses, with the small curving areas near the wall filled either with bricks cut to fit or with soil (Figure 13.3). After a period of perhaps 20–30 years, during which about 30 cm of debris accumulated on the floor, a new mud-brick floor was laid that showed considerable imagination in design but an astonishing dearth of common sense. The mason apparently decided to lay a circular mud-brick floor, utilizing the same standardized square brick throughout, beginning against the circular wall on the west side of the granary. By the time he had laid a wedge-shaped area of three rings, he found himself unable to proceed with the design. Only the outermost ring could be completed, but the laying of each subsequent ring was impossible, because each successive inner ring collided with and was stopped by the previously laid ring. To bring his initial plan to a happy conclusion, he should have made the floor bricks of each successive ring smaller than those of the preceding ring to fit the reduced perimeter and diameter of each ring as he moved from the outer wall toward the center of the floor. Rather than lift the floor bricks already laid and start over, he filled in some of the remaining areas with standard-sized bricks in straight rows, some in slightly curving rows of various lengths, and the remainder in a helter-skelter fashion to fill out the floor (Figure 13.4).

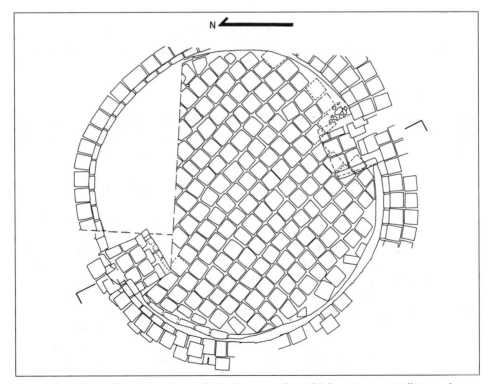

Figure 13.3 Plan of lower mud-brick floor of granary, from third century B.C., Tell Jemmeh.

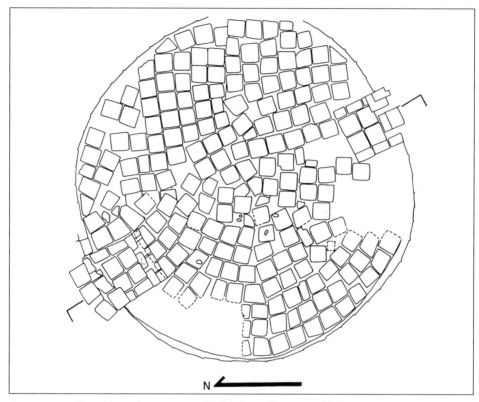

Figure 13.4   Plan of irregular, upper mud-brick floor of granary, third century B.C., Tell Jemmeh.

Fired Brick

Floors of fired or baked brick appear as early as the late third millennium B.C. in Mesopotamia. At Ur in the twentieth century B.C., fired-brick floors covered with bitumen for waterproofing were extensively used by kings Ur-Nammu and Shulgi in the gateway of the ziggurat, palace, and the royal tombs (Woolley, 1961:96, 98; 1963:142). In the following century, far to the northwest at Tell al-Rimah, the temple courtyards were paved with fired brick (Oates, 1965:69). Later, during the ninth to seventh centuries B.C., Oates (1968:136) noted that floor construction at Rimah followed the Late Assyrian tradition of laying fired brick for the perimeter areas of pavements, where floors near the mud-brick walls of buildings are subject to drainage and groundwater run-off. In contemporary royal buildings at Nimrud, most of the floors were of fired bricks in both square and rectangular (half-brick) shapes.

A splendid Mesopotamian tradition in brick-making was the stamping of the king's name on bricks destined for important structures. In the Governor's Palace at Nimrud, for example, the bricks were stamped with the name of Shalmaneser III, who reigned ca. 859–824 B.C. This ancient practice has been enormously helpful to archaeologists in sorting building phases and fixing dates of construction, additions, reconstructions, or repairs (Mallowan, 1966:42). Beginning in Roman times, floors of fired brick became increasingly common.

Today fired-brick floors are commonly laid on ground that is 5–10 cm higher than the exterior ground surface. The area is leveled and compacted, and bricks are laid directly on the prepared ground, or on a bed of dry sand. In the Beleli Customs Post near Quetta, Baluchistan, Pakistan, for example (see Figure 3.28), fired floor bricks were laid in alternating rows of headers and stretchers on the leveled ground without sand. The bricks used were molded with grooves on the upper surface to key a plastered or cement surface, either of which would be suitable in this application. Sixteen months later when we visited the customs building in operation, we saw that a concrete floor had been poured on the bricks. Floors of fired brick are, of course, more expensive than beaten-mud floors or mud-brick floors, although they are increasingly popular even in more modest homes in Southwest Asia.

In the southwestern USA, the bed for fired-brick floors is more carefully prepared. Leveled ground is treated with insecticide, over which a vapor barrier of heavy plastic sheeting in the appropriate width is spread, which in turn is covered with about 1 in (2.5 cm) of carefully leveled sand. Solid bricks—i.e., without holes in the rear surface, are laid on the sand according to the pattern and spacing determined in advance (sometimes by trying several layouts). They may be laid tightly with no real joints or laid with joints if concrete mortar is to be used. Care is taken to keep the bricks level, and any high places are corrected by gently tapping the higher bricks with a hammer. Bricks are cut to fill out the edges with a masonry saw or a wide brick chisel. With tightly laid bricks, fine sand can be swept back and forth to fill the cracks between bricks, locking them in position. If concrete mortar is used in wider joints, it is compressed with a pointing trowel. When the mortar has set, excess mortar on the bricks is cleaned with muriatic acid or similar solutions. For a fine, easy-to-clean finish, the bricks should be sealed with a sealer, oil-based varnish, or polyurethane, although the first coat should be thinned with mineral spirits to make a 50–50 mix. Finally the brick floor is coated with a paste wax, and buffed. (For details, a fuller description with useful tips is provided by McHenry, 1985:88–90.) Such floors are most attractive, adding a deep, glossy, earth color that develops a warm patina in time.

Stone

Many types of stone flooring are used with mud structures, including cobblestones and flagstones of various shapes, laid randomly or in patterns, as well as mosaics of stone tesserae. All stone floors are more time-consuming and expensive to lay than those made of earth, mud brick, or fired brick.

Excellent examples of cobblestone floors are the paved, open courtyard of a palace or elite building of the thirteenth century B.C. at Tell Jemmeh (Figure 13.5) and the identical construction of a contemporary cobblestone pavement through the northwest gateway of the town (Figure 13.6). These cobblestone floors are models of careful preparation and construction. The builders first spread a layer of chocolate-colored clay 8–14 cm thick over the leveled ground. From the stream bed of Nahal Besor along the north side of the site, they carefully selected stones of all sizes that had been rounded by centuries of tumbling in the flash floods but that had one flat surface. Larger stones were about 70–75 cm long and 50–60 cm wide, and smaller stones were about 6–10 cm long and 5–8 cm wide, with the vast

Figure 13.5 **Plan of cobblestone-paved courtyard, Tell Jemmeh, thirteenth century B.C.**

majority being of various sizes between the two extremes. The larger cobblestones were placed with their flat side down into the clay bed so that the rounded surface was up, providing the walked-on surface. By putting the flat sides down, the builders ensured that the cobblestones were stable and neither rolled nor rocked. They were

Figure 13.6   Cobblestone paving of northwest gate, from thirteenth century B.C., Tell Jemmeh.

laid close together with the edges touching, and smaller stones were wedged into the spaces between the larger cobblestones to prevent lateral movement.

This cobblestone courtyard floor is large, covering an area more than 14.7 m long (east–west) by a maximum of 8.25 m wide (north–south). Not only is it beautiful, it is durable. This area of the tell was excavated in 1927 by Sir Flinders Petrie (GVB's predecessor) to a depth of about 10.4 m, where he stopped about 65 cm above the cobblestone floor. During the 44 years before we uncovered a tiny portion of this floor in 1971, run-off water laden with eroded soil from the winter rains was allowed to pond in this area because there was no easy way—or compelling reason—to drain it off. During all the intervening years, this cobblestone floor was less than 1 m below the surface and must have been soaked several months almost every year. We were told by members of nearby Kibbutz Re`im that in many years the winter rains created a pond of standing water about 1.5–2 m deep there. With no outlet, the water remained in the bottom of the pit until it gradually soaked in or evaporated. During the eight years of our excavations of this area, we covered the floor at the end of each field season with plastic sheeting weighted down with stones, which always failed to keep water off the courtyard floor. When we returned each year at the beginning of the next field season, a thriving crop of weeds had sprouted from the interstices of the cobblestone floor riddling the plastic cover. It typically took our excavating crews a week to prepare the area for research, drawing, and photography (i.e., to cut all weeds that emerged between the stones and clean the area as it had looked at the end of the previous summer). That this cobblestone floor had not been damaged by 44 years of soaking plus eight annual cycles of wetting and drying is the best evidence of the excellent construction of the floor.[1]

At Tell Jemmeh, cobblestone paving was confined to open, unroofed areas such as gateways, courtyards, and the area outside the entrance to houses, where a reasonably heavy rain would otherwise turn a mud surface into a quagmire.

Cobblestone paving was also used in the northeast courtyard and in the workshops of Fort Shalmaneser at Nimrud during the ninth century B.C. (Mallowan, 1966:378, 402, fig. 331). As at Tell Jemmeh, the cobblestone courtyard and gate floors were unroofed and subjected to rains, as were the workshops, which were places of heavy work and foot traffic.

Dressed stone blocks were occasionally used as flooring in special structures. For example, in the ninth century B.C. at Nimrud, the floor of the podium in the sanctuary of Nabu was constructed of enormous limestone slabs 2.5 m long × 22 cm thick and set on a clay bed 16 cm thick, with a leveled base 5 cm thick. The nearly identical sanctuary of Tashmetum, wife of Nabu, was floored throughout with square limestone slabs 50 cm² (Mallowan, 1966:260, 264). Even then the quarrying and dressing of limestone blocks was expensive, but obviously no expense was spared for royal temples.

Flagstone paving was found at Soknopaiou Nesos (Dimê) in the Fayum region of Egypt in two houses, 202D and 203A. They belong to the second phase of occupation, ca. first century B.C. to first century A.D. (Boak, 1935:6).

Concrete and Cement

Concrete floors were not known in high antiquity. Durable, waterproof floors in that era were made of lime or gypsum plaster or of mud brick coated with bitumen. The invention of concrete made with cement occurred in Italy in the second century B.C. (Robertson, 1969:233). Vitruvius described Roman concrete as follows:

> There is also a kind of powder which, by nature, produces wonderful results. It is found in the neighborhood of Baiae and in the lands of the municipalities round Mount Vesuvius. This being mixed with lime and rubble, not only furnishes strength to other buildings, but also, when piers are built in the sea, they set under water. (Vitruvius Pollio, 1931 [translation]: vol. 1, bk. 2, chap. 6, ¶ 1.)

The powder cited by Vitruvius was a volcanic ash known as _pozzolana_, containing primarily silica, alumina, and lime, from the area of Pozzuoli, a town near Naples, and from other volcanic regions in Italy. This was cement, which when combined with sand and water yields concrete.

The Romans chiefly used concrete for heavy construction such as walls, domes, and vaults; these were built in wooden forms or in parallel hollow walls of stone or fired brick, in which layers of concrete alternated with layers of rubble. Concrete construction spread to many regions incorporated in the Roman Empire. There also may be contemporary examples of concrete structures beyond the boundaries of the Roman Empire in the Near East and Southwest Asia, but we know of no instances of concrete floors in those regions during either the centuries of Rome's greatness or in later centuries.

Only as recently as the late twentieth century did concrete floors become increasingly popular in the Old World, primarily as a result of the rapid expansion of concrete construction worldwide and as personal income rose. At both the government and personal levels, surplus funds are necessary for the purchase of cement, which must be imported in many countries. Moreover, all-concrete construction is about six times more expensive per square unit of measure than mud construction. Nearly all concrete floors in use now in the Near East are concrete slabs upon which mud buildings have been constructed, including most of the recently built beehive houses that we saw in Syria.

Preparing and laying a concrete slab is relatively simple. The ground must be level and packed hard. Soft spots must be compacted and filled, and the process is repeated until the surface is uniformly packed to prevent cracking of the heavy slab. Vitruvius (1934 [translation]: vol. 2, bk. 7, chap. 1, ¶ 1) noted, "if there is a made site [filled earth], in whole or in part, it must be rammed very carefully with piles." Concrete is then poured to a depth of 9–10 cm, extending 10–30 cm beyond the intended base of the house on all sides. This is leveled, often with a slight slope toward the planned position of the door for drainage, and dry cement is immediately sprinkled on the wet concrete, which is then lightly troweled or rubbed with a burnishing tool to produce a shiny floor when dry.

The inadequacy of cement plaster when applied in thin layers to mud-brick floors is well illustrated in the family house next to the Marib house under construction in Yemen. The family house was built about five years before our visit in 1991, and it was in superb condition owing to family pride, attention to maintenance, and excellent housekeeping. The sole defect was a thin coat of cement applied to protect the flat mud roof, parapets, circular mud-brick steps, and platform leading to the front entrance. During the subsequent 18 months after its application, the cement plaster had cracked badly, and many small pieces were already loose or missing, having been broken by the expansion and contraction of the mud-brick structure beneath it. To prevent further damage to the house, this coat of cement plaster should have been removed, the damage to the mud-brick base repaired, and the repaired surfaces then finished anew, preferably with lime plaster.

In the southwestern USA the laying of a slab floor involves different procedures. Surface preparation is identical to that described above. An extra step commonly required is the use of a moisture barrier—a heavy duty plastic sheeting or other moisture-resistant substance—covering the prepared ground. For maximum strength, concrete is generally poured as a unit with the foundation of the building. Although the foundation is reinforced with rebars, the slab is usually reinforced with 10-gauge, welded wire mesh with 6×6 in (15×15 cm) squares. If the size of the slab approaches 20×20 ft (6.1×6.1 m), expansion joints about ½ in (1.5 cm) wide must be used and filled with a strip of moisture-proof material—such as asphalt-impregnated fiberboard or equivalent—as wide as the slab is thick, to prevent the slab from cracking. The poured concrete is then leveled and troweled smooth. Adequate reinforcing is especially important because of the enormous weight of mud walls and in vaulted or domed houses, the additional weight of the curved mud roof (McHenry, 1984:141–142; 1985:48–49, 84).

Wood

Wood floors were apparently only used for the most important and elegant buildings in the ancient Near East. The Bible (I Kings 6:15, 30) describes how the floor of Solomon's Temple in Jerusalem (tenth century B.C.) was finished with cypress boards and overlaid with gold in both the inner and outer rooms. The throne room of the Royal Palace (I Kings 7:7) is said to have been finished with cedar from the floor to the rafters. Many temples and palaces in Anatolia, Lebanon, and western Syria may have featured wooden floors, and possibly paneling, because they were as comparable in significance to their respective citizens as the Solomonic Temple and Palace were to the Israelites. The better quality woods were expensive to acquire, whether by purchase or conquest, as were the skilled carpenters to dress, finish, and install them, and such interiors must have conveyed the impression of the high status and great wealth of the nation. Although we know of no direct supporting archaeological evidence for wood floors (due to the poor survival rate of wood through time), enough diverse fragments of wooden objects have been found to suggest the possibility that wood floors existed, and which may have been salvaged and reused in the same or the subsequent generation.

We also have not seen wooden floors in mud houses in the Near East or Southwest Asian regions we visited. Good wood was prohibitively expensive because it was not available locally; any local wood likely was of such poor quality that no tradition of wood flooring arose. In Europe and most of the USA, where fine woods have always been readily available, wooden floors are traditional, relatively low in cost, and easily installed. Apparently wooden floors first appeared in New Mexico in the 1840s, and very expensive houses now are sometimes built with one or more types of wood flooring. In mud houses with basements, wooden floor construction is essentially the same as in frame construction except that the floor joists are usually supported at each end by a ledge or by niches in the stem of the concrete foundation if there is no wooden perimeter frame to which they can be attached. In mud houses without basements, a crawl space not less than 16 in (40 cm) high is necessary for access to renew insulation or repair plumbing below the wooden floor and to prevent termites (McHenry, 1985:45, fig. 6.8).

Ceramic Tile

Ceramic tile floors have been popular since the fourteenth century A.D. in a number of regions: North Africa, southern Europe, Asia Minor, southward to the Levant and Arabia, eastward across the northern tier of Muslim countries to southwest Asia, from Iraq to Pakistan and India. The commonly used tiles were thick, like contemporary quarry tiles. Generally they were quite decorative and colorful, often featuring large designs, some of which were rendered in low relief. For the most part, such floors were found in houses of the wealthy, and some can still be seen in museums, historic structures, and older houses built during the last 300–400 years. In the USA, houses with ceramic tile floors in every room are chiefly located in regions where traditional Spanish cultural influence remains strong; but kitchen and bathroom floors of ceramic tile are extremely popular in all regions. In the Western world there is an extraordinarily large selection of ceramic tile available, so that one can choose to have floors that are beautiful in pattern and color, create warmth, and promise decades of excellent service.

Ceramic tile can be laid on many surfaces provided that they are level, smooth, and firm. To lay an attractive symmetrical floor, one should measure a center line from the two long walls and draw it on the surface. About midway in the length of the room, draw a line at a right angle to the center line. To complete the plan, do a trial layout of the tiles along both lines using proper joint widths. Then move the first line slightly to the left or right, and the second line slightly up or down, to arrange the tiles so that the outside rows at the edges of the floor can be cut to the appropriate width. On either a damp earthen or concrete base, spread a damp mixture of 4 parts sand to 1 part Portland cement. On damp earth, the mixture should be a minimum of 5 cm thick; on concrete, a minimum of 2.5 cm thick. Although the mixture is workable for several hours, one should not cover too large an area until one has sufficient experience in tile setting to know one's pace.

The tiles, having been soaked in water the previous night, are then laid with one edge exactly along the second line, with allowances for joints exactly as initially planned. Each tile should be tapped lightly in place, and a long spirit level should be used to achieve a smooth, level floor. If the floor's substructure consists of wood joists covered with plywood, thin set mortar, about 3 mm thick, can be spread on the back of dry tiles and set in place.

After the tiles dry overnight, they are ready for grouting (McHenry, 1985:84–88). Joints should be dampened immediately before applying cement based grout, and are dampened daily for several days until the joint mixture is fully cured.

Terrazzo and Mosaic

Terrazzo is a mixture of small stones or smashed potsherds of random size stirred in a matrix of lime plaster or concrete and poured into forms. Tile-size forms may be used to produce a series of terrazzo tiles, which can be laid in the same way as ceramic tiles, but generally on a bed of compacted sand. For residences and other small structures, terrazzo units about 30 cm square can be laid by a do-it-yourselfer. For large spaces, such as office buildings, stores, and large rooms and halls in private houses, a terrazzo floor is made with grids of thin metal strips fastened in place to form geometric shapes, such as squares measuring 76 × 76 cm, or free-form shapes. The terrazzo mixture is then poured into the forms, leveled, and troweled like poured concrete. When cured, the floor is ground smooth and heavily polished by machines. Terrazzo floors that are washed frequently and squeegeed become more beautiful as the colors deepen, and they develop a satin-like patina that adds warmth and richness with the passage of time. For large floors in office buildings, museums, and similar public structures, there are machines that wash and squeegee

Figure 13.7   Smithsonian geologist Richard Benson examining the red terrazzo floor with symbol of the Phoenician deity Tanit, from fourth century B.C., at Kerkouane, Cap Bon peninsula, Tunisia (1966).

the floor quickly and efficiently, and require only one person to operate. Terrazzo floors are cleaner, and therefore healthier than wall-to-wall carpeting, which almost always smells of damp dust, and which in public places can be quickly disfigured by dropped chewing gum, candy, and spilled liquids. These floors also are extremely durable and long-lasting.

Terrazzo has a long history in the Old World and continues in common use today. The earliest terrazzo floor that we have seen is in a building at Kerkouane, a Punic site on Cape Bon peninsula in Tunisia, dating in the fourth century B.C. (Figure 13.7). It is made of finely broken red potsherds in a gray matrix, and it features in a mosaic the symbol of the goddess Tanit outlined in white stone chips set in the floor. The floor and benches built along the walls were in excellent condition in 1966 when GVB visited the site.

Mosaic floors belong to this group, and differ from terrazzo chiefly in the use of specially shaped, more uniformly sized pieces of stone or glass known as tesserae, which are often arranged in designs. In terrazzo, the mortar is clearly seen; in mosaics mortar is scarcely seen because the tesserae almost touch on all sides. Mosaics are far more labor intensive—in selecting stones of the desired colors, in cutting and shaping the tesserae, and in laying them individually in the mosaic. These activities cause mosaic making to be far more expensive than terrazzo. Although mosaics are little used with mud construction, there is no structural reason why they should not be used for floors and wall panels in mud buildings. Indeed, they can add considerable beauty to elegant mud structures.

WINDOWS

In no aspect of building design and construction are there greater differences between the ancient Old World and the contemporary New World than in the quantity and quality of interior lighting provided by windows. In the Old World, windows were rarely found in archaeologically excavated buildings. All ancient buildings, including palaces as well as residences, were at best dimly lit inside. At Tell Jemmeh we found no windows, but it is much more surprising that none were discovered in the royal palaces of Nimrud or Persepolis. At Nimrud, for example, the walls were originally quite high, probably 11–12 m based on their 5 m thickness. Mallowan (1966:106) suggested that to provide even a modest amount of light, there must have been either openings at the top of the wall, or possibly some type of a clerestory, which could be closed in inclement weather.

The clerestory had already appeared in Egypt during the New Kingdom (ca. 1550–1200 B.C.), with the best known examples in the Hypostyle Hall of the great Karnak Temple, and in the Ramesseum at Luxor (Clarke and Engelbach, 1930:173, figs. 203, 204). Although the Temple is of stone, there is no structural reason why a clerestory could not be used in a mud-brick building.

Windows with mullions, some arched and others square, with vertical bars and/or hieroglyphs with backgrounds cut away were saved from the palace of Ramses III at Medinet Habu at Luxor (Clarke and Engelbach, 1930:173–176). This Palace was almost certainly constructed of mud brick, as was the tradition in ancient Egypt, and the use of stone windows, as suggested by these finds, would have been quite appropriate.

In House II 201 at Soknopaiou Nesos in the Fayum region of Egypt (ca. 100 B.C. to A.D. 100), there were "windows" to admit light into the large basement rooms. These were narrow horizontal slits, measuring 19 cm long by 5 cm high, not including the wooden frames, and positioned at the top of the basement wall. The 2 m thick wall was built with a sloping surface, resembling a chute, that extended from the bottom of the window to a point on the inner face of the wall about 1.2 m below, to permit more light in the basement. There was one window for each basement room, and the rooms were of different sizes, ranging from 9.6 to 15.36 m² (Boak, 1935:12). At any hour of the day, very little light must have entered these rooms. Such horizontal "slit windows," positioned in a variety of locations at the top of a building or through the wall just below the roof, have a long history in Egyptian stone architecture, going back at least to the Valley Temple of the second Pyramid at Giza, built for Khafre (Chephren) in the middle of the third millennium B.C. and continuing through subsequent centuries (Clarke and Engelbach, 1930:170–171, figs. 195–201).

The Romans may have been the first to increase the size of windows thanks to the invention of window glass, which was used at Pompeii and Herculaneum during the first century A.D. They also employed thin sheets of gypsum alabaster for glazing (Robertson, 1969:307).

One might explain the lack of windows in ancient sites by the fact that the wall areas where one would expect to find them have eroded away. One might also suggest that earlier archaeologists who did not adequately clean and examine the excavated walls in tell sites could scarcely have been expected to find windows. Both explanations may be correct in some instances, yet a number of walls preserved to considerable height have been excavated in sites, such as Nimrud and Tell al-Rimah, by very competent archaeologists without yielding a trace of windows.

The most obvious reason for the failure to identify windows from antiquity is that buildings were often constructed without them. If windows existed, they were generally very few, very small, and located just below the ceiling. Ancient peoples spent their lives in near darkness when inside their houses, with the only illumination coming through the narrow door or from one or more single-wick oil lamps. For them, the house was for shelter in bad weather and for sleeping at night, and most daily activities were conducted outdoors. Most dwellings in rural areas of the Near East and Southwest Asia continue to have few or no windows. Mallowan (1966:106) observed, "many of the peasant houses in the modern Near East are almost pitch dark; I have sat in almost total darkness in the halls of Yezidi chiefs in the Jebel Sinjar." We had the same experience in the beehive houses in Syria and in both Pakistan and India, where a few small porthole-like openings low on the walls add very little illumination to that entering through the open door.

The universal insistence on privacy, as discussed in Chapter 2, partly accounts for the general lack of windows. Windows were dangerous, because they might open the house to prying eyes. If there are windows, their very small size and placement near the top or bottom of the walls assures the desired privacy. Even if an individualist rebelled against accepted mores and chose to have windows, there were few materials available to cover the opening and still admit light. Two such materials are calcite alabaster and gypsum alabaster, which can be ground to thin sheets. The sheets are translucent, transmitting light but not permitting objects on the other side to be seen clearly. For centuries, this type of window was used by Romans; more recently, it is used in the tall mud-brick houses in the Hadhramaut, especially in the small, fixed-position windows just below the ceiling (see Figure 3.57). Although window glass admitted light, it failed to shut out views of the interior from the outside.

However, other factors may be partly responsible for the lack of windows, especially the cost of wood framing and window glass. There is also increased draftiness around windows because many window frames are so poorly fitted into the mud walls that long strips of daylight can be seen between the frame and the wall (Figure 13.8). Given such window construction, there is an increased loss of the insulating effects of mud construction with any increase in window sizes in South and Southwest Asian buildings.

There are no windows at all in many houses in Pakistan, India, and Syria (see Figures 3.2, 3.38, and 3.43). In other houses there may be one or more small holes 8–12 cm in diameter located 30–40 cm above the floor or base of the wall, which apparently serve as peep holes, gun ports, and fresh-air vents for the inhabitants, who sleep on the floor (Figure 13.9, and see Figure 6.10). No one outside can see inside because of their small size and low position in the walls. Many houses and mosques have windows set high in the walls just below the roof for complete privacy, as custom mandates in many Muslim societies (Figure 13.10). Windows seldom number more than two per room and are generally small. Some are 15–20 cm square, while others are rectangular, 40–50 cm long by 12–15 cm high, and sometimes hinged horizontally to deflect air to the interior. Occasionally there are larger rectangular windows 40 cm wide by 60 cm or more high. Shops sometimes have one window in the front wall, probably to permit the proprietor to see outside

Figure 13.8 Wooden window from around which the mud-mortar filling has fallen out, in the Customs Post at Beleli, Baluchistan, Pakistan (1991).

as well as to increase light in the shop.

The men's house at Qila Skarnah in Baluchistan, Pakistan, had windows and doors similar in placement and size to those of Victorian houses in the UK and the USA, the former having been copied for fine houses in India during British rule. The wooden door featured 12 square glass panes, mounted in two rows of six panes each, and bordered by a row of narrow panes on each side. Clear glass predominated in these panes, but squares or rectangles of red, blue, purple, and green glass were also placed in different arrangements in each door panel or side panel. In a typical installation, of the 24 square or rectangular panels of glass, 14 were clear glass and 10 were colored, with two panes in each of the five colors. The openings were finished at the top with a pointed mud-brick arch.

Some windows in Syrian houses are larger. A few are square, but most are rectangular, measuring 55 cm high by 36 cm wide (see Figure 3.48); another is 157 cm high by 90 cm wide. Most of the wall openings into which the windows are set have rounded edges.

In Yemen, windows have also been traditionally large and rectangular, somewhat resembling window openings in the USA. In the newlyweds' house under construction in Marib, Yemen, for example, windows are large and numerous. On the ground floor there are 12 rectangular windows about 1 m high by 75 cm wide, each crowned by a wooden lintel and an arched opening (Figure 13.11; also

Figure 13.9   Seven plugged "porthole" windows in a mud-brick house in Syria (1994).

Figure 13.10 Small windows just below the ceiling, for privacy while increasing light in the house, Pandran, Baluchistan (1990).

Figure 13.11 Windows in layered-mud house with carved-stone-filled arches, under construction in Marib, Yemen (1991).

Figure 3.51; these reminded OVB of eyelids because of their shape). Into each of the arched openings, a semicircular piece of limestone or calcite, delicately carved in intricate tracery, is fitted flush with the outer wall surface. In older houses in Yemen, a second semicircular stone piece, commonly with a different tracery design, was often fitted flush with the inner wall surface. Different colors of glass were traditionally set in the tracery, but in more recent houses, separate stained-glass pieces are often fitted flush against the inner surface of the stone. In a typical house, tracery designs differ from window to window even when only the outer semicircular piece is used, as in Figure 13.11. The play of light coming through two pieces of differently designed tracery fitted with various colors of glass creates a kaleidoscope on the walls and floor of a room as sunlight moves across it, with ever-changing designs, colors, and intensities. Such elaborate windows are traditional throughout northern Yemen.

The former Sultan's Palace in Seiyun, Hadhramaut, was converted into the regional archaeological and ethnological museum following the communist revo-

Figure 13.12   Salon with wall cushions, padded arm rests, and floor carpets against all walls in the room of the fully constructed parents' house, in Marib, Yemen (1991).

lution in Yemen. This magnificent structure is more than 100 years old. On each floor of the façade are 11 rectangular windows at floor level, plus three in each circular corner tower. Above each rectangular window is a pointed arch, in low relief, painted light blue. Above this window, just below the ceiling, is a small, rectangular, fixed window to admit more light into the room (see Figure 3.60).

Traditional houses in the Muslim world lack typical Western furniture. Floors are covered with carpets, and the occupants and guests sit on the carpet and lean on cushions against the wall (Figure 13.12; see also Figure 3.49). Bed rolls, usually stored in a separate storage room (see Figure 3.50), are spread on the floor for sleeping.

Because floor culture is traditional in Yemen, all activities, such as sleeping and eating, take place on the floor. It is not surprising, therefore, that major windows are commonly based only a few centimeters above the floor, to enable one seated on the floor to look out the window (see Figure 3.57). Most windows in the Hadhramaut are rectangular, although some are almost square. Nearly all floor-level windows in the tall houses are covered with decorative wooden screens or shutters. These panels feature elaborate cut-outs in a great variety of designs. In general, there are three sections to the larger panels, and two sections to smaller ones (see Figures 3.55, 10.8). In a three-section panel, the uppermost section has two rectangular bases with a hemispherical or pointed arch above; the middle section is divided into two rectangular open areas; the lower section is filled with narrow, closely arranged, vertical elements. In two-section panels, the middle section just described is often eliminated. The cut-out work is generally rough and unfinished like most wooden pieces in the Hadhramaut. Occasionally the panels are painted an indigo blue, especially when the exterior of the house is covered with lime plaster or whitewash, creating arresting contrasts (see Figure 3.60). Apart from the attractive design, the panels provide privacy, enabling those who sit on the floor to look out without being seen. Elsewhere in Yemen, window shutters or screens are not as large or equipped with such decorative cut designs as those in the Hadhramaut.

Small round, rectangular, or arched upper windows are positioned just below the ceiling and occasionally are set in a recessed, arched-shaped niche in the outer wall. In some houses in Marib Town, the recessed niche held both the floor-level window and the smaller, arched window immediately above it (Figure 13.13). There is also a row of small rectangular windows just below the ceiling of the lower floor.

DOORS

Ancient and contemporary earthen buildings utilized many types of doorways. The most common was and still is a rectangular entrance constructed with a wooden threshold and lintel, and generally with vertically mounted wooden jambs. The lintel must be strong and sturdy to carry the heavy load of the earthen wall above it; it is usually extended a short distance into the wall on both sides of the opening. Archaeologists seldom find these wooden members unless they have been burned, although occasionally traces of unburned thresholds survive. When found in excavations, thresholds are typically thin and fragile, at best, or have been reduced to stains on the soil. At Tell Jemmeh, we found several unburned wooden thresholds, now only a few millimeters thick.

Figure 13.13   Upper arched windows and lower rectangular windows in slightly recessed arched niches on third floor of abandoned layered-mud house (note raised corners) in abandoned Marib Town near Marib, Yemen (1991).

Although the hinge was known in ancient Egypt, it was small and used on boxes; it was never sufficiently heavy to carry wooden doors (Clarke and Engelbach, 1930:162). The most definitive artifact relating to doors recovered in excavations is a pivot stone, indicating that a door was attached to a vertical post that pivoted in the stone. These stones have a hollowed area centered on the upper surface, with a diameter of 8–30 cm and a depth of 12–18 cm, although many are much larger where massive doors, such as those in palaces and city gates, were used. The pivot hole is generally very smooth inside from the frequent movement of the vertical post. Pivot stones were set into the floor with their tops at or slightly above floor

Figure 13.14 A simple house door in village on Tell Nebi Mind, Syria, mounted on a vertical pole that turns in a pivot stone (1994). The door latch is released from inside by means of the pull cord.

level, and they held the lower end of a rounded wooden post to which the door was attached. A similar device of wood or stone projected from the wooden jamb or wall, level with the top of the door and as near true vertical as possible to receive the upper end of the door post. In Assyrian doorways, such as major gates, the wall was recessed to receive the open door so that the surface of the door would be even with the surface of the decorative orthostats on either side of the gate structure. Pivot stones are ubiquitous in both ancient sites and contemporary settlements (Figure 13.14). In Mesopotamia, Gate 7 at Khorsabad (8th century B.C.) had recessed pivot stones in place with stone floor slabs ready to cover the area around each one, when it was apparently decided not to use the gate, and it was blocked instead (Loud, 1936:10, figs. 11, 12). In Fort Shalmaneser at Nimrud, a gate-chamber had lime-stone blocks for a threshold. Pivot holes at both ends of the threshold indicate that two-leaf doors were once installed (Mallowan, 1966:393). In the Acropolis Palace, Mallowan (1966:292) noted, "Much care had been devoted to the doorways, 2–3 meters wide, closed by double doors which swung over stone-paved thresholds in deep stone-lined sockets." Elsewhere, he found stone covering slabs for pivot stones whose holes were about 60 cm in diameter, with two concentric rims. The size of the hole suggested a very large door post, such as one that would have belonged to a city gate (Mallowan, 1966:420, fig. 347).

Doors were almost always made of wood and thus are rarely preserved in archaeological sites except in those few countries, such as Egypt, where aridity permits organic materials to survive. Wooden doors of the Fourth and Fifth Dynasties of the Old Kingdom (ca. 2600–2400 B.C.) have been found in *mastaba* tombs at Meidum and Saqqara. A Fifth Dynasty tomb had a one-piece wooden door with the upper and lower pivots carved from the door itself. The upper pivot was long and cylindrical, and the lower pivot was shorter and more conical, indicating that the upper pivot was inserted first, the door lifted so that the lower pivot would slide into the floor hole. This one-piece door had warped in spite of six cleats and three heavier braces—two horizontal and one vertical—on the inner surface. The outer surface was decorated with a striding nobleman and hieroglyphs identifying the deceased as well as the name of the wood carver, Ithu, behind one of the figure's legs. It is rare in Egypt to find craftsmen signing their works (Clark and Engelbach, 1930:162, fig. 185).

Ancient wooden doors were sometimes decorated with geometric or representational art on metal strips. The Bible (I Kings 6:31–35) describes the doors of the temple built by Solomon in Jerusalem (tenth century B.C.) as made of olive wood or cypress wood and carved with cherubim, palm trees, and open flowers, and entirely overlaid with gold, i.e., gold leaf. Other examples are the pine doors of a temple at Balawat, built by Shalmaneser in the ninth century B.C. (Mallowan, 1966:378).[2] These doors were decorated with bronze bands having two registers each 27 cm high showing the Assyrian army laying siege to the city of Ashtamaku, capital of Hamath. Each register is bordered on both sides by a row of rosettes (Albenda, 1980:224-225).

The simplest closing device is a cloth hanging over the doorway. In the Afghan refugee's mud-ball house near Quetta, Pakistan, a broad strip of canvas covered the entrance (Figure 13.15). Contemporary wooden doors, however, illustrate the types that were probably used in antiquity (Figure 13.16). The Afghan refugee

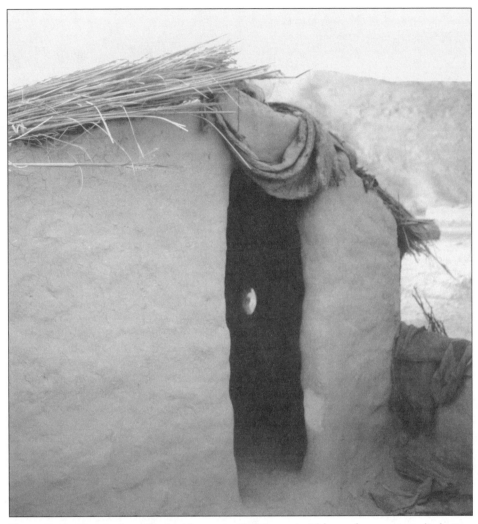

Figure 13.15 **Canvas door, lifted aside, on mud ball house in Afghan refugee community in Cantonment area of Quetta, Baluchistan, Pakistan (1991).**

settlement notwithstanding, most houses in Baluchistan use single-leaf or double-leaf wooden doors. Double doors we saw typically measured 1.68 m high by 36 cm wide (Figure 13.17). They were often made with three beveled panels, the center one being longer than the upper and lower panels, although most were of equal height in cupboard doors. They attached to wooden jambs that were wedged into the wall opening. Most wooden doors used now were made in workshops by professional carpenters.

In the Hadhramaut of Yemen, the single-leaf door is commonly used for the main entrance to a house. In Beit Jarhum in Shibam, the main entrance was recessed in the north wall.. The wooden door was large and divided into 11 horizontal panels by reinforcing battens. Each panel was decorated with either one or two short iron

Figure 13.16 Two new doors in Seiyun, Hadhramaut, Yemen (1991). Left, a two-leaf metal door with welded designs; right, a wooden door with carved battens. Note lock box to the right of the wooden door.

strips nailed to it, alternating throughout the door's height (Figure 13.18). Most doors in the region are equipped with a knocker consisting of a heavy iron ring. At Beit Jarhum, the door knocker was attached to the fourth horizontal strip from the top of the door. In the wall above the doorway was a panel with three rows of nine holes serving as a transom window, and above that was a recessed, triangular-shaped panel with a narrow vertical window in the center. (A second door on the east side served the stable and storage areas of the house.)

Doors were generally secured in antiquity by means of a horizontally sliding bolt of wood or bronze that was held in place by two or more hangers on the inner surface of the door. The bolt was shoved into a recess or hole in the jamb or wall. If double-leaf doors were used, the inner surface of the second door also had two or more hangers to receive the bolt. For massive doors, such as those of the gates of walled towns and government compounds, the sliding bolt is still used (Figure 13.19). In addition, a vertical bolt, extending from a hole in the lintel to a hole

Figure 13.17 **Simple two-leaf door of a man's room, in Pandran 1, Pandran, Baluchistan, Pakistan (1990). Note small, high window for light and privacy.**

Figure 13.18   Front door, lock, and door knocker of Beit Jarhum in Shibam, Hadhramaut, Yemen (1991).

in the threshold, reduced vertical movement in the closed doors. The ancient Assyrians wedged doors shut by cutting a small hole in a paving stone that was laid a meter or so from the bottom of the door; they placed a rod in the hole, slanting it obliquely to be inserted into a hole on the underside of a cross-member on the inner surface of the door (Mallowan, 1966:466). This device functioned exactly

Figure 13.19 Bolt hole for massive beam that locks the gate to the government buildings of the former Sultan's palace in Seiyun, Hadhramaut, Yemen (1991).

like the security rods still used by thousands of New York City apartment dwellers today!

In many regions of the ancient world, doors were secured with tumbler locks, and this type of lock in its many variations has continued in use to the present. According to Wulff (1966:67–68, fig. 98), tumbler locks go back to the second millennium B.C. in Iraq, Iran, and Egypt, the first millennium B.C. in China and Greece, and later times in Rome, from whence they were distributed throughout the Roman sphere of influence, from England to the Levant. The Arabs carried the tumbler lock as far as Indonesia, and it is still in use in the southern Arabian Peninsula today. In Shibam, Hadhramaut, the representative tall house, Beit Jarhum, was secured with a wooden tumbler lock.

A tumbler lock consists of an internal latch controlled by a series of four to six holes randomly arranged, in each of which is a wooden dowel that slides up and down freely in the hole. In a locked position, the dowels hang down and prevent the door from moving. The key, usually wood but occasionally metal, is commonly shaped in either an obtuse or right angle, with the horizontal part serving as the working key and the diagonal or vertical part as the handle. The key has a series of fixed vertical dowels, slightly smaller than those in the latch, that correspond to the number and arrangement of the sliding dowels of the latch. When the horizontal section is inserted, the key is lifted slightly, raising the tumblers in the latch so that the door can be opened. The lock is accessed from the outside through a small box built into the wall to the right of the door, which is often finished with beautiful and intricate carving (Figure 13.18; Lewcock, 1986:81).

There is also a convenient unlocking device used in the multiple-story houses of the Hadhramaut. The latch can be released from any floor inside the house by an attached chain or rope. The chain is enclosed either inside a vertical pipe or in an open channel on the wall surface, and it extends from the latch upward to the top floor. Upon hearing a knock at the door, a glance out a window to identify the visitor, and a tug of the chain or rope to unlatch the door gives entrance, so that the inhabitants do not have to run down all the flights of stairs every time someone knocks. Such latches are found in nearly every tall house in Shibam and elsewhere in the Hadhramaut as well as westward to Sana`a, Yemen.

Doors for gates and garages may be either wood, sheet iron, or corrugated iron. Entrance gates were traditionally made of wood, but more affluent properties now have iron gates often decorated with wrought iron and painted with bright colors. These gates are hung on fired-brick piers or gate posts that abut the ends of mud walls (Figure 13.20, also Figure 9.15).

All types of arch construction—corbelled, radial, pitched-brick, and ribbed or strut—can be used to form doorways without using wood, stone, or iron lintels. Additional courses in the wall can be laid over the doorway to the desired height of the wall. The most striking feature of arched doorways, however, is their beauty. Psychologically, they lift our heads as we enter, instead of forcing us to bend down when passing under a flat lintel, as is an almost universal experience in the Near East. Such arching doorways add an elegance to a house because the curves relieve the seemingly unending horizontal and vertical lines of virtually all buildings.

Figure 13.20 Iron gates hung on fired-brick piers in a mud-brick wall in Baluchistan, Pakistan (1990).

CEILINGS

Ceilings in the Near East, if finished at all, are usually painted. In the radial and pitched-brick vaults of the *mastabas* of the fourth and fifth Dynasties in Egypt, the ridges we saw formed in the vaulting were painted reddish brown to resemble the color of bundles of reeds in vaulted reed buildings. In flat-roof structures, archaeologists rarely find more than fragments of the mud roof with the impressions of reeds (see Figure 10.7), and perhaps a flake of what appears to be paint, owing to the nearly total destruction of the upper areas of most ancient buildings. However, a striking example of painted ceilings was found in the Throne Room of the northwestern palace at Nimrud (ninth century B.C.), where Mallowan (1966:105–106) discovered painted fragments of horses' heads, spoked chariot wheels, and the geometric design of a coffered ceiling in blue, red, and white with attached bits of wooden roofing beams. The more typical combination in the Near East today features heavy beams painted red, with the bamboo cross poles above painted blue or green. In a few instances, cloth with a colored print pattern is affixed to the ceiling, sometimes extending a short distance down the side walls. Apart from its aesthetic value, such a cloth covering prevents twigs, dried bits of woven matting and dried mud from the roof—as well as insects—from falling from the ceiling onto the heads of the inhabitants or littering the floor.

Figure 13.21   Gateway to extended family complex in Seiyun, Hadhramaut, Yemen (1991).

Because the coffered ceiling formed of multiple vaults we saw at Hauta, Hadhramaut (described in Chapter 11) was under construction, we did not have the opportunity to see how the intrados of the vaults were finished (if, indeed, they

Figure 13.22 Unfinished intrados of the radial, timber reinforced, vault of the gateway shown in Figure 13.21 (1991).

were finished at all). We saw a completed gateway, however, that was vaulted with similar construction techniques in Seiyun (Figure 13.21) that also had never been finished on the inside, leaving the long central beam and short perpendicular support poles on one side visible, although those on the other side were not visible (Figure 13.22). In such a fine house as the one in Hauta, it seems probable that the exposed crooked poles in the ceiling vaults would be covered in some manner.

In the southwestern USA where flat roofs prevail, exposed *vigas* (wooden beams) and the *latillas* or *cedros* decking (poles commonly of ash or split cedar) or tongue-and-groove boards above the beams are generally stained, painted, and/or varnished in combination to create a clean, finished ceiling of contrasting colors. Variously colored clay soils mixed with water are often used to stain both earthen and wooden surfaces (McHenry, 1984:134–135; 1985:127–129).

UTILITIES

As our regions of focus—from Morocco to India, and from northern Pakistan to southern Yemen—increasingly adopt twentieth century technology, the traditional ways of doing things are gradually changing. Oil lamps and candles have been replaced by ordinary and pressurized kerosene lamps, which, in turn, are giving way to electricity. Well water—previously carried in pottery jars or tin tea containers on the heads of women, in goatskin bags on people's hips, or on asses and camels—is now raised by pumps and distributed to yards and houses by pipes, much to the delight of everyone, especially the housewives. Only the disposal of wastes in rural areas, villages, and towns has so far remained the same as in the past. Wastewater is still dumped into small ditches and channels in courtyards and streets; garbage is strewn for animals to pick over and then burned daily in the street; human excrement is left in fields, along the streets, or on the waste platforms below toilet chutes (see Figure 3.59), where it is treated with lime or ash, and scavengers periodically collect the leavings to fertilize fields.

Electricity

Electricity is often distributed within villages with a minimal number of poles or supporting structures to carry a few lines (see Figure 3.42). The majority of houses have a single light fixture per room, either a dropped line with a single bulb in the middle of the room or now more commonly a fluorescent lamp fixture mounted on a wall or ceiling. In some village houses, an additional outlet is provided for a refrigerator or a washing machine.

In the house under construction in Marib, Yemen, we were able to examine the installation of electrical wiring because none of the rooms had yet been plastered. Plastic-coated electric lines had already been installed by the electrician, who had cut shallow grooves and small niches in the layered-mud walls to recess electrical lines, switches, outlets, and fixtures (Figure 13.23). If the electrician and mason coordinate their schedules to arrange several work sessions together when the appropriate mud layers or mud-brick courses are laid, they could more easily cut the wall grooves for stringing the plastic-coated wiring and installing switch boxes and convenience outlets. Otherwise, descending and ascending lines must be installed in grooves chipped out of the dried mud walls with a small hand-pick, as was the case in this house. The electrician then places the wiring in the grooves, installs the boxes in niches cut in the walls, and connects the wiring. The plastic-coated cables and electrical boxes are held in the grooves and niches by globs of lime plaster that cover the electric lines in several places and the edges of the boxes. To install a ceiling feature, a cable is run upward from the junction box in a groove in the wall and is then stapled to one of the ceiling beams from which it drops to the desired height for the fixture. Every room in the Marib house had at least one electrical outlet, which would service two or three lights and appliances, such as a refrigerator, small washing machine, or ceiling fan. The common lighting fixture was a bare or reflecting long fluorescent fixture with one or two bulbs (Figure 13.24).

Plumbing

Traditionally in the Hadhramaut, floor channels carried household wastewater to a trough or pipe that passed through the wall and extended a meter or so before dumping the water into the middle of the street. In most other countries, drainage channels naturally eroded a meandering trough in the ground, as for example in Syria, where kitchen, bathroom, and washing machine wastewater was disposed of in this manner (see Figure 3.44).

Figure 13.23 Electrical wiring installed and awaiting mud-plaster coating and fixtures in Marib, Yemen (1991).

Figure 13.24   Bedroom with fluorescent light fixture and ceiling fan in the parents' house next to house under construction in Marib, Yemen (1991), with typical beds in a floor culture. Note gypsum tracery and colored glass in the arched windows.

In one of the rooms of the Marib house under construction, a new iron bathtub finished with pink porcelain was awaiting installation (see Figure 13.23). No supply or drainage pipes appeared in the room where it stood, leading us to suspect that the tub had been delivered ahead of time and was destined for another room, perhaps in an upper floor of the house, whose walls had not yet been built to full height. A bathtub, however, with its large capacity, calls for a different method of disposing of wastewater than the common practice of draining it through a hole in the wall and onto the ground or street; although it may be directed into a large dry well several meters from the house wall, or possibly to a more modern septic tank with a wide field distribution. Both supply and waste pipes can be installed within mud walls as easily as electric wiring. Alternatively, supply pipes may be fastened above the ceiling or to the outside of the walls, as in the tall houses of the Hadhramaut. Exterior wall installation of pipes wherever freezing does not occur is acceptable, although

Figure 13.25   Square hearth at Tell Jemmeh, Israel, tenth century B.C.

it is as ugly as roof-mounted television antennas. (In this regard, twentieth century modernization has reached the mud homes of Yemen!)

Heating and Cooking

In antiquity and until recently, fixed and portable hearths provided nearly all heating in earthen houses. Fixed hearths—usually round but occasionally rectangular and placed in the center of the major room or hall known as the megaron—were already a common feature in houses in Greece during the middle of the third millennium B.C., and they are believed to have been introduced from the region north of Greece (Dinsmoor, 1950:5, 7, pl.10). At Mehrgarh, a site from about the same time near Dhardhar in central Pakistan, we saw in the center of one room a circular hearth about 40 cm in diameter, similar to a hearth in a Greek megaron, and with clear evidence of burning. At Tell el-Amarna, Egypt, during the fourteenth century B.C., three private houses of middle-class families (numbers 4, 6, and 21) featured a central court with a round hearth placed directly in front of a bench, where the family could sit, cook food, and warm themselves (Petrie, 1974:21, pls. 28:4, 6, 42:21). Square hearths were discovered at Tell Jemmeh from the twelfth to tenth centuries B.C. (Figure 13.25), but relatively few have been reported in archaeological publications in the Near East. It is probable that portable hearths were often used in place of fixed hearths because they could easily be moved where needed.

A number of scholars have suggested that a peculiar, otherwise unexplained construction in the throne rooms of many Assyrian palaces served as rails for moving a cart with a portable hearth close to and away from the throne as the king's comfort—or possibly ritual—demanded. The "rails" consisted of two parallel rows of narrow stones extending about 3–7 m from the dias, often with a central groove in each and recessed so that their upper surfaces were level with the floor. At Nimrud, such stone rails appeared in throne rooms in the Northwest Palace, the Burnt Palace, the Ezida, and the Acropolis Palace, and in Fort Shalmaneser between the ninth and seventh centuries B.C. (Mallowan, 1966:96–97, 200–204, 208, 240, 291, 443, figs. 137, 194, 195, 202, 267:AB3). Mallowan suggested the possibility that some type of heavy ceremonial objects may have stood on the stone lines in a fixed position. However, the presence of grooves in the rails, which must have been cut for a wheeled vehicle, together with the enormous size of the throne rooms and the penetrating cold of winters, argue in favor of the suggestion that these rails carried a moveable vehicle such as a cart with a portable hearth.

Wheeled carts have been found at Tell Halaf, an ancient city in northeastern Syria, and two in Cyprus of bronze, both of unknown provenience, although one is perhaps from Kition. The Cypriote bronze carts—both from ca. twelfth century

Figure 13.26   Square hearth with bin in corner for fuel in Afghan refugee's mud ball house in settlement near Quetta, Baluchistan, Pakistan (1991).

Figure 13.27   Ceramic portable hearth in Sumasar, Gujarat, India (1991).

B.C.—might serve as suggestive miniature models of the type of cart used in Assyrian palaces. Each features a ring horizontally mounted on a square frame with decorated side panels. Both carts stand on four legs with two axles and four, six-spoke wheels. Both are small, measuring 34 cm and 31 cm high, respectively; their rings are 17 cm and 15 cm in diameter, respectively, and suitable for holding a basin (Buchholz and Karageorghis, 1973:158–159, 460–461, figs. 1685a,b, 1686; Karageorghis, 1976:fig. 183).

Fixed and portable hearths must have been used continuously throughout the Mediterranean basin, the Near East, and Southwest Asia. Near Quetta in the Hanna Valley in Baluchistan, Pakistan, the Afghan mud-ball house had a square hearth sunk in the floor in the corner just left of the doorway, that served both for indoor cooking and warmth (Figure 13.26). Adjacent to it was a bin filled with dried plants for fuel. On bitter cold nights, one can imagine the bed rolls spread in concentric arcs around the hearth. In Gujarat, India, a house in Modhera had a

Figure 13.28   Portable hearth used by the Druse in the Golan Heights.

fixed hearth in each of the two dwelling rooms of the three-room house (see Figure 3.37). Elsewhere in Gujarat, the lovely two-room, narrow house in Charada was warmed by a portable hearth in the front room (see Figure 3.39). Portable hearths in western India are simple U-shaped ceramic structures, about 30 cm long, 20 cm wide, 15–20 cm high, with uniform walls about 5 cm thick. The fire is laid within the "U," the walls of which prevent wind from extinguishing the flames (Figure 13.27).

A wheeled portable hearth has traditionally been used for heating by the Druse people of the Golan Heights, in the Levant east of the Sea of Galilee and the Jordan River to the north. Figure 13.28 shows a typical brass hearth—a rectangular box about 61 cm long × 41 cm wide × 11 cm deep on four heavy, decorated legs, each 13 cm high and shaped with a reversed S-curve on each side. Its original wheels were replaced with contemporary ball casters (each with a black plastic "tire") that are attached to the base of the legs. The front panel of the box features Arabic script with a tooled background. A heavy decorated handle is mounted on each end of the rectangular box. Both handles and legs are cast to support the considerable weight of the hearth. In use, a layer of sand, 4 cm thick, is leveled in the box, and charcoal is burned on top of the sand. Inside the top of the box paralleling each long side is a rod upon which four heavy brass strips 1 cm wide slide back and forth to support a teapot, pots for food, or other utensils.

Fireplaces occur in the Near East, although they are rare. We saw a small fireplace in a "beehive" house in Slamin, a small village near Ebla, south of Aleppo, Syria (Figure 13.29). The fireplace was built entirely of mud and occupied the lower part of a corner, hiding the fan-shaped squinch behind it. The opening, an irregular, squarish circle in shape, measured about 50 cm maximum diameter.

Figure 13.29 Corner fireplace in a "beehive" domed house in Slamin, Syria (1994). Andirons are in lower left corner, and an oil lamp or candle holder hangs from the wall.

Figure 13.30   European-style fireplace in ruined guest house, Qila Skarnah, Baluchistan, Pakistan (1990).

About 50 cm above the opening and against the lower part of the squinch, the small, flat top of the fireplace was finished with a rounded mud ridge serving to prevent any object placed there from falling off. The fireplace, like the entire

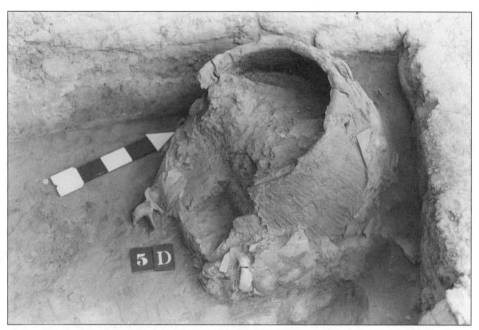

Figure 13.31 *Tabun,* **or bread oven, in a small courtyard of the thirteenth century B.C., at Tell Jemmeh, Israel.**

interior of the room, including the dome, was painted with whitewash. It was effectively vented to the outside by means of a stove pipe, with a little smoke staining around the opening. It resembled fireplaces in the southwestern USA in its corner placement but lacked the beauty of design and finish typically characterizing the latter. In the intermountain plains of northern Baluchistan, the men's house and the now abandoned and nearly destroyed guest houses at Qila Skarnah were all heated by European style fireplaces centered in either the long or end walls (Figure 13.30).

There are obvious differences between mud houses built before the development of elaborate heating and cooling systems and those constructed later. The simple heating devices, such as fixed and portable hearths, probably were barely adequate in the cold, damp winters of the Levant and the cold, dry winters of the arid regions. To be sure, the traditional houses in these regions still may not seem as comfortable as Western structures with modern amenities, but certain devices, such as space heaters, are quite satisfactory and provide important savings in fossil fuels, equipment, and operating costs.

In the Near East, most food preparation, including the baking of bread, is undertaken in the courtyard outside the house throughout most of the year because of the relatively dry weather. The vast majority of bread ovens—known as *tabuns* in the Near East—are found in unroofed courtyards in archaeological sites (Figure 13.31). Slab- or coil-built, they were usually finished with a coat of mud plaster.

During the rainy season and in regions with cold winters, cooking and baking activities must be sheltered, and occasionally a *tabun* is found in a small roofed room.

Figure 13.32   Building a *tabun* in Nush-i Jan, Iran (1974).

At Ashdod on the coastal plain of Israel, a large building—a wealthy residence perhaps, circa fourteenth to thirteenth century B.C.—had a *tabun* in one corner of the
courtyard, and a small, indoor room certainly roofed, was equipped with two *tabuns*
(Dothan and Freedman, 1967:75; plan 4:510b, 533).[3]

In the village of Nush-i Jan in western Iran, we had the good fortune to observe
one phase in the construction of a bread oven (Figure 13.32) inside a large roofed
room that already was equipped with a granary. The oven-maker was a specialist
from another village, and she brought her own soil and goat-hair temper for the
mix. Taking slip from a deep bowl, she spread it on the edges before setting the slab
in place. She then rubbed slip over the joints on the inner and outer surfaces to seal
the joint. Bread ovens built inside a house also provide a welcome source of heat
during the cold and wet months.

Other foods are normally cooked over coals in circular or elongated pits in the
kitchen. In the mountainous areas of Baluchistan, where the winters are cold,
homes have an indoor kitchen but also an outdoor kitchen for use during warm
weather (Figure 13.33); in other regions, climate permitting, outdoor kitchens are
used year round (see Figure 3.4). For grilling, a large circular metal tray, such as the

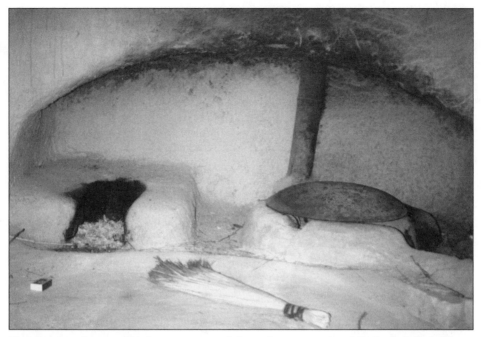

Figure 13.33 Courtyard kitchen at a women's house in compound at Qila Skarnah, Baluchistan, Pakistan (1990), with two cooking areas, one covered with a circular metal tray (right) for baking bread.

lid of a 55-gallon (~208 L) oil drum, is placed on the curbing or on a metal frame. Clay pots are used for certain foods, but most are now cooked in aluminum pots. Some still use kerosene fueled primus burners, although bottle gas burners are increasing in popularity.

Cylindrical mud granaries are kept indoors in regions of considerable climate variation, but in areas of relatively stable climates, as in Punjab, Pakistan, they may be kept outdoors (Figure 13.34). Many "beehive" houses in Syria now have refrigerators and hand-filled, hand-drained, electric washing machines.

Cooling

Before the invention of mechanical refrigeration and air-conditioning, a variety of cooling systems had already been devised, especially in regions with hot, dry summers. In antiquity as well as in our time, the orientation of buildings and the use of trees for shade and windbreaks have played important roles in both heating and cooling structures, as discussed in Chapter 4. Observations and experiments through the centuries led to architectural designs that utilize natural forces to cool buildings without mechanical, energy-consuming devices. Some of these manipulations of natural forces are altogether free, whereas others require an initial expenditure of funds. The principles involved have been explained and illustrated by Hassan Fathy (1986) in *Natural Energy and Vernacular Architecture: Principles and Examples with Reference to Hot Arid Climates*, which is the basis of the following discussion.

Figure 13.34   Outdoor mud granary in Punjab, Pakistan, raised above ground by fired bricks, with wooden lid covering the mouth and plugged bung hole at bottom (1989). The woman of the house is applying a new coat of mud plaster.

A continuous flow of air through a building can be achieved by using one or more smaller openings on the side that faces the prevailing wind, and one or more larger openings—a door, windows, or an opening covered with a screening device such as a *mashrabiya*, a lattice screen made of small, turned wooden pieces assembled to form intricate patterns)—on the lee side of the structure. The latter apertures were generally placed high on the wall to avoid drafts on people sitting or sleeping below in the room.

A device common in many Near Eastern countries from Egypt to Sind, Pakistan, is the *malqaf*—wind catcher—which has many variations. In its basic form, the *malqaf* goes back to at least the seventh or eighth centuries A.D. in Egypt and almost certainly to the nineteenth Dynasty of the New Kingdom, ca. thirteenth to twelfth centuries B.C., at Tell el-Amarna, Egypt. A tomb painting there shows the house of Neb-Amun with two triangular-shaped structures pointing in opposite directions, one serving as the catcher and the other as the exit for the air being moved by suction (Fathy, 1986:58, fig. 50).

The *malqaf* consists of a tower that rises as high as or higher than the roof of a building, where the breeze is cooler and stronger, with an opening on the windward side and commonly a shed roof to deflect airflow downward. A long narrow shaft guides the air, moving by suction, to the ground floor, and from there to the highest ceiling area, preferably in the center of the house, where several screened windows—the source of the suction—draw it out of the house. At the same time, warm air in the house rises to the high ceiling area where it too is drawn through the windows. Still more coolness can be gained by suspending wet matting inside the shaft, or even better by panels of wet charcoal enclosed by chicken wire, hardware cloth, or metal trays containing wet charcoal, which serve as buffers to increase airflow and evaporation. Because the *malqaf* collects high outside air well above the lower air laden with dust and sand, the air entering the house is cleaner. Any remaining dust and sand are largely removed by the charcoal buffers in the narrow shaft, or at the bottom of the shaft, so that only the cleanest air moves through the house.

A variant type of *malqaf* known as the *badgir* is used in Iran and other Persian or Arabian Gulf regions. It also is a tower, but with openings on two or even four sides with partitions crisscrossing from opposite corners to capture moving air from any direction. Some of the towers are decorated with trefoils, petals, and other architectural motifs, so that they somewhat resemble the traditional bell towers of the Western world.

In hot arid climates, buildings with interior courtyards surrounded by rooms are also cooled by convection. The courtyard becomes increasingly hot as the sun moves directly over it at noon, reducing areas shaded by the surrounding rooms. As evening approaches, warm air from the hot courtyard paving rises and is gradually replaced by the cooler night air. Through the night into mid-morning, the courtyard remains cool until the sun once again shines directly on the paving. At San Simeon, the monastery near Aswan, Egypt, the courtyard opens on one side into a shaded, sitting area known as the *takhtabush*, whose back wall features a large *mashrabiya* screened area, with a garden beyond. The garden becomes hotter than the courtyard during mid-day, and as its heat rises, it draws the cooler air from the courtyard through the sitting area and the *mashrabiya*. Similarly, if there is an open area outside the building, and if a window is open in each of the surrounding rooms, the rising warm air from outside the building will draw the cooler air from the courtyard through the rooms.

With low humidity prevailing in these hot dry regions, a fountain in the center of the house adds moisture that cools the air. Hassan Fathy said that the fountain is to an Arab house what the fireplace is to a house in temperate zones (Fathy, 1986:66–67).

We continue to be amazed at the empirical knowledge, imaginative designs, and elegant structures of the legion of forebearers, who learned to create superb interior comfort in an extremely hot, arid environment. Such systems reflect a high level of observation and creativity. We can benefit from their experience by accepting their patterns of thought and by using some of their constructions. Their creativity can also stimulate ours, enriching what we build by combining the best of the past with the best of the present in building with soil, this most perfect building material given to us freely by planet earth.

NOTES

1. For those who may be interested in the drawing of this beautiful but complex floor, architect David Sheehan drew it to scale, using a 1-meter string grid overlaid on the floor. He drew each grid stone-by-stone, carefully rechecking for completeness and accuracy. This task, involving meticulous detail and no little eye strain, required two weeks of full time measuring and drawing.

2. Thought at first to be cedar, when professionally identified, the beams actually proved to be pine.

3. A *tabun* also appears in sector 507b which, from its size, was probably also a courtyard in the same building.

Chapter 14

Problems and Solutions

Most people in the Western world (and increasing numbers in developing countries) have reservations about the durability and efficiency of earthen construction. In industrialized nations, this view is commonly held by people who know absolutely nothing about it. Most have never seen a mud house or read about one, never lived or even stayed overnight in one, and never talked with anyone who has. In the developing countries, doubts stem not from a lack of observation and experience but from an overwhelming desire to acquire modern (i.e., late twentieth century) housing, irrespective of vastly greater costs, increased discomfort, shoddiness, and ugliness.

For many in the western world, doubts linger about the stability and lasting qualities of mud construction. The questions invariably asked are, "What about rain? Doesn't rain melt or at least severely damage mud buildings?" For those in the northern tier of countries in western and southwestern Asia—Turkey, Syria, Iraq, Iran, Afghanistan, Pakistan, and northern India—where mud construction is prevalent (and also California, USA, where it is at least familiar), water from rain and run-off is not a serious issue because residents there learned long ago how to prevent water damage. In these regions, all of which are in seismic zones, questions always focus on the survival prospects of earthen buildings in earthquakes.

The issues of water erosion and seismic damage to mud buildings are valid concerns. Depending on where the house is located, one or both may be inevitable, but many people have survived both and lived to build again. Our creative ancestors must have spent many hours thinking about how to prevent both minor and major damage, experimenting with all sorts of ideas and devices. Those that succeeded were passed down to later generations. Some successful and lasting solutions are as applicable today as they were thousands of years ago. To these have been added contemporary ideas and discoveries. Taken together, they are useful for urban planners and builders everywhere, and especially for anyone contemplating the design and construction of an earthen house.

WATER EROSION

In 1970 when the Smithsonian Institution's excavations at Tell Jemmeh began, we conceived and financed the construction of a protective roof over what were then our core squares. Because no vehicle could negotiate the badly eroded terrain of this tell, staff and volunteers hand-carried the entire roof, a piece at a time, from the base of the site to its top some 24.4 m above; these "pieces" included prefabricated, iron A-frames, purlins, corrugated asbestos panels, and assorted hardware.

As we had hoped, the roof proved to be a god-send in preserving our excavated areas year by year in a pristine condition, including the walls, the balks and labels nailed to their layers, and the bottom surface. It also provided shaded working areas, with even, subdued light for photography and for reading the labels on the balks, and it vastly increased productivity of supervisors and volunteers working in the squares. As it turned out, our two most spectacular structures—the large circular granary of the late fourth to third centuries B.C. and the multistory, vaulted building constructed by the Assyrians late in the first quarter of the seventh century B.C.— were discovered beneath the roof. We hoped they would be preserved for people to visit for years to come. During our 12 field seasons, we repaired occasional leaks in the roof and built dikes to prevent roof drainage from entering our squares.

After we concluded our excavations, the Israel Antiquities Authority did not maintain the roof, which began to deteriorate rapidly. Asbestos panels were stolen, permitting rainwater to pond in the squares, totally destroying the mud-brick walls of the granary and eroding the soil from around and beneath two of the buried concrete-filled, steel oil drums on which the roof was founded. In 1992, conservators of the Antiquities Authority attempted to remove the protective roof at Tell Jemmeh, then in desperate need of major repairs. Workers removed the remaining corrugated asbestos panels from the entire roof, whereupon one of the concrete-filled oil drums slid free, bending and twisting the heavy angle-iron frame downward, endangering the life of a worker. The Authority workers then abandoned the project, leaving the twisted frame in place despite this author's offer (having gained experience when participating in its assembly and disassembly three times during the early 1970s) to supervise disassembly and removal of the structure.

During the rains of the following winter, water ran in a small steady stream from the bent frame onto the edge of the 16-course, rear mud-brick wall of the Assyrian vaulted building, which had remained in excellent condition during the 20 years since it was first exposed. By the following summer, the dripping water had cut several grooves, with the largest reaching about 10 cm wide and cutting about 30 cm into the outer surface of the uppermost preserved brick courses, or half the thickness of the wall, gradually narrowing and extending downward about 1.22 m. This erosion continued during subsequent winters. If the frame had been completely removed, there would have been no more than minor cracks and little or no surface erosion, because rain would have dripped over a wider area rather than poured in a concentrated stream on an area no larger than 5 cm wide. Happily, the framework was finally removed by the Antiquities Authority in 1997. The rear wall of the vaulted building still stood, although most of the vaulting was gone, like the Hellenistic granary. This is a very sad yet excellent example of the destructive power of a seasonal, minor stream of water on first-rate mud brick.

Can rain and run-off water destroy mud structures? Absolutely! During the 1961–
1962 archaeological survey of the Hadhramaut in Yemen, the remains of a small
recent farmhouse were discovered near Terim. The site had been reduced to a slight
elongated hump no more than 60 cm high near the edge of the wadi, well out of the
normal flood channel. Of course no one builds a house in or near the flash-flood
channel, but people do build along the edges near the cliffs and sometimes on the
slightly higher ground near the edge of the wadi, where floods seldom reach. Occasionally an unusually large flood suddenly spreads out of the channel, filling a part
or all of the wadi floor from cliff to cliff. Unless major changes in the valley floor
relocate the central water channel, flood waters approaching the wadi's edge move
very slowly and they eventually pond in low places. In this instance, an unusually
high flash-flood had breached its channel, and floodwater eventually surrounded the
farmhouse, gradually dissolving the lower courses of the building until it collapsed;
the mud brick returned to shapeless soil, some of which flowed downstream. However, the waters receded before everything was washed away, leaving a small hump of
earth and a scattering of potsherds to remind us that a family once lived there.

Farther west where a tributary wadi joins the main Hadhramaut flood channel
from the north, a low delta had formed rising slightly above the flash-flood channels. On this delta, a series of isolated humps outlined a rectilinear area, which was
once a large field plot surrounded by a wall or high ridge on all sides, probably
built with mud balls (Figure 14.1; see also Figure 5.12). Eventually one or more
high floods flowed over the delta, cutting through and washing away large sections
of the ridge walls, leaving only small piles of soil containing a few potsherds of a
pre-Islamic date, i.e., before the seventh century A.D.

Some 100 km west of Terim, we camped on government property where a two-
story house of mud brick had been rebuilt by agricultural authorities to serve as a
model farmhouse. This land was near the southern cliff, well beyond the normal
flood plain. The year before our arrival, an unusually large flood gradually covered

**Figure 14.1   Piles of earth left by one or more flash-floods that destroyed an earthen wall, prob-
ably built of mud balls, enclosing a rectangular field, near Seiyun, Hadhramaut, Yemen (1962).**

this area, eventually surrounding the lower courses of the original house walls. The mud-brick courses evenly dissolved one by one as the weight of the two-story walls pressed down equally on all four sides. By the time the flood receded, the entire ground floor had gradually dissolved, and the second floor had slowly and evenly settled to ground level where the first floor had been. When the land dried, government authorities and local mud-brick masons examined the house and found the original second floor—now the first floor—sound, and they proceeded to build a new second floor on top of it!

From these accounts, we learn that the most vulnerable areas of a traditional mud house are the base and lower courses at or just above ground level. This zone is attacked by run-off from rain and from domestic wastewater. Run-off water flowing along the base of a mud wall will undercut it, permitting moisture to invade it and softening or dissolving the lower courses of bricks. This undermines the wall, eventually causing it to crack, lean, and fall. A number of typical examples occurred in the large refugee camp immediately north of Tell es-Sultan (biblical Jericho) in the Jordan Valley. This settlement began soon after the 1948 war between the new state of Israel and the surrounding Arab nations. (GVB first visited the town in 1952 when participating in the excavations of biblical Jericho.) During the recurrence of war in 1967, when Israel took the West Bank following the Jordanian attack on Israel, the refugee settlers again fled, this time abandoning the camp, which had become a town. Photos from our return visit in 1978 to study the site (30 years after it was built and 12 years after it was abandoned) illustrate the effects of run-off water and erosional processes on mud construction (Figures 14.2 and 14.3).

Figure 14.2 The base of house walls eroded by run-off water at abandoned refugee town, north of Jericho, Jordan Valley (1978).

Figure 14.3 House walls splitting at corner primarily caused by run-off water undercutting the end wall, at abandoned refugee town north of Jericho, Jordan Valley (1978).

From the earliest times, builders were confronted with the problem of wall erosion at ground level, and through the centuries they developed several methods and devices to protect the bases of buildings. Many of their solutions seem obvious now: (1) Selecting a building site on high ground, or grading the site so that the ground slopes away on all sides from the building enabling water to drain away from it rather than toward it—see Chapter 4. (2) Using stone, fired-brick, or concrete foundations that extend 15 cm or more above ground level and building the earthen wall on them to prevent softening of the lower courses by ground moisture, which migrates upward by capillary action (see Figure 4.13). (3) Placing a sheet of heavy plastic cut slightly wider than the wall thickness on top of the second or third course of fired bricks to prevent the migration of salt and moisture upward in the wall (Figure 14.4). There are still other protective measures and devices not dependent on stone, fired-brick, or concrete wall stems.

Figure 14.4   Sheet of heavy duty plastic used to prevent upward migration of ground moisture and salt in a fired-brick wall in Dudhian, near Harappa, Punjab, Pakistan (1989).

Curbing

Where the base of the house meets the ground surface, curbing—commonly quarter-round in shape and made of mud or mud bricks—was often built against the wall to deflect run-off water away from the wall base. The size of curbing varies, with a radius typically of about 10–30 cm; but we saw one in Kerani, a suburb of Quetta, Pakistan, that reached a height of about 1 m and which may also have served to buttress a potentially weak area of the wall (Figure 14.5). Near Pondicherry in southern India, a rectangular, wattle-and-daub house was protected by a low, sloping curb, which may have been the slab or floor of the house extending beyond the line of the wattle-and-daub walls (see Figure 6.2). In Shibam in the Hadhramaut, a tall house was protected by curbing that consisted of a stack of five mud bricks covered with lime plaster slightly more than 2.5 cm thick (Figure 14.6). Similarly, at Tiznit, between Agadir and Goulimine in Morocco, the rammed-earth city wall also featured curbing covered with lime plaster (Figure 14.7).

In some instances, a still simpler technique was used to protect the wall base. This consisted of laying whole or broken mud bricks in a continuous line against the base of the wall to deflect run-off water. The outer wall on the south side of the large cobblestone courtyard (thirteenth century B.C.) at Tell Jemmeh was protected in this manner. When we first saw two or three mud bricks lying loose, flat, and side by side against the wall, we assumed that they had fallen from the upper courses of the wall. As the excavations were extended, we discovered that the line of bricks continued. A cross-section was cut in the wall to see the relationship of the wall to the cobblestone floor on the inside and to the narrow lane on the outside; this showed that the row of mud bricks had been deliberately laid to prevent run-off water from approaching the courtyard wall. One can scarcely imagine a cheaper, quicker, and easier method of protecting the base of a wall than this.

Figure 14.5 High curbing against property wall in Kerani, Quetta, Baluchistan, Pakistan (1990). Note overhanging fired brick with a mud capping on top of the wall.

Benches

The most elegant and efficient wall-protecting device is the mud bench. Mud benches can be built against the wall, where they serve the dual purpose of deflecting run-off water and providing seating. Normally about 40–45 cm high and about the same width, they have been finished with either mud plaster or lime plaster. At Tell Jemmeh, the large cobblestone courtyard of the thirteenth century B.C. originally had at least two mud benches, one along most of the south wall, and the second, a short one, adjacent to the bathroom. Although both benches were gone, a line of foundation stones, markedly different from the floor cobblestones in their roughness, established the length and width of the benches. In the right-angle-shaped area outside the east door of the residential quarter of this large building complex was another pair of mud benches. One was built against the west wall to the right of the door as one entered the house, and the other on the left side of the door, against the south wall. Both would have been in the shade during the day, the one on the left in the morning and the the one on the right in the afternoon. The former was more eroded, projecting only 40 cm wide in its present state. The latter was 55 cm wide and 30 cm high, and the plaster on its vertical face was intact and joined nicely the cobblestone floor of the entrance area.

Benches are such an obvious solution that they have been used everywhere through time and were probably invented independently in many places at different times, although it is possible in some instances that the idea was passed from one region to another. In the Egyptian delta, a small wattle-and-daub tea shop featured two mud benches, one on each side of the door, where customers could sit when enjoying their cup of tea (see Figure 6.13). In Beir al-Helu, near Tell Brak, in northeastern Syria, the house with the low, rounded, hipped roof (discussed in Chapter 3)

Figure 14.6 Broken curbing showing mud-brick construction inside and lime-plastered surface outside, in Seiyun, Hadhramaut, Yemen (1991).

Figure 14.7 Lime-plastered curbing protecting the base of the rammed-earth city wall in Tiznit, Morocco (1982). Lime plaster extends upwards on wall above curbing.

also had benches on both sides of the entrance, extending across the front of the house, where they were entirely in the shade from early afternoon onward (see Figure 3.48). The two-story mens' guest house in Hanna, Baluchistan (see Figure 3.17),

Figure 14.8   **Bench built of stones and covered with mud plaster protects the wall from erosion and provides seating at the political party meeting house in Hanna, Baluchistan, Pakistan (1990). Note stone-lined drain channel paralleling the end wall.**

featured a lime-plastered bench against the house wall and low curbing in front of the house. A political party meeting house, also in Hanna, had a bench against the front wall (Figure 14.8). In the village of Charada near Surendranagar in Gujarat, India, the narrow house (described in Chapter 3) had a mud-brick platform against the front wall divided only by the flight of steps leading to the door. It not only protected the wall, but also provided a place to sit in the afternoon shade (see Figure 3.38). Certainly one of the best known, heavily used examples in the USA is the long bench on the west side of the adobe Palace of the Governors in Santa Fe, New Mexico, built in 1610 (Figure 14.9).

Curbing and benches not covered with lime plaster gradually erode during wet seasons. However, both are easily replaced at a fraction of the inconvenience, time, and costs of replacing a collapsed house wall, which involves rebuilding the house.

Tops of Walls

The longevity of mud walls depends on the protection provided by the roof and drainage system. Great care must therefore be taken when constructing the roof and its drainage; both must be checked several times each year for leaks in areas where mud plaster may have separated from the wall and for soft spots, especially after major rains. Even tiny leaks around a beam that go unnoticed will soften the mud-brick wall supporting the beam, allowing the beam to settle, which permits the roof to slump and the wooden beam to eventually rot.

Figure 14.9 A fine bench along an adobe wall of the Palace of Governors in Santa Fe, New Mexico (1995). It not only protects the base of the wall from run-off water but also provides a comfortable place to rest.

The exposed tops of mud walls also can be protected in a number of ways. The cheapest and most popular method for maintaining privacy or property walls is a layer of reeds, brush, or thatch bundles laid across the top of the wall so that the ends of the bundles extend beyond the wall's inner and outer faces. If the bundles are long enough to bend slightly over the wall, rain will run down the stalks and drip on the ground away from the base of the wall. If they are also very dense, little if any water will soak through to the wall. This method is used everywhere. Two examples of property walls will suffice: one enclosing a fortress house in Najran, Saudi Arabia (see Figure 3.22), and the other belonging to a house in the mountainous areas north of Quetta, Pakistan (see Figure 4.13). The walls of unfinished—or unroofed—buildings are often protected from water erosion by placing straw across the top of the walls during the winter months (Figure 14.10). Occasionally twigs and straw are placed on top of the wall and covered with a rounded coat of mud plaster extending beyond the wall surface to form a drip molding.

A more permanent method of protecting the wall is to cover the tops with from one to five courses of mud- or fired-brick, laid to overhang slightly both faces of the wall. In the Old World, a fired-brick top is often covered with several coats of mud plaster, which must be examined frequently and recoated when cracks appear. A property wall in the suburbs of Quetta, Pakistan, suffered from a lack of

Figure 14.10 A two-room, layered-mud house left unfinished during the winter is success-fully protected from rain and snow by straw thickly laid across the walls in Hanna, Baluchistan (1989).

maintenance; the mud-plaster crown broke, revealing the mud brick beneath (see Figure 14.5). In the Southwestern USA, the Territorial Style of adobe architecture of the middle nineteenth century, which largely derived from the Neo-Classical Style then popular in the eastern USA, featured parapets finished with several courses of fired brick. From a simple coping of two or three courses of brick, more complex and imaginative designs emerged. Mixing courses of stretchers and headers with a slight overhang of courses added both weight and interest to the top of the wall while also providing excellent protection for the mud brick (Figure 14.11).

Another method of protecting the tops of earthen walls is to cover them with ceramic roofing tiles, as Vitruvius (1931 [translation]: vol. 1, bk. 2, chap. 8, ¶ 18) advised in the first century B.C.:

> When it shall be necessary to use them [sun-dried brick], outside the city [Rome] such walls will be sound and durable after the following manner. At the top of the walls let walling of burnt brick be put beneath the tiles, and let it have a projecting cornice. So the faults which usually happen here can be avoided. For when tiles in the roof are broken or thrown down by the wind (where rain-water could pass through from showers), the burnt brick shield will not allow the brickwork to be damaged; but the projection of the cornices will throw the drippings outside the facing line, and in that way will keep intact the structure of brick walls.

Ceramic tiles interlock by being placed in a layer on the wall with the concave side up, with another layer on top with the concave side down so that the edges of the upper layer cover those of adjoining tiles in the lower layer on both sides. The tiles should slope downward, parallel to the shed or gabled roof, and overhang the wall face to pitch rainwater well away from both the wall surface and the wall base. An example is a rammed-earth (*pisé*) wall enclosing a churchyard in Messimy, France

Figure 14.11   Fired-brick coping of the Territorial style, in Albuquerque, New Mexico (1994).

(Figure 14.12). Capping walls with ceramic tiles also appears sporadically in Santa Fe, New Mexico, primarily on adobe property walls.

A lime-plaster coating on the exposed tops of walls provides long-lasting, although more expensive protection. At Pishin, near Quetta in Baluchistan, Pakistan, the Qazi house has a beautiful family mosque on the estate. Before the entrance to the mosque is a porch with a small yard enclosed on three sides by a mud wall. This wall is finished with lime plaster, carefully burnished so that it is quite smooth, with no cracks or breaks on the surface, and is rounded on top (Figure 14.13). The tops of exposed walls enclosing activity areas on the roofs of the tall houses in the Hadhramaut, Yemen, are also finished with lime plaster (see Figure 10.19).

Drains through Walls

Another critical feature of mud walls that requires frequent inspection and maintenance is the area around drain spouts. Every flat-roofed, vaulted, or domed house has several drain spouts to remove water quickly and efficiently from the roof. If the drain pipe or trough is set too high above the floor of the water channel, or if the drain is too small to carry a large volume of water quickly, water will back up and pond against the wall, softening the roof or gradually eroding the wall around the pipe (see Figure 10.8) or trough (Figure 14.14). When water cuts a crack in the wall, the crack eventually widens to perhaps 15–20 cm and gradually extends down the wall, becoming narrower as it continues downward. After several rains, the wall splits along the crack and falls, destroying the structure. If a spout draining a flat roof is lost, run-off rain will cut a vertical groove in the unprotected wall, beginning at the bottom edge of the drain hole. If the spout is not replaced and the damaged wall is not repaired, the groove will deepen and enlarge with subsequent rains

Figure 14.12 *Pisé de terre* (rammed earth) wall protected by ceramic tile in churchyard of Messimy, France (1997).

Figure 14.13 Qazi family mosque with lime-plaster walls in Pishin, Baluchistan (1990).

until the wall eventually splits and collapses. An abandoned house in Marib Town is an example (Figure 14.15). Two drain pipes were lost and not replaced, so two separate streams of water flowed down one wall of the house, increasing the eroded area with each rain. Already a vertical crack extended from the end of the erosion to the ground. The longer eroded area on the right carried drainage from the roof. On the left, a second drain carried wastewater from the kitchen and was also badly eroded. Near the left corner was another vertical crack extending upward almost to the level of the kitchen drain. We predicted that the area between these two cracks would increase in breath and depth until at least half of the wall on this side collapsed, conceivably bringing down other walls and portions of interior walls and flooring with it.

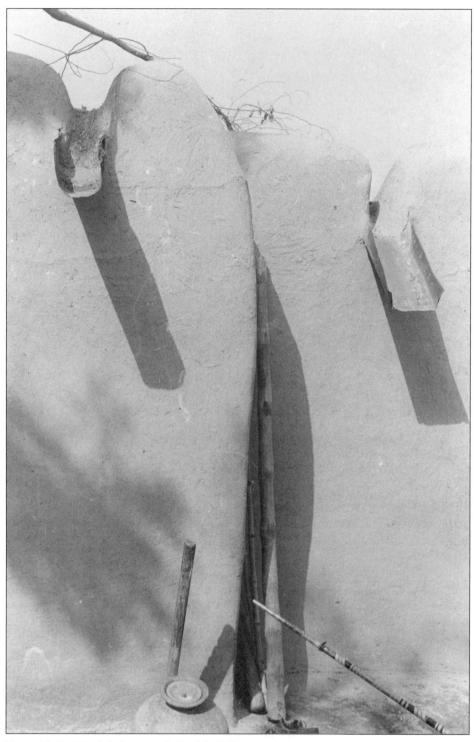

Figure 14.14   Metal drain spouts in Punjab, Pakistan (1989).

Figure 14.15 Erosion channels in a wall from a missing drain spout in Marib Town, Yemen (1991).

The best protection would be provided by coating the hole through the wall with lime plaster so that the drain pipe or trough is held firmly in place to prevent water from seeping around it and eroding the wall. In the absence of extended eaves, drain pipes or spouts should extend at least 1 m from the wall so water is dropped well away from the base (see Figure 10.8).

If a pipe or spout is not used, leaving instead only a drain hole through the wall—a vertical band of lime plaster with parallel raised edges—should be formed on the wall. This drainage panel must be wider than the diameter of the drain hole to prevent water from flowing onto the mud wall on either side (see Figure 10.9). It extends from the drain hole downward to a broad, sloping, lime-plaster-rimmed pan or plate on the ground, which slopes down toward its front edge, dispersing the water into an earthen or stone-lined channel in the middle of the narrow street (Figure 14.16).

If the drain is at floor level of a ground-floor room, and if water drains directly into a sump immediately below, no channel is necessary. If the sump is a little farther away, there must be a stone-lined or lime-plastered channel to conduct water to the sump; otherwise the drained water will pond near the wall, undermining and softening it. Examples of such drains appear in two bathrooms at Tell Jemmeh of the thirteenth century B.C. Both rooms are identical in construction: finished with lime-plaster on walls and floors and fitted with a drain hole, about 10 cm in diameter and coated inside with lime plaster, that passed through one wall of each bathroom (Figure 14.17). The perimeter of the sump of one bathroom was directly under the drain (Figure 14.18). The drain of the other bathroom directed wastewater into a lime-plastered channel that extended to the nearby sump (Figure 14.19).

Buttresses

If buildings are constructed on poorly compacted soil or if groundwater softens their foundations, the walls generally settle and cracks soon appear, often in the corners first. When groundwater undercut a property wall in the Jericho refugee town, two mud-brick buttresses were added, which kept the wall from tilting or falling for at least 11 years after the town was abandoned, even though walls had been undercut and the corner had collapsed (Figure 14.20).

Piping water into the tall houses of the Hadhramaut—without providing piped water disposal systems—has permitted vastly greater quantities of wastewater to soak into the ground with disastrous results. The increased water has softened the mud-brick foundations and caused many of them to settle and crack. To counteract the slumping and cracking, buttresses are commonly constructed to stabilize and support the failing wall. A number of Shibam's tall houses are reinforced with buttresses, including Beit Jarhum. The traditional buttress of the Hadhramaut is a huge mass of mud brick that reinforces the slumping part of the building. At the southeast corner of a house in Seiyun, the buttress reached from the ground to a point midway in the height of the third story, to the level of the top of the window. This huge box-shaped structure with battered sides measured, along the east wall, about 5 m long at the base, 3.35 m long at the top, 6.7 m high, and 1.65 m thick at the base (Figure 14.21). Run-off groundwater had already begun to erode the base of the buttress at the time of the photo.

Massive buttresses also have been used in the southwestern USA. The Mission of St. Francis of Assisi in Taos, New Mexico, of the early eighteenth century, is a well-known historic building (Figure 14.22). The back corners and end wall of the chancel of this beautiful little church are protected by massive buttresses, conical at the corners and sloping on the rear wall (Figure 14.23).

Figure 14.16 To protect walls and foundations, rimmed pans catch water from drain pipes and disperse it into the middle of the street, Shibam, Hadhramaut (1991). Note water supply pipe laid above ground in street.

The type of buttress currently used in the Hadhramaut consists of a smaller, sloping mud-brick structure reinforced with heavy wooden beams. A typical example appears at Beit Jarhum, where the buttress extends about 70 cm from the base of the wall, reaching about 2.75 m high on the wall, and finished with lime plaster.

Figure 14.17   Bathroom finished with lime-plastered floor, walls, and drain hole from thirteenth century B.C. at Tell Jemmeh, Israel.

It extends 2.75 m along the north wall on the left side of the main entrance and wraps around the northeast corner, stretching about 5.25 m along the east wall. An unusual characteristic of this type of buttress is the use of heavy wooden beams set in recesses in the mud brick of the buttress. Each extends obliquely from near the base of the buttress to a small window on the second floor where it is wedged under the lintel, which had been reinforced with a wooden block (Figure 14.24; see also Figures 3.55, 3.56). The reinforcing beams, measuring about 15 cm square and 5.3 m long, add important bracing support to the upper walls at the level of the second floor. In some applications, as in Beit Jarhum, the beams of the buttress are covered with lime plaster and are only visible above the buttress. In other instances, the beams are exposed on the buttress surface as well. The very obvious contrast between the white lime-plastered buttress and the dark wooden beam emphasizes the structural problems of the building. This type of buttress is smaller and more neatly braces the building than traditional buttresses.

Wall Surfaces in Rainy Zones

Although lime plaster is more waterproof and enduring, mud plaster—if properly maintained—has a surprisingly long life in the Near East. There are regions of comparatively heavy rainfall, such as the mountain range on the east side of the Red Sea from the Asir region in Saudi Arabia southward through the highlands of Yemen, where rainfall amounts to 762 mm or more annually (Scott et al., 1946:178). In the

Figure 14.18 Top of stone-lined sump for wastewater from the drain shown in Figure 14.17.

highlands of the Asir, layered mud houses are constructed with a row of slate slabs or thin slabs of other rocks between each mud layer, which project about 15–20 cm beyond the wall surface. The rows of stones slope downward from the wall face and function as drip moldings during the rainy season. Rainwater cannot flow up the sloping surfaces of the stones to attack the mud wall; instead it drips from the outer edges of each row until it reaches the ground (see Figure 7.17).

Eaves

Buildings with raised-frame roofs, such as gable, hip, and shed styles, can protect mud walls from damage if constructed with long overhanging eaves. When eaves extend 1 m or more beyond the wall face, the drip line is located that distance from the base of the wall. If the building site has been properly graded, all water discharged by the roof will be spilled well away from wall bases and will flow away from the house on the sloping ground. In driving rain, the long eaves also greatly reduce the amount

Figure 14.19 Sump of the south building bathroom, one-half of which has been excavated to permit detail study of the layering inside. The stone-covered channel leads from the wall on the left to the sump from thirteenth century B.C., Tell Jemmeh, Israel.

of water blown on the wall surface. Even brush or thatch used on the conical roofs of circular wattle-and-daub huts, can be extended 50 cm or so beyond the wall, in order to prevent run-off water from damaging the walls (see Figures 6.5 and 6.9).

EARTHQUAKES

Seismic motion in the earth's crust has been a sporadically occurring feature of our planet since its creation, uplifting some sections of the earth's surface and collapsing others. These seismic events produce vast numbers of stress fractures and cracks that have altered—and continue to alter—the topography of the continents. Leon Reiter, a ranking specialist in analyzing earthquake hazards, describes these complex and variable factors as follows:

> Ground motion at a particular site can be thought of as being influenced by three main elements: source, travel path, and local site conditions. The first describes how the size and nature of the earthquake source controls the generation of earthquake waves, the

Figure 14.20 Mud-brick property wall supported by small but effective buttresses, at refugee town north of Jericho, Jordan Valley (1978).

Figure 14.21 Massive mud-brick buttress reaching to the third floor, and shoring the corner of a house in Seiyun, Hadhramaut (1962).

second describes the effects of the earth on these waves as they travel (at some depth) from the source to a particular location, and the third describes the effect of the uppermost several hundred meters of rock and soil and the surface topography at that location on the resultant ground motion produced by the emerging or passing earthquake waves. (Reiter, 1990:98)

Because of the complexity of these forces and their varying patterns, earthquakes are not accurately predictable as to time, place, and severity even with the technologically sophisticated recording devices now in use, although there is optimism for greater predictability in the future.

Figure 14.22   Mission of St. Francis of Assisi in Taos, New Mexico, USA (1989). Note buttresses supporting the front gate.

Some parts of the world experience far more earthquakes than others. In the region of our focus, the zone stretching from Spain to India, including Italy, the former Yugoslavia, Romania, Greece, Turkey, Iraq, Iran, Afghanistan, and Pakistan, suffers a greater frequency of seismic activity than the parallel zone drawn across North Africa and the northern Arabian Peninsula. Crossing this region primarily from north to south, seismic events occur along a vast number of major faults, such as those extending from Lebanon and Syria to East Africa, including the formation and development of the Jordan Valley and the Red Sea trenches. There are multitudes of smaller faults oriented in other directions as well.

Figure 14.23   Enormous buttresses bracing the chancel walls of the Mission of St. Francis of Assisi in Taos, New Mexico, USA (1989).

Worldwide in the twentieth century, a number of earthquakes devastated settlements and killed nearly one and a half million people. The *World Almanac* is a handy source for a listing of major earthquakes by date, place, magnitude, and number of deaths, although the numbers of deaths cited are estimates rather than actual body counts and may vary considerably from actual counts. Three towns or cities that have prominently figured in our discussions of mud architecture in this book have been destroyed by major earthquakes in the twentieth century. (1) On 31 May 1935, the western half of Quetta, India (now Pakistan), was destroyed, killing an estimated 50,000 people, although the citizens of Quetta commonly quoted to us a figure of 25,000. (2) On 29 February 1960, 80% of Agadir, Morocco, was destroyed, killing 12,000 people as they slept, leaving behind as a memorial the resulting tell containing the buried remains of the town and its people. (3) An earthquake on 13 December 1982 followed closely by a major aftershock struck northern Yemen, killing an estimated 1800 people and destroying nearly all of Marib Town on the piggy-back tell.

Having conducted research for this book in all three towns, we feel especially close to these tragedies. In Quetta, however, none of the earthquake's devastation is now apparent, owing to the rebuilding of the city during the intervening years. At Agadir the tell remains. In Marib Town, abandonment and devastation is marked by split houses, shells of houses, and fully collapsed houses, which look much the same as they did in the days following the earthquakes, except the bodies of the dead are gone (Figures 14.25, 14.26). Among local officials and citizens of these

Figure 14.24 Mud-brick buttress with wooden beams shoring the northeast corner of Beit Jarhum, in Shibam, Hadhramaut (1991).

countries, the overriding concern about mud construction focuses on earthquakes, not on protecting houses from water erosion.

An earthquake catalog based on historical records dating from 64 B.C. to A.D. 1860 and on meteorological records from 1860 to 1952 was prepared by David Amiran for the Palestine Region. Utilizing these sources, he estimated that there had been between two and five strong earthquakes per century, one or two of which were classified as major—i.e., very strong (Amiran, 1952:48, 51). Two major epicenters were Safed in Galilee and Nablus in the hill country north of Jerusalem. Three epicenters of slightly lesser force were located at Ramle–Lod (about 15 km southeast of Tel Aviv) near Ben Gurion Airport, near Nazareth in Galilee, and in the Jordan Valley near Jericho. An epicenter of less significance but that caused medium damage was located in the southwestern coastal area between Deir el-Balah and Gaza, where the probable intersection of a north-northeast fault parallel to the coastline, and

Figure 14.25   View of the destruction of Marib Town, Yemen, abandoned after the earthquakes of 1982 (1991).

a southeast–northwest fault extending from Beer-sheba to Deir el-Balah (Amiran, 1952:62, fig. 2) occurs within 6–8 km of Tell Jemmeh.

Based on historical records, the Deir el-Balah–Gaza area epicenter has been subjected to 11 earthquakes during the last 1300 years. Four of these—A.D. 1032, 1033–1034, 1546, and 1927—caused heavy damage; three in A.D. 672, 1834, and 1903—caused medium damage; and four in A.D. 1293–1294, 1870, 1940, and 1942 caused little or no damage (Kallner-Amiran, 1950–1951:225–239). Five of the eleven earthquakes occurred within the past 160 years, with an average frequency of one every 26.7 years. It cannot be assumed that a similar frequency prevailed in antiquity, because periods of increased earthquake activity often alternate with periods of reduced activity. However, it does suggest that during the 1500 years of continuous occupation at Tell Jemmeh, many who once lived there must have experienced the terror, death, and destruction of earthquakes.

Just as those who presently live in zones of seismic activity entrust their homes and lives to construction engineers and the continuing refinements of building codes, ancient peoples who lived in such areas put their faith in their masons or in themselves to build safe and secure houses. Much thought and experimentation must have gone into developing methods of construction to withstand moderate seismic activity.

During the past century or so, and perhaps even earlier, two major approaches have emerged from the research and experiments of geologists, engineers, and architects who specialize in minimizing damage to buildings and loss of life during seismic activity. One approach advocates the construction of buildings with sufficient mass and rigidity to withstand most seismic motion. The second recommends the construction of buildings with maximum flexibility. In general, the former view prevails in Japan; the latter in the USA. Yet these seemingly opposite approaches

Figure 14.26   Another view of the earthquake destruction of Marib Town, Yemen (1991).

actually incorporate both rigidity and flexibility in different aspects of construction. Interestingly, flexibility seems to have prevailed among ancient builders.

A technique used as early as the third millennium B.C. in successive city walls at Jericho involved the placement of heavy wooden beams in vertical cavities about 91 cm wide that extended almost completely through the solid mud-brick wall of about 1.07 m thickness. During the excavations, archaeologists discovered that the cavities were placed at intervals, and that in some instances, a section of the mud-brick wall bordered by the beam-filled cavities had fallen outward, leaving the beam-filled defense wall on either side standing erect as high as 3 m (Kenyon, 1970:105–106). Apparently builders had discovered that a rigid, well-bonded mud-brick wall tended to collapse over all or most of its length in an earthquake. They devised the spaced joints to permit any one or several of the sections between the beam-filled straight joints to fall during a seismic event without pulling down adjacent sections of the fortification system. After an earthquake, it was much easier to rebuild a few sections of the wall than most or all of it.

A second example of the use of wooden beams in mud-brick structures occurs in a site in the Jordan Valley. This river valley, separating Jordan on the east bank from both Israel and Palestinian areas on the West Bank, was formed by geological faults and has been subjected to earthquakes throughout history. The remains of an ancient town, Tell Rehov, are located on the West Bank about 5 km south of Beth-shan, and was excavated by Amihai Mazar (A. Mazar, Institute of Archaeology, Hebrew University of Jerusalem, Israel, personal communication). On the citadel, he discovered a massive mud-brick fortification wall of the seventh century B.C. erected on heavy tree limbs. These beams were apparently cut to the length of the thickness of the wall and were laid perpendicular to the line of the wall—resembling the wooden ties of railroad tracks—with about the same distance between each beam. It is nearly a certainty that the beams beneath the walls functioned to provide a measure of vertical and possibly horizontal flexibility to the wall during seismic movements in the earth beneath them.

Heavy wooden post-and-beam construction, when well-joined and adequately braced, makes for a more flexible structure, much like contemporary structural steel framing for multistory structures. During seismic motion, having the capability to bend may overcome a tendency to break, leaving the basic structural framework intact. In the well-forested mountains of southeastern Europe and Turkey, people have built with timber framing for centuries, strengthening structures with wooden braces. At Shabwa and other sites in the Hadhramaut, heavy post-and-beam construction appeared as early as A.D. 200–400 (see Figure 2.8). The curtain walls (i.e., the thin, non-load-bearing walls filling in the open areas of the skeletal framework) may still collapse, whether wattle-and-daub, mud brick, or fired brick, but with results generally less injurious and destructive than the crash of the entire building (Oliver, 1987:127).

Another ancient method of minimizing earthquake damage came to light during our excavations at Tell Jemmeh. In two different applications, clean sand was used in great quantities either to cushion and isolate the building from jolts or to make the walls somewhat flexible during seismic movement. Why sand? Because sand is a homogeneous substance capable of being compressed and of flowing easily. We are all familiar with the compressed footprints we leave when walking on a dry beach, and also with the ease of heaping and pouring sand. When narrowly confined, it still retains considerable flexibility. Sand is also enduring because it is derived from hard rocks and is not destroyed by organic or inorganic processes.

At Tell Jemmeh throughout its 1500 years of human occupation, all buildings that were excavated were constructed of mud brick, including their foundations, many of which were built in foundation trenches. During the tenth century B.C., Jemmeh apparently remained a Philistine town, while the rest of the region was welded into a single unified state for the first time in its history by King David and his son, King Solomon. All buildings of this period excavated by the Smithsonian team featured foundation trenches. In square 2B, two parallel walls were separated by an open area, which probably served as a courtyard; both walls had nearly identical foundation trenches with sloping sides wider at the top than at the bottom. They typically measured 45–50 cm deep, at least 20 cm wide at the bottom, and 34 cm wide at the top, i.e., from the side of the trench to the wall face at ground level. In Figure 14.27, the trench on the right has been cleared, leaving a protective skin of the pre-existing debris layers into which the trench was dug. The trench on the left also has been cleared, and the supporting skin of debris layers has been removed. The foundation trench of another building was more shallow, only 25 cm deep.

Until we excavated these walls, all other foundation trenches excavated at Tell Jemmeh had been backfilled with the same soil that had been removed and stockpiled when the trenches were dug. Here, for the first time, we saw foundation trenches filled only with clean sand. At the bottom of the trench, before the first course of foundation bricks had been laid, builders spread a layer of sand about 5–6 cm thick (Figure 14.28). On the sand bedding layer, they laid the first course of mud bricks of the foundation, followed by at least three additional courses, which carried the foundation slightly above ground level. Workmen then backfilled the foundation trench with clean sand, instead of the previously excavated soil (Figure 14.29).

The choice of sand was deliberate despite its vastly increased costs in time and physical effort. An enormous amount of sand had to be quarried in Nahal Besor (the river adjacent to Tell Jemmeh) and transported—probably by asses climbing a slope about 30 m high perhaps thousands of times—because all buildings of this period were apparently constructed in this manner. In the 3.2 m exposure of foundation trench 47, the sand used beneath the wall and in filling the trench is estimated to have weighed about 354 kg. If we assume that the building was small, measuring only 5 m long × 4 m wide, and that the foundation trench was the same

Figure 14.27 Two cleared, parallel foundation trenches from the tenth century B.C., square 2B at Tell Jemmeh, Israel. Scale arrow points to north and is 50 cm long.

Figure 14.28 Layer of sand beneath wall 29 (right), with sand-filled foundation trench 47 (left), at Tell Jemmeh, Israel.

Figure 14.29 View of wall 29 and sand-filled foundation trench 47 after excavation in square 2B, Tell Jemmeh, Israel. Note size and homogeneity of "chocolate" mud brick.

size as it continued around the structure, the amount of sand required for this building alone would have weighed about 1991 kg! With an estimate of 200 buildings in the tenth century B.C. occupation and multiplying this figure by at least 2 metric tons, a minimum of 400 metric tons of sand would be required for all foundation trenches. A formidable task, indeed!

Incidentally, these walls were among the most beautiful walls discovered at Tell Jemmeh in terms of their state of preservation and size; even the subsurface foundation bricks were in pristine condition and showed no signs of erosion or softening (Figure 14.30). This may be due in part to the fact that all mud bricks of the tenth century B.C. thus far excavated were made of a distinctive clayey, chocolate-colored soil called paleosol A-horizon that occurs as bands in the virgin soil in buttes and other lesser eroded areas in the Tell Jemmeh region, and indeed beneath the strata of human occupation at Tell Jemmeh (Melson and Van Beek, 1992). These "chocolate" bricks occasionally appear in other periods, intermixed with the more typical, light-colored bricks made of the predominant loess soil. This is the only period in which "chocolate" bricks seem to have been used exclusively at Jemmeh, making it an extremely useful dating tool at the site, and perhaps elsewhere in the vicinity (see also Chapter 5). These mud bricks were large, measuring 56 × 35 × 11 cm, and

Figure 14.30 English-bonded mud bricks of wall 29 at Tell Jemmeh, Israel, with foundation trench sand adhering to the interstitial grooves. Note the section of foundation trench with fallen brick (left), one of several that probably had covered the top of the trench to deflect groundwater.

were laid in English bond (see Figure 14.30), which alternates courses of header and stretcher bricks.

The surface of the sand-filled foundation trench was almost certainly protected from groundwater run-off by a single course of individual mud bricks laid side-by-side against the wall face without mortar, as was used in the large cobblestone courtyard of the thirteenth century B.C. discussed earlier in this chapter. Two of these covering bricks can be seen in the balks where they were upended and settled into the sand (Figures 14.30, 14.31). Without these protective bricks, water would have quickly drained into the sand-filled trench, where it would have begun to soften and dissolve the mud-brick foundation, as well as the adjacent debris soil before being fully absorbed by the surrounding soil. Such softening did not appear either on the foundation bricks or on the debris layers below and on the opposite side of the trench.

In this application, sand provides a cushion that separates the rigid mud-brick building from the firm, compacted, surrounding soil. It provides "base isolation" for the building from seismic (P) waves that cause sharp compressive motions, (S) waves that cause rapid up-and-down motions, and surface waves that cause longer up-and-down motions, the most destructive of all. Thus the compressing sand would absorb some of the shocks of the earth moving below and around the building. To be sure, when the sand in the trench is compressed, some of it would probably be squeezed out, depositing sand on the surrounding ground surface, and perhaps displacing some of the covering bricks. That is exactly what we found on the surface of the two successive floors—layers 57 and 56—in the open area

Figure 14.31 Wall 35 and foundation trench 56 on the opposite (north) side of square 2B at Tell Jemmeh, Israel. Ground level when the building was constructed is at top of fourth course from the bottom. Note sand layer beneath wall, and another trench-covering brick that had fallen into the sand-filled foundation trench.

between the two walls. Layer 57 was the ground surface at the time the foundation trench was dug and the buildings constructed. Layer 56 was the ground surface during the early years when the buildings were in use. On both layers there were many randomly scattered, thin patches of sand. We might interpret the patches on layer 57 as accidental spills occurring when sand was being unloaded and poured into the foundation trench. Against this interpretation is the fact that sand on an occupation surface would have been trampled into the soil or kicked about rather than remaining as small discrete piles. The small sand piles on layer 56 may have been deposited during an earthquake whose motion compressed and squirted sand out of the foundation trench or squeezed it out during the sliding motion of contact surfaces. The covering bricks, shown tilted in foundation trenches 47 and 56 (see Figures 14.30, 14.31), may owe their curious positions to the same seismic event. By isolating the buildings from compacted soil, and by absorbing some of the ground motion, sand provided some protection to the structures.

Similar sand foundations—but on a much grander scale—were discovered at Khafaje (ancient Tutub) in Mesopotamia, dating between 2650 and 2350 B.C. The outer and inner enclosure walls of the Oval Temple had foundation trenches 4.6 m deep that had been filled with clean sand! It has been calculated that 64,000 m³ of sand would have been required for these foundation trenches. Here, too, there must be a reason why the builders expended such an astonishing amount of labor on this construction job. This is especially remarkable in the region where the common building practice for nearly all structures, including massive palaces, was to erect buildings directly on the hard desert surface without foundations (Lloyd, 1984:95–96). At Tell Farah South (Tell Sharuhen) on Nahal Besor, approximately 12.5 km south-southeast of Tell Jemmeh, Sir Flinders Petrie excavated a large, mud-brick gateway of the Hyksos period (seventeenth century B.C.). This structure, measuring 17.5 m long × 21.75 m wide and with outer walls 2.6 m thick, was constructed on a bed of sand in what appeared to be a shallow, excavated base for the gateway (Macdonald et al., 1932:29–30, pl. 77).

The second use of sand in construction at Tell Jemmeh was discovered when we excavated the multistory, pitched-brick-vaulted building of the seventh century B.C. This unique structure, described in Chapters 11 and 12, also featured a curious construction technique. In erecting the exterior and interior mud-brick walls, which were laid in English bond, wet sand was substituted for mud mortar in the bedding and rising joints of the horizontal courses (Figure 14.32). This method of laying mud bricks in sand was found in all contemporary, seventh century buildings at the site, including those excavated in 1927 by Petrie (1928:6, fig. 9). While excavating the buildings of this phase, we soon learned, as we troweled the debris layers, that a trickle of sand indicated we were within a few millimeters of a wall. If there was no mud plaster remaining on the walls, the sand would trickle from the joints when we exposed them. All of us were accustomed to mud mortar, and we did not understand the substitution of sand for mud. The sand was not as clean as that found in the tenth century B.C. buildings because it included some silty soil, suggesting that a mixture of ¼–⅓ soil and ¾–⅔ clean sand was used.

Clearly the sand had to be wet when laid as mortar, because dry sand would have been squeezed or fallen out immediately, as it did when we were excavating. Moreover, the mud bricks probably would have forced dry sand out of the rising joints

Figure 14.32 The well-preserved rear wall of the seventh century B.C. Assyrian vaulted building at Tell Jemmeh, Israel, in which wet sand was used as mortar.

even faster than from the horizontal bedding joints, causing the wall to collapse on its own were it not for the bonding pattern in these 60-cm thick walls, which prevented sand in the inner joints from falling out. To prevent loss of the wet-sand mortar, after four or five bricks had been laid, masons would have dampened the mud bricks for good adherence and then covered them immediately with a coat of mud plaster, perhaps as much as 6 mm thick. When dry, the sand would have been tightly sealed in place; evidence of this was found in several areas (see Figure 12.2).

When we excavated this building more than 2700 years after it was built, a task requiring three field seasons to complete, large patches of mud plaster were visible on the interior walls, but no mud plaster remained on the outer surface of the exterior walls. Even with the fallout of sand from the bedding and rising joints during excavations, and continuing in diminishing amounts afterwards, enough sand mortar remained to keep the walls sturdy. They withstood the excavations on top, inside, and outside, as well as the weight and movement of the staff and visitors for more than 20 years.

When walls are built with mud bricks laid in mud mortar, they become rigid when cured, and shock waves generated by earthquakes often break and topple them. The sand-filled horizontal and vertical joints in this building seem to have provided a measure of flexibility, enabling it to survive some seismic motion by minor sliding, slightly adjusting to and absorbing some of the shock. Bricks could withstand slight shifts of position, more horizontally than vertically. If the bricks were shifted out of alignment by an earthquake, the sealing of the mud plaster would break. It may have been possible to manipulate some of the bricks back into their proper position by tapping and sliding them on the sand mortar. If they had to be removed because they were fractured or would no longer fit, new wet sand could be placed on the upper surface of the bricks below, and a new brick inserted. In both examples, it would be necessary to force wet sand into the upper bedding and rising joints, and immediately apply a patching coat of mud plaster over the area. The ability to repair walls instead of destroying and rebuilding them would at least partially repay the builders for the greater costs, time, and effort expended in using wet sand as mortar in the first place.

During the 1976 field season, we saw convincing evidence of the yielding or cushioning effect of sand-filled joints. A large portion of the north end of the tell at Nahal Besor has been lost through the centuries. The flash floods that rush down the stream bed during winter and spring rains undercut the butte beneath the tell, causing gradual collapse of the massive debris site above. Some of the soil forms a scree slope at the base of the tell, with the remainder washing downstream. As frequently happens on the top surface immediately behind the vertical edge of the tell, rainwater infiltrates insect and rodent holes, causing cracks to develop, expand, and deepen seasonally. After the rainy season, the soil dries and contracts, causing the fractures to widen. From time to time during the early summer, chunks of the tell topple and fall onto the scree slope and into the stream bed 26–30 m below. The enormous impact breaks fallen sections into relatively small chunks, usually less than about 1 m across.

At the beginning of each field season, the scree slope and stream bed were examined for artifacts exposed when chunks of the occupation layers in the site fell to the wadi floor. In 1975, we were astonished to see a large block of debris had fallen at least 24 m and survived the impact without breaking up. This multi-ton block remained upright (Figure 14.33). It consisted of a substantial portion of a mud-brick wall at the top with a sequence of debris layers below. The mud-brick courses of the wall were somewhat jumbled in a slightly jagged horizontal line, but both bedding and rising joints were easily identifiable, and both still contained sand. From the method of construction, we knew immediately that the wall belonged to the seventh century B.C. It seems clear that the sand-filled bedding and rising joints provided enough cushioning to enable the wall to withstand the tremendous shock and stress of impact.

It may be that the intact sections of vaulting in the seventh century B.C. building owe their survival to the flexibility of the supporting walls, whose brick courses were set in sand. As described in Chapter 11, the pitched-brick vaults were not only constructed with thick mud mortar, but were made stronger and even more rigid by the deep grooving on the lower face of each vault brick, which increased the surface area and suction in the mud mortar. The amount of vaulting surviving intact in the five rooms excavated varied from as little as two courses of about 30 cm in room A to 1.0–1.5 m in rooms B, C, and E, to 4.75 m in room F. A major section of the vault in room F broke in antiquity and fell as a unit about 50 cm, where it caught on the side walls, held, and continued to hold even after the interior of the room beneath it was excavated. Possibly a minor or moderate earthquake occurred between ca. 650

Figure 14.33 A portion of the enormous block of seventh century B.C. tell debris that fell upright into the wadi from the top of Tell Jemmeh without breaking up. The sand-laid bricks were jumbled by the tremendous impact but survived to be recognizable in their courses.

and 630 B.C. that shook down some of the vaulting in these rooms, after the Assyrians relinquished their hold on the Levant and Egypt and evacuated their military troops from the forward base at Tell Jemmeh.

Whence came the use of sand as mortar in this application? Possibly it was introduced in the seventh century B.C. at Jemmeh by the Assyrian builders who accompanied King Esarhaddon's armies and constructed the buildings at this base. No instances of the use of sand in this manner were found by GVB in contemporary ancient buildings in Iraq, Iran, or northern Syria, although that region is subject to frequent earthquakes like the southern Levant. It would not be surprising if this method of construction originated there.

Two other instances of similar use point to southwestern Israel as the place of origin. At Ashkelon, a coastal site on the Mediterranean Sea, mud bricks were laid in sand bedding joints in a wall of the tenth or late eleventh century B.C.[1] Also at Tell esh-Shari'a (Tell Sera') about 24 km east of Tell Jemmeh, mud-brick walls of the tenth to ninth centuries B.C. were built "with alternating courses of mud brick and sand" (Oren, 1993b:1332). Clearly, the Ashkelon and Shari'a application are contemporary with the tenth century B.C. example at Tell Jemmeh. It is most unlikely that memory of the Khafaje (Mesopotamia) and Tell Fara South usages of sand in the third and second millennia B.C., respectively, were passed down to the tenth century B.C. in the Levant. It seems far more probable that this method represents an independent invention by local masons in southwestern Israel and the Philistine coastal plain.

As for the seventh century B.C. application by the Assyrian masons at Tell Jemmeh, it remains without parallel. The laying of mud bricks in sand must reflect another experimental approach to minimizing earthquake damage. With more archaeological excavations of sites with mud construction, and with greater attention to detail by archaeologists, we may eventually know with certainty the place or places of origin, the path of development taken by this method of construction, and its function.

While we very much doubt that either of these sand methods would have prevented destruction of the buildings by a major earthquake of the magnitude of the Northridge, California, event of 1994, or the Kobe, Japan, event of 1995, they may have saved the Jemmeh buildings, reducing the damage that would have occurred during minor or even moderate earthquakes. If so, many local citizens may have escaped death and serious injury and faced a simpler, easier task of repairing the buildings rather than completely constructing them anew. Either of these two beneficial consequences would have more than justified the expenditure of time, hard work, and funds involved.

To be sure, we cannot prove beyond doubt that these applications of sand in earthen wall construction were conceived as a means of minimizing earthquake damage. However in our experience excavating ancient mud buildings, investigating contemporary earthen structures, and learning materials and procedures, we have weighed every possible explanation that we could think of for the use of sand in foundation trenches and mortar in walls of mud brick. Arguably, the use of sand beneath mud-brick walls and in filling foundation trenches to improve drainage of rain and groundwater may seem to be the best alternative explanation. That water is the greatest enemy of mud-brick foundations and walls where they meet hard ground is exemplified by the tall houses in Shibam, Hadhramaut, and the buildings in the refugee town near Jericho. One would therefore expect the tenth century B.C. foundation walls and foundation trenches at Tell Jemmeh to show signs of the erosion of both the mud bricks below ground level and the debris layers on the other side of the foundation trench by the sand-laden water, as it was slowly absorbed by the mud bricks and the debris layers. But no evidence of erosion has been found. It seems, therefore, that these locally new applications, which were expensive and time-consuming, must have served a very important function. One can scarcely imagine a more useful function than reducing minor earthquake damage to people's houses.

Why did this method of construction disappear? Perhaps it did not provide the hoped for protection in some instances, causing people to decide that it was not worth the effort. Possibly there was an extended period with little or no seismic activity, leading townspeople to assume the protection was no longer necessary. If we have learned one thing about people, however, it is that they typically have little practical, historical memory, seldom spanning more than a generation. We discard efficiency and productivity by failing to profit from what our parents and grandparents learned, because each generation arrogantly sees itself as the only knowledgeable generation in human history. The truism that those who ignore history are condemned to repeat it is overlooked and ignored by people in every generation.

In this context, people probably forgot the methods used by their forebearers to protect their homes from earthquakes and, as a result, were condemned to lose their houses and possessions, and often the lives of their families as well as their own. In the absence of oral tradition and without excavating their ancestors' homes to learn how they were built, how would they know? Of course, they might reinvent the techniques that had been lost, but reinvention seldom occurs immediately; it sometimes requires generations if it happens at all. It seems likely that a combination of all of these causes—i.e., failures of the two sand methods to provide total protection, a period of reduced seismic activity, and the inability of people to pass on the knowledge of their ancestors—led to the disappearance of what may have been a valuable way of protecting lives and property. Unless reinvented by an imaginative builder, it could not have been recovered without archaeological excavation and observation.

In the southwestern USA, concerns about earthquakes led to experimentation, which resulted in a number of structural recommendations that are primarily concerned with strengthening the mud structure itself so that its walls do not break and collapse during an earthquake. Smith and Austin (1989:22) cited an experiment featuring the construction of a slightly reduced-size adobe building on the 20×20 ft (6×6 m) platform of an earthquake simulator at the Richmond Field Station of the University of California, Berkeley, where different adobe construction features were tested. In addition to bond—or tie—beams, recommendations included enclosing the walls inside and out with welded wire mesh, stucco netting, or chicken wire; steel reinforcing rods bent to right angles to be placed in every third horizontal mortar joint in wall corners; and the use of buttresses at points of stress at corners.

McHenry (1984:178–181) provided an excellent summary, "Design for Earthquake Loads," which is "must reading" for anyone contemplating an earthen building in zones of probable seismic activity. The most important single item is the bond—or tie—beam, which ties the walls together. The New Mexico building code requires a bond beam on the top of walls or at regular intervals, such as at the top of each floor, to stabilize the walls. It may be made of reinforced concrete or wood. If concrete, it must be a minimum of 6 in (15 cm) wide, or as wide as the wall is thick, plus 6 in (15 cm). The concrete must be continuously reinforced through its length, especially at corners, with a minimum of two no. 4 reinforcing rods. Wooden tie beams must also be a minimum of 6 in (15 cm) in width or as wide as the wall, plus 6 in (15 cm). They can be built of solid wood or built up in layers of lumber, with no board thickness less than 1 in (~2.5 cm). Bond beams are anchored with bolts to the top three courses of mud-brick walls.

Although few if any of these recent devices for strengthening buildings against seismic action are used today in the Old World, all should be incorporated into the construction of earthen buildings. It would be interesting to combine such ancient techniques employing wooden beams and sand for base isolation and mortar for adding flexibility, with modern methods such as reinforcing corners and using bond beams, especially when constructing more massive walls 60–90 cm thick.

Thanks to the experiments of ancestors who pioneered earthen construction and to those of specialized builders in more recent centuries, we now have mud buildings that can withstand most of the destructive forces of nature: rain, hurricanes, tornadoes, and at least some earthquakes. With increased interest and continuing testing, we might greatly improve the chances for survival of both our earthen houses and ourselves.

NOTE

1. Colleague Egon Lass called GVB's attention to the wall in 1993; Director Lawrence Stager provided full details in a subsequent conversation (L. E. Stager, Department of Near Eastern Languages and Civilizations, Harvard University, Cambridge, Massachusetts, USA, personal communication).

Conclusion

MUD ARCHITECTURE IN THE TWENTY-FIRST CENTURY

At the beginning of the twenty-first century, earthen architecture is slowly growing in some of the wealthier industrialized nations—France, Austria, Australia, and the American Southwest, among others. This is due largely to greater interest by environmentalists, architects, and adobe enthusiasts who want the prestige and comfort of elegant houses and community buildings that by their very nature contribute significantly to improving the environment through saving natural resources and reducing pollution. People who take time to visit such houses are often likely to build or buy one. By contrast, in many of the developing nations where mud construction has been common for thousands of years, it is losing ground in the cities, where concrete has been adopted because it is "modern." Only in the villages and countryside does mud remain the building material of choice.

At the lower end of the economic spectrum, when people build their own earthen houses, the concept tends to spread throughout the neighborhood. International organizations, government bureaus of housing and development, and mortgage banks worldwide must be educated about the fantastic characteristics and features of earthen construction and its many advantages over contemporary construction materials so that they will provide funds and loans to both professional earthen builders and do-it-yourself families. If construction of mud structures was to increase rapidly, not only would a major industry be born, but this development would aid in addressing two critical problems facing our world: the shortage of affordable housing for a burgeoning human population and the degradation of our environment.

A Need for Affordable and Environmentally Friendly Housing

Consider the progressive increases in world population through time. It took 1800 years, from the Roman period to A.D. 1830, for world population to reach one billion; only 100 years, from 1830 to 1930, for the population to double to two billion; and only 50 years, from 1930 to 1980, for it to double to four billion. It is probable that in about 35–40 years, from 1980 to about 2015–2020, the population will double again to eight billion. If this growth rate is sustained, the world population can be expected to double again to 16 billion by 2050!

Although population growth has slowed in developed countries, growth rates have increased rapidly in the many underdeveloped countries, which account for a majority of the world's population. Factors that have promoted population growth include medical discoveries that greatly reduce mother and infant mortality at birth and prolonged life for youths and adults; religious beliefs that oppose family planning methods or abortions to terminate unwanted pregnancies; and traditions in cultures that place high value on a large family as a source of pride, added income, and security for the aged.

In polygamous societies, the size of the nuclear family and the number of children born into it is almost beyond our comprehension in the West. In 1994, Ora and I met a young woman from a typical Bedouin family in Israel's Negev region. Her father had four wives, 20 daughters, and 10 sons. If each of these 30 children remained monogamous and each had only seven children, the family would increase by 210 grandchildren. Thus the first-generation nuclear family of five adults that grew to 35 members (65 when counting the 30 spouses) in the second generation would number 275 members in the third generation! This potential number of grandchildren is likely to be unrealistically low, because some of the sons would almost certainly have additional wives, each of whom would add still more children to the total. This illustrates the dimensions of population growth in traditional or fundamentalist Muslim regions.

Mechanisms such as family planning, societal controls (such as China's one-child policy; Tickell, 1993), epidemics, war, societal violence, and natural disasters have slowed world population growth to some extent, but indicators for continued increases far outstrip them.

Humans are the greatest destroyers of the environment. As a result of industrial promotions in advertising and our materialistic desire to get the latest and newest products, we throw away things before they are broken or completely worn out, creating enormous land fills, many of which may never be returned to cultivable soil due to the toxicity of the waste in them. Many cities in the Western world can no longer find nearby sites for landfills and must transport their waste to distant places. In developing countries, the destruction and loss of arable land, the stripping and cutting of forests, the development of new industries without pollution controls, the polluting of aquifers and rivers, and the daily burning of household garbage and trash all contribute to worsening environmental conditions worldwide.

The Intergovernmental Panel on Climate Change (IPCC), organized by the United Nations Environment Programme and World Meteorological Organization, issued their Second Assessment Report (IPCC, 1995) based on data supplied by 2500 scientists from more than 60 nations representing many disciplines, chiefly including climatology, ecology, oceanography, economics, and medicine. As cited in *Nucleus* (Goetze, 1996) and *The Geographical Journal* (Tickell, 1993), the report indicated that since the late nineteenth century, average world temperature increased 0.25°C–0.61°C. Since 1860, the 10 warmest years all occurred during the past 15 years. The IPCC projected a worldwide temperature increase of 1.0°C–3.5°C during the twenty-first century.

Global warming will raise sea level worldwide. The IPCC predicted a rise of as much as 0.5 m in the next 100 years, which would have serious consequences for beaches, low-lying urban areas, and shallow estuaries, and thus, the residences of millions of people living in these regions.

Notwithstanding the potential natural disasters caused by either gradual sea level rise or sudden severe weather events that could render vast populations homeless, it is a sad fact that ongoing political, racial, and/or religious strife and violence in some regions cause thousands of people to flee their villages, rendering them homeless refugees.

Obviously mud construction cannot stop the population explosion or political strife, nor can it alone stop the global warming and all its predicted dire consequences. However, it can ease demand on our natural resources by creating a focus on the renewable building material most readily available—earth. Not only will this help alleviate the increasing future demand for shelter, but it can also vastly improve living conditions for those now living in perhaps 500 million to one billion dwellings of gunnysack, cardboard, scrap wood, and corrugated metal slum shacks throughout the world, in refugee tent camps, as well as in sub-standard tenements and public housing in cities everywhere.

To meet this enormous housing demand with "modern" materials, building industries would have to increase their production many fold. In the developed world, traditional home construction consumes vast quantities of Earth's natural resources in a continuing cycle that begins with obtaining materials (usually at considerable expense) and ends with the ultimate destruction of buildings and burial of their components in rubble landfills.

Consider wood-framed houses in North America. Scarcely anyone cuts trees on one's own land and mills them anymore. Instead, we depend on timber industries to provide materials for houses. Trees in distant forests must be felled, transported to mills where they are prepared for use, packaged, transported hundreds or thousands of miles to lumberyards, and then locally transported to construction sites. Similar complex operations are involved in acquiring stone, concrete, fired brick, ceramic tile, steel, aluminum, copper, plastic, and all other materials that go into the contemporary house. The amount of fossil fuel—non-renewable energy—consumed in quarrying, manufacturing, transporting, and installing operations is enormous (see Chapter 1). For example, it has been calculated that 300 times more commercial energy is required to produce a concrete block than to make a sun-dried mud brick of the same volume (Wright, 1978).

Contemporary homes also require the continuing use of these materials and fuels for improvements, maintenance, heating, and cooling year-round. When a house finally deteriorates or is torn down, significant amounts of energy are again expended by wrecking equipment to clear the site and to haul the debris in trucks to rubble dumps. Because these materials are not suitable for recycling, and because it is doubtful that rubble fills would ever be appropriate for future building sites, this cycle is the ultimate in wastefulness.

The cycle of producing, transporting, constructing, and destroying occurs throughout the world, although in somewhat different ways and usually in lesser quantities than in the USA. In much of the underdeveloped world, growth of a middle class during the 1980s–1990s and the concomitant desire to become "modern" have led to a surge in manufacturing and building that, in some instances, parallels the pace of these activities in developed nations. I shudder to imagine what will happen to our forests and supplies of oil, gas, coal, metals, and plastics with so many contemporary-style houses to build.

To protect planet Earth for humanity for the next 150 years or so, we must find as many ways as possible to conserve our natural resources. One way is the worldwide adoption of earthen buildings.

As we have seen, earthen buildings are built of soil that is commonly quarried as near the site as possible; generally mixed with water, straw, and/or sand; baked by the sun; and erected either as wet mud or dried mud modules—i.e., bricks. Buildings can also be constructed of soil with or without adding water. Both types of soil construction can be used for foundations, walls, floors, and even roofs, virtually eliminating all manufactured building materials and their transport, except for doors, windows, kitchen and bath plumbing and fixtures, and electrical supplies and appliances.

For convenience and efficiency, earthen houses will continue to require many items that draw on the natural resources of our delicate environment. Yet even if many prefer to use concrete or stone foundations, ceramic tile or wooden floors, and wood trim in mud houses, there still will be a significant overall reduction in the devastation of forests, ore beds, and oil and gas deposits, and in the pollution resulting from their manufacture, distribution, and installation.

It is clear that mud construction cannot provide many types of buildings essential to the modern world—gigantic factories, large office buildings, shopping malls, stadiums, theaters, orchestra halls, truly high-rise apartments, and other structures designed to accommodate vast numbers of people. Conventional building materials and construction techniques will continue to be used for such buildings. But not only is mud construction ideal for residential housing (including large apartment houses with as many as six to eight floors), it is also a plausible alternative for service stations, small- to medium-sized strip shopping centers, schools, meeting halls such as neighborhood places of worship, multiplex cinemas or small theaters, and other commercial or municipal structures in this size range.

Earthen construction is not the whole answer to all our environmental and societal problems, but it can contribute significantly to the redemption of the environment of our planet while increasing the availability of affordable homes. One cannot conceive of a more "natural" or environmentally friendly building material than soil. Unlike other natural materials—e.g., grass, trees, rocks, caves—soil is the only material that could meet a demand for the required number of substantial dwellings that are inexpensive to build, comfortable to live in, and friendly to the environment.

Transitioning to Mud

All people deserve to live in decent houses. Ideally, all houses should be environmentally acceptable, that is, they should provide comfort to the inhabitants while significantly limiting the use of forest materials and fossil fuels in their construction and also reducing pollution resulting from the manufacture of "modern" building components, construction, and use. They should be affordable to build, suitable for a family to construct with their own hands under competent guidance, and easy to maintain. They should also be aesthetically pleasing to the human spirit, and durable enough to last three lifetimes, at the very least. These goals have been almost totally ignored by government planners, architects, engineers, corporations such as those involved in forest products and cement manufacture, oil producers, and home builders in our time. If we take these aims seriously, we will find only one material that meets all these requirements—soil.

I do not intend to advocate that only mud or earth be used in buildings. We in the Western world have been brought up on many conveniences and luxuries provided by modern technologies, and most inhabitants of the developing world are driven by an insatiable desire to share our good fortune. We are presently combining those technologies with earthen construction to please ourselves and, as these combinations become known, they will equally delight people everywhere. In addition to those features we take for granted, such as concrete foundations and slabs, basements, plumbing, and the numerous electrical appliances in our houses, there are other items that our lifestyle demands, such as large windows and doors with superb insulating glass and long-lasting, well-insulated roofs. This is, of course, the direction taken in the southwestern USA. Yet the porcelain bathtub in the layered-mud house at Marib proves that combining modern amenities with traditional methods is a growing trend among peoples of more distant nations as well. I hope readers everywhere will peruse books on Southwestern earthen construction for popular designs that appeal to American homeowners and for ideas to improve all traditional house designs. In terms of basic house design, almost any style of building can be constructed of rammed earth or sun-dried mud brick.

Earthen house designs are competitive in cost and, depending on labor costs in a given area, may prove to be less expensive in the long run than current wood framing, vinyl or aluminum siding or facades with a veneer of fired brick, and the adequate insulation necessary with each. For a do-it-yourselfer to build earthen house walls not only reduces costs but provides tremendous satisfaction and pride.

Although some forms of construction are more durable than others, all types can be long lasting if they are well built and carefully maintained. When we see structures built as early as ca. A.D. 900, 1450, and 1773 that are still occupied in the twentieth century, we are assured of the longevity of mud construction. By recalling that the walls of such buildings are fireproof and that the thickness of rammed-earth walls—24–36 in (~61–91 cm)—could surely withstand hurricane-force winds, we can be reasonably certain of their safety. Similarly, the effect of sand-filled foundation trenches and wet-sand mortar between bricks should be experimentally tested in all seismic zones.

GLORIOUS MUD!

We began with Mother Earth and we end with Mother Earth. Indeed, we have been intimately involved with her on every page. Within the last 150 years, humans developed the capability to alter many of nature's rhythms in ever-expanding areas with increasing force. Of all living creatures, we are most endowed with boundless curiosity, imagination, and logical thought. Through time we developed the ability to record knowledge as an aid to memory so that we could share it with our contemporaries as well as those who came after us. The process of preserving information enables each generation to build on the achievements of its forebears. It was my desire that this book contribute to our knowledge of how various societies solved their housing needs with earthen materials—and also that it may address a current problem that will likely increase greatly: How do we shelter an ever-increasing population worldwide?

After all is said and done, many people of both the industrial West and developing countries harbor a prejudice against mud construction, thinking it old-fashioned or primitive. Can we change this opinion? And if so, how? I suggest that we emphasize the "modern" earthen house, using as examples the up-scale, beautiful adobe houses from the southwestern USA, France, Germany, Egypt, and Yemen that feature striking decorative motifs and design elements. I wish that model earthen houses would be built in every state in the USA and in every country in the world. When people begin to recognize that mud houses are associated with a comfortable, affordable, and secure lifestyle, they may be more receptive to the notion that mud houses are desirable.

By showing what human beings have accomplished in sheltering themselves with soil throughout history in different regions of the world, I hoped to spark an interest in houses made of earth. The history of mud design and construction is a glorious triumph of human creativity. Yet except for a few scholarly studies, most publications have treated ancient mud construction incidentally, and many not at all. Historians of architecture and construction have had little to say about earthen architecture, and even archaeologists have largely overlooked it in practice, by both failing to study it in detail and later lacking information to include in their publications. This is an area ripe for additional research. I am humbled by the thought that I too have failed to do justice to my mud structures due to my own incomplete knowledge, yet here I have attempted to share my experience in excavating and interpreting ancient structures with fellow archaeologists as well as lay persons, who I hope will find this approach to mud buildings interesting and compelling.

To me, "Here's mud in your eye!" means "May beautiful mud architecture be in your eye and in your mind's eye forever!"

Appendix A

Maps

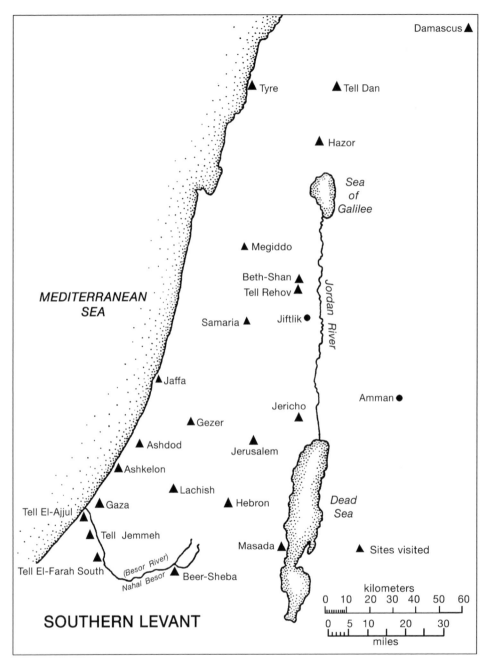

Map 1 Towns and sites visited and other important archaeological sites in the southern Levant.

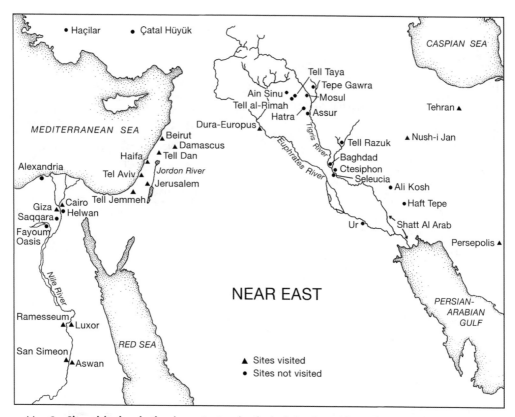

Map 2   **Sites visited and other important archeological sites in portions of Egypt and the Near East from the Levant to Iran.**

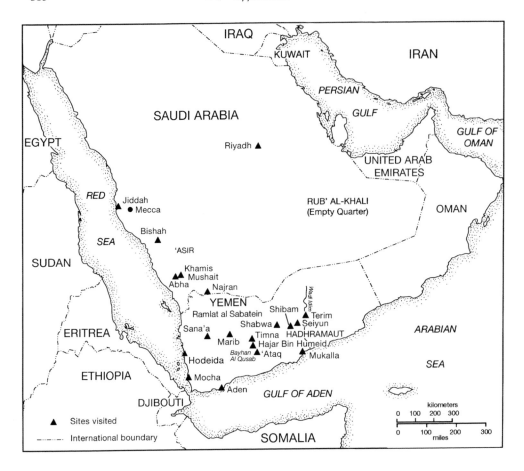

Map 3   Places of research in southern Saudi Arabia and Yemen.

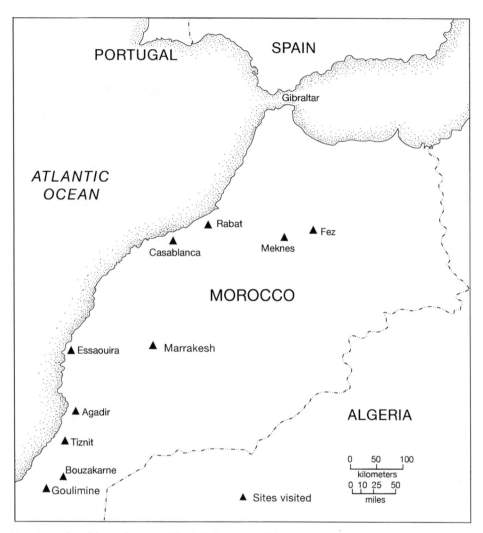

Map 4   Major cities and towns visited during research in Morocco.

Map 5   Towns and villages visited during research in Baluchistan and elsewhere in Pakistan.

Map 6 Places of research in India, especially in Gujarat State.

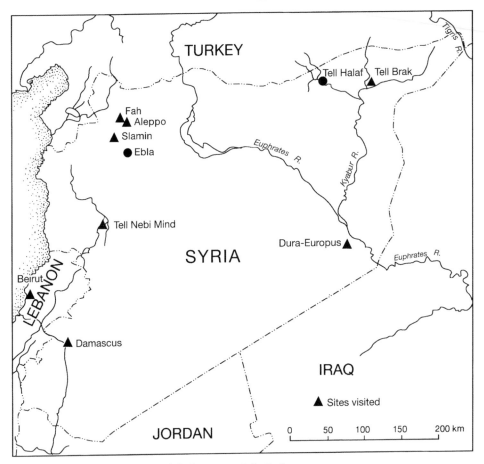

Map 7 **Towns and villages visited during research in Syria.**

Appendix B

Excavation Techniques

EXCAVATION OF ARCHAEOLOGICAL FOUNDATIONS

When a pit, hole, or trench is dug in the earth, the natural layers of soil are destroyed by this disturbance. Even if the pit or trench is subsequently filled with soil and well tamped, it will not have the same density and sequence of layers as the surrounding undisturbed soil. The cutting line of the original hole or trench can usually be found with careful inspection because such cuts in the soil always leave telltale scars, much the same as cuts in human flesh. These principles are important for identifying foundation trenches in archaeological excavations.

During excavation, it is important to carefully scrape the constantly changing work surface with a trowel, cleaning and smoothing the surface so that any intrusive features, such as pits or trenches, will stand out clearly. For example, if a circular line separates grayish-brown debris soil from dark gray or black ash, it should be instantly recognized as an ash-filled pit (Figure B.1). Similarly, when digging near the side of a wall, the appearance of a line or a slight change in color and texture of the soil suggests a foundation trench. Although it may require an extra hour or so, the only way to be certain is to excavate carefully a small, rectangular test pit about 1 m long and 0.5–0.75 m wide at right angles to the wall face and to a depth of perhaps 0.5 m. When the vertical sides of the test pit are dressed smoothly, an archaeologist can almost always recognize a vertical line separating two different layer patterns. One pattern will appear in the solid ground more distant from the wall, and a different pattern will appear in the soil near and against the wall in the backfilled foundation trench. The vertical line, either straight or ragged, will mark the edge of the outer side of the trench (Figure B.2). Sometimes an excavator must dig as many as three or four such test pits along the face of a wall to locate the foundation trench, because the rough trench sides often were not dug in a straight line. The edge of a foundation trench is rarely parallel to the wall surface because such trenches were seldom dug with care and exactness. The foundation laid in the trench, however, will be much straighter and its corners more square. Thus the width of the trench on both sides of the foundation may be as narrow as 1.5–3.0 cm in one area and as wide as 20–30 cm farther along.

515

Figure B.1   Circular pit cutting through a mud-brick fortification wall from the eighth century B.C., Tell Jemmeh.

Such careful digging and observation of foundation trenches slows the progress of an excavation. Is it worth the time and effort spent? The answer is an emphatic "yes!" Foundation trenches are of the greatest importance in excavating tells with successive occupations because they help us to unravel the intricate stratigraphy of the site by placing buildings in their proper sequence among debris layers through time. Assume, for example, that the base of wall A stands on the ground surface; the pottery and other artifacts from the layers immediately above that surface provide a date for the construction of the wall—e.g., ca. 1300 B.C. Assume next that a nearby house

Figure B.2 Foundation trenches backfilled with clean sand, into which a mud-brick fell or was placed, Tell Jemmeh, tenth century B.C.

wall B was built in a foundation trench 40 cm deep but was not preserved more than two courses above ground level. Based on the pottery and other artifacts in the layer associated with the base of wall B (down in the foundation trench), an archaeologist would assign it to an earlier period, 1400–1375 B.C., and would therefore draw wall A on one plan and wall B on a chronologically earlier plan. Because the foundation trench was not recognized, the fact that walls A and B were contemporary—and should have been on the same architectural plan—was missed.

DIFFERENTIATING WALL TYPES

Basic principles and techniques that apply to the excavation of mud walls include special treatment to preserve wall surfaces. Key to this is the ability to differentiate among the types of earthen construction and to recognize the one used in the area being excavated. Care must be taken to note the characteristics of layered-mud and rammed-earth walls (see Table 7.1), which are more difficult to identify during excavation than mud brick. For any earthen wall excavation, the following techniques are recommended for the preservation of important features that will aid in identification of the construction method.

We must be attentive to our walls when excavating. Very gently brush the outer and inner wall faces with both horizontal and vertical strokes, keeping a sharp eye for remnants of mud plaster, for the bedding and rising mortar joints of mud brick, and for small random pits and imperfections on the wall surface, such as those in concrete walls. This step should be completed before troweling the wall surfaces, so that any residual marks and impressions will not be cut away. If joints do not appear quickly, the wall should be left to dry until the following day. Then the wall should be scraped lightly and gently with a trowel, followed by a light brushing with a soft-bristle brush, alternating these operations.

It may be profitable to dig a small test pit about 60 cm square flush with the wall, keeping the sides of the pit vertical, smoothly dressed, and at a right angle to the wall. The two sides of the pit perpendicular to the wall (and the corners they form at the wall) should be examined for thin vertical cracks marking the separation between debris and the wall surface. Be vigilant also for the possibility of a coat of mud plaster between the two materials. If no cracks are seen, carefully trowel the vertical sides of the pit and search for a crack again. At a distance about 7–14 mm from the wall face, using the point of the trowel, gently try to flake off a tiny bit of the debris; if it does not come off easily and cleanly, let it dry for a few hours and try again. Examine the flakes of debris for tiny potsherds, bones, and other artifacts that distinguish debris from mud plaster. If there are artifacts in the matrix, the material is obviously debris; if instead of artifacts there are tiny hollow impressions of straw or seeds, the material is mud plaster.

It is not likely that mud plaster will still cover both surfaces of the wall, although it is remotely possible. If plaster covers the entire wall, slowly and patiently remove an area of plaster about 30 cm high × 60 cm wide to expose the underlying surface. An area of this size will generally disclose the bonding pattern of mud brick if the wall was built with it. Examine the exposed wall surface in detail. If there are no clear individual bricks and mortar joints, the wall was probably constructed of layered mud or rammed earth.

CARE AND DOCUMENTATION OF MUD-BRICK WALLS

When the composition of a wall has been confirmed as mud brick, further care must yet be taken. One should clean mud brick walls gently using a trowel and lightly with a soft-bristle brush, just before—or immediately after—the surface of freshly exposed brick has begun to dry.

I frequently reminded our staff and students at Jemmeh that they must "lovingly tickle" the mud wall surface so that we may learn its secrets. They did, and the walls responded. Indeed, our Jemmeh architects, Brian Lalor and David Sheehan, would not draw a brick unless all four corners were visible; if a corner was missing, the line of the fracture was clearly defined in the sketch.

Such care as this, together with the curiosity and patience to gather all sorts of data on mud brick, will vastly increase our knowledge of ancient mud construction in building techniques and typological dating, and will probably provide clues to the movements of ancient people, their ideas, and their technology.

References

Abu-Bakr, Abdel-Moneim. 1953. *Excavations at Giza, 1949–50*. Cairo, Egypt: Government Press.

Albenda, Pauline. 1980. Syrian–Palestinian Cities on Stone. *Biblical Archaeologist*, 43(4):222–229.

Albright, William Foxwell. 1949. *The Archaeology of Palestine*. Harmondsworth, Middlesex, UK: Penguin Books. [Pelican Book A199.]

Amiran, D. H. K. 1952. A Revised Earthquake-Catalogue of Palestine—II. *Israel Exploration Journal*, 2(1):48–65.

Anonymous. 1960. *The Thatcher's Craft*. London: Countryside Agency.

Association pour la promotion de l'Institut international de la Construction in Terre dans la Ville Nouvelle d'Isle d'Abeau. 1987. In *l'Isle d'Abeau: Le Domaine de la Terre*. Paris: Ministère de l'Equipement du Logement, de l'Aménagement du Territoire et de Transports, République Française.

Bader, N. O. 1993. "Results of the Excavations at the Early Agricultural Site of Kültepe." In *Early Stages in the Evolution of Mesopotamian Civilization*, ed. N. Yoffee and J. J. Clark, pp. 7–40. Tucson: University of Arizona Press.

Biran, Avraham. 1984. The Triple-Arched Gate of Laish at Tel Dan. *Israel Exploration Journal*, 34(1):1–19.

Boak, A. E. R., ed. 1935. *Soknopaiou Nesos: The University of Michigan Excavations at Dimê in 1931–32*. University of Michigan Studies Humanistic Series, 39. Ann Arbor: University of Michigan Press.

Boak, A. E. R., and E. E. Peterson. 1931. *Karanis, Topographical and Architectural Report of Excavations during the Seasons 1924–28*. University of Michigan Studies Humanistic Series, 25. Ann Arbor: University of Michigan Press.

Boswell, James. 1931. *The Life of Samuel Johnson LL.D.* Modern Library edition. New York: Random House.

Braidwood, R. J. 1952. Matarrah: A Southern Variant of the Hassunan Assemblage, Excavated in 1948. *Journal of Near Eastern Studies*, XI(1):1–75.

Breton, Jean-François, Leila Badre, Rémy Audouin, and Jacques Seigne. 1980. *Le Wādī Ḥaḍramawt: Prospections 1978–1979*. Aden, Yemen: Ministere de la Centre Culturel et de Recherches Archéologiques.

Brunskill, R. W. 1970. *Illustrated Handbook of Vernacular Architecture*. New York: Universe Books.

Buchholz, Hans-Günter, and Vassos Karageorghis. 1973. *Prehistoric Greece and Cyprus: An Archeological Handbook.* London: Phaidon.

Bunting, B. 1964. *Taos Adobes: Colonial and Territorial Architecture of the Taos Valley.* Santa Fe: University of New Mexico Press.

Canty & Associates. 2004a. "Historical Weather for Lahore, Pakistan." *Weatherbase.* http://weatherbase.com/weather/weather.php3?s= 004614 (accessed 10 June 2004).

———. 2004b. "Historical Weather for Quetta, Pakistan." *Weatherbase.* http://weatherbase.com/weather/weather.php3?s= 006614 (accessed 10 June 2004).

Clarke, Sommers, and R. Engelbach. 1930. *Ancient Egyptian Masonry.* London: Oxford University Press.

Copeland, Paul W. 1955. "Beehive" Villages of North Syria. *Antiquity,* 113:21–24.

Courtney-Clarke, Margaret. 1990. *African Canvas: The Art of West African Women.* New York: Rizzoli.

Creel, H. G. 1937. *The Birth of China, A Study of the Formative Period of Chinese Civilization.* New York: Reynal and Hitchcock.

de Sutter, Patrick. 1984. Presentación de la cartilla manual para la construcción popular en adobe, "hagamos nuestra casa." *Hagamos nuestra casa, 2.* Quito, Ecuador: Instituto Nacional de Patrimonio Cultural.

Denyer, Susan. 1978. *African Traditional Architecture: An Historical and Geographical Perspective.* New York: Africana Publishing Co.

Dever, William G., H. Darrell Lance, and G. Ernest Wright. 1970. *Gezer I: Preliminary Report of the 1964–66 Seasons.* Jerusalem: Hebrew Union College Biblical and Archaeological School.

Dinsmoor, W. B. 1950. *The Architecture of Ancient Greece: An Account of Its Historic Development.* Revised, enlarged edition based on first part of *The Architecture of Greece and Rome,* by William J. Anderson and R. Phené Spiers, third edition. London: B.T. Batsford.

Dothan, M., and D. N. Freedman. 1967. Ashdod I: The First Season of Excavation, 1962. *Atiqot,* 7:1–171. Jerusalem: Department of Antiquities and Museums in the Ministry of Education and Culture; Department of Archaeology, Hebrew University; and Israel Exploration Society.

Easton, David. 1996. *The Rammed Earth House.* White River Junction, Vermont: Chelsea Green Publishing Company.

Emery, Walter B. 1961. *Archaic Egypt.* Harmondsworth, Middlesex, UK: Penguin Books. [Pelican Book A462.]

Farooqi, M. A. 1986. *Shelter for Low Income Communities: Project Preparation: Balochistan: Appendices.* Government of the Islamic Republic of Pakistan, Ministry of Housing and Works, National Housing Authority.

Fathy, Hassan. 1973. *Architecture for the Poor: An Experiment in Rural Egypt.* Chicago: University of Chicago Press.

———. 1986. *Natural Energy and Vernacular Architecture: Principles and Examples with Reference to Hot Arid Climates.* Chicago: United Nations University by the University of Chicago Press.

Fisher, Clarence S. 1924. *The Minor Cemetery at Giza.* Philadelphia: Egyptian Section of the University Museum.

Fisher, Nora, ed. 1993. *Mud, Mirror, and Thread: Folk Traditions of Rural India.* Ahmedabad, India: Mapin Publishing; Middletown, New Jersey: Grantha; Santa Fe, New Mexico: in association with Museum of New Mexico Press.

Fitch, James M., and Daniel P. Branch, 1960. Primitive Architecture and Climate. *Scientific American,* 203(6): 134–144.

Ghirshman, R. 1954. *Iran: From the Earliest Times to the Islamic Conquest.* Harmondsworth, Middlesex, UK: Penguin Books. [Penguin Book A239.]

Gibson, McGuire. 1980. The Hamrin Expedition, Chicago–Copenhagen Expedition to the Hamrin, Iraq; Second Season 1979. *The Oriental Institute, Annual Report, 1979–80*:19–28. Chicago: The University of Chicago.

Goetze, Darren. 1996. The Climes, They Are Achanging. *Nucleus* 18(1):1–3, 12.

Guillaud, Hubert. 1983. Earth Architecture in France: History, Localization, and Prospect. *Adobe Today*, 39:30–39.

Güntzel, Jochen Georg, 1988. Zur Geschichte des Lehmbaus in Deutschland. 2 Volumes. Ph.D. diss., Kassel-Universität, Hessen. Staufen: Ükobuch Verlag.

Hansman, John F., and David Stronach. 1979. Excavations at Shahr-i Qumis, Iran, 1971. *National Geographic Society Research Reports*, 1970:237–258. Washington, D.C.: National Geographic Society.

Hole, Frank, Kent V. Flannery, and James A. Neely. 1969. Prehistoric and Human Ecology of the Deh Luran Plain: An Early Village Sequence from Khuzistan, Iran. *Memoirs of the Museum of Anthropology, University of Michigan*, 1:1–438.

Huyler, Stephen P. 1993. "Creating Sacred Spaces: Women's Wall and Floor Decorations in Indian Homes." In *Mud, Mirror and Thread: Folk Traditions of Rural India*, ed. Nora Fisher, pp. 172–191. Ahmedabad, India: Mapin Publishing; Middletown, New Jersey: Grantha Corp.; and Santa Fe, New Mexico: in association with Museum of New Mexico Press.

Intergovernmental Panel on Climate Change. 1995. *IPCC Second Assessment—Climate Change 1995*. Geneva, Switzerland: IPCC.

Jakob-Rost, L., E. Klengel, R.-B. Wartke, and J. Marzahn. 1987. *Das Vorderasiatische Museum*, Berlin: Staatliche Museen zu Berlin.

Jefferson, Thomas. 1990, *Papers of Thomas Jefferson*. Volume 24 (1 June–31 December, 1792). ed. Julian P. Boyd, pp. 634–635. Princeton, New Jersey: Princeton University Press.

Johnson, Douglas A. 1992. Adobe Brick Architecture and Salado Ceramics at Fourmile Ruin. In *Proceedings of the Second Salado Conference*, ed. Richard C. Lange and Stephen Germick, pp. 131–138. Tucson. Arizona Archaeological Society, Occasional Paper.

Kahn, Lloyd, ed. 1973. *Shelter*. Bolinas, California: Shelter Publications.

Kallner-Amiran, D. H. 1950–1951. A Revised Earthquake-Catalogue of Palestine—I. *Israel Exploration Journal*, 1(4):223–246.

Karageorghis, Vassos. 1976. *The Civilization of Prehistoric Cyprus*. Athens: Ekdotike Athenon.

Kenyon, Kathleen M. 1970. *Archaeology in the Holy Land*. Third ed. London: Ernest Benn.

———. 1976. Jericho. In *Encyclopedia of Archaeological Excavations in the Holy Land*, ed. Michael Avi-Yonah, 2:562. Jerusalem: Israel Exploration Society.

———. 1981. *Excavations at Jericho, 3: The Architecture and Stratigraphy of the Tell*. Parts 1 and 2, ed. Thomas A. Holland. London: British School of Archaeology in Jerusalem.

Kirkbride, Diana. 1972. Umm Dabaghiyah 1971: A Preliminary Report. An Early Ceramic Farming Settlement in Marginal North Central Jazira, Iraq. *Iraq*, 34(1):3–15.

Lee, A. B. 1937. *Houses of Earth*. Washington, D.C.: A. B. Lee. [Privately published.]

Lee, J. R. 1978. "Tuleilat el-Ghassul." In *Encyclopedia of Archaeological Excavations in the Holy Land*, Volume 4, ed. Michael Avi-Yonah and Ephraim Stern. p. 1208. Jerusalem: Massada Press.

Levy, Thomas. 1993. "Ghassul, Tuleilat el-." In *The New Encyclopedia of Archaeological Excavations in the Holy Land*, Volume 2, ed. Ephraim Stern. pp. 506–511. Jerusalem: Israel Exploration Society.

Lewcock, Ronald. 1978. "Architects, Craftsmen, and Builders: Materials and Techniques." In *Architecture of the Islamic World: Its History and Social Meaning, with a Complete Survey of Key Monuments*, ed. George Mitchell, pp. 112–143. London: Thames and Hudson.

———. 1986. *Wādī Ḥaḍramawt and the Walled City of Shibām*. Paris: UNESCO.

Lloyd, Seton. 1984. *The Archaeology of Mesopotamia: From the Old Stone Age to the Persian Conquest*. Rev. ed. New York: Thames and Hudson.

Lloyd, Seton, and Fuad Safar. 1945. Tell Hassuna: Excavations by the Iraq Government Directorate General of Antiquities in 1943 and 1944. *Journal of Near Eastern Studies,* 4:255–289.

Loud, Gordon. 1936. *Khorsabad, Part I: Excavations in the Palace and at a City Gate.* Oriental Institute Publications (OIP) 38. Chicago: University of Chicago Press.

Lumbreras, Luis G. 1974. *The Peoples and Cultures of Ancient Peru,* trans. Betty J. Meggers. Washington, D.C.: Smithsonian Institution Press.

Maas, Pierre. 1990. Djenné: Living Tradition. *Aramco World,* 41(6):18–29.

Macdonald, Eann, J. L. Starkey, and Lankester Harding. 1932. *Beth-Pelet,* Volume 2. London: British School of Archaeology in Egypt.

MacLeish, Kenneth. 1967. "Journey unto Canaan." In *Everyday Life in Bible Times,* ed. Merle Severy, pp. 56–105. Washington, D.C.: National Geographic Society.

Mallowan, M. E. L. 1966. *Nimrud and Its Remains.* Volumes 1 and 2. London: Collins.

McHenry, Paul Graham, Jr. 1980. "Adobe Comes Full Circle." In *Desert Housing: Balancing Experience and Technology for Dwelling in Hot Arid Zones,* ed. Kenneth N. Clark and Patricia Paylore, p. 115. Tucson: University of Arizona Press.

———. 1984. *Adobe and Rammed Earth Buildings: Design and Construction.* New York: John Wiley & Sons.

———. 1985. *Adobe: Build It Yourself.* Revised edition. Tucson: University of Arizona Press. (Reprinted 1992.)

Mellaart, James. 1967. *Çatal Hüyük: A Neolithic Town in Anatolia.* New York: McGraw-Hill.

———. 1970a. Excavations at Haçılar I. *Occasional Publications of the British Institute of Archeology at Ankara,* 9. Edinburgh: Edinburgh University Press.

———. 1970b. Excavations at Haçılar II: Plates and Figures. *Occasional Publications of the British Institute of Archeology at Ankara,* 10. Edinburgh: Edinburgh University Press.

Melson, William G., and Gus W. Van Beek. 1992. Geology and the Loessial Soils, Tell Jemmeh, Israel. *Geoarchaeology,* 7(2):121–147.

Merpert, N. Y., and R. M. Munchaev. 1973. Early Agricultural Settlements in the Sinjar Plain, Northern Iraq. *Iraq,* 35(2):93–114.

Miller, Lydia A, and David J. Miller. 1982. *Manual for Building a Rammed Earth Wall.* Greeley, Colorado: Rammed Earth Institute International.

Miyagawa, Ellen. 1985. *Bulletin of the Fluvanna County Historical Society,* 4 (October):21–23.

Moore, Molly. 1993. "My Children, Grandchildren—Gone: Official Estimate of Death Toll from Indian Earthquake Rises to 21,000." *The Washington Post,* 2 October 1993, A1.

Morris, Kelly Jon. 1973. "Tin and Thatch in Togo." In *Shelter,* ed. L. Kahn, pp. 44–45. Bolinas, California: Shelter Publications.

New Mexico Commission of Public Records. 2003. New Mexico Earthen Building Materials Code. *The New Mexico Administrative Code,* 14.7.4. http://www.nmcpr.state.nm.us/nmac/parts/title14/14.007.0004.htm (accessed June 8, 2007).

Oates, David. 1965. The Excavations at Tell al Rimah, 1964. *Iraq,* 27:62–80.

———. 1966. The Excavations at Tell al Rimah, 1965. *Iraq,* 28:122–139.

———. 1967. The Excavations at Tell al Rimah, 1966. *Iraq,* 29(2):70–96.

———. 1968. The Excavations at Tell al Rimah, 1967. *Iraq,* 30(2):115–138.

———. 1970. The Excavations at Tell al Rimah, 1968. *Iraq,* 32:1–26.

Oates, David, and Joan Oates. 1959. Ain Sinu: A Roman Frontier Post in Northern Iraq. *Iraq,* 21:207–242.

Oates, Joan, 1969. Choga Mami 1967–68: A Preliminary Report. *Iraq,* 31(2):115–152.

Oliver, Paul. 1987. *Dwellings: The House across the World.* Austin: University of Texas Press.

Oren, E. D. 1993a. "Haror, Tel." In *The New Encyclopedia of Archaeological Excavations in the Holy Land,* Volume 2, ed. Ephraim Stern. p. 582. Jerusalem: Israel Exploration Society.

———. 1993b. "Sera', Tel." In *The New Encyclopedia of Archaeological Excavations in the Holy Land,* Volume 4, ed. Ephraim Stern. pp. 1329–1335. Jerusalem: Israel Exploration Society.

Patty, R. L. 1942. Soil Admixtures for Earth Walls. *Agricultural Engineering,* 23(9):291–294.

Petrie, W. M. Flinders. 1928. *Gerar.* London: British School of Archaeology in Egypt.

———. 1974. *Tell el Amarna.* Warminster, UK: Aris and Phillips. [Reprint of 1894 edition published by Metheun and Co., London.]

———. 1977. *Gizeh and Rifeh.* Warminster, UK: Aris and Phillips. [Reprint of 1907 edition published by British School of Archaeology in Egypt, London.]

Pliny the Elder. 1961. *Natural History.* Volume 9. Trans. H. Rackham. Cambridge, Massachusetts: Harvard University Press. Loeb Classical Library.

Powell, Robert. 1999. *Earth, Door, Sky, Door: Paintings of Mustang.* London: Serindia Publications.

Reade, J. E. 1968. Tell Taya (1967): Summary Report. *Iraq,* 30(2):234–264.

Reiter, Leon. 1990. *Earthquake Hazard Analysis: Issues and Insights.* New York: Columbia University Press.

Rice, D. Talbot. 1962. *The Byzantines.* Ancient Peoples and Places Series, 27. New York: Praeger.

Roaf, Michael, and David Stronach. 1973. Tepe Nush-i Jan, 1970: Second Interim Report. *Iran,* 11:129–140.

Robertson, D. S. 1969. *Greek and Roman Architecture.* Second edition. Cambridge, UK: Cambridge University Press.

Rosen, Arlene M. 1986. *Cities of Clay: The Geoarchaeology of Tells.* Chicago: University of Chicago Press.

Ruşdea, Hedwiga. 1986. "Vine-yard Press-House with Cellar." In *Museum of Folk Technology Guide Book,* ed. Corneliu Bucur, Cornelia Gangolea, Dan Munteanu, and Irmgardd Sedler. Trans. Eugen Gergely. Sibiu, Romania: The Museum.

Saggs, H. W. F. 1967. "The March of Empires." In *Everyday Life in Bible Times.* Washington, D.C.: National Geographic Society.

Salim, Shakir Mustafa. 1962. *Marsh Dwellers of the Euphrates Delta.* London: University of London, Athlone Press. (London School of Economics Monographs on Social Anthropology, 23.)

Santillanes, V. 1994. Volunteers Replicate Indians' Home-Building. *Albuquerque Journal,* 14 August, 1994:3.

Sarre, Friedrich, and Ernst Herzfeld. 1911. *Archäologische Reise im Euphrat- und Tigris-gebiet.* Volume 3. Berlin: Dietrich Reimer.

Schick, Wilhelm. 1987. *Der Pisé-Bau zu Weilburg an der Lahn.* Weilburg an der Lahn: Alt-Weilburg.

Schmidt, Erich F. 1937. Excavations at Tepe Hissar Damghan. *Publications of the Iranian Section of the University Museum,* 32. Philadephia: University of Pennsylvania Press.

———. 1939. The Treasury of Persepolis and Other Discoveries in the Homeland of the Achaemenians. *Oriental Institute Communications,* 21. Chicago: University of Chicago.

Scott, Hugh, Kenneth Mason, and Mary Marshall. 1946. *Western Arabia and the Red Sea.* Oxford, UK: Naval Intelligence Division, under authority of HMSO at the University Press. (Geographical Handbook Series.)

Seigne, Jacques. 1980. "Les structures I, J, et K à Mašga (Mashgha)." In *Le Wādī Ḥaḍramawt: Prospections 1978–1979,* ed. Jean-François Breton, Leila Badre, Rémy Audouin, and Jacques Seigne. pp. 22–32. Aden, Yemen: Ministere de la Centre Culturel et de Recherches Archéologiques.

———. 1992. "Le château royal de Shabwa: Le bâtiment, architecture, techniques de construction et restitutions." In *Fouilles de Shabwa 2: Rapports Préliminaires,* ed. Jean-François Breton. pp. 111–164. Institut Français d'Archéologie du Proche-Orient: Publication Hors Série 19. Paris: Librairie Orientaliste Paul Geuthner.

Singer, Charles J., E. J. Holmyard, A. R. Hall, and Trevor I. Williams, eds. 1979. *A History of Technology.* Volumes 1–2. Oxford, UK: Clarendon Press.

Smith, Edward W., and George S. Austin. 1989. Adobe, Pressed-Earth, and Rammed-Earth Industries in New Mexico. *New Mexico Bureau of Mines and Mineral Resources Bulletin,* 127:1–60. Socorro, New Mexico: The New Mexico Bureau of Geology and Mineral Resources.

Smith, Philip E.L. 1972. Survey of Excavations in Iran during 1970–71. *Iran,* 10:165–186.

Southwick, Marcia. 1965. *Build with Adobe.* Chicago: Swallow Press.

Speiser, E. A. 1935. *Excavations at Tepe Gawra.* Volume 1. Philadelphia: University of Pennsylvania Press.

Stager, Lawrence E. 1993. "Ashkelon." In *The New Encyclopedia of Archaeological Excavations in the Holy Land,* Volume 1, ed. Ephraim Stern. p. 106. Jerusalem: Israel Exploration Society.

Stronach, David. 1969. Excavations at Nush-i Jan, 1967. *Iran,* 7:1–20.

Stronach, David, Michael Roaf, Ruth Stronach, and S. Bökönyi. 1978. Excavations at Tepe Nush-i Jan. *Iran,* 16(1):1–28.

Sweet, Louise E. 1960. Tell Toqaan: A Syrian Village. *Anthropological Papers, Museum of Anthropology, University of Michigan,* 14. Ann Arbor: University of Michigan.

Thomas, Dana. 1998. "Tibetan Huts May Descend from Long-Lost Kingdom." *The Washington Post,* 12 January 1998, A3.

Tickell, Crispin. 1993. The Human Species: A Suicidal Success? *Geographical Journal* 159(2):219–226.

Todd, Ian A. 1966. Aşikli Hüyük: A Protoneolithic Site in Central Anatolia. *Anatolian Studies,* 16:139–163.

Ussishkin, David. 1983. Excavations at Tel Lachish 1978–1983: Second Preliminary Report. *Tel Aviv,* 10(2):97–175.

———. 1993. "Lachish." In *The New Encyclopedia of Archaeological Excavations in the Holy Land,* Volume 3, ed. Ephraim Stern. pp. 907–908. Jerusalem: Israel Exploration Society.

Van Beek, Gus W. 1974. "The Land of Sheba." In *Solomon and Sheba,* ed. James B. Pritchard. pp. 40–63. London: Phaidon Press Ltd.

———. 1983. Digging Up Tell Jemmeh. *Archaeology,* 36(1):12–19.

———. 1984. Archaeological Investigations at Tell Jemmeh, Israel. *Research Reports, National Geographic Society,* (1975)16:675–696.

———. 1987. Arches and Vaults in the Ancient Near East. *Scientific American,* 257(1):96–103.

———. 1992. The Rammed Earth Revetment at Tell Jemmeh. *Eretz-Israel 23.* pp. 4–9. Jerusalem: Israel Exploration Society.

Van Hafften, Claes Joris. 1988. "Details of Architecture and Construction." In *Hammam et-Turkman I: Report on the University of Amsterdam's 1981–84 Excavations in Syria,* ed. M. N. van Loon. pp. 129–139. Leiden: Nederlands Historisch-Archeologisch Instituut te Istanbul.

Vitruvius Pollio. 1931–1934. *Vitruvius, On Architecture.* Volumes 1 and 2. Ed. from Harleian Manuscript 2767. Trans. Frank Granger. Cambridge, Massachusetts: Harvard University Press; Loeb Classical Library 251, 280.

Waterman, Leroy. 1933. *Second Preliminary Report upon the Excavations at Tell Umar, Iraq.* Ann Arbor: University of Michigan Press.

West, Trudy. 1971. *The Timber-Frame House in England.* New York: Architectural Book Publishing Co.

Wolfskill, Lyle A., Wayne A. Dunlop, and Bob M. Gallaway. 1979. *Handbook for Building Homes of Earth.* Greeley, Colorado: Rammed Earth Institute International, Report E 14-63.

Woolley, Leonard. 1934. *Ur Excavations, Volume 2: The Royal Cemetery.* London: Oxford University Press.

———. 1953. *A Forgotten Kingdom.* Harmondsworth, Middlesex, UK: Penguin Books Ltd. [Pelican Book A261.]

———. 1961. *The Art of the Middle East including Persia, Mesopotamia and Palestine.* New York: Crown Publishers.

———. 1963. *Excavations at Ur: A Record of Twelve Years' Work.* London: Ernest Benn.

Woolley, Leonard, and D. Randall-Maciver. 1910. *Karanòg: The Romano–Nubian Cemetery.* Volumes 1 and 2. Philadelphia: The University Museum.

Wright, David. 1978. *Natural Solar Architecture.* New York: Van Nostrand Reinhold.

Wulff, Hans E. 1966. *The Traditional Crafts of Persia: Their Development, Technology, and Influence on Eastern and Western Civilizations.* Cambridge: Massachusetts Institute of Technology Press.

Yadin, Yigael. 1966. *Masada; Herod's Fortress and the Zealots' Last Stand.* New York: Random House.

———. 1993. "Hazor." In *The New Encyclopedia of Archaeological Excavations in the Holy Land,* Volume 2, ed. Ephraim Stern. pp. 597–600. Jerusalem: Israel Exploration Society.

Yoffee, N., and J. J. Clark, eds. 1993. *Early Stages in the Evolution of Mesopotamian Civilization: Soviet Excavations in Northern Iraq.* Tucson: University of Arizona Press.

Index

527

About the Author

Gus W. Van Beek, PhD, has melded his passion for archaeology and architecture with the highest scholarship in this unique book, *Glorious Mud!* His thorough research, photo documentation, attention to detail, and masterful interpretation render a work that is deeply insightful as it uncovers many years of findings by Dr. Van Beek with colleagues and his wife and research partner, **Ora Van Beek**, an ethnologist. In a manner of true gifting, Gus draws readers from many disciplines with clear and compelling writing and does so without sacrificing the seriousness and excellence of his profession.

As a curator of Old World Archeology of the Department of Anthropology of the Smithsonian Institution, Gus has overseen many major exhibits, including the Dead Sea Scrolls of Jordan Exhibition. In it, he showed not just scrolls, but the scrolls in their cultural setting, and therefore organized the exhibition in a series of sections: the discovery of the scrolls; an overview of the people of the scrolls and their community at Qumran; the famous Psalms Scrolls with fragments of other biblical books, apocryphal, pseudepigraphical, sectarian works and commentaries, and a section on scrolls research. This didactic exhibition proved to have one of the greatest average daily attendances of any large exhibition in the history of the Smithsonian.

Dr. Van Beek earned a PhD in Near Eastern Archaeology and Semitic Languages from Johns Hopkins University; a bachelor of divinity degree from McCormick Theological Seminary, Chicago; and a bachelor degree with honors from University of Tulsa. He also was an Archaeological Fellow at the American Schools of Oriental Research in Jerusalem, Jordan, and has received many honors and recognition for his work, especially in mud architecture.

In addition to many significant articles such as "The Arch and the Vault in Ancient Near Eastern Architecture" (*Scientific American* 257(1):96–103), Dr. Van Beek is the author of *Hajar Bin Humeid: Archaeological Investigations at a Pre-Islamic Site in South Arabia* (1969) and editor of *The Scholarship of William Foxwell Albright: An Appraisal* (Harvard Semitic Monographs, 33). Cambridge: Harvard University. ***Glorious Mud!*** celebrates this author's career of nearly half a century, telling a story of ancient yet timeless architecture that is full of intrigue and delight.